THE SILENCE OF GREAT DISTANCE

Courtney,

I will miss your sweet smile and laughter so much. You have truly put fun into all of our lives.

Have a blast in college. Please keep in touch.

Love,
John

THE SILENCE
OF GREAT DISTANCE

WOMEN RUNNING LONG

FRANK MURPHY

WIND⚡SPRINT
PRESS

KANSAS CITY, MISSOURI

For information, address:

WindSprint Press
116 W. 3rd Street, Suite 304
Kansas City, Missouri 64105-1203

Library of Congress Cataloging-in-Publication Data

Murphy, Frank, 1952-
    The silence of great distance: women running long / written by Frank Murphy
    p.cm.
    Includes bibliographical references and index.
    ISBN 0-9629243-2-6 (pbk.)
    1. Marathon running. 2. Women runners. I. Title.

GV1065.M87 1999
796.42'52'082--dc21   99-053861

FIRST PRINTING

Cover Design by River City Studio
Book Design by Susan Ng Williams

To Mary
and to the memory of Tom Dowling

Preface

One day in Oxford, Mississippi, I stuck my hand in my coat pocket and found a note I put there long before: don't forget Stephanie Herbst, it said. I put the note in my pocket as a reminder, some day, to write a book about Stephanie Herbst. I had the idea that Stephanie was a great runner for whom victories came with ease, and to whom records fell casually, but I also recalled that in a moment she was gone. I wanted to know about that moment. Any time being all time, I wanted to know the time rolling into and away from Stephanie. In short, I wanted to know how it was that Stephanie, and other women of her age, were permitted to run long distances when that activity had been denied earlier generations, and I wanted to know what caused Stephanie to run, and I wanted to know what caused Stephanie to cease to run.

In the development of Stephanie's time, I had in mind a bomb with a long fuse, which was lit. The fuse burned slowly, largely ignored, and then it exploded. I had in mind a fault line. Unseen, one block of material slid over, under and against another block of material until the ground became unstable and the earth moved. I had in mind social progress, made gradually but revealed in sensation. I had in mind women athletes, forced to disguise themselves until the time for truth arrived. I had in mind one generation of women who were there when the bomb went off, there when the ground shook, there without disguise, there when social progress created opportunity. I had in mind the nature of that opportunity, its promise of gain, its capacity for reward, and its inseparability from loss.

ONE

It is not wisdom to be only wise
and on the inward vision close the eyes.

George Santayana

A dream of great achievement arrives like respect from a stranger, like thunder on a warm day, like new life. It is the first step in a long walk, which, when taken, transforms time into energy, failure into experience, pain into suffering, loss into penance, and tribulation into trial, with vindication surely at hand. A dream stirs an ember into flame and it sweeps contentment into a new shape, making restlessness a charm and relaxation a task. A dream barters today for tomorrow, willingly. It lives in occupation and in reverie, and it endures a measureless age. The age complete, a dream dies the way the light of day gives way to darkness. It dies the way a cool day becomes cold, the way love goes, the way forgiveness comes, the way the sound of a train drifts slowly away. It dies the way mourning ends; and the way old friends fail to return. It dies the way footfalls recede on a quiet path. It dies the way faith is lost and as youth ends. The dream gone, doubt slides into the vacant space, holding it until the next dream, the next life, and the next certainty arrive. The dream is like a race, which begins and ends in the same place, which, however, is no place at all but all places.

. . . . .

Although she was immersed in them and captive to them, the young woman running this afternoon with uncommon grace gave no thought to dreams. She gave no thought, even, to her motion or to her path. She did not see the traffic that surrounded her early in the run, and she did not hear the occasional calls made to her. She did not see the forest trail when she entered it, and she did not notice the softness of the terrain or the green branches and the blue sky overhead. She was withdrawn entirely to herself, and she was pre-occupied with the single question whether she should stop.

The activity in question was competitive distance running. Such a silly pointless thing really, just so much distance covered in so much time, but it hid great complexity. She had seen the thing up close. In the activity, some people grew strong and some collapsed, and there appeared no order to the result in either case. Anyway, silly or not, running was important to her. For many people it defined her. If she stopped, some part of her would be gone forever. Against that sure loss, she imagined a part of her that would be regained, a function and practice that she had avoided for years. And if she continued? There was no answer for that as she ran. Sun changed to gentle rain and she did not notice.

Men would pause today and stare as she ran past; they always did, some stepping off curbs they forgot were there and stag-gering for a step or two in embarrassed surprise, others distractedly dodging stop signs and mailboxes, happy to pay the slight price. She took no interest, and felt neither insult nor grievance. In all they saw, they saw nothing. She was moving. She continued her calculation, marshaling the relevant facts as she ran. Some she collected from six years of her own experience, and some she borrowed from other people she knew or watched. Gathered together, the facts sailed past each other like particle waves. Although apparently related, every wave distorted every other wave. None of this was any good for reckoning and conclusion. She simply could not see a pattern. By now, even words, much less full thoughts, clashed: opportunity, folly, pride, responsibility, arrogance, temerity, habit, self-respect, duty, fear, safety, enjoyment, fulfillment, strength, ambition, fitness, illness. Playing at the edges of an analysis they should have dominated were risk and benefit. Her head throbbed.

All around her life was full. Nearing home, stopped dead at an intersection, she looked up to see a friend smiling. It choked her. Why was everyone else happy, and she confused and lost! Deep in the sea, she imagined, a swimmer could panic and forget which way was up and which way was down, and swim away from the light and toward the dark. How was the choice made? Dumb luck and damn chance, some would say. That possibility horrified her, and she rejected it. On instinct, she ran faster. For the first time today, she turned herself to the details of mechanical movement and efficiency. As she did, the rain, which had been gradually slowing, was replaced by translucent mist. Fully engaged, the woman ran now with great force, driving from the hips, lengthening her stride, increasing her cadence, and pulling herself forward with consciously relaxed arms. The hands were low, and her thumbs just creased the lower corner of her shorts—each rocking motion, down, across, up, across; down, across, up and across. This, at least, was a pattern she recognized.

The ground skimmed beneath her, and she punched again and again, finding no resistance to the increased pace. Once more and she was at top end. She held the pace, settling in as if the earlier languid rhythm had been an aggravation, as in fact it had been, given her usual vigor. Occupied with the new activity, it took her a mile or two to realize that her mind had grown silent. Turning back into herself and away from the run, she listened for the familiar arguments and counter-arguments that had raged within her. She heard only the pounding of her own heart and the deep draughts of her own breath. The next deep draw, the last of the journey this day, was a sigh of relief. The runner was at peace.

No decision had been made, but the struggle was ended. If cognition is the act of knowing, this was the beginning. The rational mind was issuing an invitation to the willing heart. Listen, it said. If you do not hear the sound of the train, you must stop. If the footsteps are quiet, you must stop. If the day is grown cold, if the light is given way to dark, if your old friends have abandoned you, if faith is gone, and youth is lost, you must stop.

. . . . .

At the moment of her decision in 1987, Stephanie Herbst was a junior at the university. She was 20 years old. She was a five-time all-American, the women's collegiate record holder for 10,000 meters, unbeaten at that distance, and the leading runner on a cross-country team that won national titles twice in her three years on the team. She was an Academic all-American. Summing it up, a national publication had described her situation as "a nice place to be when you remember that women will contest the 10,000 in the Olympics for the first time in 1988."

Olympic fervor would continue. That was certain. Physically, she was made for the challenge—tall and thin with extraordinary natural strength and balance. Her father had said she "runs like a deer," and indeed no one would dispute the characterization. Descriptions of her reflected remorseless grace, lap after lap of hard running until the race was run. She had once said simply, "I like to see how far and how fast I can go." Her coach, Peter, in whom she had absolute faith, said that another feature of Stephanie's success was her trust "in what we ask her to do. She listens and believes in us." This was structure, and Stephanie was comfortable within it. She controlled everything else in her life, but decisions about running she left gratefully to Peter.

Perhaps it would be better to say that she left all decisions about running to Peter, save one: should she run at all? That question she reserved to herself. She had always viewed running at arm's length. Early in her college career, she said that she would "like to take running as far as it will take me, but I don't want it to interfere with what I'm here for and that's to get a business degree and eventually a graduate degree. I'll use running as much as it will help me reach those ends." She candidly admitted that she avoided contact with runners when she wasn't training and racing. She had two lives, and wanted it that way. She needed, for her own good, to hold a private person secure from the unwanted attention and pressure created by the public one, the one who ran.

In fact, the pressures were accumulating despite Stephanie's attempts to control them or to compartmentalize her activities. It was not sufficient to transfer responsibility for running to Peter. It was not enough to avoid runners and wasteful chatter about running during the remainder of her academic and social day, nor to ignore the times and condition of her rivals, which she also did. Success, notoriety—fame of a sort—overrode all attempts to control it. This was a matter of growing concern. Already, people she ran with had been hurt. Some had injuries. Others were unnerved, perhaps to the point of clinical severity. Some women were obsessed with eating and thinness and with running in general. Others grew exhausted and quit. "Is it safe?" the dentist asked the marathon man, "is it safe?" The anxious question answered itself. It was not safe, not entirely, but why not? Considering the events that surrounded her, Stephanie reminded herself of something she knew but sometimes forgot, having buried it in emotion: not every problem experienced by a runner was caused by running. It was worth repeating: not every problem experienced by a runner was caused by running. She was not fooled by an analysis that placed an event and a circumstance in close order and presumed causal relationship, "because this, therefore this." That kind of thinking was for the grave diggers and carnival barkers who came to women's sport for controversy rather than understanding; people who were looking for trouble, or hoping for scandal. Her own analysis was finer. Within the general context of competitive sports, her individual nature was nevertheless at issue, she knew. How was she doing? Why did she hesitate when others plunged forward? Why did she fear? What in the mix of general and individual issues encouraged her to such watchfulness? This approach, this self-questioning, drew all the impulses into one and made the analysis more complex. But it was scrupulous. In that way, it was consistent with Stephanie's expectation of herself.

Under pressure, she was intense—a "loner." That much she recognized in herself without question. The social isolation was a problem, perhaps measured most starkly by the great variety of experience the campus offered and from which she, by her choice and too often from her caution, turned away. Could she attach a price? Impossible, really; but it was an enchanting idea: to swing the deal the other way, to trade her one experience, her one life, for many experiences and many lives. Who would she date if she did not rise every morning to run? What would it be like to join a sorority? Would her studies improve if she was less tired when she came to them? What would it be like to rest deeply and think nothing at all at the end of a long day? What else was out there that she was missing?

There was more, of course, to think about. She herself was thin. Sometimes she was thin enough that Peter grew concerned about her. She watched her weight carefully, but she gave no quarter. She designed and adhered to a strict diet. Her goal was to be as light as she could be—to draw all possible advantages out of carrying less weight over great distances—but not so light that she lost strength, a result that would defeat the entire purpose of the exercise. From time to time, she knew that she went too far and she adjusted.

But few people noticed her slight adjustments. In fact, her weight was a topic of conversation among strangers, people who had no basis upon which to state an opinion but who could cause offense by the public distribution of their remarks. "Willowy," one said, meaning sick, she understood. It was presumptuous and insulting, no less so because that remark and others like it were coated with solicitude for her safety and her welfare. This was her life they were talking about. What gave people the right to comment? And where were the limits? More important, who controlled the process?

In such moments, she was overcome with disquiet. At other times, it was pride that overcame her, not in herself but in her friends, her teammates, her coach, her university, and the many women with and against whom she ran. Too often, she saw the women from a distance. Having once withdrawn, she could not find a way to draw close. Nevertheless, she watched with respect and admiration. One teammate in particular amazed her. This teammate was two years younger, but she seemed of an entirely different world. While Stephanie turned in, this woman turned out, capturing and controlling the entire atmosphere on the team without any contrivance or intention. Relaxed and gentle off the track, combative and uncompromising on it, the younger runner was the future, not merely for herself but for the sport. Stephanie was not jealous of her younger teammate nor covetous of her position on the team; she was just a bit rueful, almost wry in her response. Stephanie had gone a different direction because it had been necessary, but the cost was high. Perhaps only now did she fully realize how much she paid for so little. Nobody's fault but her own! Nobody's triumph but her own?

All of these things now tumbled together; the positive and the negative pulled in so tightly that it was hard to distinguish them. The original goal of academic and professional success, the superb athletic performances, her sense of accomplishment, the regard of her family, her sense of obligation to the university, the camaraderie with her teammates, her loyalty and respect for her coach, the accompanying pressures, the threat of injury or illness, the isolation, the emphatic "lone-ness" to her life, her weight, her sense of direction, all made it difficult for her to remember the incantation she sometimes used, or was it a prayer? "All I can do is the best I can do." Was it, in fact? Did she believe that any longer? There it was, then. The decision was at hand. For a young woman of twenty with an enticing prospect in front her, it was an awkward time to strike such an intersection. It was too early, some would say. She should delay. Just as long as peace of mind permitted the deception, she would agree. But soon the terrible pressure would be on her again. It was early, if they said so, but unbidden, dark in the night, she got a glimpse of the past nestled against the future, saw them both at once, and knew. The time, in fact, was terribly late.

TWO

Some blind instinct, for he was past reasoning,
must have driven him to take the river bank
in the direction of the sea.

Orlando,
Virginia Woolf

The photograph is more revealing than a single moment in
time ought to be. It shows three young girls on the track in shorts
and tee-shirts leaning slightly forward, all awaiting the starter's pis-
tol to send them away. The girl on the right in the inside lane stands
somewhat higher than the two figures on her outside. She is taller,
leaner, and bends forward less dramatically. Her arms hang straight
down, betraying neither tension nor nervous readiness. Her face is
relaxed with no muscle drawn and no concern in her expression. Her
gaze has no close focus but is directed far down the track. If anything, the face shows disinterest. Meanwhile, the two girls in the
second and third lanes crouch lower, muscles at the ready, with a
tightness in the jawline of each of them. Their arms are held high
and they are ready to swing into action. Yet, the two girls do not look
down the track but to the inside lane. They look toward Stephanie
Herbst, upon whom their concentration is total. The race is yet to
begin, but it is over.

. . . . .

Late in the summer of 1980 in a suburb of Minneapolis, Michele and Stephanie Herbst waited for high school classes to begin. Michele was entering her sophomore year while Stephanie was an incoming freshman. Michele, the veteran, was training for the cross-country team at Chaska High. Stephanie, who had run a decent half-mile in junior high, was doing nothing. Time will affect the memory of both girls, but Michele did say to Stephanie on an otherwise undistinguished afternoon, "I can run five miles in one stretch, and you can't." Of course, that would never do, not between sisters. Stephanie slipped on her loafers and went out to meet the challenge, apparently resolved but secretly in doubt.

When Michele took off at a trot, Stephanie settled in beside her. From time to time, she gave her sister an admiring glance, but for the most part she just hung there, in lockstep. The two sisters were like ships tied together in tow, with the water rippling along-side each of them—stirred and sifted until it receded, finally, into the calmness of the distance downstream. Permitting Michele to carry the initiative, Stephanie waited for the moment to arrive when she would be forced by fatigue and by the surrender of pridefulness to pull over and sit down. But for now the course was clear. She would run a block, and then another block, and then another block. She would take one stride after the other until something happened that forced her to the side.

As Stephanie concentrated on her task, however, she began to notice something so plain that it was odd. The distance was falling away and she was getting closer to the end. In fact, now that she thought about it, the whole endeavor, the idea of running five miles without stopping, was beginning to make a weird kind of sense. There was a great distance, and there was a finish line. The distance encouraged caution. "You better slow down because you have a long way to go!" But the finish line inspired audacity. "You better run faster because you need to get there first!" Somewhere in the middle of all this was a chance to do something special, to get it right, to find the precise balance between the impulses, and to do it so well that no one noticed what was happening. Two apparently hostile impulses were being integrated seamlessly. Done properly, you could miss one for the presence of the other, and just the reverse.

Sorting this out, Stephanie remembered that only moments ago she thought she would have to quit. But she had not quit, and now she was running strongly. She was doing it! Not just running; that, it turned out, was the easy part. No, she was doing the more difficult thing. She was running hard and running easy all at once. And there was Michele, still moving with her. As good sisters do, she had given Stephanie a little boost to get her moving. And she had given her more than that. Somewhere on the road, Stephanie had caught sight of her future self. She was running on a path that shimmered like blacktop at first light and, along that path, the whole world opened up with promise.

. . . . .

In the fall, Stephanie joined Michele on the Chaska High School cross-country team. The school, with approximately 900 students, was one of the smaller teams in Minnesota's Division II. That fact would make every step on the way to the state meet, and every state meet, more competitive. It made Stephanie nervous to think what might happen, but she decided the reward was worth the risk.

As Stephanie moved to high school, Michele warned her that it would be harder than junior high. If it was, Stephanie barely felt it. She quickly left the girls behind and began running with the boys' team. While she initially satisfied herself with the assigned workouts, she soon began to add distances and workouts. By the time she graduated from high school, she would be running every morning and doing five to eight miles every afternoon. Some of the

Stephanie Herbst, an early study in concentration and relaxation.

distance was on the track in short intervals; some of it was on the roads. She lifted weights three times a week. She never missed a day of training, no matter what Minnesota's harsh weather might bring.

Training hard and regularly permitted Stephanie to feel that she controlled her own fate. She also knew the great gulf that existed between potential and performance. She would not be lulled into contentment because the activity felt natural to her and she was good at it. Alone, natural ability would get her to the starting line, which, of course, was not the point. Stephanie had to win. Thinking through this, she might have been tempted to say, "Stephanie wanted to win," but she knew that would be a lie, a deception by lack of force and power. Stephanie had to win. Working through it one more step, she knew that her determination, while it increased the likelihood of success, also made the sport more nerve-racking. It would have been easier to give herself a "back door," to find satisfaction even on days she did not win, but she did not do that.

In the first season of cross-country, Stephanie, after sharing the spotlight with a teammate for several early meets, became the team's leader. Although she did not reach the state meet in cross-country, she ran well. When track season arrived, she did even better. Without the undulations and rough surface of cross-country courses, her smooth, uniform stride was most effective. Minnesota high school rules permitted an athlete to compete in more than one race of 800 meters or longer, and Stephanie often ran both the 800 meters and the 1,600 meters. In at least one meet, she ran the two events within 15 minutes of each other and won them both. When she ran 5:18.8 for 1,600 meters, the local paper reported that the freshman had "absolutely destroyed" the school record. Perhaps the most startling performance was a race in which she climbed over and around 68 other runners to win a 1,600-meter race in 5:24, which qualified her to run in the state championship. Her best time of the year was a win at the regionals in 5:04.5.

At the state meet, Stephanie faced 20 runners in the 1,600-meter final. By the second lap, she was among the leaders; she moved to third at the three-quarters mark, and held on until the last homestretch where she was out-sprinted by two other runners. Typically hard on herself, she commented later that, "I don't know what it was. I just didn't have it today." Nonetheless, the performance was sufficient to alert the local press, which announced, "Chaska High School may have a future state champion miler in its midst." For her performances, Stephanie was named to the all-State team. Her 1,600 time was the fourth fastest in Minnesota.

Encouraged by her record freshman year, Stephanie trained throughout the summer. The University of Minnesota maintained an arboretum near her home. As her father Dan later said, "It's a great place to train. There is a three-mile path that undulates in and around hills. Stephanie worked that path to death." In fact, the arboretum was beautifully landscaped with mature trees and an attractive pond, but Stephanie never noticed. Each morning she got out of bed, dressed appropriately for the weather, stepped outside, and started running at a brisk pace. The idea of jogging her distance, or of long, slow distance, or of accumulating mileage for its own sake never occurred to her. She ran alone most days, except Sunday when she might join a friend; and every day she ran the same course, which she timed religiously, comparing her performances one day to the next. When running her course, Stephanie dreamed her future. She rehearsed the coming performances with such precision that when they arrived they were like memories.

On the arboretum course that summer, Stephanie had time to think about the flaw in her competitive running. The problem was that she tended to fight once with a rival, and, if she lost, to concede to that person in subsequent races. She even lost several races early in the cross-country season to another freshman at Chaska. Only when illness removed the girl from a later race did Stephanie assert herself and run as fast as she was able. A girl who wanted to be a champion could not afford such quirks, and Stephanie knew it.

After the summer's work, Stephanie won most of the cross-country races in her sophomore year. In her first state cross-country championship late in the fall, Stephanie went to the front of the 3,200-meter race. She said, "I try to keep a consistent pace, so to end up first I have to start fast (to get the lead) and keep it about the same." On this day, two other girls ran in her wake and out-sprinted her. Stephanie finished third, and said simply, "I was hoping to do a little better than that." If she was to do "better than that," however, it would not be at the state track meet later in her sophomore year. After a season filled with victory after victory in both the 1,600 and the 3,200 meters, she fell in the state meet's 3,200-meter race and finished fifth. The best that could be said was that she got back up while others might have stayed down. She was eighth in the 1,600 meter.

Notwithstanding the occasional upset, like that at the state meet, Stephanie's first two years in high school were successful. The first run with Michele, and the succeeding ones with the high school team, continued to indicate the same positive prospect. What's more, she had developed a context for her running: it was a means to an end, and the end was a good job. To assure that result, she studied regularly and devoted some of her remaining, available time to social activities. When she got the chance to meet someone from the local business community, she took it. As time progressed, those chances would become more formal. For example, Stephanie was invited as a guest to a local Rotary meeting and to functions of a similar nature. The invitations and appearances were consistent with Stephanie's functional view of her sport.

She had also continued to grow and mature physically. While some of her friends developed hips and thighs, Stephanie remained straight and narrow, or as she says, "tall, thin, and gangly." Her light build went well with her raking, relaxed stride. And although she claims that she was not "exceptionally attractive" and that she did not date in high school, other indicators are that she was popular. In the next year, Stephanie would enter the Chanhassen, Minnesota Junior Miss Contest. Not surprisingly, she was a winner, finishing first runner-up. In the picture taken after the contest, she holds her trophy easily, as one would who has a shelf full of them at home. In all, Stephanie was growing into the woman who would soon be labeled by one young writer—a guy, of course— as "the answer to every male runner's dreams." The sentiment was awkwardly expressed, but the meaning was clear.

Stephanie trained regularly after her sophomore season and entered her junior year with high hopes for cross-country. The two girls who beat her the previous fall had been seniors and were gone. Stephanie ran well throughout the cross-country season and was favored to win the State Championship. Still, on race day, she was nervous. She was also bothered by the weather, which was blisteringly cold and windy. Misjudging the situation, she decided to run without tights, a decision she regretted as she struggled all day to feel the ground under her frozen feet or to get loose. This was her own carelessness, she knew, which made things worse.

Stephanie sometimes claimed that not even her best friend knew that she was a runner and that no one in her high school knew she was an athlete. In truth, she was something of a sensation and had been ever since that all-State award in her freshman year of track. The previous year's third place in the cross-country meet only sharpened the attention upon her. Now, as Stephanie warmed up for the big race in her junior year, she could feel the pressure and expectation building. Closing out her warm-up and getting ready to race, struggling to get the feeling into her feet and legs, criticizing herself for a decision already made, Stephanie Herbst was everybody's favorite to win the State Championship but her own.

When the race started, Stephanie once more did the pace

work. Although she left most of the field behind almost immediately, one girl stayed with her. Stephanie could tell that the girl was a good runner and that she would not fade. The girl was also wearing warm tights, a fact that Stephanie noted ruefully. Would it have helped to have warm legs, a little blood running through there? The question was useless. Stephanie pressed along, trying to win, running stiffly and with little of her customary smoothness, all the while knowing, or at least suspecting, that she would lose. When the two of them turned into the final stretch, the other girl ran away, and Stephanie did not answer. She was second in the big race people expected her to win. Afterward, some people used the bitter cold to excuse Stephanie's loss. Stephanie herself admitted that she "thought her teeth were going to shatter." But she also knew that nerves were part of the problem. She should have won. This was one of those races about which she would say, "I was inhibited by my brain!"

Her "brain" was no problem in the track season later that junior year. She ran through a record-breaking year before winning the state championship at 3,200 meters in 11:08:70, about 10 seconds slower than her season best. She also came back for second in the 1,600 meters. Stephanie was given general credit for even attempting the double in record-breaking heat and humidity. The 1,600 meters was especially praised, as the second effort and the one in which she fought most tenaciously before losing by 2 seconds. One reporter tried to make Stephanie feel better about the loss by saying she "couldn't have come much closer than 2 seconds to the winner," but Stephanie curtly cut him off, "Oh, I could have." Implicitly, she was saying, "I should have."

Whatever the disappointments of her junior year, Stephanie washed them away in her senior year. Stephanie had always respected her elders. Now that she was the senior runner, the championships were rightly hers and she set out to get them all. First up was the long-sought and cherished State Cross-Country Championship.

This time she dressed appropriately for chilly weather and described herself as "a little less nervous than last year." As customary, she grabbed an early lead. She was ahead by 50 meters at halfway and increased the lead from there until she crossed the finish line as the new state champion. The goal accomplished, her post-race remarks were self-deprecating and graceful. "I always felt there was somebody back there who could catch me. For the last 100 meters, I couldn't believe it," she said. "There had to be somebody coming. But there wasn't. It must have been a miracle."

If it was a miracle and not merely a result of talent and hard work, the miracle repeated itself in the spring. The road was not without difficulty, however. After a uniformly successful track season, the state meet was supposed to be a triumph for Stephanie. She knew it, and so did everyone else. But Stephanie's nerves savaged her as the meet approached. Friends said they had never seen her so affected. The night before the first race, Stephanie lay awake, her mind spinning, at once considering all that was behind her and all that was ahead of her, and never able to find a reconciliation between the thoughts, and always the recognition that every moment lost was lost forever, that sleep once forfeited was irredeemable and unforgiving. Still, she lay there tossing about until 5:00 a.m. when she finally fell asleep. She woke at 9:30 a.m., feeling like she'd been beaten with a stick. To make matters worse, she missed the bus to the meet, could not get the car to start, and had trouble finding the stadium. After all that, the race over 3,200 meters was uneventful. She just ran to the front and stayed there. She won in 10:56:16, more than 20 seconds faster than her nearest pursuer. The 1,600 followed the next day. For once, Stephanie was relaxed. She again took the lead and again increased it as the distance unwound. She ran a controlled 5:01:45 to win by more than 10 seconds. With that, Stephanie had swept the board in her senior year: cross-country, 1,600 meters, and 3,200 meters. She was champion of them all.

Stephanie Herbst: Chaska Girls Athletics

At the close of her high school running, Stephanie Herbst could look back on four years in which she was a nine-time all-State performer in track and cross-country. She held school records in the 800 meters (2:21:90), 1,600 meters (4:58.97) and 3,200 meters

(10:50.3), as well as taking part of a 3,200-meter relay record. In all she owned 1,600 meters and 3,200 meters records at conference, sub-region, and regional levels. She ran 52 cross-country meets and won 43 of them. She ran 15 races at 800 meters and won 13 of them. She ran the 1,600 meters 64 times and won 59 times. She won 47 of 48 of her races over 3,200 meters. This record documents what Stephanie said about herself: I have to win. In her case, that desire, it must be said, only rarely revealed itself by pitched, back-and-forth battles along the finishing straight, pushing and clawing to exhaustion. That was not Stephanie's style, nor was it necessary. Rather, her competitive quality revealed itself in thorough preparation, and, on race day, the methodical elimination of all competition. Most often, her homestretches all looked alike, the last lap distinguished only by the fact that Stephanie stopped at the end of it.

In a short essay she wrote in high school, Stephanie said "[t]he greatest challenge and thrill is experienced in the race, but the practice is where it all happens. It (participation in sport) began and existed through the will and commitment I made to myself. Running is life, filled with effort and risk, uncertainty and tension." Remarking on the nature of triumph, Stephanie said in her essay "There is that brief wonderful moment that accompanies every race when I realize my accomplishment. For that brief moment I have sacrificed hours of psychological and physical pain."

It was a bargain she made willingly in high school, but not innocently. For Stephanie, the "sacrificed hours" were measured regularly. If they failed to produce a complementary gain, she would adjust. That much was clear from the start.

With all her accomplishments in high school, however, Stephanie would have been disquieted by a survey of the results. Looking back to a freshman year when she ran 1,600 meters in 5:04, there was only 5 seconds improvement in the next three maturing seasons. It had been sufficient, that much had to be admitted, but there was no explosive improvement. The 3,200 meters was good, at slightly faster than 11:00, but it was not overwhelming. Stephanie was merely the best woman distance runner in Minnesota's high schools. She was not one of the best high school women runners in the nation. At 1,600 meters, she was a full 5 seconds from inclusion on the national lists. She was so far back that she would not have noticed the sophomore from Stevens Point, Wisconsin, named Suzy Favor who was already safely established with the fifth-fastest time in the country. Nor would she have been aware that her 10:50 for 3,200 meters was 12 seconds away from national ranking, and a full 44 seconds behind Suzie Tuffey, a junior from Peoria, Illinois, who ran 10:06.6 to lead the list.

The high school girls were tough enough, but Stephanie would have been even more shocked to look at the college teams she might have to run with and against in the next year. In cross-country, Stephanie would have found teams from Oregon, Stanford, North Carolina State, Tennessee, and Wisconsin out front. At the National Collegiate Athletic Association (NCAA) meet, Betty Springs of North Carolina State edged away from Nan Doak of Iowa, while Cathy Branta and Katie Ishmael from nearby Wisconsin were solid all-Americans. During the 1984 track season, Stephanie would have found Ms. Branta even more impressive. At the NCAA, Branta surged the last two laps—allegedly because she feared the short kickers—to win the 3,000 meters. Outstanding competitors trailed her, including PattiSue Plumer, Shelly Steely and Sabrina Dornhoefer. At 10,000 meters, the 1983 The Athletics Congress (TAC) national champion Katie Ishmael fought hard before losing narrowly to the talented Kathy Hayes of Oregon. And in the 5,000 meters, Plumer, doubling back from the 3,000 meters, picked up her own championship. In Plumer's race, back in seventh, was Kathy Ormsby of North Carolina State, just a freshman but already running 16:19.79. Times like that were so very fast that trouble was ahead if

The reward for all her work.

Stephanie dared to approach, which she would, of course, as quickly as possible.

Statistics and comparisons aside, Stephanie reflected on her experiences in a telling high school interview. She was most proud, she said, that she had been friends with her competitors, and that so many had wished her well before the state meet. She was pleased that she had never been a bad winner or a sore loser. Perhaps thinking back to that first five-mile run, she expressed regret that her sister Michele never got the attention that she deserved for the running she did at Chaska. Stephanie also said she was sad when other people criticized her devotion to winning. She was mature enough, she proclaimed, to make her own decisions about how she wanted to compete. She would not bend for the people who thought her single-mindedness, her purpose, and her ambition were unseemly. Stephanie's attitude to such criticism was dismissive.

And well it might have been. Stephanie had earned the right to make her own way in the world. When she was two, her parents, Michael and Sharon Boll, flew away in a private plane for a planned trip. The plane disappeared. Forty days later, it was found crashed far off course in the hilly terrain of eastern Oklahoma, and Stephanie's parents were dead. Stephanie and Michele spent some months with their grandparents before Mike's sister and her husband, Dan, provided a home for them.

Even with that comfort, Stephanie had learned early one of life's hardest lessons. Security is always at risk. It is the flying kite tethered by twine to a fixed, safe point on the ground. On a good day, it gets so high that only the movement of the twine gives warning that the kite is crashing now, or that the twine is broken and the kite is released. Knowing this—so deeply as to be beyond the requirement of language or conscious thought—Stephanie would draw the elements of her life into close order. She would permit herself to dream, to aspire, to work hard in order to bring those dreams and aspirations to achievement. At the same time, and with sensitivity born of experience, she would reserve herself and she would watch. She would be cautious even in triumph. And when danger came, she would see it.

All this, of course, was remote from Stephanie's high school experience. She excelled there. Now graduated, she prepared for the next stage. She would find it had been set for her, years earlier, by girls long since grown to womanhood. These were the girls who would not cease the playing of games, who would run and jump and throw so long as it seemed right to them, whatever the consequences. These were the women who fought for and won the right to compete in sports. Although Stephanie did not see them, they were near.

THREE

Without the fact of the past, we cannot dream the future.

Brother to Dragon
Robert Penn Warren

In the city, absolute darkness is difficult to imagine. From downtown buildings, from street posts and individual houses, from cars, and from beams flashed in the sky to mark the spot where products are purchased and religion acquired, light is diffuse but palpable. Look at the sky and see how dim the stars are, and the point is made. Deep in the country, however, with twilight gone, when true night has arrived, a person can walk onto an isolated lane or into the middle of a field, and see nothing. The sight is shocking by virtue of being no sight at all. In the event, dark is not a description; it is a noun. Furthermore, as a noun, darkness is not merely the absence of something positive. It has its own values, its own impulses, and is capable of independent meaning. Its apparent nothingness says something and must be attended. Now, if you will, imagine women generally in sport at the beginning of the century. It is the city and light is diffuse. Now, imagine women running for sport at the beginning of the century. The darkness is total.

· · · · ·

Stephanie Herbst came to maturity in the middle of history. She was not a person who participated in revolutionary change, because she was born too late for that; but neither was she a person who competed after the changes wrought by revolution were fully absorbed and assimilated, with expectations settled and adjustments made. To understand Stephanie's time, then, a person looks backward and forward—backward to history and forward to the lessons her generation could teach based on the peculiarity of their experiences.

In looking backward to the history of women in competitive sports, an older quote serves as a point of reference. "In women, inferiority of the locomotive apparatus, the apparatus of physical labor, is apparent in all parts...The brain is both absolutely and relatively smaller than in men. Women have an abundant supply of soft and semifluid cellular tissue which creates softness and delicacy of mind, low power, nonresistance, passivity, and, under favorable circumstances, a habit of self-sacrifice." This quote is reputed to be from an 1840 lecture given by Chandler Gilman, M.D. to medical students at New York's College of Physicians and Surgeons. It marks the spot from which to orient a conversation about women in sport. Sport, after all, does not exist in isolation, but reflects cultural values then in place. If that is true, perhaps it can be agreed that women in athletics, so far as Dr. Gilman was concerned, started at ground zero.

The process from that arbitrary point in 1840 was one in which women in sport met objections and overcame them. The objections, when overcome or reshaped, permitted women to participate in sports unevenly. Which is, some women could participate in some sports at some times. Other women could not compete in any sports at any time. The sports in which any woman could participate changed and evolved over time. Always, some sports were favored for women and others were disfavored. In the later part of the nineteenth century and into the early part of the twentieth century, for example, it was not unusual to find women archers, tennis players, golfers, swimmers, equestriennes, and cyclists. Although early participation in even these sports was limited to society women, who had leisure, money sufficient to finance recreation, and status suffi-cient to protect them from criticism, participation in that kind of sport eventually made its way into the colleges and, finally, into the lives of working-class women.

While early participation centered on traditionally "female sports," the list of such sports slowly expanded, most prominently to basketball and track and field. Within track and field the degree of acceptance varied with the event, some being more acceptable than others. Eventually, the "athletic girl" emerged as an identifiable fig-ure. The athletic girl was defended—and defense was required—by the argument that sport made her more attractive, that it promoted healthy childbirth, and that, used by the "right types," it could have a eugenic benefit for the entire country. The athletic girl of the early part of the century merged into the flapper of the 1920s to create a model for the "new woman." In all, the period before the Depression witnessed an expansion of opportunity for women in athletics. Sport both pushed and was pulled by the general social progress.

The progress of the 1920s, although helpful as a founda-tion, barely touched the question of vigorous sports like long-dis-tance running, or, for that matter, any sports that had the potential to cause exhaustion or that emphasized the putatively manly qualities of strength and power. Sports of that nature differed in pedigree and intensity from activities like golf, archery, and tennis, and they remained distasteful. As late as 1967, when considerable progress had already been made and more was imminent, this sentiment was expressed, "It would probably be culturally unacceptable for girls to participate in a collision sport such as football," said one expert. He added his belief "that the great bulk of American people would be reluctant to see girls go into weight lifting or wrestling. At the same time, there is something very appealing about a woman in swimming, golf, or tennis, even at a national championship level. We value in this country certain attributes in men: bravery, strength, capacity to compete in vigorous sports. But in a woman we value social graces and femininity more. These are not necessarily lost in vigorous sports, but some sports are more graceful than others." The same article noted that mothers of young girls approved of swimming, tumbling and gymnastics but had doubts about other sports. "Anything that makes too many muscles is bad," one mother was quoted as saying, while another said that "Many sports are simply too mannish." Full opportunity in sport demanded that women crash through the barriers between favored and disfavored sports, between the sports that were considered consistent with femininity and those that were not. They had to claim the right to exhaustion, to severe and prolonged effort, to disheveled dress, to sweat, to odor, to harsh language, to physical familiarity, and to collapse.

With regard to vigorous, contested sports, old and new objections were drawn into battle as it heated up in the 1950s and 1960s, driven in part by an emphatic and comprehensive women's movement. Even a partial list of the objections illustrates the remaining controversy. Women should not compete in sport because to do so will cause damage to the reproductive organs. Women should not compete in sport because it will require them to dress immodestly. Women should not participate because competition requires an aggressive response that is masculine. Women should not participate because men will create a sexual spectacle of their participation. Women should not participate because it will produce muscles, which are manly. Women should not participate because to do so invites sexual interest, and leads to promiscuity. Women should not participate because they easily give way to the powerful impulses of competition and they will over-indulge. Women should not participate because women are of an essentially nervous temperament and will be damaged. Women should not participate because they will become Amazons, attractive only to other women. Women should not participate because sport will interfere with menstruation. Women should not participate because of the danger of physical injury to their light bones and otherwise delicate physical characteristics. Women should not participate because the specific sport requires arduous training, which, sustained over the long term necessary for success, is incompatible with femininity and with the proper social role of women. Women should not compete because it may cast them into direct conflict with men. Women should not compete because women are instinctively nurturing, which competitive sport is not. Women should not participate because women who participate in sports threaten men. In sum, women should not participate because the implications are just so complex that they threaten the social order in some way that is not properly understood at this point, or will cause some kind of harm or disharmony or physical injury or emotional dislocation or general frenzy, or exploitation or sexual revolution or confusion that would be altogether regrettable.

Some of the objections were nonsense. They do not encourage or bear scrutiny. Some of the objections, however, are worth a closer look either because they were based on fact, on supposition of fact, on distortion of fact, or by the projection of fact into fear. Others should be evaluated solely because, without regard to fact, they had a persistent effect on the rate at which progress was made. Of the objections, arguably the primary and most obdurate is that sport produces musculature and that musculature is inconsistent with womanhood. This allegation was most damaging when it was used as the first step in a syllogism, rarely spoken but often implied: sport produced muscles; muscles were manly; sport produced manly women; or sport attracted women who by their nature were manly. In either case, manly women could not attract a man; therefore, manly women would become spinsters; spinsters were pitiable, wasted people; or, alternatively to spinsterhood, manly women would "become" lesbians.

Before and during the growth period of the 1950s and 1960s, women often contested the stereotypes. They played sports but made special efforts to emphasize femininity. At the very least, these women distracted men who might otherwise have stated an objection had they not been slack-jawed at their good fortune. The attempt to enhance femininity suggested, however, sexuality. Unfortunately, as women who participated in sport were already "acting like men," women who enhanced their sexuality in order to gain acceptance raised the further suspicion that they would "act like a man" in social life, which is to say, they would pursue sexual relationships serially and for pleasure. Women who were African-American particularly found themselves prey to this alternative, and no less demeaning, stereotype. This was so because black women were generally stigmatized sexually. "North American and British scientists of the nineteenth century described black sexuality as lascivious and apelike, marked by a 'voluptuousness' and 'degree of lascivity' unknown in Europe." That image continued into the twentieth century and worked in tandem with the general idea that participation in sports would masculinize a woman's sexual behavior. No matter what they did, women generally and African-American women specifically hit the tripwire of one of two social objections. Either they were too manly, or they were wanton females.

Clearly, the arguments against participation, including but not limited to the ones based on physical appearance and sexual conduct, were not in good faith. Had people been in good faith, a different syllogism would have controlled the case of women in sports: men enjoy and benefit from sport; women would also enjoy and benefit from sport; the participation of women in sport should therefore be encouraged as it is for men, and to the full extent it is for men; if, in the course of women's participation in sport, specific issues arise, they should be addressed as they are for men when similar issues arise concerning their participation in sport; no statement arguing in favor of the disqualification or limitation of women in sport will be honored until it is established in fact, and until all less intrusive remedies (than disqualification or limitation) have been explored and exhausted. In all but the most extreme cases, the autonomous choice of the woman who proposes to participate in the sport will control.

Absent good faith, no one had much interest in seriously analyzing the question whether participation in sports created muscles, much less the question whether muscles were inherently inconsistent with female gender, or any of the other frivolous objections. Absent analysis, progress would have to be made by women in the field doing things that other people thought they should not be doing. Some women athletes pressed the issue by remaining absolutely true to their own nature and personality despite criticism, while others contested the issue incrementally, by taking what was offered, seeking to accommodate criticism by changes in appearance, demeanor, or attitude, and slowly but incessantly inching forward. At each progressive step, earlier criticism would fall away, having been proved by application to be untrue.

· · · · ·

Track and field is running, jumping, and throwing. None of this is particularly ladylike. In sprinting, the nose starts near the ground while the backside is up. In long jumping, the legs split wide, and the face gets close to sand. In high jumping, the old western roll is provocative, while the flop is beyond comment. The throwers emit shockingly rude noises, and the thrust—the wild swinging of arms and legs amid a barely controlled balance—is altogether wrong if the goal is good manners. Quarter-milers and half-milers occasionally vomit, such is the force of their exertion. Distance runners move lap after lap with the skin progressively flushing and mottled; when they finish they may totter. Sometimes, they crumple to the ground and sit still—for long periods of time with the gaze of spectators upon them—with no concern for comportment or the placement of their exhausted limbs. In fact, everywhere a spectator looks on track or field, a woman is assaulting the notion of ladylike behavior. If ever a sport was doomed to disfavor, track and field is it; and much work would be done before attitudes changed perceptibly.

Any conversation about the history of women in track and field can begin with Babe Didrikson. Ms. Didrikson was the greatest multiple-sport athlete that the United States has ever produced. According to one account, "[Babe] didn't confine herself to the things young women usually did. She never wore stockings and found they were the most uncomfortable things she had ever put on. She was an exuberant tomboy whose life was athletics. She ran, she threw, she swam, she jumped. She played baseball, basketball, football, tennis, lacrosse, handball. She boxed, bowled, fenced, skated, golfed, shot, cycled." Physically, she was 5' 4" tall and competed at 105 pounds. "She was a jut-jawed, raw-boned girl with the muscles of an athlete, not pretty, but not unattractive." Another sportswriter put it this way: "This chin of the Babe's, the thin, set lips, the straight, sharp profile, the sallow suntan, undisguised by rouge, regarded in connection with her amazing athletic prowess at first acquaintance are likely to do her no justice." Attempts to feminize Babe Didrikson by referring to her baking and sewing ability largely failed, unable to overcome the vision of Babe Didrikson in competition. The idea that she could look like an athlete, including a full complement of muscles, and also look like a woman, never occurred to anyone. Really, it was one or the other, muscles or femininity. Even late in life, when she married and more often wore dresses than shorts or softball outfits, it was muscles unavoidably. And when she was stared at, and judged, Babe Didrikson persevered. If Babe is legend today, it is as much for her defiant truth to herself as for pure athletic talent.

Many other women athletes in track and field competed in Babe Didrikson's model, straight-ahead, with neither apology nor stratagem. Other track and field athletes took a different path. They emphasized femininity while trying to minimize the effects of training and competition. This, of course, may have reflected the personal choice and characteristics of the competing women—who felt more comfortable with makeup and restrained manner than the unvarnished look and attitude of a Babe Didrikson—but it was also more acceptable to the viewing and funding public. For example, when Tennessee State women athletes dominated world sprinting in the 1950s and early 1960s, Coach Ed Temple enforced a dress code and otherwise facilitated a protective, feminine appearance for the runners. Wilma Rudolph, nicknamed the "black gazelle" after winning three gold medals in the 1960 Rome Olympics, was often described first in terms of her physical beauty and grace. A 1961 article in *Newsweek* captures the public image of Wilma Rudolph. After first assuring readers that Ms. Rudolph "would rather sleep than run," the writer identified her appeal as two-fold: "Unlike most American female sprinters, she wins; and, unlike many American female athletes, she looks feminine." Uniformly, Ms. Rudolph was perceived as the perfect model for a woman athlete: a combination of speed, grace, and appearance, and all without excess ambition or drive.

Furthermore, African-American female sprinters in the late 1950s and early 1960s drew advantage from an historical oddity. It was the Cold War era, and the United States was competing in dual meets with track and field teams from the Soviet Union on a yearly basis. Crowds more nearly associated with professional football games—50,000 and 60,000 people at a time—came out to watch. Because African-American sprinters were our best hope for victory in the women's events, it was easy to approve of their participation, whatever the sexual implications may have been and however much they may have been ignored in other competitions.

As late as 1965, *Sports Illustrated* covered the national indoor track and field meet almost entirely in terms of how attractive the female competitors were. The article, which consisted of four large photographs of individual women and a short narrative, reads like a boy's adventure, an ogler's delight. One woman sprinter was shown lounging in conversation with a man who was in the foreground. The woman's face was crossed by a wide smile and the posture of the woman and the framing of the photograph suggested flirtation. The woman herself was described as a "blond German," a suitably evocative image. An Asian hurdler was also pictured. She was shown in mid-flight, an image of power and speed. She was described as "comely." The fourth-place finisher in the 440, Pat Winslow (Connolly), was pictured in an expansive stretch, her arms held high above her head with sufficient tension to excite a single, admiring, celebratory word: "buxom!" Finally, the reigning Olympic champion in long jump, Mary Rand from Great Britain, inspired the narrator to close examination and meticulous judgment. Ms. Rand had, the writer opined, "a nose that is too long, a mouth that is too wide and a haircut that is too short," but, the writer continued, "somehow they [the singularly objectionable features] fit niftily with a smooth, pink complexion, a dazzling 36-24-36 figure, and a buoyant irresistible charm." So much for that Olympic gold medal.

More generally, the article described the scene at the meet in the following terms: "lithe young women leaping, running and soaring in a colorful selection of Capri stretch pants, turtlenecks, blouses, Bermuda shorts, leotards and bikini short shorts." If that doesn't bring in the crowds, nothing will, the article seems to intimate. Amid all this came the passing statement that some of the women outperformed their male counterparts, but who noticed that with all the heavy breathing? Arguably, by 1965, the images reported from the national meet were a result of the general, liberalizing shift in fashion and sexual mores that characterized the 1960s, and not necessarily the result of women who decided, consciously or subconsciously, to do whatever was necessary to defeat old stereotypes. Effectively, however, it came to the same thing; and historically, it owed a debt to other women at other times who were required to contrive appearance as the price of admission.

Women sprinters, hurdlers, and jumpers could all emphasize femininity within the context of their events, which lend themselves to such characterization, as the 1965 article proved. Shot-putters and discus throwers faced a more difficult challenge. They competed in events that rewarded size, strength, and explosive quickness, all characteristics associated with the aggressive male. While many of these women were, in fact, coordinated, graceful, and feminine, most critics had no understanding of that fact. For women in the throwing events, there was no way around the central question whether size, strength, muscularity and power were naturally inconsistent with womanhood, a question that, even now, persists although the line between acceptable and unacceptable may have been moved a bit.

Distance runners are, for the sake of this discussion, a case unto themselves. This is so because for most of the century, the question of women running long-distance events was academic only. They were not allowed to participate. The history of Olympic track and field is illustrative. Women were first permitted to compete in the Olympic Games in 1928. They were offered five events: the 100 meters, the 800 meters, the 400-meter relay, the high jump, and the discus throw. The inclusion of an 800-meter run was controversial because many people doubted that women could run that far without damaging themselves. The race itself was admirably run, as Lina Radke of Germany set a world record for women by running 2:16.8, but the immediate aftermath stirred controversy. The *New*

York Times reported that event in these terms: "The final of the women's 800-meter run, in which Frau Lina Radke of Germany set a world's record, plainly demonstrated that even this distance makes too great a call on feminine strength. At the finish, six out of nine runners were completely exhausted and fell headlong on the ground. Several had to be carried off the track. The little American girl, Miss Florence MacDonald, who made a gallant try but was outclassed, was in a half faint for several minutes, while even the sturdy Miss Hitomi of Japan, who finished second, needed attention before she was able to leave the field."

The London Times was only slightly more reserved: "The half dozen prostrate and obviously distressed forms lying in the grass at the side of the track after the race may not warrant a complete condemnation, but it certainly suggests unpleasant possibilities." Although an official at track side later termed this "one amusing little incident," and verified that there was nothing wrong with any of the participants, the harm was done. The 800 meters was removed from the schedule in later Olympic Games. It was not returned until 1960. The years between 1928 and 1960 might therefore be called "the wilderness years" for women's distance running. Events were contested, and progress was made, but few people knew of it, and even fewer appeared to care. Without a presence at the Olympic Games, interest in the events was diminished. The sport awaited its awakening.

So far as the national consciousness was concerned, the first stirring occurred in the late 1950s, and early 1960s. The consciousness was largely a matter of the national press, which, in that time, was dominated by several mass circulation periodicals. *Life, Look, Newsweek, Time* and *Sports Illustrated,* and perhaps a few others, occupied the field. Those select publications had the potential not only to reflect cultural experiences, but, by reporting them either one way or the other, to sculpt them. They are, therefore, disproportionately important in understanding how things happened.

An early example is seen in a 1961 article of *Life*. On the back pages were pictures of Julia Chase, described as a 19-year-old sophomore at Smith College. Ms. Chase was dressed casually in sweater, shorts, knee socks, and tennis shoes, and she was climbing a tree. She was also shown in the company of her brothers chasing a dog across a field. The writer assured the readers that the photographed activity was preceded by some tumbling, a game of tag and a game of ping-pong doubles, and revealed, rather remarkably, that the point to all this "monkeyshines" was to prepare Ms. Chase to run marathons. "I may be a runner," the article quoted Ms. Smith as saying, "and a girl....and something else." The "something else," the article said, was a tomboy who routinely ran four miles a day, topped off her jogs with cartwheels and calisthenics, and frequently followed that with some tree climbing. The article then reported that Julia had run two Amateur Athletic Union (AAU) marathons and finished ahead of a total of 18 men. Of course, she was not permitted to enter officially, could not begin the races on the starting line, and sometimes was required to give the men a block headstart, a collection of circumstances to which no objection was voiced, the entire body of them being accepted as natural—certainly more natural than what this girl was doing. As to her family's reaction, her mother is quoted as saying only that "I don't know what she's doing out there, but she does it all the time."

The article on young Julia Chase is instructive because it trivializes Julia's activity as a way of approving it, or of at least withholding disapproval. So long as the training was the rough equivalent of other "monkeyshines" like tree climbing, and so long as it was done by a 19-year-old "tomboy" who might be expected to grow out of the strange phase, it was acceptable, even amusing. One can only imagine what the reaction would have been if people had acknowledged that Julia Chase was a serious athlete engaged in the business of running long distances at the peak of her physical and mental ability. Socially, it also did not hurt that Julia was at Smith College, a highly respected women's school, and that her mother was quoted from the family home in Groton, Connecticut, a very proper neighborhood that could provide insulation from criticism. When the article mentioned that Julia formerly rowed a canoe to her high school classes, the comforting image of eccentric privilege was complete.

Later in the 1960s, other girls and women emerged from the wilderness with an interest in distance running. Occasionally, influential national publications noticed. Viewed with a jaundiced and judgmental eye, all of the early articles were sexist, patronizing, flippant, trivializing, and insulting. On the other hand, most of the articles, read with an understanding of the times and the developing culture, validated the subject's participation in the sport, and encouraged other girls and women to join in. Furthermore, the fact that the articles appeared at all was important for the development of interest.

If you go today to a cross-country meet and see hundreds and thousands of young high school girls most of whom are white, running with enthusiasm and pride across well-marked and attended courses, and you notice that the girls are healthy and vigorous and attractive and secure, you should think of a young girl who competed long ago named Marie Mulder. Marie Mulder came to prominence in 1965, when *Newsweek* magazine introduced her as a pretty 15-year-old from North Highland, California, who was learning to sew, got good grades in school, and had an "unusual ambition for an American girl." She wanted to be a long-distance runner. After noting that Marie had set an American record of 2:07 for 800 meters in finishing second at the US-USSR track meet, that she could do 70 push-ups, and that she religiously ran three to seven miles every day—performances that might be expected to suggest seriousness of purpose and dedication—the article darted in the other direction.

"When asked about her unusual regimen, Marie gushes like a typical teenager. 'It's fun,' she says effusively." The juxtaposed messages about Marie Mulder were clear. To a general audience, she was just a kid whose preoccupation with sport was not a matter of concern. To her peers, she was a pretty and popular girl whose example was encouraging.

The next time Marie appeared in the national press, she was on the cover of *Sports Illustrated*. With her signature dark hair and long, tan legs, she was running with a friend, an equally attractive blonde girl. They were striding evenly across a colorful, flowered field. Both seemed happy to be where they were, doing what they were doing. The magazine cover read: "Remarkable US Teen-Age Distance Runners Marie Mulder and Janell Smith." Inside, the refrain was familiar. The story was titled "This is the Way the Girls Go" and the caption read "Two strictly feminine teenagers from towns and backgrounds widely separated are proving that running for distance is not so un-American after all." The article itself chronicled a comfortable combination of good looks, excellent grades, steady families, sewing, working around the home, traditional teenage responsibility at school, and, of course, extraordinary running. The photos of Marie and Janell were equally familiar. Marie was at sewing class. "Californian Marie Mulder sews as well—but not as fast—as she runs." Janell, seated among her classmates back in Fredonia, Kansas, "is like any all-round high school senior—except that her sport is middle distance running." And, again, there was the reference to graceful athleticism. Both girls ran "like boys," if not better, and both worked very hard without sacrificing the qualities of young girls. Marie's workouts were given in detail. She ran five times a week with workouts such as three miles of 220-yard sprints. Surveying a scene of Marie and her teammates practicing, Marie's coach expressed his satisfaction. "And look at 'em. Not a dog in the bunch. Every one as neat and feminine as you'll find."

For a mother or father who thought of sending a daughter to track practice, the message was reassuring.

The article on Marie and Janell was interesting in another respect as well. It included a sign, consciously or unconsciously, that someone had decided to draw white girls who ran distance away from their counterparts who sprinted and threw, some of whom were black, but all of whom presented different challenges in terms of social acceptance. The article, which was designed to introduce a new generation of American girls competing in track and field, included a short paragraph that followed the statement that Marie and Janell were "excellent examples of the present and future of American women's track and field." The short paragraph acknowledged that there were "others," and identified several sprinters, hurdlers and throwers. Lynn Graham, a 17-year-old from Pasadena, had just set the American indoor and outdoor records for the shot-put, and was one of the noteworthy. Ms. Graham was shown in a photograph with the caption "unseasoned shot-putter," along with the further notation that she was "catching up" with Russia's Tamara Press. Ms. Graham, who is African-American, was posed with her head resting in one hand while the other hand gripped a large shot. Her hair was uncombed and her expression was disinterested. The mention of Tamara Press was unflattering. Informed readers recognized Ms. Press as a massive Russian thrower surrounded by rumors that she was, in fact, a man. In narrative and photograph, the reader was allowed none of the grace and strength that must have characterized Ms. Graham's performances. There was nothing alluring in the short paragraph about her and the sprinters and hurdlers, and no discernible invitation for other young girls to join them.

In fairness, it should be noted that other articles did speak of the sprints and throws with more detail and in greater context. The importance of this part of the Mulder/Smith article is that it arguably illustrated a theme that was crucial to the development of women's distance running in the United States. Commentators and academic scholars now detect in that development a design of "virtue by association." Succinctly, one writer said "Rather than credit the achievements of African-American athletes who had overcome sexual and racial barriers to excel in their sport, athletic leaders legitimized track and field by treating it as a sister sport to 'feminine' and overwhelmingly white sports like gymnastics, swimming and diving, and the recently adopted sport of synchronized swimming." The distinction can be made finer by saying that the virtue was particularly ascribed to the formerly unthinkable act of running long.

The emphasis on grace, beauty, and youth in long-distance running was also prominent in a *Sports Illustrated* story about Roberta Bingay, who ran the Boston Marathon in 1966. The story was titled, "A Game Girl in a Man's Game." The subtitle reported that Boston had been "unprepared for the shapely blonde housewife who came out of the bushes to crush male egos and steal the show from the Japanese." A photograph of the finish line showed Ms. Bingay—a "tidy looking and pretty 23-year-old blonde"—finishing the marathon in relaxed fashion, with her arms swinging smoothly above newsworthy legs. In fact, Roberta Bingay, having discarded a bulky sweatshirt at three miles, ran the full marathon in 3:21, a creditable time for men and women alike more than 30 years later. The article about Ms. Bingay's marathon contained the blend of elements that was becoming traditional in the early writing about women who ran distance events. The elements included an admission that the women trained hard and consistently—in Ms. Bingay's case it was 2 hours a day, seven days a week with an occasional 5-hour run thrown in "to keep her from getting lazy"—but with the assurance that they ran for fun. Ms. Bingay, for example, was quoted as saying competition did not interest her, but she ran to absorb the beauty of nature. Also noted was the fact that Ms. Bingay had not been permitted to enter the event officially, thus the necessity to come out of the bushes. Like Moses, one surmises, a long way from the Promised Land, but making a start of it.

Marie Mulder was back in *Sports Illustrated* later in 1966 to carry the women's case. She joined 107 other women in St. Louis' Forest Park for the third ever National AAU Cross-Country Championship, an event the article said was one "everybody was not talking about and the papers were not full of," and at which "there was hardly anybody around but chicks." The article began with a graphic description of the perils of cross-country running, especially when conducted on a challenging, muddy course, and the effect on young girls who competed. Quickly, however, the article tracked back to comforting images of "shaved legs, the singlets that actually do a service, all that symmetry, that fragrant hair." Marie again was an object of attention. She was a "pretty little thing" who had "thinned out a little and is running very well." She had grown her hair long to "please the latest target of her big brown eyes," the article noted. All of the contestants were called girls. The most prominent among them was a 24-year-old physical education teacher from Seattle, Washington, who was described as "the girl for now." This was Doris Brown. Doris said that she didn't like races much, but she did enjoy training. She worked out with her husband, who was also a runner. The article said that Doris held the world indoor record for the mile in 4:52, but that, the author added, was like "setting a record for peaches canned or trading stamps licked." More to the point, the writer thought that Doris was "handsomely feminine," whatever that means. In any event, the description presented the opportunity to ask Doris directly about the femininity issue, essentially whether the other runners were like her. Aware of the subtext, Doris said flatly, "I do not know any girl running who is not feminine." Whatever that means, either, for that matter, but everybody got the point. "Come on in, the water's fine; no big muscles here; nobody here but us normal girls, having fun." This article, paren-

Marie Mulder: 1966, Forest Park, St. Louis, Missouri.

thetically, was titled, "Chasing Girls Through the Park." What could be more normal? As for the championship itself, it was quickly over. Doris beat Marie by 200 yards over the 1.5-mile-long course in 7:51.2, the first time anyone could remember a woman being under 8 minutes for the distance, and a time fast enough, surely, for many boys and men to worry—for maybe the first time—that these "girls" could outrun them given a fair opportunity.

Marie was in action again in February, 1967, at a major indoor meet covered by *Sports Illustrated*. She had not been training well, and she was threatened by Canada's "curly haired Abby Hoffman" and by Charlette Cooke, "the strawberry blonde with a dancer's body." Actually Marie got beat by Ms. Hoffman who set a Canadian record, but it was all right, because Marie was improving, the story offered reassuringly, and she would be fine. Anyway, she had let her hair grow out yet again. "Her soft brown hair, once cut in a boyish bob, now hangs down to her shoulders, flowing behind her when she runs, like Batman's cape." Marie said she grew her hair out because she got tired of people thinking she was a boy in need of a haircut. "Now they know for sure I'm a girl," she said. They might also have known because Marie and her friends were by now becoming familiar sights, as many young girls were turning to distance running. "All of a sudden," said Marie, "a whole lot of girls were running in the meets, especially 12 and 13 year olds." Meanwhile, the reader found out that Doris Brown wasn't running the meet because "the arches in her fast little feet were aching from overwork." But this too was fine because Doris was still married, and still teaching school, and still running on both tracks and trails. The reader was also told that Doris "keeps her 5'4", 108-pound figure svelte by training twice a day." Perhaps other women, reading the article, would like to share Doris' good fortune by engaging in a little exercise?

Too soon, Marie Mulder finished running, or rather, she

stopped competing on the national and international level. Doris Brown continued. In other articles, she and her coach, Dr. Ken Foreman, made the case that women could run and remain feminine. In a 1969 *Sports Illustrated* article, Doris got the opportunity to discuss a five-mile run through the Arboretum at the University of Washington. She described the maples and red pines and katsura trees whose beauty was typical of what runners see along the way, and consistent, she said, with her view that "running is a matter of enjoyment and a means of fulfilling your needs, to at least partially give back to others what they have given to you." Doris spoke while at the National Cross-Country Championship which, that year, had grown to 542 girls age seven and older. Doris now had a fight from such young runners as the emerging Francie Larrieu, then described as a "bouncy" 17-year-old, but destined to be one of the most important and enduring contributors to women's long-distance running in this country, and by Cheryl Bridges, and Pat Cole. All these women were pioneers who had been disqualified from their high school teams on the basis of gender, but had persisted. At this race, Doris won, as she always seemed to do in those years, but that was not the story. The story was that she faced increasing competition.

The increased number of girls and women competing as runners did not mean that the environment was free of bias. Runners and coaches still had to defend themselves. Commenting on the 1969 National Cross-Country Championship, Dr. Foreman volunteered, "The women running are tremendously sensitive people. They are an amazing transition from the typical brute, from the archetype that all those who don't know women's track claim them to be." Couched as denial, the comment proves that the spectral figure—the masculine female—was still out there, and a force to be reckoned with.

· · · · ·

The figure was still out there, in part, because the question whether women could compete in arduous sports while remaining feminine was getting tangled up in two other questions. The first question was "when is a woman not a woman?" The second question was what happens when a women takes steroids, or other performance-enhancing drugs, thereby further, and in this case unnaturally, closing the distance between men and women.

The question of womanhood arises when women compete against women, and when the charge is made that one competitor has gained an advantage by bringing to the competition the advantage of masculinity, based as it is on the fixed notion that to be male is to be stronger and faster. Unfortunately, sports administrators, from time to time, have lost sight of even that marginally defensible excuse to question the gender of women. Too often, while allegedly looking for unfair advantages, they have wandered off into characteristics that bear no logical relation to the issue. When she was 17 years old, Francie Larrieu was required to submit to a sex test. Referring to the doctor who would check her, she said, "My gosh, couldn't he see?!" Her reaction makes more sense than much of what was happening then or has happened since on the issue.

Regarding sex testing, it is first important to know how rare the source of true concern is, that is, men dressed up as women, binding themselves and slipping through undetected so that they can compete for self and country. Certainly, that happened once without question because the perpetrator, Hermann ("Dora") Ratjen from Bremen, Germany, admitted publicly that in the 1930s he had been forced to pose as a woman by officials of the Nazi Youth Movement. As a woman, he finished fourth in the women's high jump in the 1936 Berlin Olympics and in 1938 set a world record in the event.

More frequently, people are affected by physical irregularities that create for them a twilight existence which is neither wholly male or female. The Czech athlete Zdena Koubkova, who set a world record of 2:12.8 for 800 meters at the World Games in London in 1934, is a case in point. Reportedly, medical authorities later determined that Koubkova was a man, and operated to correct the abnormality, thereby making it possible for him to marry and live as a man. Aleksandra Chudina of the former USSR also competed as a woman. At 6' 2" tall, she set world records in the high jump and the pentathlon before being retired, reputedly to compete in Moscow on a volleyball team composed entirely of others of "her own kind." Shim Geum Dan of North Korea is also mentioned in reports on this issue. Shim held the record for the women's 400 meters in 1967 at 51.9 and held unratified records of 51.4 for 400 meters and 1:58 for 800 meters. At her prime, the gap between Dan's performances and other competitors was 6.3 seconds in the 400 meters and 19.3 seconds in the 800 meters. Of Shim, it was said that Olympic coach Payton Jordan saw her compete in Moscow in 1963, and characterized her hip action and development as that of a man. Allegedly, a South Korean recognized Shim later as the son from whom he had been separated in the Korean War, a remarkable circumstance since it was later claimed that Shim married and had two children!

Finally, accounts refer to Claire Bresolles and Lea Caurla who competed for France at the European Championships in 1946. Of Bresolles, a 1967 report said that she answered to the name Pierre and was a father. Lea Caurla was said to have had an operation that was so successful that she/he served in the French airforce, an occupation reserved for men at the time. Finally, the Eastern Bloc nations contributed a number of prominent instances. Tamara and Irina Press of the Soviet Union competed between 1959 and 1965. Between them, they took five Olympic gold medals and set twenty-six world records. They competed at a time when it was commonly rumored that Eastern European men bound their genitals and took estrogen in order to develop breasts and compete as females. When sex tests were first initiated at the European Outdoor Track and Field Championships at Budapest in 1966, the Press "sisters" failed to appear. Suspicion and mistrust has dogged their accomplishments ever since. Iolanda Balas of Romania also failed to compete in Budapest. Balas was the Olympic women's high jump champion in 1960 and 1964, and set the Olympic record on both occasions. Her record jump in 1964 was 6' 2-3/4". Even with the assistance of Mexico City's high altitude, the best the winner there could do was 5' 11-3/4". Ms. Balas was suspected primarily because she withdrew from the competition at Budapest by claiming injury, and because she retired from all international competition just as sex tests were generally instituted.

It is impractical, and perhaps impossible, to know the truth to any of these allegations without considerable and confidential inquiry. In some instances, the evidence is stronger than in others. With regard to the Press sisters, for example, the head coach of the Soviet track and field team was quoted in *The London Times* as saying that his team had voted in favor of tests when the issue came up at the Olympic Games in Tokyo, 1964. Tests were subsequently made at the Soviet Championships in 1966, and the decision was made that the Press sisters should not compete as a result of those tests. This decision was made, in words attributed to Soviet coach Korobkov, so that "no unfair advantage would be taken." In other instances, the evidence is circumstantial and correspondingly less reliable. Individual situations may never be understood, and the allegations never established as either true or false. That the issues arise, however, is independently instructive. It reveals that the question of gender haunts women's athletics.

The test in Budapest in 1966, which the Press sisters and Iolanda Balas skipped, was a so-called "nude parade." Apparently, 234 women competitors were required to walk naked past an assortment of gynecologists for a visual inspection. They all passed. Subsequently, International Olympic Committee members decided to impose more sophisticated tests. Beginning in 1967 on a trial basis and in 1968 on a regular basis, international competition for women included a sex test. The International Amateur Athletic Federation (IAAF) joined the International Olympic Committee (IOC) in imposing sex tests, thereby emphasizing the seriousness of the issue and the resolute quality of the response. The prominent measure required by both IOC and IAAF—the key to a "fem card," certifying eligibility to compete as a woman—was the buccal (inside of cheek) smear test. This test has nothing to do with appearance, or strength, or even sexual function. It is simply a microscopic analysis of cells to determine whether the person has chromosomes in the correct pattern, XX for females, and XY for males. When the test reveals an abnormality, further testing and evaluation can be ordered for verification.

The first person to run publicly afoul of the chromosome test was the Polish sprinter, Eva Klobukowska. Ms. Klobukowska was a member of Poland's 1964 Olympic gold medal 400-meter relay team in Tokyo, and was the co-world record holder for 100 meters at the time of her disqualification in 1967. She passed the visual test at the European Championships in 1966, along with everyone else there; but in 1967 the buccal smear test, which was used for the first time as a trial, said that she had a chromosomal irregularity. Subsequent evaluation concluded that she had been "unwittingly competing" as a female when she was, for purposes of competition, ineligible. To keep the results confidential, the international committee suggested that Ms. Klobukowska compete in meets subsequent to the test, but withdraw at an appointed time, citing injury. However, when Poland contested the test results, the incident became a public scandal. Dr. Max Danz, president of the West German Track and Field Association and a member of the European

Committee of the IAAF, was quoted as saying "It was absolutely firmly established that she is no female." Ms. Klobukowska, the central figure of a spectacle she did not create and for which she bore no responsibility, spoke for all women, presumably, when she said: "I know what I am and how I feel....It's a dirty and stupid thing they do to me."

As it happens, Ms. Klobukowska may have been right when she said it was a "stupid" thing they did to her. Stupid, that is, because the chromosomal tests, and the configuration of X and Y chromosomes, often confer no competitive advantage on the person so constructed. A second scandal, and one is tempted to say outrage, illustrates the point. The woman involved was Maria Jose Martinez Patino, and the year was 1988. Ms. Patino was in Kobe, Japan to compete for Spain as a hurdler in the World University Games. In the ordinary course, she reported to "sex control," and permitted cells to be scraped from the inside of her mouth to determine the sexual pattern of her chromosomes. This was not a matter of concern to her; she had been tested previously at the World Track and Field Championships in Helsinki in 1983 and was certified. She had a "certificate of femininity," and was being retested only because she forgot to bring it to Japan. On this occasion, however, the tests revealed an irregularity. Ms. Patino was told moments before her event that she would be required to fake an injury in the preliminary round and withdraw, which she did.

After an anguished week in Japan waiting for the meet to conclude, she went home. As in Ms. Klobukowska's case, an arrangement was made that Ms. Patino enter an additional competition notwithstanding the result of the sex test, but contrive another injury. If she did not, the test result would be made public. This time, however, Ms. Patino refused. Although sick with worry that officials would stop the race, she ran and won. The next week, a story about her situation appeared in Madrid's leading daily newspaper and many more articles followed. Ms. Patino was expelled from the national sports residence, lost her coach, many friends, and her peace of mind. All this occurred because a chromosome was out of order.

Ironically, Ms. Patino derived no athletic advantage from the irregularity detected by the so-called sex test. Deviations from the usual XX or XY chromosomal patterns occur in approximately one out of every 1,000 births. In the development of gender, however, more is involved than the composition of chromosomes. Ms. Patino would soon learn from her own endocrinologist that she was, in fact, initially conceived with an XY pattern (i.e., male), and developed testes, but that thereafter she was subject to a genetic mutation by which she was rendered completely and totally unresponsive to testosterone. In the developing fetus, this condition always leads to female gender. In Ms. Patino's case she had no uterus and was sterile, but otherwise she looked and functioned entirely as a female. The testes, which might otherwise have suggested ambiguity, were internal and atrophied. Furthermore, because Ms. Patino remained unresponsive to testosterone, her condition created disadvantage not advantage to her participation in sports. Faced with this evidence, officialdom recanted and restored Ms. Patino to eligibility. The harm, however, could never be undone.

The condition to which Ms. Patino is subject is called androgen insensitivity. Androgen insensitivity, because it mocks the significance of chromosomes in gender development, supports the argument that chromosomes should not be used to distinguish men from women in the context of athletic competition. Finally in 1991, the IAAF accepted this argument and stopped using the buccal smear test. The IAAF determined to rely on visual inspections made incidentally when women were providing urine for drug screens. The IAAF also referred to national federations and the advisability of conducting medical examinations "for the health and well-being of all athletes," including a "simple inspection of external genitalia."

The IOC continued to use the buccal smear test and conducted them for the 1996 Olympic Games in Atlanta.

The question of gender is, however, far from resolved. No one wishes men to compete as women, and therefore most would wish for a bright line to separate the genders. On the other hand, no one wishes to stereotype the female gender by reference to less strength, less speed, less musculature, less power and less endurance. Therefore, any reference to those characteristics to establish the bright line would be inappropriate; and, it can be said, any reference to naturally occurring physical or hormonal characteristics that lead generally to greater strength, speed, musculature, power, and endurance, but which do not essentially change women to men, are also inappropriate.

. . . . .

If sex testing raises (or lowers) questions of fairness to an ambiguous level, the same cannot be said for the second specter that affects both men and women in sports: chemical and other artificial enhancements. Here the question is not what nature provided and what the individual developed, it is cheating. If an accepted group has decided that some assistance to competition, like proper nourishment, adequate medical care, secure housing, and good coaching are acceptable, and other assistance, such as steroids, is not, it is incumbent upon all in the group to comply. Otherwise, unfair advantage is taken.

Admitting that people who cheat, like people who steal, will always find a way around any impediment, and are therefore constantly locating new and better ways to enhance performance inappropriately, such as the use of human growth hormones and various methods to manipulate oxygen levels in the blood, anabolic steroids nevertheless remain a central part of the problem. Anabolic steroids are a synthetic form of male hormone, called androgens. They are taken because they increase strength and endurance, and they increase oxygen uptake (VO2 Max) and red blood cell count. Steroids also permit an athlete to recover faster after hard efforts, and therefore to train more consistently at high levels.

Steroids were first used in the 1950s, but popularized, if that is the term, in the 1960s by weight lifters, shot-putters, and discus throwers. Soon, the use of steroids exploded from this narrow group into wider circulation. Women athletes found steroids particularly tempting. This was true, in part, because steroids had special benefit for women. At the time of the 1996 Olympic Games in Atlanta, the USOC Drug Education Handbook stated that: "Excessive amounts of testosterone [the naturally occurring male hormone] above the levels normally found in the urine can be detected. A drug test is positive for testosterone if the administration of testosterone or the use of any other manipulation has the result of increasing the ratio in the urine of testosterone to above six." Dr. Don Caitlin of the USOC testing laboratory explained the guideline this way: "Everyone, male and female, naturally has some testosterone, and the normal ratio of testosterone to epitestosterone (a hormone similar in structure to testosterone, but one that does not function as a male hormone) is one-to-one, for both men and women. In order to avoid false positives in drug tests and allow for naturally occurring variations, the IOC medical committee agreed to allow a six-to-one ratio of testosterone to epitestosterone before banning an athlete, male or female." However, the ratio used to detect steroid use works better for men than for women. Simply, the test catches more men than women because when a man uses "out of body" testosterone, his own natural production lowers and he has to compensate by taking even more, thus raising his ratio and increasing the possibility of detection. However, because the natural testosterone level in women is low, even minor increases in the level significantly enhance performance. This fact permits women to take testosterone in low doses, but with little chance of exceeding the permitted ratios. The chance of detection is slight. In the meantime, according to one expert, "Even slight changes in male blood hormone (testosterone) levels can convert mediocre female athletes into champions." For women, the attraction is obvious: low risk, high gain. The situation for women who cheat is further improved by newer drugs that are so transient they cannot be detected one day after being taken. On the other hand, the benefit of taking those drugs—enlarged muscles and strength—continues after the drug is out of the system.

In 1997, Dr. Caitlan announced the development of a testing method that was more reliable than the "ratio" method and did not, apparently, distinguish between men and women in its efficacy. The new test directly measures carbon isotopes in urine samples. The carbon isotope ratio of pharmaceutical testosterone is lower than testosterone that occurs naturally, a fact that provides the key to detection. Assuming that no inconsistency arises in the procedure and that other variables do not cloud the results, the new test may help validate future performances, even if it does not address the myriad other ways athletes and coaches seek the short way home.

On the specific question of anabolic steroids, moreover, current scientific methods permit effective measurement and detection. Women could take blood tests, which would show the actual amount of testosterone in the body. Bearing in mind that even the blood test would establish only an effect and not a cause for higher testosterone levels, and acknowledging the need to study aberrant results separately, the use of blood tests could permit women to compete more evenly.

. . . . .

Women distance runners are carried along by the contro-

versies of gender and drugs. Especially when times drop precipi-
tously, either or both issues can be raised, particularly when the
progress comes from a closed society that defies scrutiny and regular inspection, as it did historically behind the Iron Curtain and more
recently in China. Some North African countries also pose difficulties. But in the ordinary course, women distance runners are not the
principals in such controversies. This is because women distance
runners typically do not look like men. They are not big, not muscle
bound, not explosive in their movements. As a result, while people
knowledgeable about the sport might fret and worry whether the
female distance runners from the former Eastern Bloc or from China
are, or are not, taking steroids or doing something else to enhance
performance artificially, the general population does not react to that
controversy the way it would if the women began to bend gender
visually, as occasionally happens in a more pronounced way in the
strength and sprint events.

Aspiring women distance runners are often thin, conscientious, and dependable in the activities related to performance. The
sport rewards those virtues, so it attracts people with them and
develops them in people who lack them. Certainly, Stephanie Herbst
was in the fold when she graduated from high school: tall, thin,
introspective, careful, perhaps tightly strung, but no man by any
measure and certainly not in appearance, in fact rather the reverse
judged by the result of the Junior Miss contest and other affirma-
tions of her femininity. But the thinness of women distance runners
like Stephanie, which protects them from some controversy,
envelops them in others. Too often, they hear the whispers that they
are too thin; they are too nervous; they are bulimic; they are anorexic; none of them has a period. Not only do they look like boys, they
live like boys.

On one level the boyish look, the relative paucity of curves
on a woman who runs hundreds of miles a month is, or at least has

been, a social advantage for women distance running. It fit into the look of the 1920s flapper, the tomboy, the waif, and other relatively non-threatening gender images. However, athletic amenorrhea, anorexia, bulimia and other eating disorders are a grave concern among women distance runners and others involved in the sport. Many fine runners work at the edge, trying to be as thin as possible without sacrificing endurance and strength. Occasionally, the end is lost to the means, which becomes an end in itself, pulling from the woman all her reserves of discipline and self-respect. The situation is aggravated by the illusion of control. Studies suggest that women who value achievement, higher education, and professional careers are more likely to be obsessed with thinness and suffer from eating disorders. For these and other women, a surrounding culture sells the idea that if a woman can control her body, she can control her life. For women distance runners, the fixation on weight and body shape is doubled, which is to say that the song they hear is twice as loud, emanating as it does from two sources—one the general culture and the other a sport for which thinness is a valuable characteristic. One summary of the situation points out the depth of the problem by saying, "In Western society, women are consistently and obsessively concerned not with the process of becoming more physically adept or expressive of the needs of their own participating bodies, but instead with the body and the self as products and conveyers of information to the observer. Since the body is never a finished product, but only as good as it is at the moment, only a work in progress, women must be eternally vigilant about appearance." Granted that many women athletes, including distance runners, do in fact use their "participating bodies," the question of impermanence remains. If success in distance running comes and goes depending on fitness, and if a woman's body is constantly subject to change, then women distance runners are twice told: you need to be thin and, to be thin, you must be vigilant. No wonder, then, that some women distance runners—

many of them fitting the stereotype of ambitious people who "value achievement" and hold professional ambitions—have occasional trouble remembering that "too thin" is a legitimate concept.

Some studies place the minimum percent of body fat at which women should run at 10 or 12 percent, although many women should run at significantly higher percentages. Numbers that fall steeply below the norm may promise short-term benefit and long-term risk, a bargain only a fool knowingly makes. If eternal vigilance is demanded, and it may be, the question of health should be its center rather than performance or appearance. Increasingly, the popular media now includes women with muscles and size, but those messages are not particularized to distance running for women. In fact, many elite women distance runners continue to record body fat nearer to 6 percent than 10 percent, a fact that is, rather unfortunately, linked to excellent performance, and which tempts some women to walk a fine line indeed.

Of course, the risk of weight loss or eating disorder is a cautionary note; it is not an objection to participation itself. Nor are other objections sufficient to stop a woman from participating. Some objectors, for example, placed damage to internal sex organs and interference with pregnancy on their lists. In the usual circumstance, these objections are baseless. The uterus is one of the most shock-resistant organs. Generations of women have now proved that the alarm was false. The same may be said for pregnancy. Practice outran social and medical concern. Women ran, and they had healthy babies after uneventful pregnancies. On the list, too, was the idea that competitive sport was inconsistent with the naturally nurturing female. The idea that females and males "care" differently is controversial. That fact notwithstanding, some respected scholars argue that girls are taught concepts of "relatedness" and carry those lessons into a nurturing adulthood, epitomized by traditional motherhood; and, correspondingly, that boys are not taught the same nurturing lesson: "One of the repeated injunctions to young boys is not to pay much attention to others' feelings and needs, not to be empathetic, not to be concerned with feelings or relationships—those domains are for girls." Accepting, for purposes of discussion only, that girls are nurturers by nature or learning, it would stand to reason that competitive athletics would carry exaggerated pressure. To compete is to defeat, not to enable, encourage, soothe, or facilitate. Phrased another way, coming at the woman in sport from one side is her instinct and her instruction to nurture; coming at the woman from the other side is her relatively new instruction: win.

On a page devoted to fashion on October 31, 1996, a day no different, really, than any other before or since, *The New York Times* remarked on "the tension emerging this season between hard and soft, masculine and feminine." Within the careful phrasing is nuance; a woman may wear clothing with a masculine quality, but that clothing must reach back and refer to the essential nature of woman. It must be soft, perhaps pliant, with just the suggestion that it will give way to force. So it is with women as they enter ever more strenuous sports. Advances are made; they are permitted, but they are also qualified by reference to the continued expectation that women will yield. The injustice of requiring women to define themselves in feminine terms while competing in masculine terms creates a false dichotomy based on gender; it wrongly links essentially asexual qualities to gender differences; and it promotes conflict, both for the woman who attempts to meet the demands made of her, and for men who may presume the right to enforce the stereotypes.

That said, however, something in the injustice makes women's athletics more fascinating than men's athletics. If running itself creates a conflict between the contradictory impulses of exertion and relaxation, women's running adds a second layer of complexity based on gender and social expectation. Measured by reconciliation as well as athletic performance, the skill required for success is vastly more subtle, and the women who accept the challenge are, to that degree, more fascinating, if not more admirable.

FOUR

Not for delectations sweet; Not the cushion and the slipper, not the
peaceful and the studious; Not the riches safe and palling, not for
us the tame enjoyment/
Pioneers! O Pioneers!

Leaves of Grass
Walt Whitman

Opening your eyes, fall from the near dawn into the new
day, silent and unknowable. Ignore the meek who hesitate. They
prefer the dark for its stillness, its isolation, its promise of identity.
The stillness is no life; the isolation is no protection. The identity is
monstrous, composed of people at ease—before ambition, before
accomplishment, before failure, before cruelty, even before kindness that must be repaid. That is not for you. Step out: be the first
person into the last darkness, the one bold enough to draw the light.
This is the courage of desire. This is the willingness to see something and to want it, and, wanting it, to go and get it. This is the
courage of morning, with boundless possibility. Darkness has no
hold. It is not permitted. And you, being first in the light, shall have
no true companion.

. . . . .

No one told Doris Brown to run. She just did. She had been
born Doris Severtsen in 1942, took a few years to get her legs under

her, and then took off. While other kids rode bikes back and forth to visit each other, Doris ran. When she needed quiet moments alone, or merely to shake out the nervous energy, she ran. On the beaches and forest trails near her home, she often ran as far as ten miles with no notion of training. The long runs were simply a way of feeling alive. Asked what her parents thought of this behavior, she says they didn't know. They did know later, when Doris decided to join a local track club.

The small club had been started by an older man who knew nothing about running except that the girl next door had talent but no opportunity. He was the kind of coach who would run onto the track just before the gun went off and offer his girl a doughnut, "for the energy." Although the offer was sweet, it was unnecessary. The longest distance any of his girls ever ran was 75 yards. As for Doris, all she had in mind was the long jump. She chose that event because, as far back as she started, it was longer than the 75-yard dash and she wanted the extra distance. At first, her parents refused to let her join the team—surely there were more productive and appropriate ways for a young girl to spend energy than running up and down and jumping—but Doris persisted. Eventually they not only agreed but helped and encouraged her.

In deferring to Doris, Mr. and Mrs. Severtsen were wise. If ever a person was bound to run, with all the sense of obligation and inevitability that word—"bound"—conjures, it was Doris. A spirit moved within her and she would move with it. Truly, she could do no other. Restless, athletic, and to all appearances a tomboy waiting to grow out of the phase, Doris first played softball, one of the few organized sports available for girls and young women at the time. She enjoyed being a member of the team and the experience. But softball was just a fun thing she did in the summer. It would never become part of her life, never give her the opportunity to win or lose on her own merits, to define herself by her planning and her effort, or take her where she needed to go. Running could do those things.

Still, Doris' introduction to organized running was not without inconvenience. She was surprised to find, for example, that she would be required to wear shoes when she competed. She preferred barefoot because it was natural to her, and the feel of the surface directly beneath her was part of the pleasure of running. Nevertheless, after some thought, she made the sacrifice. She put the shoes on and jumped well. She might have stayed with the long jump if success in local meets, where she excelled, was the criteria. But it didn't happen that way. Instead, her age-group team traveled the short distance to Canada, and there, Doris was given the chance to run a whole quarter-mile. She only did it because a teammate who might have run the event was out of town, and somebody had to fill the spot. It is not hard to imagine Doris churning around the dirt track, and it comes as no surprise that she covered that first quarter-mile in a shade under 60 seconds, sensational running for a girl so inexperienced. Needless to say her jumping career was over.

Within two years of her first track meet, Doris moved up to the half-mile. The year was 1960, and her inspiration was the Olympic Games to be held that year in Rome. The schedule included a women's 800-meter run for the first time in 32 years. Doris meant to be there. It sounded like a wish and a prayer, but her chances were realistic. Not many girls ran the 800 meters in 1960, and fewer trained for it. Even if Doris failed to make the Olympic qualifying standard established for the event, she might still go to Rome because every country got one entry. The National Track and Field Championships for women were held in 1960 in Corpus Christi, Texas. With the help of local civic organizations, Doris raised the money to make the trip. On a day that looked like any other day, distinguished only by the fact that she was leaving Seattle for a track meet a great distance away, young Doris climbed onto a train and quietly entered the stream of history.

. . . . .

The separation between Seattle and Corpus Christi was greater than the measured distance between two points on the map, and more surprising than the exchange of green for brown. Corpus Christi was the western edge of the old south, and it was the old south that attracted Doris' dumbfounded interest upon her arrival in Texas. Nothing in her life prepared her for a social and legal system that separated people by race and ethnicity. Noticing her angry reaction, the other athletes, particularly those who were black, said, "Doris, you be discrete," but the instruction was lost on her. She recoiled against the situation, as did many of the other athletes. They all avoided restaurants that would exclude any of them, and they raced for the back of the bus when they traveled together. The athletes, like Doris, many no more than children, knew that the gestures were slight but they expressed a natural and profound regret for the way things were.

As for running, the thing that caught her attention was that no one seemed to train. In fact, no one quite knew how, or so it appeared to her at first. Doris certainly didn't know what she was doing. Her idea was to leave the house, run as far and as fast as she could manage, and then trail back in, exhausted. The idea of warming up occurred to her only vaguely, defined perhaps by the first stiff steps out the door and then forgotten in the onward rush of her ambition. That kind of training was sufficient to make Doris one of the best of the few half-milers convened in Texas, but she was anxious to do better. She turned eagerly to the few knowledgeable coaches available to her.

One was Ed Temple, the coach of Tennessee State's famous Tigerbelles, of whom Wilma Rudolph was about to become the most celebrated member with three gold medals at the Rome Olympics.

Doris was impressed enough with Coach Temple that she asked whether she could come back with him to Tennessee State to run. He didn't have the heart to tell her that Tennessee State was a black school. He just told the little white girl that it wouldn't work out and left it at that. He must have shaken his head in wonder and with affection that such a person could exist.

At the national meet, Doris ran so hard that she passed out in the homestretch—within yards of the finish line—after a fierce fight with a 17-year-old named Billie Pat Daniels, who won. Billie Pat was much bigger and stronger than Doris in 1960, and even a terrier-like tenacity could not change the result. Billie Pat proved the point later in the summer when she beat Doris again at the Olympic Trials in Abilene, Texas. In that race, Billie Pat ran 2:15.6 for an American record in the 800 meters, Rose Lovelace from Cleveland was second in 2:15.7, and Doris was third in 2:17.6. As Doris now says in admiration for the victor, Billie Pat Daniels "could just climb out of bed and beat me every time!"

Be that as it may, Billie Pat, Rose, and Doris were not running world-class times. In fact, none of them ran fast enough to have an automatic qualifying time for the Olympic Games. That was not a problem for Billie Pat because every nation could send one entrant regardless of time or quality, but anybody else who wanted to represent the United States at 800 meters would have to meet the standard. To give Doris a chance, she was invited to join the United States women's Olympic team at the training camp in Emporia, Kansas. Races would be organized as part of the camp activity.

Living, socializing, running, and racing with the other members of the team in Emporia, Doris got her first real taste of life away from home and her first organized coaching. Personally, Doris was shocked to find that some of the runners and jumpers became habitues of the local tavern and that they were capable of outrageous pranks directed against each other and the townspeople, including one masquerade designed to gently mock race-conscious Kansas. Doris was taking it all in, but she was not distracted from her work. The first thing that required attention was her form. She ran on her heels and her arms were wild. With instruction, she became conscious of what she was doing with her body and worked to make her motion smoother and to become more forceful. On a cinder track at Emporia, Doris ran her first interval workout. Asked to run a set of 300s, Doris ran them as hard as she could go with no idea of pace or control. The coach merely shook his head, and said dolefully, "You girls are all the same; you just don't listen." Of course, Doris was listening, but her enthusiasm got the better of her. Doris particularly welcomed the advice of team manager Juner Ballew, a knowledgeable and caring woman.

Unfortunately, the work in Emporia did not produce an Olympic qualifying time. When the US team left for Rome, Doris dragged back to Seattle. Actually, she flew! It was her first time on an airplane. The flight went well except for one short conversation with a US team official who expressed surprise that Doris was not on the Olympic team. He said to Doris, "We just didn't work it out right." From this, Doris understood that it would have been possible to fudge the times a little and get her under the qualifying standard. Of course, Doris knew she was unprepared for an Olympic Games and she would not have wished to get there dishonestly. Still, she hurt and couldn't help wishing things had worked out differently. As for Billie Pat Daniels, she, too, continued with the sport long after that first Olympic Trials in Emporia. She eventually made three Olympic teams, the last two in the pentathlon. Over time, she became better known by married names, first as Pat Winslow, and, more recently, as Pat Connolly. Perhaps her greatest fame came as coach to Evelyn Ashford, a double Olympic Champion in 1984, and the only Western sprinter to contest the supremacy of East Germany's women between 1976 and 1985.

All that however was many years away. In 1960, Doris graduated from high school and was thinking about college. At first she thought she might attend a state-supported school. But after seeing the wide world of Texas and Kansas, and after hearing first-hand stories of taverns and casual socializing, she decided she would be more comfortable in a private school with a religious orientation. She enrolled in Seattle Pacific University, not far from her home. Like most colleges at the time, Seattle Pacific was governed by the in loco parentis model, which placed the school "in the place of" a student's parents and made the school responsible for the student's welfare during the term of the enrollment. An obvious reflection of that concern was a formal dress code at many private colleges and universities, including Seattle Pacific. For women, dresses and skirts were the rule. The rule was enforced closely enough that, when Doris wanted to run in shorts or sweats, she had to avoid the campus boundary for fear of violating the dress code.

Of course, Seattle Pacific did not have a women's track and field team. Almost no university or college did. Doris had heard that the University of Hawaii did have a program, but thinking of that she could only gasp, "When you got over there, you were alone! I mean, alone!" In those early days, airplanes did not swing people back and forth across oceans at the same rate they do today, nor did they offer cheap airfares. Although bold in many ways, Doris was not prepared to set her course so far from friends and family. As for scholarship assistance, as late as 1967 the only schools that financed women's track programs were John F. Kennedy College and Pepperdine College, and some of the traditional black schools in the South, including Tennessee State.

Going to Seattle Pacific did not mean that Doris abandoned running. It meant only that she had to continue on her own. On those terms, she approached the men's coach to ask whether he could be helpful. He said, "Doris, I don't coach women, but if the men will let you run with them, it's OK with me." She wasn't looking for coaching—that would have been too much to ask—just for this man to look the other way while she followed an uncommon pursuit. As for the runners, they were, in Doris' experience, never the problem, and neither were these young men at Seattle Pacific. They accepted her efforts in good faith, and helped when they could. For Doris, the association required special dedication because training with the men left her with little room for error or relaxation. In short, she had to run hard every day in order to keep up with them. Even the men's warm-up pace over three or four miles could be exhausting for her. As to the workouts, she just shoved herself into the middle of them and ran her heart out and her legs from under her. She knows now that the mileage and intensity of those workouts was excessive. She should have backed off some days, taken some days off, and worked very hard on the others, rather than banging them out one after the other. To do that, however, might have been viewed as capitulation or compromise rather than the exercise of discretion, judgment, and wisdom. In either course, Doris never considered backing off, even for a day. As a result of her determination and the resulting immoderate training, Doris suffered one injury after another: hamstrings, tendons, and stress fractures. Other times, she was simply exhausted. Nonetheless, she pressed on, alone in the early years, doing a thing no one else was doing and few people understood. The isolation of such a venture is impossible to exaggerate.

Competition was hard to find. In the absence of college programs, Doris was sometimes allowed to run a half-mile as part of a high school boys mile, but much of the time she was just out there by herself on the cinder or dirt tracks trying to hit one qualifying time or another. She recalls entire seasons dedicated to running faster than 2:10 for a half-mile. Without the encouragement of competition, that time loomed as a major challenge, and she often did not make it. Even with disappointment, though, Doris kept at it. She ran long runs of ten miles at maximum effort, added intervals, and did challenging hill work, pounding up and down hills that would have caused other people to at least wonder what they were doing. It is worth remembering that in Doris' early days, even men did not run without criticism and ridicule. No one—male or female—was normal if they spent time exercising on public streets; and no one was praised for continuing such activity after school days marked their normal end. Doris was, in that environment, a shock of such severity that many people would have rubbed their eyes in disbelief. She ran in the traditional uniform of a physical education major— longish shorts with a zipper down the side, a blouse, and general purpose recreational shoes, far removed from the colorful and functional running shoes that the most casual jogger owns today. Even now, Doris says softly about those days, "If the men weren't with me, I was treated awful. People threw things at me from cars, and they yelled at me." She seems to disbelieve the scenes she created by the simple act of running down a street.

Finally, one day while running hills, she just broke down physically. "They had to carry me off that hill," she says, clearly enjoying the memory of her own persistence. Of course, as soon as she could manage it, she went back out and started all over again, a cycle of injury and effort that particularly marked her first several years as a runner. Much of this changed midstream at Seattle Pacific when Dr. Ken Foreman returned to the school. During Doris' first year, Dr. Foreman had been completing his graduate degree. On his return, he offered Doris something few other women had: a knowledgeable person with a specific commitment to women's athletics. Dr. Foreman encouraged his athletes to excellence. In the decade of the '60s, Dr. Foreman as coach and Doris as star gradually formed the center of a colony of women distance runners, including such standouts as Vicki Foltz, Trina Homer, and Judy Oliver, who competed as the Falcon Track Club. Doris describes Dr. Foreman as bril-

Doris Brown at full power.

liant, the person most responsible for her success, and a person with
the proper mixture of knowledge, common sense, and sensitivity
that women's distance running required in its developmental stage.

Gradually, Doris started to run better. By 1964, she hoped
for another chance at the Olympic team in the 800 meters. She qualified for the trials, but she broke her foot before the meet. Still hoping she could put the pain out of her mind long enough to make the
team, she went to the meet. Even that dismal prospect ended when
she cut her foot badly while using the hotel swimming pool. Doris
admits without a hint of chagrin that she was trying to jump into a
plastic boat at the pool and hit it wrong! Thoroughly dedicated to her
sport and competitive on the track, she also enjoyed herself along
the way. This time, she had the bad luck to get hurt, but she did not
question herself. In 1964, unlike 1960, there was a bemused quality
to her disappointment. As she went home again, she thought to her-

self, "All you people will be dead and gone, but I'll still be out here trying to get it right!"

Her determination was more than words. She had always trained hard; now she began to train smarter. Like all runners of her time, she was starved for information about the sport, so when a piece of information did make its way to her she grabbed and held it fast. One such piece of information, which she received in either 1965 or 1966, was that the young Kansas miler, Jim Ryun, ran twice a day. Doris had not approached that volume, but when she saw the article she said to herself, "Oh, I better try this, too!" A favorite course was from her house, around a nearby lake, and back. The path was five miles—one hilly mile, three relatively flat ones around the lake itself, and then the hilly mile back—so she started to run that five miles almost every morning. She never jogged this or any other workout mileage. She ran vigorously. She figured that the longest she ever had to run in races, even taking cross-country into account, was two or three miles; that being the case, she might as well run hard for that two or three miles in practice, and then hang on. This theory made each workout race pace, but it also meant that, every day, Doris was looking for the chance to stretch out, to do more than she had the day before, to do it better and with greater strength, so that race day would be that degree easier.

The first time Doris ran in the morning was a critical day for her. She worried about the effect of the morning run on her afternoon workout. She did not want to exchange intensity for volume. On that first day, she happened to have scheduled her toughest track workout for the afternoon: three 660s in 1:30 with a full rest interval of approximately 10 minutes between each run. The times were pace work for a 2:00 half-mile, which was her goal. Despite her anxiety, the 660s went well. That was the confirmation she needed that the new regimen could work, and it was the beginning of a new approach to training. "The good thing about running twice a day,"

Doris said, "is that if, for some reason, you don't get one of your workouts in, you can still have a good week. You're missing only one workout from twelve or thirteen, depending on what you do on the weekends. But if you're just running once a day, and maybe not running but once on the weekends, losing a day can decimate your week." With five miles every morning at a good pace, she felt she had a head start of thirty miles every week. To that, she added her basic workouts. On Mondays, for example, she extended her morning workout by running ten miles in the morning to the school where she was teaching after graduation from Seattle Pacific; then she ran ten miles home. If she got back there soon enough she sometimes ran again with the team from Seattle Pacific. Some days she added fast track work. She pushed her mileage over a 100 miles a week on a regular basis, getting stronger and stronger.

Quickly, Doris' times started to come down at every distance as she entered the last half of the 1960s. The major breakthrough came in 1966. In Canada, organizers put together an indoor mile for women, which was almost unheard of, and invited her. Doris won in 4:52, which was a world indoor record for women. The result helped her confidence. As she increased volume and maintained intensity in her workouts, she became the dominant American woman distance runner. In cross-country especially, she was virtually unbeatable in the 1960s. Her only complaint was that the cross-country courses were too flat and too short, both unwelcome adjustments men made for women.

Doris added more international experience in 1967, including a stirring race at the Pan American Games in Winnipeg when she and teammate Madeline Manning staged a back and forth battle up the home stretch before Manning won with the last move. The times were 2:02.3 for Madeline and 2:02.9 for Doris, while Abby Hoffman of Canada was third in 2:04.6.

One of the most interesting and instructive races, however,

took place in Montreal, when the United States faced a combined team from Europe. The women's 800-meter race was one of the few in which the best representatives from each team were present. The Europeans sent Vera Nikolic, a 19-year-old Yugoslavian, and Karin Kessler, a powerful runner from West Germany. The United States had Doris Brown and Madeline Manning. Before the race, speculators anticipated a conflict between two accomplished front runners, Doris and Vera Nikolic, and two kickers, Kessler and Manning. At the gun, however, Madeline Manning shot to the front, carrying Nikolic in her wake through a 59-flat first quarter with Doris content to sit five or six yards off the pace, with Kessler a stride farther back. Into the second lap, down the backstretch and entering the final turn, Nikolic challenged for the lead, but Madeline held her off. The two runners came into the homestretch together. Both of them were in the first lane, neither conceding an inch, mutually depleted, and finally so close to each other that they collided. Madeline careened a stride or two into the infield before regaining her balance and climbing back into the fight. Up the long straight, Nikolic used short, quick strides; Madeline used long, raking strides. Nikolic looked surprisingly energetic and Madeline looked like she might fall over at any minute. After an agonizing stretch run, the two champions hit the tape together, but Madeline Manning won. One report of the race credited Manning with a "heart the size of a whale," presumably meaning that she was a woman of great courage. Both Vera Nikolic and Madeline Manning ran 2:02.6. Doris finished third in 2:05.3. Women's 800-meter running, although virtually ignored during the years the Olympic agenda omitted it, was heating up in 1967, as evidenced by such a contest.

Another important event in 1967 was the Little Olympics, held in Mexico City as a rehearsal for the Olympic Games in 1968. In part, the meet was designed to measure the effect of high altitude on the middle- and long-distance events. Doris did not worry much about the altitude because she was running just two laps. She remembers more vividly the cheap movies made available to the athletes and the jai alai contest she witnessed for the first time. As for the race, Doris intended to run it in her customary manner, which was to take the lead as soon as it was practical, and try to get so far ahead that she could not hear the pursuing footsteps. In the silence, she could relax and run easily.

In Mexico City, however, Doris was not the favorite and was in no position to dictate the pace. The leading competitor was Vera Nikolic of Yugoslavia. Paoli Pigni of Italy was also in the field, along with Abby Hoffman of Canada, and Charlette Cooke, the United States champion at 400 meters and the winner of that event at the previous Little Olympics in 52.3. In the event, five runners, including Doris, streamed past 200 meters in 30 seconds before Nikolic moved into the lead, carrying the field through the 400 meters in 64.5. With the pace slowing, Doris made a strong move on the backstretch of the second lap. She actually got three or four yards ahead before hitting 600 meters in 1:35.5. At that point, however, Nikolic took the race back, and charged past for a clear victory in 2:05.3. Doris trailed in 2:09.6, having dropped back to sixth. Charlette Cooke finished second in 2:07.5. By comparison, Doris' best time in 1967 for 800 meters was 2:02.9.

With her victory at the Little Olympics, Vera Nikolic became the early choice to win the 800 meters at the next year's Olympic Games, a position she fortified in early 1968 when she ran 2:00.5. Nikolic would carry that pressure uneasily as her country raised its expectations. For Doris, the Little Olympics was simply another good experience. For one thing, she got to run in a pack, which was important to her because she often ran far ahead of her competition in the United States. She needed to learn how to race in a crowd, bumping up against other people, hearing them throughout the race, responding to moves they made suddenly. She also wanted to see the difference between racing in the States, which she described as a "touch-me-not" experience, and racing against Europeans, who considered middle-distance running a contact sport.

Doris came back from Mexico City and immediately got back into her training for the cross-country season. In the absence of long-distance events on the track, cross-country was Doris' favorite sport. She was permitted to use her strength, tenacity and endurance, as well as her comfort in conditions others found uncomfortable, to maximum advantage. The fall of 1967 was particularly important because the first World Cross-Country Championship for women was scheduled for Wales. The women's event would be held coincident with the men's event. The United States sent its military team to compete for the men's title, but it sent no women. Doris could afford to go only because the principal at her school and another man who lived down the street from her house put on a spaghetti dinner and raised the money to pay her way. At the same time Doris was training for the first World Cross-Country Championships, the 1,500 meters was introduced as an approved track event for women. In October of 1967, Maria Gommers of Holland set a new world record of 4:15.6 for the distance. The acceptance of the 1,500 meters as a championship event was good news for Doris, but it would not be added to the Olympic Games schedule for women until 1972.

The World Cross-Country Championship in Wales was a joyful experience for Doris. This, for once, was real cross-country. "We're talking messy, muddy fields, off the soccer field and into the pasture," she says now. The English had an advantage because they had more women who regularly ran cross-country, and they were accustomed to the rough conditions. For this meet, the Lincoln sisters from England were favored. The women would race a course of approximately three miles, although no one much cared for that trifle, exact distance not being the point of a sport that distinguished itself by so many other variables: terrain, weather, surface, and configuration among them. As Doris prepared to race the large field of more than a hundred women, she wanted to win not only as a personal accomplishment but as a way of encouraging—goading might be as good a word—the American authorities to send a full team the next year.

Of course, Doris was in full flight at the sound of the gun. After following the Lincolns early in the race, she went to the front and worked as usual to put the sound of the other runners behind her so that she might run comfortably and relaxed. The only noise she wanted was the regular breathing from her own body, the soft sound of her feet as they struck the relatively few dry patches, and the squish and pull of those same feet on the more prominent wet spots. She didn't want to hear those sounds from her pursuers, nor their gasps and coughs, and throats clearing. She wanted to be alone, and in the event, she was. At the close of this race of approximate distance, Doris Brown, a woman apart, won the first World Cross-Country Championship for women. No one deserved the honor more.

Looking back at the event, Doris does not speak often or long of the race itself. It is the ceremony after the race that captures her emotion. It is the large hall filled with men and women who, together, shared the field and the weather, the exertion, the dreams of triumph and the expectancy of disappointment. It is the people who wondered to themselves each night, as they went out to run after a day's work, whether this made any sense, and realizing it didn't, went on anyway, laughing in satisfaction at themselves and at the folly. In that large hall where the athletes cheered, and stamped their feet, and jeered at each other, and praised the accomplishments of their fellows and made false threats and promises of revenge, and calculated plans that might or might not be kept, Doris holds her memory. At the time, she wished to share the room and the experience with other women from her country. This year she was joined only by Pat Cole among American women, and the two ran as individuals. Next year, she was determined to come with teammates. That was her wish and her vow.

Doris herself learned something important in Wales. Race promoters chided her for not answering the invitations they had issued to her to run in other events. "You could at least have done us the courtesy of a reply," they said. This embarrassed Doris because she did not know what they were talking about. She would have been thrilled to receive invitations to run! Upon inquiry, she learned that the invitations had gone to the governing United States athletics federation, which simply tossed them aside. Smartly, Doris arranged to receive notice of the invitations herself so she could respond to them.

In the Olympic year, 1968, Doris continued to train hard. The 800 meters was a stacked deck, and not in her favor, because it was too short for her, but it was the longest race on the schedule so she hacked away at it. She continued to run more than 100 miles most weeks. Sunday she ran long, and on the track she ran intervals of 440, 660 and 880 yards. As before, she ran in the mornings. Once, she moved the morning mileage from five miles to eight but was not satisfied with the results so she dropped back down. Later in the early summer, she received an invitation to run in Ireland and England. The promoter of the event in Ireland, which would serve as the springboard for other races on the same trip, was the famous Billy Morton of Dublin. In order to comply with the Amateur Athletic Union rules, Doris contacted them and told them about the trip. They, in turn, told her that she had to have a chaperone with her and that it would take two weeks to make arrangements, by which time it would be too late, of course, for her to go. Tenaciously, Doris continued to ask questions. She finally learned that if she was paying her own way, the chaperone would not be required and she could go. Faced with the faint prospect, Doris borrowed the money and went alone. It took years to pay off that loan.

Still, there in Ireland and in England was the world for which Doris yearned. In Ireland, she ran 2:05 for 800 meters on a grass track mowed out of a pasture. She then crossed the Irish Channel to England. In London, she ran the English National Championships at the famous Crystal Palace. The field was deep and fast. Most prominent among the entrants was the reigning European champion Vera Nikolic, continuing to run well after the Little Olympics of the year before and, as always, an habitual front runner, not rash but methodical and punishing. Nikolic was only 20 years old in 1968, but she ran with great maturity. She was a strong runner who was 5' 6" tall and weighed 123 pounds. Vera Nikolic was joined in London by England's Lillian Board, a woman who could range back and forth between 400 meters and 800 meters with virtually equal success. And there was Doris, of course, running two laps when four, eight, twelve, or even twenty-five would have been better suited to her.

Doris now says that the 800 meters she ran in London was the best she ever ran. But she did not win. The honor went to Vera Nikolic who forged to the lead and ran nearly even 400-meter splits of 60.5 and 60.0, and 200-meter splits of 28.9, 31.6, 30.1, and 29.9, for a final time of 2:00.5, breaking the world record of 2:01, which had been held by Judy Pollock of Australia. Lillian Board was second in 2:02.0, while Doris finished third in a personal record of 2:02.2. She had carried none of the pace, but just ran as hard as she could in Nikolic's path. Her time was more impressive than it might have appeared to outsiders because, as frequently was the case, she was fighting an injury. Her hamstring was strained even before the trip to Ireland and England, and she had been carefully nursing it along. It was, in context, a fine run against two women of extraordinary ability, both of whom were running their best events. It was also a good setup for the United States National Championships, the Olympic Trials, and the Olympic Games themselves.

Before Doris went home, she had a lesson to learn about amateur athletics. For races she was willing to run for nothing, she was offered money. Remembering that this woman had borrowed the money for the trip, the temptation must have been extreme, but Doris said, "No, I'm not taking any money." Even when the promoters repeated their refrain, "No one will know. It will be in cash. Take the money. It can't be traced. Take the money," the answer stayed no. Doris was carrying the standard for herself, her country, and the women who would follow in her footsteps. She could not take chances.

Doris was well pleased with the results in Ireland and England, but she was still anxious for the Olympics. If anything, the glow of her European running made the training even harder. The morning run of five miles now dropped to sub-six-minute pace, with the idea that training should be "sport specific." In Doris' case, that meant that as the cross-country season ended and track season approached, the need for speed replaced the need for strength. She broke away from training one time in order to run a mile in 4:42.2, an American record.

Because the Olympic Games in 1968 were held in the high altitude of Mexico City, many runners were anxious for places to acclimate. Doris went to Los Alamos, New Mexico, which was the training camp for women. Doris lived much of that summer with a Los Alamos family and was able to hold costs down. Madeline Manning was there, too, only 20 years old, the defending national champion at 800 meters and a lean, long-striding runner at 5' 9", 126 pounds. While Doris tended to run over-distance, Madeline did sharp, intense speed work on the track. The training itself marked the difference between the two athletes. Doris makes nothing of this today, but the fact is that she did not have quite the basic speed she needed for 800 meters and she tried to compensate with strength and stamina. On the other hand, the 800 meters was Madeline Manning's natural event, and her training was one indication that she knew it. Speed over 800 meters has no substitute.

Nevertheless, it was Doris who won the American National Championship 800 meters on August 17, 1968. The track in Aurora, Colorado was wet, and Doris' strength prevailed. She sprinted for home with 300 meters to go, an extended drive she learned while in England, and beat Madeline to the line. Later, Madeline and Doris finished in a dead heat in the Olympic Trials, both women running 2:03, and both, also, safely on the Olympic team.

Doris thought she had a good chance for a medal at the Olympics in 1968 and that a gold medal was possible if everything went just right. Vera Nikolic would be there, of course, but Doris had been close enough to her to make an upset possible. Lillian Board had decided to run only the 400 meters (in which she would finish with a silver medal), Australia's Judy Pollock, the former world record holder, was pregnant and would miss the Games entirely, and Madeline Manning, although a great runner, was not necessarily better than Doris, who had beaten her at Nationals and run her to a standstill at the Trials. Doris' case was made stronger by the Olympic schedule, which called for three successive races, one each on October 17, 18, and 19. That schedule might eliminate the sprinters who were moving up to 800 meters, but lacked endurance. At the Games themselves, Doris' chances were further enhanced when Vera Nikolic walked off the track after 300 meters of her semi-final, the victim, in various views, of too much pressure or of punishing workouts.

For Doris, a gold medal was not to be. The Olympic Games 800-meter final belonged entirely to Madeline Manning who, with the impetuosity of youth, joined Romanian Ileana Silai for a 59.1 first 400 meters before busting up front on her own, resisting attacks from Silai and Maria Gommers, and finishing an Olympic champion in 2:00.9, a time that equaled the world record. Doris was in the final with Madeline, having qualified uneventfully, and she hoped for a medal as she rounded the final bend and turned toward the homestretch. Runners were bunched in front of her, she was moving well, and, although Madeline was out of reach, the other two medal positions were not. It had to be perfect, however. She had to run that bend without incident and she had to gather force as she entered the homestretch and she had to sprint as she had never sprinted before. She did not have 300 meters to go this time, and no chance to drive the starch and the strength out of runners clinging to spaces behind her. This time, Doris had to move quicksilver, and this time, it didn't happen. As Doris ran that final turn, another runner, probably seeking balance or awash in oxygen debt, reached out and just briefly, but enough to make a difference, grabbed her arm and wrenched it down. With that pull, it was over. Running is balance. It might be said that it is entirely balance—the right combination of long running for endurance and short sprinting for speed; the fine tune between enthusiasm and preoccupation; physically, the concerted movement of arms and legs to the purpose of horizontal movement. And now the balance was gone. With it, so also was speed. Doris strove down the homestretch at the sprint she could manage, but it was not the sprint she needed, and it was not the sprint she might have produced had her balance been protected. That quickly, the dream of many years was dashed.

For Madeline, however, Doris was exultant. She was as happy for Madeline as she would have been if she had won herself. Doris had hoped for the day when an American woman would win an Olympic distance event. This was no distance event, but it was all that was available, and an American had won! That, for Doris, was enough to take home with her. An American woman won the 800 meters in Mexico City. Doris had finished fifth in 2:03.9. The silver medal was won in 2:02.5.

After the Olympics, Doris returned to her first love, cross-

A European experience: Doris Brown finishes.

country. Quietly, her sport was maturing, and she was its north star, showing the way by her example, nurturing young girls who came up to join her, and holding the fine line between competition and camaraderie. In 1968, the AAU National Cross-Country Championships for women were held in Frederick, Maryland on November 30, only five weeks after the 800 meters at the Games. The course was to Doris' liking. It was liberally sprinkled with hills, some as long as a quarter-mile; and it included a number of tight and challenging turns that might disrupt the rhythm of a less experienced athlete. For Doris, by now a secure veteran at 26 years old, the race was a simple matter of claiming the lead in the first 200 meters, lengthening the lead to 35 yards, and holding it. She finished an easy winner, 5 seconds in front of her teammate Vicki Foltz. The team championship went for the second consecutive year to a team from Sacramento, California, Will's Spikettes. In prior years this had been Marie Mulder's team, but in 1968 she ran for the Long Beach Comets, for whom she finished ninth. A look at Will's Spikettes shows that women's cross-country was still based on age-group running and not on university participation or open athletics typical of today. The runners on Will's Spikettes included Judy Walker, 16; Rose Mary Gilbert, 14; Debbie Dobbins, 14; Debbie Otten, 16; Glenna Stephens, 14; and Diane Smith, 15. Only Dino Lowrey at 20 years and Carol Hughes at 27 were adults. Doris says today that "Just because you are not a child anymore doesn't mean you can't do these things," but that view had not entered the mainstream in 1968.

In 1968, Doris led a full team of American women to England for the World Cross-Country Championships. Doris won again. And this time her US team won, too. Doris gives much of the credit for this victory to Cheryl Bridges, who finished fourth at the US National Championships, but picked up a bunch of places with a strong drive late in the international race. The victory of America's women at the World Championships reflected a general growth in the sport in the United States. From that point, participation and interest continued to grow throughout the decade and into the beginning of the next. In 1969, for example, at the National Cross-Country Meet for women, 542 girls and women competed, compared to the 40 girls and women who had competed in the same meet only five years before at the second AAU Championship. As one girl said in 1969, "It's like pierced ears. A few years ago only certain people did it. But now, it's acceptable. Same with cross-country." With each year, the number of people who ran continued to increase, and Doris Brown continued to lead the way. By 1972, 830 girls and women competed in the five age-group divisions at the National cross-country meet, and only in that year could it be said that Doris passed the baton to the new generation. Francie Larrieu, after four years of trying, finally won at nationals, beating Doris over the 2.5-mile course by 50 yards.

Between 1968 and 1972, however, Doris secured her place in athletics history. She was the unyielding person who could run a series of hills during her workouts, carefully apportioning them: one hill for Francie Larrieu, with whom she always enjoyed tough competition, one hill for Maria Gommers, the strong Dutch woman, and one hill for herself. "I knew that if I was going to win," she says, "I had to work on that final climb." Whether referring to a specific race or a specific hill, Doris did work and did win. In five consecutive World Cross-Country Championships from 1967 to 1971, Doris Brown was the champion. Only Grete Waitz of Norway, another legend, equaled that accomplishment in later years, and no woman has beaten it. Fittingly, Doris' cross-country string ended not because she was beaten in the field, but because the AAU asked her to run an indoor meet against the Russians in 1972 instead.

From this distance it may seem that progress for women was inevitable, but at every step of the way Doris and others who worked with her were cutting a path through deep resistance. She was hard on herself and on other girls and women who ran, saying, "There is a difference between running and racing, between being an athlete and being a person who wants to stay active. As soon as you cross that line between training and racing, you do belong to the public." For Doris, this meant that as her sport grew, she would accept conditions as they were and change them as she could. With regard to the early articles that tended to emphasize the appearance of women—the pretty ones, the young ones gathering the most positive coverage, for example—she says, "I wouldn't want to say I totally resented this. My first attitude was that I was doing this because I wanted to. People had said women don't do this, when you are out of school, you need to move on." When Doris refused to move on, she accepted that other people had the right to comment. "If you're going to be different than other people, you're going to be noticed. It comes with the territory, so you want to take care of yourself." For Doris, this meant a balanced approach. During competition, she didn't bother about her appearance, knowing that at such times her hair would be unkempt, her muscles strained, and her face would show fatigue. Nothing would change any of that, and she wouldn't try. People who criticized her on that basis would get nothing from her by way of adjustment. On the other hand, when she was finished with competition, she would clean up and present a more conventional image. With just a hint of irony and a great deal of good humor, she says, "When I went to the starting line, I was there to run a race. I didn't care what I looked like. But otherwise, I tried to put on a reasonable face!" With regard to the people who wrote early articles on women's running, which might now be seen as patronizing or sexist, she gives credit where credit is due. "Any coverage was better than no coverage in those days." The tone of the articles, she felt, was consistent with the times. "These people weren't being mean," Doris says, "They were working from their context, looking through the knothole in the fence that was available to them. So you have to look at it from their view."

That, then, was Doris Brown: pioneer, social rebel, conventional student, rigorous worker, conscientious leader, empathetic mother to a generation of young runners in a sport that was entirely new. The sport, however, was changing in ways that even Doris Brown did not entirely recognize. She saw the addition of a 1,500-meter race to the Olympic schedule in 1972 as an advance, but she could not predict that, behind it, stood an army of people training behind an iron curtain. As Munich approached, the Eastern European countries surged to the front of women's middle-distance running. When that happened, Doris was still there, bridging the gap between days when merely to race was triumph and the days when triumph became everything, or apparently so.

In January 1972, the summary list for the prior year ranked Doris seventh in the world for 1,500 meters. Her best time for the mile in 1971 was 4:39.6, and her best time for 1,500 meters was 4:14.6. At that level, Doris was in the pack. The fastest time in the world for 1,500 meters was 4:09.6 by Karin Burneleit of the German Democratic Republic (East Germany) in winning the European Championship. In that run, Burneleit showed unusual strength and pace by holding virtually even splits throughout: 68.5, 68.5, 67.0, and a final 300-meters in 45.6. She did not lead until the final 40 meters of the race. Rumor had it, however, that Burneleit won only because her GDR teammate, Gunhild Hoffmeister, waited for her at the line. Officially, however, Hoffmeister was second to Burneleit and ran 4:10.3, a good recovery from the 800 meters at the same championship, where Hoffmeister collided with Hildegard Falck of the Federal Republic of Germany (West Germany), thus leaving the way free for Vera Nikolic to win in 2:00.0. On the yearly lists, Burneleit was first, Hoffmeister third, and Tamara Pangyelova of the Soviet Union split the two, with a season's best of 4:10.2. Of the 19 ranked athletes at 1,500 meters in 1971, 11 were from Eastern Bloc

Doris in her element.

countries. Back in the eighth slot was Lyudmila Bragina of the Soviet Union. Actually, Doris might have achieved a higher rank in 1971 if she had had more opportunity for competition. As it happened, she ran the mile or the 1,500 meters only seven times, and won six times. The only loss came to Pangyelova of the Soviet Union, 4:13.8 to 4:14.6, a race in which Doris beat Bragina, who ran 4:19.9.

In March 1972, Doris joined her American teammates in a dual indoor track meet against the Soviet Union. This was the race she ran when officials asked her to skip the World Cross-Country Championships. The matchup revealed how quickly the Soviet women had distinguished themselves from their Western counterparts. "You go against the Russians," said 16-year-old Debbie Heald from La Mirada, California, who joined Doris in the mile, "and you hope to catch them on an off-day. I figure I'll finish fourth." Debbie also noted Doris' special position, saying that she felt sorry for Doris because Doris was her country's best miler and "people expect it." Doris, however, was not taken in by the hysteria about Russia, which, although abated from the days of the Cuban missile crisis, was still intense. She reminded people, "This is a chance for some very fine competition against friends. Hey, look, they're people, too, just like you. Why make something else out of it?" Why, indeed, because in the event, Debbie Heald swept past a surprised Tamara Pangyelova to set a world indoor record of 4:38.5. Doris meanwhile ran well until two laps from the end when she blacked out. Instinct kept her running so swiftly that she eventually finished in a personal record for the distance but she was not the victor nor first American finisher.

Doris was not concerned about her performance against the Russians. In fact, she was pleased with it as an excellent run in difficult circumstances. In the week prior to the meet, she helped organize the National Cross-Country Championships in Seattle, ran the trial race herself and won it, completed the oral part of the examination for her master's degree, and flew late in the evening to Richmond, Virginia, for the competition. In short, she was very tired.

Later in the outdoor season, she re-established herself as America's leading miler, and led a contingent of three athletes into the 1,500 meters at Munich for the Olympic Games: herself, Francie

Larrieu, and Francie Kraker. All three athletes were products of age-group running. In Munich, the three women ran into a buzz saw. Doris went out unceremoniously. She never even got the chance to run. In the parade of competitors to the first heat of the 1,500 meters, she stepped on a curb that had been moved to allow room for the high-jumper's warm-up. She broke five bones in her ankle and foot, and tore a tendon. She was devastated, saying now that her adrenaline went from over a 100 percent to zero. "You can run on a bloody stump," she says, "but I just could not run."

Surely, Doris would have enjoyed the chance, and in all probability she would have devastated her personal bests given what happened at Munich in her absence, but it is difficult to imagine her winning the 1,500 meters. Runners in the first heat were stunned by the performance of Lyudmila Bragina of the Soviet Union. Bragina was a 23-year-old woman with a smooth, economical stride directed to maximum forward movement. "Distinguished by its economy," said the Soviet sports journals. She had advanced erratically in the years prior to Munich, running for 800 meters and 1,500 meters respectively, 2:05.8 and 4:22.2 in 1967; 2:07.3 and 4:17 in 1968; 2:06.4 and 4:13.2 in 1969; 2:08.1 and 4:13.4 in 1970; and, for 1,500 meters, 4:13.8 in 1971. Speaking of her development as an athlete, Bragina described an inauspicious beginning during the first year of her instruction at the Sverdlovsk Teacher Training Institute: "When for the first time I ran two laps in 2:30 and asked to be admitted to the running group, the instructors merely shrugged their shoulders, as if to say, 'What did this overgrown girl need this for?'" From that point, however, she benefited from an uninterrupted 12-year period with the same coach, Victor Kazantsev. Under his care, she employed what Kazantsev called "rational techniques," which included 15 to 20 kilometers of running each day. She also aimed exclusively, and from the start, for the 1,500-meter final in Munich. "Another important element was the fact that my trainer did not psych me up for a series of secondary victories," Bragina said, "but immediately set me the strategic goal of preparing for the 1972 Olympics. From that moment on, however things went, I saw before me a single stake: the Olympics. Increasing the amount and intensity of training sessions, elaborating various tactics, we did our best to be fully armed for 1972."

While Bragina anticipated a great improvement in 1972, virtually no one else was prepared for her explosion. She started the year by running a world-record 4:06.9 for 1,500 meters in a heat at the USSR Championships, and by becoming the first woman to run 3,000 meters faster than 9:00 with 8:53 in August at the Soviet Physical Culture Day Holiday. At the Olympics, Bragina and her coach Kazantsev decided she should "put on a maximum of speed in each preliminary heat, putting all my cards on the table as it were, and exhaust my main rivals before the finals." Putting this plan into effect, Bragina coasted her heat in a world record of 4:06.5 after front-running splits of 63.1, 2:09.6, and 2:43.6 (1,000 meters). Amazingly, a 17-year-old Canadian, Glenda Reiser, finished second in the heat with a Canadian record of 4:06.7, while three others were also under 4:09. In the second heat, Francie Kraker survived a more temperate pace, finishing a qualifying fourth in 4:14.7. In the third heat, Francie Larrieu also advanced after running 4:11.2. Both Americans, however, were eliminated in the semifinals, as Kraker ran 4:12.8 and Larrieu ran 4:15.3, both admirable performances but pale by comparison to what was happening up front. In the first semifinal, Pangyelova, beaten by a teenaged American nine months earlier, now ran 4:07.7 to win, while in the second heat, Bragina set yet another world record by running 4:05.1. In doing so, she carried Burneleit to an almost equally astonishing 4:05.8. In the two semifinals, fourteen women ran under 4:10 for 1,500 meters. Only five of the eighteen semifinalists failed to run faster than 4:09.6, which had been the world record six months before the Olympics began.

In the final, Bragina was content to let others lead through 400 meters in 62.5 before taking the pace at 700 meters. She led through 800 meters in 2:10, and accelerated. Her final 800 meters was covered in 2:06.1, and her final time was a scintillating world-record, 4:01.4. Bragina pulled the GDR's Hoffmeister to a 4:02.8 time, and Paola Pigni-Cacchi of Italy to 4:02.9 while Karin Burneleit ran 4:04.1 for fourth. The final, too, had been according to plan, as Bragina later described it, "For the finals we decided to change our tactics somewhat. I should not immediately take the lead, but make my rivals think I was tired and incapable of active competition. The plan was successful. When my main rivals had slowed down their speed, I tore ahead and reached the finish line well ahead of the pack." Manifestly, Bragina was like a cat toying with mice.

The 800 meters at Munich was not as breathtaking as the 1,500 meters, but it did produce extraordinary depth. Hildegard Falck of West Germany won in 1:58.55 and was followed to the line by four women under 2 minutes: Niole Sabaite of the Soviet Union in 1:58.7; Gunhild Hoffmeister of the German Democratic Republic in 1:59.2; Svelta Zlateva of Bulgaria in 1:59.7; and Vera Nikolic of Yugoslavia in 1:59.98. Ileana Silai of Romania finished next in 2:00. Rosemary Stirling of Great Britain was seventh in 2:00.2, and Abby Hoffman of Canada also ran 2:00.2 but finished eighth.

Munich ended, then, in a great rush for women middle-distance runners. For Doris in particular, an age was ending. By the next Olympics, she would not be the leading American middle-distance runner. Gradually over the years, her competitive opportunities would shrink in direct relationship to the increasing administrative responsibilities she undertook for her sport. During those years, American women would run faster than Doris had. They would win their own championships and make their own statements of principle. That fact being admitted, they could not really overtake Doris.

In the early years, she endured when others faltered. Later, she thrived when others endured. Meanwhile, with the success of Bragina of the Soviet Union and the other Soviet satellite athletes, the development of women's distance running withdrew behind the veil. Every few years it would be possible to see the results, but the process itself was hidden. As the years passed, curiosity grew. That curiosity being unsatisfied, Eastern Bloc women eventually became magnets for mistrust and suspicion. Not only did the nature of the sport change, but so also did the nature of nature. If people had believed that women in sports could produce, naturally, one set of results, how would it be possible to explain another set of results wholly at variance with and in excess of what was predicted? If it happened that women's performances were manipulable in response to virtually limitless stressors and enhancements, which ones were ethical and which ones were not? Absent effective monitoring, the choice would fall by default to each country, each coach, each club, and each athlete, and the effect of each choice would ripple through the entire field of competitors. In the west, the youngest girl dreaming of long distance running would feel the impact. At the least she would know, or soon learn, that someone out there was intent on smothering her dream before it drew first breath.

What was being smothered was the idea that a woman's performance was valuable in and of itself. In the West, historically, few people had cared what happened when women raced, even internationally; so women did not receive much recognition, but neither were they exploited. The Soviets and their ideological counterparts changed that by attaching to women the duty to represent the greater society. That is, the Soviets exploited women for a purpose other than sport. This idea—that women athletes could be used in a wholesale, programmatic way—was new, except, perhaps, for the unusual period in Hitler's Germany immediately prior to and during the 1936 Olympic Games in Berlin, and it constitutes a loss of innocence for women athletes, or at least a loss of detachment from what was otherwise happening all around them. Soon, women would represent the Western democracies scurrying to catch up with the East, and they would represent commercially funded, corporate clubs, and they would represent themselves in competition for money provided by sponsors. They would also represent colleges and universities as scholarships became available. All these new, representational states were of a piece: they were like each other in essential ways. They heightened interest in and expectancy for women athletes. Thus, the continuum that starts with Doris Brown and her clubmates plunges through the Soviet states and comes out the other side in America's colleges and universities, with pressure building at every level. In sum, women began to carry the great weight of ambitions other than their own, beginning with the women of the Soviet Union.

FIVE

And the prisoners in ranks of five separated from the rest and marched ahead, so that they could be watched from front and behind: five heads, five backs, ten legs.

One Day in the Life of Ivan Denisovich
Alexander Solzhenitsyn

A monolith is a single great stone often in the shape of an obelisk or a column. Things are said to be monolithic if they exhibit massive uniformity. Countries and cultures that express apparently absolute and consistent values and practices are often described as monolithic. Reference to an individual within a monolithic state or culture is oxymoronic. Prior to its dissolution, the Soviet Union was often described as monolithic. One aspect of its massive uniformity was an insistence that women carry some of the social burden, including physical labor—at all times—and dangerous service at and near the front during times of war when resources were totally mobilized. As a result of the generalized treatment of women in its society, the Soviet Union was more receptive to women's athletics than western countries and enjoyed a correspondingly high degree of success. When the leadership exhorted the country's "young physical culturalists" to remember, "From you must come our new Masters of Sports who will surpass bourgeois sports records and will raise the banner of Soviet physical sports culture to new unprecedented heights," as they did in 1935, the message was for women as well as men, and activity jumped. Over 800 meters, for example, while the Western countries hesitated to offer full opportunity, Soviet women were active and dominant for almost five decades. Because they participated in a monolithic structure, however, the individual runners were seen as products of the system rather than creators of it. Too often, they were accorded only slight and ephemeral notice before being buried by the larger system within which they competed.

That anonymity was, however, the view from the outside looking in. From the inside looking out, the athletes knew that they were part of a proud continuum of champions: Oyelizavyeta Kuznyetsova, 2:24.5 (1927); Olga Mamotyeva 2:19.0 (1935); Yevdokiya Vasilyeva, 2:19.4 (1935); Vasilyeva, 2:15.3 (1938); Kensiya Shilo, 2:15.3 (1940); Vasilyeva, 2:12.0 (1943); Vasilyeva, 2:13.0 (1950); Valentina Pomogayeva, 2:12.2 (1951); Nina Otkalenko, 2:12.0 (1951); Otkalenko 2:08.5 (1952); Otkalenko, 2:05.0 (1955); Lyudmila Lisenko-Shevtsova, 2:04.3 (1960); Niole Sabaite, 1:58.65 (1972); Valentina Gerasimova, 1:56.0 (1976); Tatyana Kazankina!

She is not the end of the line. In fact, in some ways she is nearer the beginning than the end. But pause here with Tatyana Kazankina, the impossible Soviet runner. She was a woman who shined so brightly that her light penetrated the darkest monolith, the closed society. Let your mind wander for a moment through Soviet history, feel the hope and chaos, fear and shame, the pride, the resentment. Feel the terror of a country born from Marx, birthed by Lenin, formed by Stalin, built on bodies and bones. Hear hopeless voices. Imagine inexpressible thoughts. That done, look, finally, into the eyes of Tatyana Kazankina, resident of Leningrad—heroic, indomitable Leningrad—and citizen of the Soviet Union. Withdrawn into a thin, sharply sculpted face, itself the result of privation, effort, and intensity, those eyes invite approach, but are wary.

They promise kindness, but anticipate fierce competition. They have seen sorrow and triumph, and do not know which of the two is to be cherished. They know the present, and value its worth. They hope for something more even as they doubt it. Those eyes ache and they rejoice, they despair and celebrate. Tatyana Kazankina was an uncommon individual crafted to athletic perfection by a totalitarian regime. Throughout an international career that began in 1974 and continued through 1985, Kazankina was the mighty atom, the Russian dragonfly, the mouse that roared, the original large engine in a small frame, the keeper of an extraordinary calm, a confident woman bent on survival, the master kicker. Acclaim and praise poured down on her.

Tatyana Kazankina was born on December 17, 1951, into a working-class family in Petrovsk, a small town in the Volga area of the Soviet Union. Petrovsk is southeast of Moscow and midway between Gorky to the north and Stalingrad to the south. When Tatyana was a girl, she took her physical education in the basement of a small school without a dressing room or a shower. Outdoors, she used the stadium in the town or the surrounding country for her idle exercise and sporadic sport. She enjoyed basketball and volleyball, which she could play for hours without getting tired. She did not like running, a fact that did not deter an instructor of the town's Children and Youth Sports School who thought that Tatyana could become a good middle-distance runner. Beginning in her eighth of ten year's of general education, he coached Tatyana toward that end. He was correct in his appraisal of the strong young woman, for she soon became champion of the Russian Federation over 800 meters.

In 1965, Tatyana moved to Leningrad and began her active sporting career. She also studied economics at the Leningrad State University, which in turn led to post-graduate studies at the Leningrad Institute of Physical Education. Eventually completing a Ph.D. at the institute she reportedly wrote her thesis on "The Study

The great Tatyana Kazankina of the Soviet Union: those eyes.

of Some Aspects of Subsidizing Sports Under Developing Socialism." Describing her training at the university, Tatyana said, "Track and field sessions were very exciting. Everyone used to take part in them: runners, jumpers, throwers and experts in combined events, beginners and celebrities. With all that mixed together, they were highly emotional for us all. Later, at the main session, each athlete practiced with his own instructor, but the spirit of communication lingered somehow. We all went to exhibitions and theatres together. If someone was lagging behind in his studies, all his sport colleagues would come to his rescue. There were physicists, mathematicians, historians, and economists among us, even some assistant professors." In Leningrad, the work of P.S. Lesgaft and I.P. Pavlov was well known. The two men were scientists whose work had direct application to the Soviet athletic system. Lesgaft's philosophy was based on the idea that the human organism develops uninterruptedly, changing under the influence of physical conditions, while Pavlov's theory of conditioned reflex supported a similar outcome, which is that an organism's development of higher nervous activity comes in response to external challenges.

Chief among the more direct influences in Tatyana's development was the coach who would take her to glory, Nikolai Malyshev. When he first met Tatyana, Malyshev thought that her running form, which consisted of long, bounding strides with her feet held high, was unrefined. He worked to smooth out that motion. He also gradually increased the volume and intensity of her workouts. By the time she ran in the Olympic Games in Montreal in 1976, Tatyana was devoted to her sport. "I train twice a day as a rule," she said. "I run between 20 and 30 kilometers (12 to 18 miles) daily. The degree of loading depends on the stage of preparation I am at, naturally." Referring to a year in which the Olympics occurred in the fall, she said that March was her heaviest month and that she was frequently dead tired. Kazankina also worked specifically to develop "speed strength" which would produce the ability to vary her stride length to the circumstance, and to develop the highest speed during the last 100 meters of any race by increasing stride length and stride frequency.

Tatyana did not appear on the yearly list of best Soviet performances until 1971 when she ran 1,500 meters in 4:19.0. She was then 19 years old. In the years between 1971 and 1974, inclusive, she continued to run well, recording bests of 2:05.2 and 4:13.6 in 1972; 2:03.5 and 4:14.2 in 1973; and 2:03.1 and 4:05.9 in 1974. In 1974, Tatyana was the fourth-ranked women's 1,500-meter runner in the world, a position she held in 1975, albeit at the slower time of 4:07.9. However, in 1975, Kazankina did improve at 800 meters by running 2:01.7. That time, though, was only equal to the 15th fastest time for the year. A total of 19 women ran faster than she did that year for 800 meters. Interestingly, among the 18 women who ran faster than Tatyana did for 800 meters in 1975, 14 were from the Eastern Bloc, as was the woman who ran the same time. In the middle of the mix, Madeline Manning, now running as Madeline Jackson, clung to a precarious position as the sixth-fastest woman for the year with 2:00.3. At 1,500 meters, where Tatyana was higher ranked in 1975, a notable performance belonged to Grete Waitz who ran 4:07.5, fighting hard against the Eastern tide. For these Western runners, it was hard to know what to make of their counterparts. When Tatyana, for example, was sought for interviews after one meet, she was unavailable. Her friends said only, "She's a nice girl. She went to the movies."

None of this prepared the sporting world for what Tatyana Kazankina did at the 1976 Olympic Games in Montreal. Measured against later standards, she began gently by running a personal best of 4:05.2 approximately six weeks before the Games. She then stepped up the intensity by winning the 1,500 meters at the World Games in 4:02.8, which was then the third-fastest time ever recorded

Sometimes the cat, sometimes the mouse, Kazankina (2) lays in wait.

for the distance. Small matter, however, because on June 28, 1976, at Podolsk, USSR, Tatyana Kazankina drove women's middle-distance running into a new era by smashing the four-minute barrier: 3:56, a full 5.4 seconds under the world record Lyudmila Bragina established so shockingly in Munich. At that, Tatyana dragged a second Soviet runner, Raisa Katyukova, under the old barrier with her, at 3:59.8.

While Tatyana was busy with the 1,500 meters, her Soviet teammates were making similar progress at 800 meters. In particular, 27-year-old Valentina Gerasimova was crashing barriers. First, she broke the Soviet national record by running 1:58.6 in Moscow; she followed that with 1:58.4 in Munich; and she then finished things off by shattering Bulgarian Svetlana Zlateva's world record with an extraordinary 1:56.0. She pulled countrywomen Svetlana

Styrkina and Tatyana Providokhina to times of 1:56.7 and 1:59.7 respectively. These three Soviet runners would have been favorites in Montreal had it not been for other Eastern Bloc runners, notably Anita Weiss of East Germany who ran 1:57.7 and Nikolina Shtereva of Bulgaria who ran 1:58.8. America's reigning Olympic champion Madeline Manning-Jackson was also entered in the 800 meters and talked of running 1:52. By 1976, she held the American record for 800 meters at 1:57.9.

If that was not enough talent for one race, Kazankina found herself jammed into the 800 meters at Montreal. It was her own fault, of course. Had she not run 1:56.6 in the run-up to the Games, it would not have happened, but she did. Kazankina's argument that she lacked speed for an event dominated by women who could run a very fast 400 meters was brushed aside by the Soviet coaches. They figured she was fast enough. They also thought she was so strong that, no matter the outcome of the 800 meters, Kazankina would be unaffected in the 1,500 meters, which was scheduled later in the program. Finally, the coaches rejected the suggestion that Kazankina would be second-string to Gerasimova, and unnecessary to protect the interest of the Soviet Union. Tatyana Providokhina, who had originally been entered, was deleted from the list, and Kazankina was added. She was entered because other people had more faith in her than she had in herself. She still wasn't satisfied, saying later that the decision risked her fair chance for a gold medal at 1,500 meters for a "highly dubious chance to get a medal of less noble metal." Nevertheless, Kazankina had her orders, and she set her strategy: she would distribute her energy over the entire course of the 800 meters and rely on strength in the homestretch.

The 800 meters for women at Montreal was astonishing. In some respects, it was like a river overflowing its banks, an excess of nature that inspired awe but also suggested the need for greater con-trol. In the middle of the flood was 5' 3-3/4", 104-pound Tatyana

Kazankina. In the heats, she was indistinguishable, just one of eleven women who ran faster than 2:01 and advanced to the semifinals. She would not have noticed America's Wendy Knudson run 1:59.9. Tatyana's eyes were already focused on the semifinals, where the action really started. In the first semifinal, Anita Weiss, who had run an open 400 meters in 51.4, showed what that kind of speed meant in an 800 meters. She slashed through the first 400 meters in 54.4, passed 600 meters in 1:23.9, and finished in an Olympic record 1:56.5. Kazankina was in the semifinal with Weiss, but she and four other runners stayed 15 to 20 meters behind Weiss through 400 meters, after which Kazankina moved up to take second in 1:57.5. The fourth and last qualifier was Doris Gluth from East Germany who ran 1:59.3. Judy Pollock of Australia, by now 36 years old, recorded 1:59.9 but missed the final by finishing fifth. The second semifinal lacked the single amazing performance that Weiss had produced, but nonetheless brought extraordinary depth. Svyetlana Styrkina of the Soviet Union finished first in 1:57.3; two others finished within three-tenths of her; and the fourth qualifier ran 2:00, the only person to make the final who did not break two minutes.

When the qualifications finished, no Western runner remained. The entire field of eight came from behind the Iron Curtain: two from the Soviet Union, two from Bulgaria, three from East Germany, and one from Romania. Madeline Manning-Jackson, who ran in the second semifinal, admitted that she had been "psyched out" by Weiss' run. She could manage only 2:07.3, a performance nowhere near her ability on a normal day. Also eliminated was the world-record holder Valentina Gerasimova, who was in position to qualify in the second semifinal before fading in the stretch. In fact, the second semifinal saw the elimination of the defending Olympic champion, the current world-record holder for the event, the British Commonwealth champion, and the European champion. A new order was not only imminent but unavoidable.

On the day, the 800-meter final was run in remarkable silence. Watching a field with unfamiliar names, the crowd apparently did not know who was who or what was what, only that nobody they knew was running. Instead, there were people with names like Shtereva, Zinn, Styrkina, Koleva, Gluth, Suman, Weiss and Kazankina with no break for a Smith or a Jones. All of this horde ran in assigned lanes for two turns and then broke for the pole, passing 400 meters along the way in 55:05, not much slower than the scintillating pace Weiss had run in her semifinal. The leader at 400 meters in the final was Svetlana Styrkina of the Soviet Union. Anita Weiss and Elfi Zinn of East Germany were the closest pursuers, and the last was Kazankina, who was hoarding her resources. She simply hoped to "stick with the leaders as much as I could." As the race progressed, however, Kazankina was astonished to find that she was handling the pace, and she stayed in contact around the third bend and into the backstretch. Doris Gluth of East Germany lost contact there, but the rest of the field clung together through 600 meters. Styrkina and Weiss were the leaders there in 1:25 but five other runners passed within the next second, and all remained in contention. Kazankina was sixth on the backstretch, started to make a move, but surprisingly cut back into the field and into a box as Weiss, followed quickly by her teammate Zinn, swept past Styrkina going into the final turn. Weiss led into the straight, Zinn challenged, and so now did Bulgaria's Nikolina Shtereva. Kazankina meanwhile was forcing herself out of the box and through traffic. Finally, she got outside and had a clear run to the tape. Attacking powerfully and without apparent distress, Kazankina moved into the lead for the first and only time 80 meters from home but finished ten meters ahead. Her time was an Olympic and world record 1:54.9. Behind her, the silver and bronze medals went to Shtereva in 1:55.4 and Zinn in 1:55.6. Weiss missed a medal, but ran 1:55.7. Four women had run faster than the world record in one race!

Kazankina assessed her performance modestly (and inaccurately in its particulars), saying that her finish was a "bit lucky. Shtereva, Zinn and Weiss were all battling for the inside lane, busy with each other, while I had three lanes to myself on the outside. I was coming full steam, and just caught them ten meters from the tape. They wore one another down, and were all wilting when I caught them unawares." Explaining the lateness of her winning move, she claimed that she "just could not sprint" and that it was best for her to "hope the pace is fast for the others, and make my move in the home straight." Or, as she also said, "To start off calmly and speed up." In fact, however, she did not speed up but slowed down less than her competitors. Her last 200 meters was 29.4, which was slightly slower than the average pace of the run. That, however, is the stopwatch talking and catches none of the power of Kazankina in the last 100 meters.

The race won and the world record set for 800 meters, Kazankina could now look forward to her favorite event, the 1,500 meters. Preparing for the race, she might have been aware that the international press had no fixed spot for her, no explanation for the woman who could run with such power, who could do it with such precision, and then demurely, quietly, shyly answer their questions. As *The London Times* said, "Look at her winning time of 1:54.94 seconds and wonder how many male British runners would be delighted with the same performance. But is this a robot straight off the conveyor belt from some Soviet sports factory as our American cousins or envious British officials might have us believe? Hardly."

Kazankina even got a bit of the old feminization technique so popular with runners of an earlier generation. While commending her power and strength, as well as her sudden bursts of speed, the reports also said that she and her husband were "culture vultures," and that Tatyana's marriage was "a highly successful one." Her activities off the track included keeping house, they said. Kazankina was quoted as saying, "I love to shop, to cook, and always find the time to look after things on this front, too." Asked after one of her Montreal performances whether she expected to continue her sporting career, she replied: "Well, I would like to, but I will have to consult my husband on the subject before deciding." What could be more comforting, and what more calculated to draw Tatyana Kazankina away from and out of the mix of Eastern Bloc ideology. She was like us! Or so the stories seemed to suggest. They even approved when she later changed her mind about her future sporting career and said that she hoped to be in Moscow for the 1980 Olympics and would do her best to stay on top. By then, the small, shy woman had conquered all reservations.

She still had, however, the formality of the 1,500 meters in Montreal. This was her event. She had been favored before the Games, and was more so after the 800-meter victory. In the heats and semifinals, Kazankina was untroubled. In the third of four heats, she slipped quietly into the second qualifying spot behind East Germany's Ulrike Klapezynski in 4:12.1. The other heats were characterized by numerous times between 4:07 and 4:11, including that of defending champion Lyudmila Bragina who ran the fastest time, 4:07.1. In her semifinal, Kazankina was an easy winner in 4:07.4. The other semifinal was faster, as Soviet teammate Raisa Katyukova led through laps of 62.5, 67.5 and 65 before fading to a non-qualifying sixth. Her pacesetting, however, permitted Klapezynski to run 4:02.1 with four others also under 4:03, including Bragina who finished third in the heat and qualified automatically, and Jan Merrill from the United States who finished fifth in an American record 4:02.6 and qualified as a fastest loser. Merrill's time beat the prior American record Francie Larrieu had set in her prelim, 4:07.2.

For the final, expectations for a world record were high. Kazankina's finish in the 800 meters, taken together with her world record for 1,500 meters before the Games and the ease of her qualification, heightened the sense of possibility. Notwithstanding that fact, however, the East German coaches planned a slow pace for the final. They believed that their athletes, Hoffmeister and Klapezynksi, would be slightly faster than Kazankina in a sprint finish. As to Klapezynski, the coaches compared her best race of 3:59.9 with Kazankina's 3:56, and found that Klapezynski ran the last 300 meters of her race 1.6 seconds faster than Kazankina had run that distance in hers. Despite the faster overall time of Kazankina's run, they thought they had a chance in a sprint.

Perhaps the opposing coaches had been too credulous in listening to Tatyana describe her lack of speed after the 800-meter final. In the longer race, five runners from the Eastern Bloc joined four runners from the West. One of the Westerners, Nina Holmen of Finland, led a desultory 68.2 first 400 meters followed closely by the 33-year-old Hoffmeister and the 23-year-old Klapezynksi. The second lap was even slower. Holmen ran 70 seconds for a 2:18.2 split. No one was lost at this pace and no one was surprised that Italy's Gabriella Dorio decided to pick things up. She moved up at 900 meters and accelerated. Again, the two East Germans attached themselves closely to the leader, a position they held entering the penultimate homestretch until Bragina moved to the front and began a long drive for home. Later, she and Kazankina denied that this move was planned between them, but certainly the injection of pace worked well for Kazankina. When Bragina hit the bell, Kazankina was relaxing in her wake, resting fifth or sixth on the outside. Bragina's 1,200-meter split was 3:23.4, but she held the lead only 200 more meters before the two East Germans moved. Hoffmeister passed Bragina on the inside; Klapezynski passed her on the outside, and the race was on. The two East Germans entered the homestretch in tandem and were perfectly positioned for the stretch run.

After the race, observers noted that when Hoffmeister entered the straight and caught sight of the potential gold medal, she

Kazankina completes the double in Montreal.

switched immediately and obviously to a wilder, more exuberant sprint finish. In those same moments, however, Tatyana Kazankina asserted herself. After running in sixth for most of the race, she drifted up on the outside, and, as in the 800 meters, collared her victims in the last 100 meters. This time, she reached the lead with 50 meters left, and won by three. Her winning time was slow at 4:05.5, but she did not care. After the race, she professed herself overjoyed with the result, as well she might have been. Her last 200 meters took less than 28 seconds, and was itself part of a final 800 meters of 2:03.5, a final 600 meters under 1:29, and a finishing 400 meters in 56.9 seconds. This was not the plow horse the East German coaches might have expected!

One post-race anecdote explained the mystery of Tatyana

Kazankina's kick. The story goes that the day after the event, Gunhild Hoffmeister, the silver medalist, and Ulrike Klapezynski, the bronze medalist, visited the track and field room at the International Center in the Olympic Village. They came to look at the film of the prior day's race, in which they had been outsprinted so handily. Watching Kazankina's charge up the homestretch and their own flailing, energetic but futile attempts to resist her, Hoffmeister spoke in German to her teammate and made a circular motion with her hands. As the witness put it, "What Hoffmeister saw was that while she and Klapezynski were fighting hard down the straight, sprinting with forceful, driving, piston-like strides, Kazankina almost seemed to flow past them, her legs moving effort-lessly in an economical rolling action." Often described as desiccat-ed, frail, emaciated, or merely thin, and sometimes as tiny, Tatyana Kazankina, in fact, had strong, muscular legs which appeared to do most of the work as she ran, leaving her relatively light arms and upper body for reaction and balance. As she said, "My strong finish is the result of special training methods. There is nothing surprising about it. It was all planned." There, then, was the tiny giant, who years before covered as much ground with each stride as she could—in a bounding, high-footed action that required correction. There, the Russian wonder who said she had no speed but out-sprint-ed the best in the world at Montreal. Behold!

The Olympic victories were the close of a spectacular year for Tatyana Kazankina. She did not lose a final that year at either 800 meters or 1,500 meters. She ran two of the eight fastest 800 meters ever run, including a resounding world record, became the first woman to run 800 meters under 1:55 and the first to run 1,500 meters under 4:00, ran two of the four fastest 1,500 meters ever run, and became the first woman in 35 years to hold both the 800-meter and 1,500-meter world records. Her illustrious predecessor was countrywoman Yevdokya Vasilyeva, who ran 2:12 and 4:38. While the difference between Vasilyeva's times and Kazinkina's times show the improvement in standards, some reports highlighted another aspect of Kazankina's performances, which was that she had closed the gap between men and women. Over 800 meters, what had been a 32.4-second differential 50 years before, narrowed to 11.4 seconds. At 1,500 meters, the separation moved from 59.4 seconds to 23.8 seconds. And the gap was closing, according to Tatyana, who predicted that times for her two events would soon move to 1:52 for 800 meters and 3:53 for 1,500 meters. "But it may not, of course, be me who will break the current records," she added cautiously.

After her double victory in Montreal, Tatyana was clearly the woman of the year in athletics. Her 1977, by contrast, was quiet. She ran the 800 infrequently. She lost the USSR championship race to Svyetlana Stryrkina, but won the dual meet with the United States and finished second at the World University Games. She was ranked third in the world for the distance. At 1,500 meters, she remained the top-ranked runner in the world but her standard fell. Her fastest time was only 4:04.2 while winning the USSR Championships. She also won the European and World Cup Championships. In all three major events, she showed the same firepower in the homestretch that she had in Montreal. If 1977 was subdued, 1978 was more so, but for reasons that had nothing to do with middle-distance running. Tatyana was pregnant for much of the year before giving birth to her daughter on November 6, 1978. In her absence, women from the Soviet Union dominated the middle-distance events at the European Championships in Prague. They went one-two-three in the 800 meters and won both the 1,500 meters and the 3,000 meters. In both 1,500 meters and 3,000 meters, Grete Waitz represented the West. She ran particularly well at 3,000 meters where she bravely tried to run her rivals off their feet. She held the lead until 200 meters to go before being forced back into third with 8:34.3 to Svetlana Ulmasova's 8:33.2.

It would have been hard for Tatyana Kazankina to watch the events of 1978, but for the fact that no runner came near her performances from 1976. She still owned the field. And while others might have reasonably asked whether she could get back to world class by 1980, much less defend her Olympic titles, she worked to assure the result. "All that time," she said, "I was seriously involved in a building-up routine, naturally under strict medical supervision. This helped me regain my form quickly." By May 1979, she was running in competition and doing well. She did not, however, race seriously, and was not world ranked, nor were any of her performances fast enough to be listed.

Even in the absence of Kazankina, however, the set-up in 1979 for the Olympic year 1980 was daunting. From a Western perspective, the most obvious feature at 800 meters was that only one of them, Christina Boxer of England, ranked in the top fifteen in the world. Ms. Boxer scraped in at fourteenth with the first sub-2:00 800 meters by a Briton. Otherwise, the lists were full of Eastern Bloc runners. The Soviet Union itself had seven of the fifteen runners, while athletes from Romania, Bulgaria, and East Germany shared the other spots. Notably, this was a year steroid disqualifications had a major impact. The fourth-ranked runner, Totka Petrova of Bulgaria, and the eighth-ranked runner, Ileana Silai of Romania, were nabbed. In fact, the disqualified Petrova was top ranked at 1,500 meters with a fastest time of 3:57.4 at the Balkan Games. The second ranked 1500-meter runner, Natalia Marasescu of Romania, was also disqualified for steroid use. In all, the 1,500-meter rankings for 1979 included only three Westerners, Grete Waitz of Norway in the tenth slot, Chris Benning of England in the eleventh place, and Francie Larrieu of the United States at number fourteen. Otherwise, as at 800 meters, the list was dominated by Bulgarians, Romanians, East Germans and Soviets. Glancing up to 3,000 meters, which was increasingly being contested, the rankings were much the same, as runners from the Soviet Union held seven of the fifteen spots, and only five Westerners broke the stranglehold. Francie Larrieu was in the sixth position with a best time of 8:51.1. Her time was only the fifteenth best time recorded for the year.

Shortly after the 1976 Olympics in Montreal, Tatyana had suggested that major revisions would be made to the 800-meter and 1,500-meter records. She thought that the records would come sooner than later, but she eventually changed her mind. Now she said that they would come in the Olympic year. "It will come in preparation for Moscow in 1980. And I think it will be a very good record," she said. Modest by nature and intention, she would not have been talking about herself with that prediction, but she might have been thinking it. Quiet Tatyana was planning an assault. In the winter of 1980, she occasionally covered more than 200 kilometers (approximately 125 miles) a week. This was prodigious training, but it was arguably proportionate to the challenge. Even in her own country, new runners had emerged in her absence. They would grant Tatyana no concession for past glory. Rather, they would take that glory as their own by bringing her down.

In the woods around Moscow, Nadyezhda Olizaryenko was training. At 26 years of age and with more than ten years experience in the sport, she could look back on steady if unspectacular progress, moving from 2:11.4 as a 16-year-old girl to 1:55.9 in 1978 when she was ranked equal first in the world with Tanya Providokhina, a training partner and best friend to Tatyana Kazankina. Olizaryenko could also see, however, that too often she was second, just short of the strength and speed necessary to win. In the 1978 European Championships at Prague, where she ran her fastest time, she lost narrowly to Providokhina and had only silver rather than gold to show for her effort. At other races, too, she showed second rather than first—the Spartakiad in Moscow in 1979 where she finished second in her year's best of 1:57.5; in both the 1978 and 1979 USSR

Championships, in each of which she finished second. It was a pattern and looking forward now, she saw only one way to break it. She, too, drove her volume up in the winter of 1979-1980. Some reports said 125 miles a week while others described a more cautious 75 miles per week. Most of the work was done with her husband, a steeplechaser who would join her on the Soviet Olympic team at Moscow, or with her coach, Boris Gnojevoi, with whom she had been working since she was 14. Olizaryenko's objective was to gain the strength and speed necessary to dictate the pace in a championship race while holding the ability to finish furiously. In short, she hoped to become the ultimate racer, ready for any tactic or eventuality. To that end, she held Tatyana Kazankina at no great distance, but drew her in for comfort and inspiration. Tatyana was no queen, and she could be overtaken.

As the 1980 season approached, Olizaryenko left her job as an office worker and moved into a training camp in the Caucasus mountains to do her final preparations. She honed her 5' 5", 119-pound body—sometimes described without glamour as "square"—to capture the divergent requirements of strength and speed. In early June of 1980 at the Pravda Prize meet in Moscow's Lenin Stadium, she gave persuasive proof that success was near. Running against an impressive international field that included Fita Lovin of Romania and five top-flight Russians, including Kazankina, Olizaryenko boomed to the front, covered the first 400 meters in 57.1, rebuffed repeated efforts by Kazankina to get past her beginning 250 meters from home, and finished the 800-meter race in 1:54.85. In a stroke, she had removed Kazankina from the record book at 800 meters! She also gave notice in the post-race interviews that this run left her unimpressed and unruffled. Describing Kazankina's challenge, she blandly answered that, having run 1:56.7 in the heats, "I knew that I was in top form and had plenty in store, and was deliberately taking it a bit easy up front, awaiting and anticipating an attack. So I was more than ready with my own surge when it came, and knew that there was no way in which she could pass me. It was pretty satisfactory."

After the Pravda Prize, Tatyana took herself out of contention for the 800-meter Olympic Championship. There would be no "double-double." "I will concentrate on the 1,500 meters in the Olympics," she said, "and leave alone the option to run the 800 meter, too, mainly because my best friend, Tanya Providokhina, deserves her own Olympic chance. In 1976, I was in great form partly because Tanya helped me so much, and last year we made our comeback jointly, after a year's rest." When she was later encouraged by the media to admit that it was Olizaryenko, not Providokhina, who prompted her to leave the 800 meters alone, Tatyana staunchly held her position, "I have known of Nadyezhda's potential for some time. I had ample opportunity to assess it during the selection's training session. But I believe this is going to be Tanya Providokhina's year at 800 meters. She richly deserves it."

Be that as it may, Olizaryenko was not satisfied with her victory at the Pravda Prize. She moved up to the 1,500 meters at the Znamensky Memorial in Moscow on July 6, 1980. Kazankina was entered in both the 800 meters, which Olizaryenko did not contest, and in the 1,500 meters. After Kazankina ran only a non-qualifying eighth-place 2:04.6 in the 800-meters heats, Olizaryenko stepped forward in the 1,500 meters as favorite. At least, that would have been her view. Run in driving rain, the race nevertheless began auspiciously as Raissa Belousova hared through 400 meters in 60.0 and 800 meters in 2:07. Belousova was joined closely by Romania's Ileana Silai and Maricica Puica, and occasionally overtaken by one or both of them. Kazankina tucked in behind, always in contact, closely monitoring changes of pace and rhythm. Olizaryenko meanwhile, in only the second 1,500 meters of her career, stayed back in the field. As a result, she was not where she needed to be when

Belousova accelerated one more time at 800 meters and not where she needed to be when Kazankina launched a long punishing drive for home at the 950-meter mark. Only teammate Lyubov Smolka followed Kazankina through 1,200 meters in 3:09.2, and even she dropped away when Kazankina sprinted the last 300 meters in 45.8. The time was a new world record of 3:55, a full second under the prior time. Behind the winner came other astonishing performances: Smolka, 3:56.7; Olizaryenko, 3:56.8; Zamira Zaitseva, 3:56.9; and Yekaterina Podkopayeva, 3:57.4. Even with this result, Olizaryenko was in no mood to concede Olympic gold to Kazankina. "There will be no Belousova in the Olympics," she said.

Perhaps to underscore her point, Olizaryenko went out the next week and ran a 400-meter race. She beat the best women in the Soviet Union by running 50.96. When asked what this speed might mean at the approaching Games, she spoke brusquely, "How should I know? OK, it may mean that my finish will be stronger, which is important... More generally, it will mean that I will probably have greater reserves of both speed and stamina." As to her competition, Olizaryenko spoke candidly. "So who is there?" she asked, "Kazankina, Mineyeva, and several other possibilities from the home side, plus people like Totka Petrova and Shtereva from Bulgaria, Lovin, Marasescu, Puica and perhaps even Silai from Romania, and whoever the GDR comes up with. Comprehensive enough?" Of course, it was not comprehensive enough. It included no Americans and no runners from the other countries who boycotted the Olympic Games in 1980. But that was a small matter to Olizaryenko and Kazankina and the other Eastern Bloc athletes. They had their hands full with the group that was there, never mind the exception who might otherwise have troubled them.

Kazankina had run 800 meters in 1:56.5 at the same meet that saw Olizaryenko's 400-meter victory, and five times she ran faster than 1:59 for 800 meters in 1980, but true to her word she stayed out of the event in Moscow. She left it to Olizaryenko, and Olizaryenko destroyed the field. Normally a nervous person, Olizaryenko slept easily the night before the final. "For the first time in her life," said her coach. No wonder, because her mind was at ease and her tactics were simple and direct. She was the fastest and strongest runner in the field, she figured, and she dared anyone to match the pace she would set. Facing a field in which no qualifier ran slower than 1:59.0, she simply dived into the lead at the break and maintained a fast, even tempo. At 200 meters in 27.2, only 0.5 separated first from last in this strong field, which included only Gabriella Dorio from the West among an otherwise entirely Eastern Bloc field. Around the second bend and through 400 meters in 56.2, Olizaryenko continued her steady assault. Dorio hung with her. Olga Mineyeva of the Soviet Union came up on her shoulder. The entire field went through under 58.0. None of that made an impact on the dispassionate leader. She accelerated through a third 200 meters of 28.5. The field was no longer bunched behind her, but single file as in a queue, or, perhaps better yet, like a game of "pop the whip" as the tailenders were dislodged one at a time by the energy in front of them. With 300 meters to go, Mineyeva, a woman with 400-meter speed, moved up and tried to pass. For perhaps a split second, the question lingered before Olizaryenko answered. She would not let her teammate past, and she surged down the backstretch, into the homestretch, clear now by 5 and then 6 meters. In the long finish, she showed some sign of the pace. She chopped her stride; she leaned back slightly. But her arms still swung easily, and she lost no appreciable power. Finishing, she was 10 meters ahead of silver medalist Olga Mineyeva of the Soviet Union and 15 meters ahead of Kazankina's best friend, Tanya Providokhina, also of the Soviet Union, thus completing a one-two-three sweep. Inevitably, Nadyezhda Olizaryenko smashed the world record by running 1:53.42. In doing so, she dragged Mineyeva to 1:54.9 and

Providokhina to 1:55.5. The eighth and last finisher was Dorio of Italy, who ran 1:59.2.

After the race, Olizaryenko was characteristically blunt. "I wanted to win the race," she said, "and saw pretty good prospects for doing just that. I wanted to run a world record, because that seems the best way to ensure that I would come out on top. It was the safest variant. The 56.41 for the first lap was not fast at all though; it was slow, in fact. I was playing it by ear there. Had Mineyeva stayed closer on my tail, I would have gone down to 55 or even 54. But there was no real pressure, so that I decided to keep my final surge intact. This world record being the human limit? Not at all. This sort of time had been due, in fact, for a while, and there is plenty of room left for improving on this result." Equally confident with other reporters, she also said, "The 400-meter split was excellent, and I was in front, as always. I was really feeling easy. I knew then that I was capable of breaking the world record."

Next up for the confident Nadyezhda Olizaryenko was Tatyana Kazankina, the legend from Montreal. Kazankina was watchful of her rival, saying of her prior to the Games: "Her secret? Simply—acceleration and tempo. Olizaryenko tried all sorts of tempos with her coaches, persevered, and now she has a strong formula. In sprint events, talent is the main thing you have to have in order to be able to explode into 10 to 11 seconds of unmitigated action. With us middle-distance runners, it's different. We have to work out, mature into, optimal patterns." Olizaryenko said much the same thing but with a threatening effect. "Uncompromising tempo and a scorching finish," she said, "these are the ingredients of middle-distance supremacy. And now I have both."

Notwithstanding Kazankina's favorable appraisal of her, Olizaryenko would find in Moscow a confident competitor well prepared to defend her title. To Kazankina, the situation was encouraging. "Naturally, just like at Montreal. I had beaten the world record and then I won the Games," she said. "It was a good augury." Kazankina was also helped by the fact that she had only two races to run. In Moscow, the heats at 1,500 meters were eliminated in favor of two cutthroat semifinals, in which 26 women were separated into two fields with the first four across the line in each race advancing. Kazankina handled her semifinal calmly. She followed Maricica Puica of Romania for 1,100 meters, and then rushed past her, covering the last 300 meters in 45 seconds and finishing in an Olympic record 3:59.2. Olizaryenko, however, stayed close by running 3:59.5 in second.

That would be the race, everyone assumed, for the final: Kazankina vs. Olizaryenko. In the event, Olizaryenko did the early work, but more gently than at 800 meters. She led through a relatively calm 65.5 400 meters and 2:13.7 800 meters. Kazankina moved along in sixth place through the first lap, then gradually moved up one place at a time until she was ready. With 600 meters left to run, she darted to the front and turned on the power. At the bell, she was two meters ahead of Lyubov Smolka who was a meter ahead of Natalia Marasescu. Olizaryenko, who got caught in the wave of runners chasing Kazankina, lost the momentum of the race and fell into last. Twelve-hundred meters passed in 3:12.3 and still Kazankina was accelerating out front. The 400 meters after she took control was run in 58.7! By the last turn, she was 20 meters in front and completing a final lap in 57.7, for a final 800-meter split well under 2:00. Finally, Olizaryenko came alive and gave chase, but she was too late even for silver. That prize went to Christiane Wartenberg of East Germany. Olizaryenko got bronze for all her strong talk and hard work. For all three medalists, the times were fast (3:56.58, 3:57.8, and 3:59.6, respectively) but not record-breaking. On the other hand, Kazankina's finish, taken in itself, was running of such power that no one could deny it. Her crown, lately challenged, was firmly in place.

Explaining her tactics, Kazankina said that she thought only of winning the Olympic title. "I didn't care about times," she said. "I've been aware these past few months that I've lost some speed and that's why I didn't attempt the 800 meters." She also said that she had changed her usual tactics because she was "obliged" to do so. "Usually I start my kick near the end of the race, but today I knew that my only chance was to kick from farther out." She also said, however, that she had more speed available to her if she needed it, "if it had come down to a fight."

Four days after the Olympic Games, Kazankina wound down with an easy 1,500 meters in Rome. The race was fairly fast at 3:58.94 and, of course, Kazankina won, but it meant little to her. The next race was the big one. Kazankina would run a signature race, the one that defined the time and put her enduring mark on it.

SIX

Without science, no Communism.

VI Lenin

But, dear readers, you must think, at least a little. It helps.

WE,
Eugene Zamiatin

The English can speak with conviction of Walter George or William Cummings, Albert Hill and Alfred Shrubb, but for most people the world of middle- and long-distance running begins—long before women took up the sport—with Paavo Nurmi of Finland. A memorial stands in front of the Olympic Stadium in Helsinki as a reminder of his accomplishment. Among many races, the memorial honors a day three weeks before Nurmi went to the 1924 Olympics in Paris and won four gold medals. On that earlier day in Helsinki, Nurmi dispatched token opposition by running the first 400 meters of 1,500 meters in 57.3, tempered the rhythm to 2:01 at 800 meters, passed 1,200 meters in 3:06, and finished untroubled in 3:52.6, a new world record. Without the ambitious first lap, he thought it was possible to run 2 seconds faster for the distance, but he never did. Advancing now to 1980, one considers his reaction to Tatyana Kazankina, the woman who, being queen, would be king. In Zurich for a 1,500 meters on August 13, 1980, Kazankina went to the line in the blood-red jersey of the Soviet Union with Paavo Nurmi in her sights. If she ran well, she would surpass him. How might he have reacted to that prospect—always so stern, so proud? Upon her success, might he have said: "Pull down the statue. I require no memorial. A gaunt, pale Russian woman has revealed me. Pull me down." Or might he have bridled with indignation and injustice? After surveying the increasing dominance of Eastern Bloc women over the middle-distance events, after learning of the stunned silence in Montreal during the 800 meters when women from the Iron Curtain countries ran alone, after the extraordinary performances in Moscow, after hearing too much about scientific method and receiving too little detail, after detecting an increased murmur of suspicion, discontent, and rumor, might he have said: "I accuse."

If Paavo accused, he would level his arm and point his single finger east—toward the Union of Soviet Socialist Republics, and to the countries trapped by the Soviet Union after World War II and forced to accept its fantastic nightmare. Within those countries, he would point to sport, which was not sport, but realpolitik. Doing so, he would ask in rectitude the question that begins much ethical dialogue: "what is going on here?"

Some of the evidence was spread out before him. Sport as an instrument of the socialist states had produced extraordinary results in women's middle and long distance events after 1968 and during 1980. In 1968, the finalists in the women's 800-meter run at the Olympic Games included two women from the United States, two from Britain, and one each from Canada, France and the Netherlands. Only Ileana Silai of Romania represented the East. By 1972, the finalists in the Olympic 800 meters had assumed a different character. The field included one Canadian, one West German, one Briton, and five women from Eastern Bloc countries: one each from the Soviet Union, East Germany, Bulgaria, Yugoslavia, and Romania. At 1,500 meters, which was offered for the first time in 1972, only four of the ten finalists were from the East, but they filled three of the top four finishing positions and won the gold and silver medals. Lyudmila Bragina was particularly astounding, as she lowered the world record from 4:06.9—a record that she already owned—to 4:01.4 in the space of days. By 1976, Bragina was a footnote, reduced to fifth place in the final of the 1,500-meter race, which Kazankina, who had already smashed the world record down to 3:56.0, supremely dominated. Only five of nine women in the 1,500 meters at Montreal were from the East, but, significantly, they filled the first five slots: Soviet, East German, East German, Bulgarian, and Soviet, leaving nothing for Western athletes. In the 800 meters, of course, the domination was even more striking. Kazankina sprinted her world record of 1:54.9 from a field composed of two Soviets, two Bulgarians, three East Germans, and one Romanian. At Moscow in 1980, Gabriella Dorio was the sole Western athlete to make the finals in either the 800 meters or 1,500 meters. Among the boycotting nations, only runners from the United States or West Germany might have otherwise intruded. Surely, no one from a boycotting nation could have run with Olizaryenko or Kazankina.

World rankings emphasized the growing strength of Eastern Bloc countries after 1971. For the year *1972, Women's Distance Running News* ranked the Olympic champion Hildegard Falck number one in the world for 800 meters, but followed her closely with six women from the East before a Briton appeared in the eighth position. In the 1,500 meters the domination was less pronounced but Bragina was first and she was joined by three other Eastern Bloc women in the first five slots. In 1973, women from the Eastern Bloc took four of the first five positions at both 800 meters and 1,500 meters; and in 1974, six of the first seven positions at 800 meters went to Eastern runners while the top three at 1,500 meters also were Eastern Bloc runners. In 1975, only Madeline Manning Jackson prevented Eastern Bloc women from taking all ten of the first positions at 800 meters, while at 1,500 meters Grete Waitz of

Norway, Francie Larrieu of the United States and Nina Holmen of Finland performed similar duty. Waitz, remarkably, took the first ranking in the pre-Olympic year and spoke hopefully of running "near 4:00." All this of course washed away in 1976, as the East asserted itself at Montreal. And in 1977, 1978, and 1979, similar results were recorded in annual lists maintained by *Track and Field News*, which had long chronicled men's performances and more recently added women's performances. In 1977, the first ten athletes over 800 meters were from Bulgaria, East Germany, the Soviet Union, the Soviet Union, Romania, Romania, East Germany, Bulgaria, Romania, and, finally, West Germany. At 1,500 meters, it was the Soviet Union, Norway (as always this was Grete Waitz, who battled the high tide for years before moving up to the marathon), Romania, East Germany, Romania, Bulgaria, the United States (Francie Larrieu), East Germany, Romania, and East Germany. The year 1978, if anything, saw an even more pronounced left lean. Of the top 29 fastest runners for the year over 800 meters, only two were from countries outside the Eastern Bloc, and they were 24th and 26th fastest. At 1,500 meters, the West did better as Grete Waitz and Gabriella Dorio again wedged themselves into the top ten, as did Ulrike Bruns of West Germany, but otherwise the top-twenty performers were from the other side of the curtain. In 1979, the first 13 runners in the world over 800 meters were Eastern Bloc, and six of them were from the Soviet Union; at 1,500 meters, 12 of the first 15 ranked runners were from the East. Only Grete Waitz broke into the top ten, at tenth. Meanwhile, as soon as the 3,000 meters was contested, Eastern athletes moved there, too, producing similarly dominant performances.

To this survey, a snapshot is added. The month is August, 1980. The top ten performances in the world for each of the women's middle-distance events show the domination of the Soviet Union (SU) and its allied countries:

800 meters		1,500 meters		3,000 meters	
1:54.85	Olizaryenko (SU)	3:55.0	Kazankina (SU)	8:33.6	Sipatova (SU)
1:55.1	Mineyeva (SU)	3:56.7	Smolka (SU)	8:33.9	Sycheva (SU)
1:55.9	Providokhina (SU)	3:56.8	Olizaryenko (SU)	8:34.0	Fraznova (SU)
1:56.5	Kazankina (SU)	3:57.4	Podkopayeva (SU)	8:36.6	Smolka (SU)
1:56.7	Olizaryenko (SU)	3:59.3	Sorokina (SU)	8:38.73	Decker (US)
	Lovin (Rumania)		Puica (Rumania)	8:40.23	Waitz (Nor)
1:56.9	Veselkova (SU)	3:59.9	Liebich (East Ger)	8:40.4	Yaneyeva (SU)
1:57.0	Vakrusheva (SU)	4:00.1(i)	Decker (US)	8:46.2	Romanova (SU)
	Ruchayeva (SU)	4:00.3	Shesterova (SU)	8:47.0	Sadretdinova (SU)
1:57.3	Gerasimova (SU)	4:01.79	Wartenberg (E.G.)	8:52.8	Skripkina (SU)
	Rigel (SU)				

This is the kind of domination that causes some people to shield their eyes, to look away from the obvious. The act of judging fairly would seem unkind.

Courage would be required to raise the question directly— What is going on here?—and to follow it to its conclusion. It was not enough to identify cultural and historical differences between East and West, and to suggest that women from the Eastern Bloc were permitted to do more work, were less inhibited by the Western woman's stereotype of appearance and behavior, were selected for sport at an early age, were sent to specialized settings for education and athletic development, had coaching from one person or one group of persons over the course of a career, took succor and confidence from each other as they succeeded, and had considerable material advantage from success, in that they became part of a privileged society within the larger totalitarian state. All these things were arguably relevant to the analysis, but they did not settle the account. To suggest that it did, and to make remarks like "Our girls just aren't doing enough," was insulting to the women in the West who were, in fact, dedicating themselves to the task at hand assiduously and deserved protection from competitors who cheated.

In point of fact, something else was going on behind the Iron Curtain and everybody knew it. Information about drugs leached out of the East—figuratively, from under and around and over the wall—long before testing began to reveal and to prove it in individual cases. Sometimes, admittedly, it was mere rumor, as when Gordon Pirie alleged in 1962 that his Russian rival, Vladimir Kuts, used drugs to win gold medals at 5,000 and 10,000 meters at the Olympic Games at Melbourne. If Kuts was using drugs to enhance performance, his denial was among the more disingenuous of the genre, "Neither the thousands of spectators during and after the race," said Kuts, "nor the scores of correspondents to whom I gave interviews for 40 minutes immediately after the finals, noticed anything strange in my behavior." This sounds like a man accused of being high on cocaine, not one accused of taking performance drugs!

More frequently, the evidence of doping was based on observation, on gathered, collected, collated experience, and on infrequent admission. Sometimes, the information skirted along the edge, leaving ambiguity where accusation might have stood, as when one commentator from the vantage point of 1979 watched a documentary film of the 1964 Olympics and noted, "They (i.e. women) used to run with adipose tissue. As Ann Packer led the runners to the tape, I was amazed to note the almost complete lack of definition in their legs. None of the 'cuts' (to use the bodybuilding term) so evident today." Drawing closer to the real theme, the writer observed, "Remember 'massive' Tamara Press? She was a wimp compared to today's putters. Probably hadn't heard of 'roids." This was not an accusation. Neither, however, was it a joke. It was an innuendo, a veiled or equivocal observation on character and reputation.

Other times, the visual evidence was packaged openly, as when Ken Steward, the head coach of the Australian Olympic team, was purported to say that "European"—meaning Eastern European—hurdlers, sprinters, and long jumpers were taking drugs prior to the 1972 Olympic Games in Munich. The evidence: "It may be coincidence, but among certain European countries there were no lean women sprinters, hurdlers, or long jumpers. Whether tall or short, they all had heavy buttocks." That may be going too far, and women might object that the statement denies them the full range of body type at the risk of losing femininity, but it was a point of evidence and inquiry. It was fair game to ask whether appearance, whatever it might have been, was being adjusted to the demands and requirements of competition, and to ask how that was being done.

By 1976, the answer was coming. It was more than heavy buttocks, and much more threatening. It was science. It was reported that prior to Montreal, the East German athletes in the weight events underwent a sophisticated regimen that started with 100-milligram (mg.) injectable Deca-Durabol or Winstrol, both banned steroid substances; added daily injections of four to eight 5-mg. administrations of Dianabol, Neurobol, or Winstrol, all of which were steroids; and included legal assistance from vitamin supplements, mental training sessions, caffeine before training sessions, dance and ballet, massage, technique films, biorhythm awareness, and "psychic regeneration" of an undisclosed nature.

At the same time this revelation was made, others retreated to the basic question whether there was anything inherently wrong or unethical with doping, apparently on the dual theory that such interventions might not, in fact, assist performance, or, if they did, they were not substantially different from other enhancements to warrant their distinction in law and regulation. To this was added an uncertainty whether steroids carried the risk of adverse reaction. Amid reports that much of the talk in the Olympic Village at

Mary Decker, right, hangs on as the Soviets accelerate.

Montreal was of drugs, the United States Olympic Committee set up an Olympic Drug Study Panel in late 1976. Irving Dardik, M.D., a member of the Olympic Committee's medical staff at Montreal, reportedly said that the purpose of the panel was to "look into areas considered taboo," such as blood boosting and steroids. At or near the same time, a group of medical doctors attending a conference in Freiburg, Germany directly posed the question whether steroids and other performance-enhancing drugs should be permitted. The report of this conference included the statement that anabolic steroids were harmless to physically mature athletes if dosage was controlled; that there were 18 Olympic disciplines, including the weight events in track and field, for which drugs were "necessary" in order to meet the "norms" in the events; and that "the group also felt that the drugs had been secretly approved years ago by the Soviet Bloc nations." One doctor said that three options existed for the Western countries: "One, we formally announce that we won't prescribe steroids and surrender the world sports standards to the East Bloc. Two, the Olympics ban all 18 sports in which the muscle pill is used. Three, we, as doctors, decide to support every measure that helps improve the athlete's performance without injuring his health." The doctor who made this list favored the last option, in part because steroids had been outlawed "in the West" on the basis of "highly emotional arguments about sports ethics."

As to women, the conferees included one physician who had worked with the East German women swimmers before he defected to the West. The physician said that the East German women were on a program of steroids, and that they needed much less than the men did in order to improve performance. "This is one of the reasons for the high superiority of East German sports in women's disciplines," he concluded.

Reports and inquiries like these two are interesting for a number of reasons. First, they confirm a deeply held belief that the

Eastern Bloc nations and the Western democracies had gone different directions on the question of drugs. The East, so the story went, determined that ethically and medically there was nothing "wrong" with taking performance-enhancing drugs, while the West said there was, and acted to ban such enhancements. Second, having taken this action, the West, in athletic terms, had fallen behind the East and had ceded the field in some events. Third, testing for drugs would never catch all the users, and competition would remain uneven and unjust. Fourth, the only way for the West to catch up was to look back to the essential ethical and medical questions and determine that an error had been made—that, in fact, it would now be permissible for all athletes to begin taking drugs openly. Finally, and fifth, the remarks reveal an essential misunderstanding of performance drugs. People were still talking about "muscle" drugs and thinking in terms of the power events. The idea that middle- and long-distance runners might be taking drugs was unmentioned.

This all changed in October, 1979. That month the IAAF, which tested athletes at major competitions, announced that seven women from the Eastern Bloc countries had recently tested positive. This was news in itself, but a genuine furor attended the further news that among the seven were the three fastest women over 1,500 meters for the year: Bulgaria's Totka Petrova, and Romania's Natalia Marasescu and Ileana Silai. If people previously thought that drugs were for men only, or for field-event competitors, now they knew better. Four-time Olympic champion Emil Zatopek was quoted to explain the situation. "It's a matter of conditioning," he said. "An athlete can do more in training, recover faster from hard training, and generally become fitter. Any athlete who can do that will benefit." Perhaps the saddest commentary on these suspensions came from Grete Waitz of Norway who, having battled Eastern Bloc athletes for years, knew what she was talking about. "These are not the only girls who aren't clean," she said in the same article that quoted Zatopek. The IAAF used the occasion to trumpet its dedication to finding the violators. It promised to redouble its detection efforts in 1980 by using $10,000 in development funds for the purpose. This compared favorably to the $6,000 that was expended in 1980. Expenditures at this level were sufficient to prompt Adriaan Paulen, the IAAF president, to say, "Our battle against doping will be ruthless."

The organizers at the Moscow Olympics announced similar get-tough measures for drugs, but it hardly mattered. In what was mistakenly taken as good news, no one got caught doping at Moscow—not a single disqualification "despite the heaviest regimen of testing yet." Simultaneously, however, with this news was evidence of its meaninglessness. Many athletes apparently avoided detection by taking testosterone, which the tests could not detect at the time.

Thus it was that Tatyana Kazankina moved from the triumph of Moscow to Zurich for her epic 1,500-meter race, a solitary figure pressed forward to do the work of multitudes. The stadium was filled with 26,000 appreciative and enthusiastic spectators; the night air was calm, ruffled only by expectancy. There was no mendacity, no subterfuge, no doubt this time, no tactic, and no concern beyond that which trailed her accomplishments like a shadow. That matter being beyond repair, Kazankina let it go. When the race began, she paid no heed to any competitor. She merely tucked in behind her teammate and friend Tatyana Providokhina at the gun and worked behind her through a ferocious first 400 meters of 58.3, a good time even for a men's race over this distance. She stayed there, too, through the slightly slower second 400, which brought the two Soviet stars through 800 meters in 2:04.5, a time faster than the men had run for this split in the Olympic final at Moscow. The crowd was by now in an uproar, encouraged by the announcer who told them at the 800-meter mark that the pace was faster than world-record rhythm. One hundred meters later, however, Kazankina lost her rabbit. Providokhina pulled over, her job done, especially impressive when one considers that earlier in the evening she had finished third in the 800 meters by running 1:59.80. That fact aside, she was gone now, and it was left for Tatyana Kazankina to forge her own pace. Through the last 600 meters, she held her form, accompanied by clapping and cheered encouragement, an enclosure of sound that compelled her to do what she had set out to do in any event. With one lap to go, the time was 2:51.6, and Kazankina needed only 63.3 to break her prior record. She accelerated after the goal, passed 1,200 meters in 3:07.1, and fought to hold her flawless form. In fact, she was sprinting. The last 300 meters were run in 45.4, and the last 400- meter split was 60.9. The last two laps had been covered in 2:05, and the final time was a record-slashing 3:52.47. The time was roughly equivalent to a mile in 4:09. For purposes of comparison, the world record for the women's mile was 4:21.68. Tatyana Kazankina's time for 1,500 meters was also, incidentally, 0.2 seconds faster than Paavo Nurmi ever ran in his life.

The deed was done. It had been swift, ruthless and remorseless. If Paavo pointed, no one saw.

SEVEN

Fear death by water.

The Wasteland
T. S. Eliot

When Tatyana Kazankina was running it would have been wise to anticipate the later Cold War slogan: Trust but verify. At the time, the sporting world did not trust but neither did it effectively and timely verify. This was unfair to Kazankina and her cohorts if they were competing within the rules, and it was unfair to their competitors if they were not. In either case, it did not change things. Kazankina's records and those of the other Eastern Bloc women were ratified in due course, and they set the standard for the generations that followed. In point of fact, those records distorted women's middle-distance running by moving the marker too far out. Essentially, Kazankina and her friends fixed a point in time and reference that appeared unattainable by anyone else as drugs were increasingly monitored; and as the possibilities narrowed. They therefore threatened to leave the sport without reliable history, without transition, without gradualism, and without the promise of dynamic growth and progress. It was another conundrum courtesy of the East; that which looked like progress was, in fact, stasis. This prospect loomed especially in the West, which in the early 1980s was pitiably claiming moral authority—for having refrained from systematic drug use—but not victory itself, which might energize and inspire young girls like Stephanie Herbst back in Minnesota. And it would have remained that way but for one exceptional Western woman who would not permit it. Virtually alone among her peers, the woman braced herself, challenged, and eventually overcame the best runners the Eastern Bloc had to offer. By her courage, by her resolve, by her indomitability, she reclaimed her sport for young girls of Stephanie's age and for all who came after her. She created for them a more reliable point of reference than the "records" did, and she crafted for their emulation not just the image of athletic grace but its reality. The woman was Mary Decker.

If you remember Mary Decker only as a woman crying tears of pain, frustration, disbelief, and anger on the floor of the Los Angeles Coliseum at the 1984 Olympic Games, step back and take another look. Better yet, dig. Concentrate your first energy where you find remnants of teams like the Los Angeles Mercurettes, Will's Spikettes, the Long Beach Comets, the Blue Angels, and the Southern California Cheetahs. Nearby you will see evidence of a gangling, hyperkinetic, 11-year-old girl who joined an equally untrained girlfriend for her first cross-country race in 1969. While the girlfriend dropped out, Mary won easily and attracted the attention of a former racewalker who coached an age-group track team for girls. From that point the layers mingle finely. One moment she is a girl running in the park for fun; almost literally the next she stands on the line representing her country against the best women runners in the world. Turn the soil again and she is adrift, nursing injuries and ignored; one more time and she is running for her college in the first years that activity was encouraged but she, ironically, is distinguished largely by her past. Look again, she is returned to prominence, triumphant and richly rewarded for her gifts. A small shift and she is down hard. In raw anguished gulps of hopeless air, she is grieving beyond comfort, shedding public tears for an essentially private wound. That, too, passes, and she emerges as the person she had always been. She is the pig-tailed girl, the tomboy, the flapper, the girl next door, and the resilient, strong-willed woman who drew all the impulses of a developing sport to herself and made them her own.

In 1969, few areas in the country offered young girls the chance to run against each other. Southern California was one of those few places. That would not have mattered to Mary Decker, who was born in Bunnvale, New Jersey, on August 4, 1958, except that her parents moved to the area when she was 10. At 11, she and her friend saw the notice of a three-quarter-mile cross-country race and decided to run. Her inspiration was boredom. "In the sixth grade," she said, "my best friend and I were sitting around one Saturday saying, 'What can we do?' We had a flyer from the Parks Department and saw there was a 'cross-country' that day. We didn't know what 'cross-country' was. We went down and found out it was running, so we ran. My friend dropped out. I won—by a long ways. I don't remember it being very hard." It would not have been for a young girl who has since been described as a "physical genius," an "elegant mover on the track," and a remarkable natural talent. To her credit, Mary saw it immediately. She knew. So, too, did Don DeNoon.

DeNoon was the unpaid coach of an age-group girls' and women's running club, the Long Beach Comets. With a strong background in track and field generally and in racewalking particularly, where he excelled as an athlete, DeNoon was influenced by the coaching methods of Mihaly Igloi, who emphasized highly regimented interval training, and also by his own favorable experience with interval training. For the period of slightly more than four years between roughly 1970 and 1974, Don DeNoon and Mary Decker worked together to mine the deep deposit of talent in the girl. It was a precarious adventure. The upside was that the young girl had limitless potential; the downside was that the young girl had limitless potential. For a coach, this is a losing proposition. If the talent converts to accomplishment, it is the result of genetic predisposition, for which the coach gets little credit; if the athlete fails to develop through injury, illness, changing body type, or disinclination, the blame belongs to the coach. In Mary Decker's case, the situation was made more difficult by the disharmony between her body, which was light, fine, and fragile, and therefore susceptible to injury, and her boundless enthusiasm and willingness to absorb work, without which she might not succeed, but with which, in excess, she might be injured. Perhaps as important was DeNoon's coaching philosophy. He believed strongly that every athlete had an essential right to explore his or her potential fully, and that it was his job to challenge them to maximum effort. He felt that this approach worked well with young athletes, who would respond affirmatively to hard work as they never would to gradual increases and speculative achievement, which might never occur. He pushed willing minds and bodies, a paradoxical approach that left him open to criticism. Nevertheless, the two began.

Decker began her running career as a sprinter, stepped up to the mile, and then settled in as a half-miler. Although DeNoon's team sometimes went to the beach for a longish run, and other times used the perimeter of a local park for two miles of warm-up, most of the training was interval work done on the track. Interval training was the predominant method for training middle- and long-distance runners in the United States at the time. It consisted of fast running on the track, alternating periods of stress and relaxation, volume generated by the number of repetitions, and distance added to the program incidentally through warm-up and warm-down. DeNoon's youth teams ran workouts four days of nearly every week, generally held the total mileage to approximately 35 miles per week, and raced on weekends. Running repeats of 220 yards, 330 yards, 440 yards, 660 yards, and occasionally longer individual runs bundled into sets, Decker, in particular, made the running harder than it otherwise would have been because she absolutely hated to "lose" an interval such was her competitive nature. Effectively, she was racing all week.

The Long Beach Comets, Decker's team, was one of the larger clubs operating in Southern California and one of its most successful. The Comets were not associated with a school system and were privately funded. The girls and their families provided most of the money that drove the program, and businesses occasionally added sponsorship. From time to time, the girls would solicit donations from people leaving local banks and shops. Each person would receive a decal from the club in exchange for a small contribution: Support the Long Beach Comets. Mary Decker took her place with the other girls on the sidewalks, stoops, and parking lots, asking for money so she and the other girls could run. In order to get the girls to practice, DeNoon and the parents organized car pools. For uniforms, the girls modified boy's shorts and swimsuits until commercial products finally became available. When they ran in the park, the girls shared the field with other recreational and social activities. Helter skelter, they skittered and dodged in and out of pedestrian traffic, around trash cans, past the grandstand, and near the benches and tables. Sometimes the young runners gave fair warning of their approach and sometimes perhaps not. The streets, where the team might have run over-distance, were dangerous because of traffic, and DeNoon was reluctant to send the girls out. One time he took the chance, and a young girl was struck by a car and injured. The track was safer.

DeNoon once said of Decker, "No one knows Mary like I knew her in those days. She ran only what she wanted to run and when she wanted to run. She loved the excitement, the spotlight and the rewards." The rewards and the spotlight came quickly. When she was 12, she set a world age best by running 2:12.7 for 800 meters; at 13 she ran a 4:55 mile. The summer of 1972, however, Decker was inactive, hobbling around on casts. DeNoon said that the "curtailment...was the result of Seaver's disease which is an inflammation of bone growth tissue in her feet. Her hyperactivity made rags out of those casts in a matter of days, necessitating their replacement." Be that as it may, Mary Decker sprang back sensationally when she was 14 years old. The year was 1973. It was the advent of "Little Mary Decker," a worldwide sporting phenomenon. For Mary it was the end of the beginning.

The year started well when she was selected to represent the United States against the Soviet Union at the Senior International in Richmond, Virginia. There, Decker finished a close third in a mile won by 1972 Olympic 1,500-meter champion Lyudmila Bragina. Bragina ran 4:38.7, while Mary ran 4:40.1. Most boys would have been overjoyed to run an indoor mile in 4:40 when they were 14, but for Mary Decker greater things were in store outdoors. She finished second to Wendy Knudson in the US Championships while running 2:05.9 for 880 yards, and then stepped it up by winning the Pan-Pacific Games Championship in Toronto. In that race, she used her 53.9 400-meter speed—remember that this girl was only 14!—to outkick Australia's Charlene Rendina in 2:05.1. Gathering force, Decker then joined the US national team touring in Europe where in her first race she was beaten by 1972 Olympic 800-meter champion Hildegard Falck, 2:01.4 to 2:02.43, before winning an 800 meters in Turin against Italy's best. She was now ready to try her luck against the Soviet team again. The occasion was the 11th track and field meet matching the US against the USSR in Minsk on July 23 and 24, 1973. Facing off with Olympic silver medalist Niole Sabaite, with a personal best of 1:58.7, Mary made an unprepossessing adversary: 5' 0" and 86 pounds, a kid from California, to all appearances fresh meat—and bones, mostly bones—for the Soviet grinder. In the event, Mary ran last at the bell, moved up to third at 600 meters, and then surged into the lead on the homestretch with Sabaite in hot pursuit. In memorable phrasing, one witness said that "Sabaite chased after the skinny little Californian, all arms, legs and forward lean, but Mary actually accelerated brusquely over the final 15 meters to win by a couple of meters in 2:02.9."

As it happens, America was watching these events with interest. While the tension from the Cold War was perhaps a notch lower than in the '50s and '60s, people enjoyed seeing one of their own, especially a child, bring down the manufactured runners from the Soviet Union. It was nature's way! It was also the passing of a torch from Marie Mulder to Mary Decker because here, again, was a young and attractive American girl who could compete well while maintaining decorum. In order to make this point, Mary Decker was suited out in the media with the appropriate references and quotes as she completed the 1973 athletic year, passed her 15th birthday in August, 1973, was ranked fourth in the world over 800 meters for the year, and began the 1974 season. The coverage of Decker was the usual drill of giggles, boys, good legs, and casual excellence. When, for example, Mary ran the 1,000-yard run at the Sunkist Invitational in Los Angeles, *Newsweek* reported that she had been shooed away from the starting line by an official who mistook her appearance ("only 5 feet 3 inches tall, weighs all of 93 pounds and has brown puppy dog eyes") for that of an interloper, "Come on, little lady," he said, "your race isn't being run yet." When Mary refused to yield, the official took her by the hand and walked her off the track while she dissolved in tears. Of course, when the mess was sorted out, she "calmly shucked her sweatsuit, took her mark—and easily outdistanced a tough and class field of older women to set a new world indoor record of 2 minutes 26.7 seconds."

Referring to the *Los Angeles Times* indoor meet, which followed in three weeks, Mary was said to have breezed past her rivals to win easily. "I just went out and ran," she shrugged afterward.

"There wasn't anybody there." In preparation for her races, she was reported to run a "tough" training program of five or six miles after school every day. But should anyone grow concerned, the article continued, "I'm not running so fast in workouts because of my boyfriend," Mary giggles innocently. "I'm not going to sleep early enough. Our conversations are too stimulating." She also was permitted to say that her life was "normal," indeed, that it was better than normal because of all the traveling and meeting different people, "even though boys can sometimes think of nothing cooler to say than 'Lemme see your legs.'" Similar language appeared in a *Sports Illustrated* article that focused on her developing career, her extraordinary talent, and on the mix of people who took an interest in her life, either helpful or disruptive. In that mix, there was, however, a feminizing (but not feminist) reference to her personal habits, "Off the track she is a bewildering mixture of styles and attitudes, like so many of today's youngsters. She plucks her eyebrows and replaces them with thin pencil lines, but she also wears braces on her teeth. She painted her nails maroon until recently, when she started biting them. She loves strawberries, but before a race she dutifully eats spaghetti—without sauce or salt—to stock up on carbohydrates." The obligatory declaration was also present. "I am a typical 15-year-old. I swim and sew and bike and do all sorts of other things, just like any normal kid." This kind of language was the old code, designed to reassure parents and encourage young girls. It was also image building, not for Mary Decker who, like all persons of celebrity was an interchangeable part, but for her sport. Simply, the sport of girls and women running middle and long distances was being packaged and sold using Mary Decker as the medium.

As an image, Mary Decker's impact was more pronounced than that of any of her predecessors. Television made the difference. While Doris Brown and Marie Mulder attracted the print media, as Mary also did, they did not appear regularly on television. Decker did. The effect has been described succinctly, "Primarily through television, the great American public followed [Decker's] stunning progress and the combination of her extreme youth, slight frame and outstanding success against rivals so much older and bigger, made the pig-tailed Miss Decker a wildly popular figure. Much like Olga Korbut in Munich the previous year she inspired hordes of young girls to try and emulate her, and the tremendous growth of women's running in the USA must owe much to the publicity surrounding Mary in 1973 and 1974. Suddenly, it was 'respectable' for white, middle-class American girls to run. Previously it had been widely held that whereas swimming or tennis was socially and physically acceptable, running wasn't." Other American women also ran well during those years and attracted young girls to the sport. Robin Campbell was only 14 years old when she beat the Soviet women Valentina Gerasimova and Tamara Kazachkova over 800 meters indoors at the same meet in Richmond, Virginia, where Mary Decker made her international debut. Francie Larrieu was referred to as "Little Francie Larrieu" even when she was 21 years old and an Olympian, having made the 1972 team. But the primary focus remained on Decker. Arguably, demographics made the difference. Decker was white while Robin, a remarkably blessed athlete with a captivating smile and easy charm, was black; and Decker was a girl while Francie Larrieu was a young woman. Neither point discounts or minimizes a third, and that is Decker's charisma. The word is devalued by overuse, but it is apt to describe a girl who command-ed the light to follow where she went.

In the indoor season of 1974, as the publicity machine revved, Decker ran 2:01.8 for 800 meters and 2:02.4 for 880 yards in the same race, the latter time an indoor world record. She also changed her racing tactics. While previously she tended to follow and kick, she now started going to the front. As one report said, "Mary no longer dazzles crowds with breathtaking, last-lap heroics.

Now she just runs better and faster than everybody else. Last summer, she wasn't fully aware of her capabilities, and so she dropped back, held on to gauge the competition—and put everything she had into the end of the race. More experienced and confident now, Mary streaks for an early lead with uncommonly long strides for one so tiny—and thus also avoids the punishing bumps and shoves that are an inevitable feature of races run on narrow indoor tracks." Or as DeNoon said, "She runs a secure race right now because she has no competition. When somebody moves up on her shoulder, Mary just zips right away from her."

In the biggest meet of the 1974 indoor season, Mary Decker did run from the front when the United States challenged the Soviet team in Moscow. She won easily in 2:04.5. Back in fourth and last place was an obscure performer from Leningrad, Tatyana Kazankina. At this same meet, Decker revealed her youth and her petulance by permitting herself to be elbowed and bullied into a failure of concentration on the anchor of the 4 x 800 meter relay. Bumped out of contention, she flung her baton not once but twice at her discourteous but surprised rival. Much has been made of this event, but it would have passed unnoticed if she had not been where, chronologically, she had no business being, which was center stage of the international sports world. There may also have been additional pressure on her that indoor season because she had a new coach, having separated from Don DeNoon. With his team, now called the Blue Angels, Mary said the workouts were no longer fun. Other versions of the decision referred to Mary's mother, Jackie, who wanted to have more control over her daughter, including the right to choose what track meets her daughter ran, and the right to negotiate expenses for Mary and for herself as chaperone. Mrs. Decker was quoted as saying that she was concerned about the "long distances" Mary was running. DeNoon did not accept the changes and he was replaced. Outdoors, under her new management, Mary had a successful season against domestic competition and she beat the Soviets again in the outdoor dual meet—running 2:02.3 in Durham, North Carolina—but that effectively was the end of her season. She did not tour Europe for personal reasons, including the divorce of her parents. Despite the turmoil in 1974, Mary Decker was ranked ninth in the world for 800 meters.

It was the end of a turbulent two years. Decker had started the process as a child with a variety of possibilities in front of her. By her excellence and her notoriety as well as her own desire, she had swiftly narrowed the possibilities to one. She was Mary Decker, runner. The box may have been the correct one for a young girl of her potential, but it was still a box and no less confining for being appropriate. She had also become public property with everyone pulling and pushing her, all of them anxious for an association with the new star, tomorrow today. Many people meant well and spoke from concern, including Steve Prefontaine, who feared for her well being. "She's the greatest female 800-meter runner in the world right now at 15," he said. "She can be the greatest for quite a few years. But she's not going to make it if she keeps going like she is now." Much the same admonition came from George Frenn, a hammer thrower on the United States team at the indoor meet against the Soviets in 1973. Frenn interrupted one of Decker's workouts to warn her that she would "burn out." Switching metaphors, he told her "You can only take so much out of the cash register without going bankrupt." Whether the hard training was cumulatively excessive is an open question. Even Mary later said that she was not pushed beyond her willingness, "People think DeNoon pushed me; they think my mother pushed me, but I can't honestly say I was ever pushed. I trained and raced hard because that was me. It was something within myself." What is undeniable, however, is that Mary Decker was changing. Between the ages of 15 and 16, she grew 6 inches and put on about 25 pounds, leveling off at 5' 6-1/2" and 110 to 115 pounds. As she later said, "I didn't know what to do with all this body." The new body ran less well than the old one, the young one. The new one, the older one, had injuries.

Trouble began early in 1975. In February at the Sunkist Invitational indoor Meet in Los Angeles, promoter Al Franken planned a match race between Mary Decker, world record holder for 800 meters, 880 yards, and 1,000 yards indoors, and Francie Larrieu, world record holder for the indoor mile, two mile and 3,000 meters. The two would race 1,000 meters, a rarely contested event in 1974, and an inviting prospect for a world record. One report from the race is sufficient to convey that Mary Decker's hot, first light had blinked: "Wearing a new Patriot Track Club uniform which resembled an Evel Knievel outfit, Decker moved quickly to the front while Larrieu was having difficulties getting past Anne Danboy of the South Bay Striders who occupied second position. Larrieu patiently tapped Danboy on the haunches a few times. Danboy got the message, moved over and Francie took out after the leader. By the end of the third lap Larrieu had assumed command and gradually built up her big lead. With two laps to go, Cyndy Poor finally mustered enough courage to pass Decker and she continued to pull away. Poor was five seconds back of the winner, Decker ten." In the race, Francie Larrieu broke the world indoor record previously held by Tamara Kazachova of the Soviet Union. Mary Decker, meanwhile, was stricken by a burning pain in her shins. Subsequent rest and therapy did not help, and the entire season washed away. In 1975, Mary Decker's best 800 meters was only 2:08.2. In 1976, still beset by injuries, she did not compete at all. And in 1977, her fastest 800 meters was an indoor 2:15.2. Obviously, Decker was off the charts when world rankings were assigned in those years. Looking back, she said, "At 16, I was a has-been."

Those are the lost years, 1975, 1976, 1977. As Mary said in one interview, "My injuries started when I was about 15. The bad ones hit when I was 16. I had a stress fracture in my right ankle. After six weeks in a cast I started back training and that's when my shins started aching." Ironically, after all the concern that Decker would break down under DeNoon's tutelage, the serious and persistent injuries came after he stopped coaching her. Coaches who followed DeNoon had Mary do more mileage, perhaps in response to the intense interval work DeNoon favored. The additional distance either caused the injuries or was coincident with them. It hardly mattered in either event because Decker was hurt, and she stayed that way for a long time—long enough that other people would have drifted away from the sport and satisfied themselves with middle-aged stories about vaunted, departed youth.

Mary Decker never quit. DeNoon had once said that Mary's whole life was running, even though the articles referred to girlish activity like sewing and diversions like boyfriends. Other people noticed her fierce desire to win, so complete that it seemed to carry self-esteem along with it. For this young girl, there was only one road open and she stayed on it through all the hard years. Her road, unfortunately, detoured around Montreal in 1976 where, once, she had hoped to compete for Olympic gold medals. It did lead her finally in the summer of 1976 to Boulder, Colorado, a safe distance from which to survey the scene. Internationally, it was the Eastern Bloc women, many of whom she had beaten when she was a child, who now dominated her events. In Boulder, it was the University of Colorado, which now had a women's track program; and it was Frank Shorter, who lived there and served as the epicenter for an incipient running boom.

EIGHT

*In war more than anywhere else things
do not turn out as we expect.*

On War, Book Three
Carl von Clausewitz

In the summer of 1976, Mary Decker arrived for a vacation
in Boulder, Colorado, the quintessential college town full of erratic
cottages, inspired campus architecture, liberal orthodoxy, and casual privilege. Liking what she saw, she stayed. Boulder had high altitude, which would be helpful if her bad shins permitted her to train;
it had a friendly student population; it had the reality of a job in
Frank Shorter's running store on the mall; and it offered refuge for
a fallen star who desperately needed new dreams. In Boulder,
Decker was a fugitive of her fame and from the Olympic Games in
Montreal. The Olympic Games hurt sharply. "It was difficult to sit
and watch. It's hard to watch the Olympic Trials or the Games
knowing that you've run with those people before. Now you can't
because of some stupid injury," she said. "I had run against the
'names'—Francie Larrieu, Cyndy Poor, Wendy Knudson. I'd beat-
en them before. I can't say I would have beaten them in any particular race, but what hurt so bad was that I knew I had the potential to
be out there." In Colorado, she found that it was nice to be unknown.
"In California, people were always coming up and saying, 'You're
really healthy. You just don't want to run.' Not many people know

me here and that makes it easier."

Rich Castro, the coach of the women's team at the University of Colorado, also made things easier. He knew that Mary could not be force-fed a diet of hard running, but must be permitted a chance to heal, and must be afforded the opportunity for surgical intervention if that was necessary. When Mary joined his Colorado women's team in January, 1977, he said, "We're trying to be very low key. She's always been pushed into the limelight. We don't want that. We may even suggest that she not even run an individual event in our first really 'big' meet at Albuquerque." Whether she was pushed into the limelight or ran for it was arguable, but Castro's philosophy was wise in either event. "Right now," Decker said, "I wouldn't want to push myself to the point that I might hurt myself so that I would never run again." Referring to the pain in her shins, she said that if she didn't want to compete again, "there probably wouldn't be any problem. I could jog around the track twice a day and not bother them. But that's not what I hope to do. If I have surgery, will it work, or will it leave me so I can't run? I look at it as a final alternative. I want to try everything else I can."

In fact, Decker ran very little for Colorado in the winter and spring semesters of 1977. Her major contribution came at the Big Eight Indoor Championships at the University of Missouri in February. With all her injuries, and without much training, she still had the speed to win the quarter-mile in 56.7, a meet and Big Eight indoor record at the time. She also pushed herself to a third in the 880, running 2:15.9 behind Cindy Worchester of Kansas State, who won in 2:10.9; and she ran a leg on the mile relay, which finished second in 4:01.9. This was impressive running in the circumstance, but it was a heart-rending distance away from Little Mary Decker, the young girl with the elegant, preternaturally long stride who—once—could kick from the back or run the legs off the best runners in the world. Later in the year, the outdoor season was ruined by the

Mary Decker, arrived in Colorado for a new start--but with an old question.

recurring pain in her shins and by the futile attempts at remedy. *Track and Field News* carried a cryptic report: "Mary Decker probably won't run this spring following the recommendation of a podiatrist. What seemed to be persistent shinsplints are in reality a series of stress fractures. Ouch!" Actually, that turned out not to be the case, but not before Decker spent ten weeks in a cast. Finally, in May 1977, Mary Decker met Dick Quax of New Zealand. The meeting suggests that Decker's time in Colorado served one central purpose. It put her in the right place at the right time to meet the one person who could point her in the right direction.

In memory, Dick Quax is a man fixed forever in time, place and circumstance. The time is the early evening of July 30, 1976. The place is Montreal. The circumstance is the final of the Olympic 5,000-meter run. Quax has extricated himself from a box on the near backstretch and is poised on the shoulder of three-time Olympic champion Lasse Viren, who is hopeless surely. It only remains for Quax to sweep past him. If not Quax, then countryman Rod Dixon, also in close attendance; if not Quax and not Dixon, perhaps then Klaus-Peter Hildenbrand of West Germany or Brendan Foster of Great Britain. In any case, the moment has arrived for Lasse Viren to lose an Olympic final. He has permitted the early pace to slow, and even an injection of speed over the final four laps cannot save him from the kick of faster men. Quax has run 3:38 for 1,500-meters. Dixon owns an Olympic bronze medal from the 1,500 meters in Munich. Foster has many times run the mile faster than four minutes. Hildenbrand is running an inspired race and is full of vim. With the bunched runners collected for a strike behind him, however, in that instant of hopefulness and expectation, Viren seized the day for himself, pulling it away from the others as truculently as a child reclaiming a favorite toy. Simply, he did not give way and the runners who pursued him stayed where they were and where they always would be. Caught by the camera, Quax is nearest the prize, his mouth open wide, his eyes closed, his hair wild, knees high. He is a traveler who would never arrive. Accelerating casually, skimming over the ground with no wasted movement, Viren got to the finish line first and changed everything. The place for which Quax and the others strove was gone before they could get there.

Dick Quax had the solace of an Olympic silver medal for his effort. In a career damaged by injury, it was a good result, if not the one he wanted. Resiliently, he planned an assault—eventually successful—on the 5,000-meter world record in the year after the Olympics. In his new pursuit, he visited Boulder in May 1977, for a month of altitude training. In the small town, he would naturally meet Mary Decker, which he did in time. To her good fortune, Quax listened to the story of her injuries not with compassion, or commiseration, but with recognition. As it happened, his own shins were scarred by an operation that released his calf muscles from the sheath that had bound them too tightly and crippled him. He told Decker and Decker, taking hope, had the same operation in July, 1977. Within weeks she was running without pain. It was more than muscles that had been unbound. It was Mary Decker herself.

The University of Colorado was the first beneficiary. In the fall of 1977, Decker started gently by running a local 15-kilometer road race in a winning time of 58:59. She then continued her training for the cross-country season. Often, she trained with the Colorado men's team, saying that she thought it was an advantage. "It pushes you," she said. "It makes you run faster without realizing it. You may end up running in the back of the pack, but that's because you're running with people who normally run faster than you." Coming from a long way off, she slowly regained condition. She finished second in the Big Eight conference meet and helped the "Lady Buffs" qualify for the AIAW National Championship meet in Austin, Texas on November 19, 1977. Commenting on his team's chances, Rich Castro said, "We really don't have a superstar right now. But give her another year, and Mary Decker will challenge everyone. That's a year away. What she lacks just takes time, and only time can give it back to her after the surgery. But after that, look out." On race day, Castro's appraisal proved accurate. Mary Decker was a year away. On an overcast, windy day, Decker finished seventh in a talented field. Kathy Mills of Penn State won. She was followed by Brenda Webb of Tennessee, Julie Shea of North Carolina State, Ellison Goodall of Duke, Sue Shafer of Eastern Kentucky, and Karen Bridges of Oklahoma State. Only Colorado teammate Dana Slater separated Decker from the ninth place runner, Joan Benoit of North Carolina State.

If Rich Castro was right in thinking that Mary Decker was "a year away" from winning the AIAW National Cross-Country Championship, he was wrong in thinking that, in the meantime, he would not have a superstar. Decker had a sense of this herself. Asked by Castro to establish goals for the outdoor season, she listed 1:58 for 800 meters and 4:05 for 1,500 meters. The times approached the standing American records of 1:57.9 and 4:02.6 and showed that Decker's confidence in her ability was undimmed.

Decker finished the semester at Colorado and then accepted an invitation arranged by Dick Quax for her to train and race in New Zealand in late 1977 and early 1978. While there, she trained using a schedule written for her by Quax. She won all seven races she ran in New Zealand and Australia. Most significantly, her times were fast. Four times she ran and won at 800 meters: 2:05.2, 2:04.6, 2:04.2, and 2:01.8. She won slow, easy races at 1,500 meters and 1,000 yards. Finally, in January 1978, she cruised a breathtaking 1,500 meters in 4:08.9. Down in New Zealand and Australia, Decker had reconstructed herself. She was ready now to retake her old position: the Darling of American track and field.

The *Los Angeles Times* indoor meet on February 3, 1978, was Mary Decker's re-entry to premier domestic competition. The

WOMEN RUNNING LONG

distance was 1,000 yards. The competition was good. Francie
Larrieu was there, as were Wendy Knudson, Julie Brown, and Ellen
Wessinghage of West Germany. Decker was nervous before the meet
because she was returning home to southern California, and did not
know whether the fans would remember her, or, if they did, what
response they would give. Before 16,333 cheering fans—who did
remember her, after all—Decker settled the question early. She went
directly to the front, had a 25-yard lead at the quarter, passed the
880-yard mark in 2:05.2, and, as the crowd lifted itself to a deafen-
ing roar, cruised home with a world record of 2:23.8, more than 6
seconds ahead of Francie Larrieu, who finished second. When Mary
Decker finished, the crowd gave her a standing ovation. Slumped
happily in a chair after the race she said, "This is elation!" She had
not run for a record, she said, but just hoped to get out front and run
away. "Because I haven't run indoors for so long I wanted to avoid
all the pushing and shoving." She also claimed her future: "No more
injuries and no more losses. I'm looking only upwards."

Back home in Colorado after the race, Decker spoke expan-
sively of her future, saying that while she still wanted to combine
school with training and competition, running now came first. "It's
like I told everyone else—all over the world—after that race [the LA
Times meeting]: running comes first in my life now. I want to work
and achieve my goals in running. I won't settle for less than I'm
capable of." She said that her plans called for a heavy competitive
schedule in March 1978, a period of long-distance training in late
spring, and a return to national and international competition in the
summer, where she hoped to run more 1,500-meter races. She
thought the longer races were now her best ones. "I really think that
I'm more suited to the longer race," she said, "because in competing
on a world level, I'm more strong than fast." From a woman who
could run 200 meters in 23.7, her alleged lack of speed was doubt-
ful, but there was no question about her strength. She proved that

point again on February 10 in Toronto, Canada for the *Toronto Star* Maple Leaf Games. Once again running before a sell-out crowd—this time it was 16,267—she joined a "match-off" of America's three leading 1,500-meter performers: herself, Francie Larrieu, and Jan Merrill. It was vintage Decker. Running in the black, silver-ferned vest of New Zealand, she moved to the front after a quarter, opened a gap, calmly observed a last-lap challenge by Francie Larrieu, and, as one report of the race described it, "sort of shrugged her shoulders, and sprinted away to win by five yards." The winning time was only 4:12.6, but it was enough to make a point. Francie Larrieu said after the race that "Mary is just too strong right now." Barring injury, the situation was not likely to change. To emphasize the point, Decker added Big Eight Indoor Championships to her list of accomplishments. She ran a conference record 2:05.29 in the 880-yard event—taking more than 5 seconds off the record set the previous year when she had finished third while running 10 seconds slower—and cut the mile record to 4:41.2, 8 seconds faster than the prior record.

Simultaneously with Decker's return to competition, a new image began to take shape. She had been a child star. Then she had been injured. Upon her return to form, she was recast as a victim of childhood abuse, no less, who had overcome it all by virtue of her talent and courage. One article in 1978 started dramatically, "As a child studies a thing—smashing it to see what is inside—people shook Mary Decker and rattled her, and bounced her a couple of times, curious about the inner works. That the damage probably was done as innocently as a child would do it did not undo it. Decker broke and was forgotten." In this version of events, Don DeNoon did not offer Mary Decker the opportunity to run with his team; rather, he "spirited her away to his track team," where she was thereafter subject to training and racing that were unsuited for her age and condition. Long quotes attacked the training to which Decker was subject without specifically saying what the training was; and the question of causation—what actually caused the injuries from which Mary Decker suffered beginning as a 15 year old?—was only superficially treated. Innuendo and suggestion replaced hard fact and rigorous analysis, which might have either proved or disproved the supposition. Opportunity became abuse. Youthful accomplishment, which arguably has value in and of itself, was dismissed as inconsequential; indeed, it was harmful if it did not lead to adult performance of equal or greater value. Very quickly, in this and many similar articles that followed, the people who volunteered time and energy to Decker's youthful pursuits became suspects. Meanwhile, Decker herself was victim and survivor. With her enhanced image, Mary Decker was established as a feminine icon for a new age.

Interestingly, just as her childhood injuries were being used to redefine her, Decker's adult training injured her. After getting behind in her classes during the indoor season, she withdrew from the University of Colorado, and dedicated more time to her running. Still working with Dick Quax, she adopted a program of stamina training, doing over-distance twice a day on the roads and in the country. Reportedly, she raised her mileage to a high of 90 miles a week and developed tendinitis. She did manage a third-place finish in the US National Championships with an 800-meter time of 2:03.1, but otherwise the outdoor season in 1978 was disappointing and she was not listed in the world rankings. To make matters worse, her shin problems returned and she had to undergo a second surgery for the condition in August 1978. Nevertheless, Decker came right back, enrolled again at the University of Colorado, and represented the school in cross-country. The AIAW national meet was held in Boulder in 1978. In pleasant 60-degree weather, Decker let Julie Brown, who was running for Cal State-Northridge, set a blistering pace of 4:58 through the mile, closed up as Brown faded, and was third in the homestretch when the defending champion and leader Kathy Mills of Penn State veered slightly off course. Seizing the

Mary Decker of Colorado and Kathy Mills of Penn State
fight for a national championship.

opportunity, Decker sprinted from 30 yards back to win in the last quarter-mile. She beat a strong field, which included many women who would run well for years: Julie Shea from North Carolina State, Ms. Mills, Margaret Groos of Virginia, Brenda Webb of Tennessee, Joan Benoit from North Carolina State, Debbie Vetter of Iowa State, Martha White from Virginia, and Lynn Jennings who represented Princeton at the meet and finished ninth. The field was so deep that a runner as fine as Judi St. Hilaire from Vermont could finish only 20th. Still, none of these distance runners could beat Mary Decker, best known as a half-miler, over 5,000 meters on rough terrain at altitude.

From that high point, Decker hit another low spot. When she traveled to New Zealand within weeks of her victory at the AIAW, she was troubled by pain from the sciatic nerve. She made things worse by falling on wet pavement. Later in 1979, she was bothered by a torn back muscle that cost her almost half the competitive season. Despite the injuries, she ran well. For 800 meters, she recorded a seasonal best of 2:03.5 (eighth fastest American for a year in which Essie Kelly of Prairie View was the national leader in 2:01.2). Confirming her move to slightly longer distances, Decker ran an American-record mile of 4:23.5 (with a 1,500-meter time en route of 4:05). She also won the Pan-American Games 1,500-meter championship with 4:05.7. She was not, however, the top-ranked American at year's end. That honor went to Francie Larrieu who had a slower seasonal best at 4:06.6 but a stronger overall competitive season. And while Larrieu was ranked 14th in the world for the year, Decker was an also-ran. Among the fastest runners, her 4:05 for 1,500 meters left her buried beneath two Bulgarians, four Romanians, eight Soviets, one East German, and three women from the West, Grete Waitz from Norway, Chris Benning from Great Britain, and Brigitte Kraus of West Germany. The best time in 1979 belonged to Totka Petrova of Bulgaria, who ran 3:57.4. That time, of

No. 1: Mary Decker paddling along in Eugene, Oregon.

course, was tainted by Petrova's positive drug test late in the year, but it was nonetheless the standard. Measured by that standard, Decker had not arrived in the first echelon of international athletics in 1979. She was merely on the horizon.

She arrived finally in 1980. Located by now in Eugene, Oregon, Decker continued to accept advice and coaching from Dick Quax until late in the year when she switched to the legendary Bill Bowerman, who, according to one account, felt "honored to be entrusted with her talent and a little burdened with her temperament." The temperament to which he referred was one which, discussed discreetly and carefully, was said to require a great deal of attention and nurturing, affirmation and assurance, aspects of personality often attributed either to her traumatic athletic youth or to an equally unsettled domestic life, marked by a mother and father who were, in her words, "never close." In any case, it made for a lot of hand-holding. With specific regard to her performance as an athlete, it meant that her self-concept remained tightly connected to her success as a runner. When she felt good about herself, she tended to run well. And when she ran well, she tended to feel good about herself. By that measure, 1980 was apparently a good year for Mary Decker's delicate equilibrium. She began like a champion and ran well all year despite occasional pain on the heel of her right foot from an inflammation of the plantar fascia.

That does not mean, however, that the year went entirely to plan. A day and a place were missing. July 30, 1980. Lenin Stadium. Moscow. As it happened, they didn't leave an empty lane where Mary Decker should have been standing in that stadium on that day in that city, but they should have. She had earned the right—by her talent and by her persistence, by her dreams and hopes, by her toughness under pressure—to run a heat in the Olympic 1,500 meters. She had earned the right to look over and see Tatyana Kazankina, who already owned something that Decker might once have considered her own, the accolades from Montreal. She had earned the right, even, to be thrashed if that was the result. She had earned the right either way, victory or defeat, to run in the Olympic Games of 1980. All her season was pointed to that day. How many hours, how many quickened heartbeats, how many times did she see 100,000 people watching her every move? How many red vests did she imagine surrounding her as she ran to the front? How many lifetimes were intrigued by the outcome and moved by the possibilities? Jimmy Carter is a good man, but he took that day, those lifetimes, away from Mary Decker and the other deserving American athletes when he organized a boycott of the Olympic Games in response to the Soviet Union's military incursion into Afghanistan. With that, it is possible to review the year only as it was, rather than the year as it was intended to be.

The year began auspiciously. Visiting New Zealand for the

third successive early winter— summer in the Southern Hemisphere— Decker ran a mile in 4:21.7, her first outdoor world record. She followed that with an astonishing indoor season in the United States. She set a world best of 4:00.8 for 1,500 meters, ran an 800/880 race in 1:58.9/1:59.7 with a first lap in 56.9, and ran a mile on the huge track in the Houston, Texas Astrodome—five laps to the mile, boards, banked—in 4:17.55. Outdoors, her momentum was interrupted in April when she hurt an achilles tendon while running a road race, but she covered the situation by roller skating six miles a day and swimming, alternative exercises she dismissed as "not as much fun as running." When she was able, she went quickly back to her work. The Olympic Trials, made a mockery by the boycott of the Olympic Games, was a formality she completed by winning the 1,500 meters in 4:04.91. In that race, she shot to the front, ran the first 400 meters in 62.4, had a 25-meter lead by 800 meters, and coasted through the second fastest time ever by an American outdoors. After the race, Decker said she would look for a "good one" in August. She wanted to break the world record for 1,500 meters. "I would love to win an Olympic gold medal, but if it isn't possible, it isn't possible. Maybe I can prove I'm the best in other ways."

World records aside, the first task was to take Jan Merrill's aging American record for 1,500 meters, a relic from Montreal. Decker accomplished that on July 12 in Stuttgart, West Germany. Against undistinguished competition, she dived straight into the lead, ran undisturbed for the entire distance, and finished in 4:01.17, a 1.44-second improvement on the old mark. Buried in the congratulations was the acknowledgment that the new American record was only 20th fastest on the world lists. Undaunted, Decker moved to Oslo for her next race. On July 15, she ran her premier 3,000-meter run in 8:38.73, also an American record. Finally, she flew back to Philadelphia to run another 1,500 meters. The so-called Liberty Bell

Classic meeting was hastily organized to assuage the pain of the Olympic boycott, an ambition completely unrealized, but it did draw a decent international field and 20,111 spectators. In her race, Decker faced Julie Brown, Francie Larrieu, and Rose Thomson, a Kenyan running for the University of Wisconsin. In hot and humid weather, she sprinted the first 400 meters in 61.6; dispatched Julie Brown, the only runner who tried to go with her, by running through 800 meters in 2:07.2; hit 3:13.4 at 1,200 meters; and finished in 4:00.87, another American record and almost 10 full seconds ahead of Brown. After the race, Decker admitted that she had hoped for sub-4:00 but was not disappointed given the weather conditions and her fatigue from travel and racing. She also repeated the audacity of her goals, "The world record is definitely on my mind—and not way back either." She wanted, she said, to race the Olympic gold, silver and bronze medalists after the Games. Even after Kazankina scorched the Olympic 1,500-meter final in 3:56.6, with Wartenberg of East Germany and Olizaryenko of the Soviet Union following in 3:57.8 and 3:59.6 respectively, Decker retreated only grudgingly, saying, "I don't think I would have won a gold medal—3:56 is a little fast for me—but I do believe I would have won a medal." It was important for her to think in those terms, not only for herself, but for the other women in the West who too often looked down rather than East, who grew despondent and stopped trying. Even if she failed, Decker would have the satisfaction of McMurphy in One Flew Over the Cuckoo's Nest who, upon failing to dislodge a control panel he intended to use later in an escape attempt, could roar at the other mental patients on the ward, "But I tried, though! Goddammit, I sure as hell did that much, didn't I?"

Mary Decker had her first chance in Rome on August 5. It was only days after the Olympics closed, and she drew Kazankina herself, as well as Gabriella Dorio of Italy. Unfortunately, Decker was slightly affected by a twinge in her achilles tendon and could only manage 4:03.15 while Kazankina, who was tuning up for her big race in Zurich, ran 3:58.96, and Dorio became the first Western woman to break 4:00 for 1,500 meters by running 3:59.82. Three days later, Decker ran 800 meters in a personal best of 1:59.10 before trying one more time to get under 4:00 for 1,500 meters. In Budapest on August 11, she just missed. She did run another American record but it was 4:00.4.

All eyes turned next to Zurich for the Weltclasse. In fact, Mary Decker was in Zurich with Kazankina in 1980 and she took a beating that evening, although she did finally get under 4:00 by running 3:59.43. The new American record stung a little because Decker was 50 meters behind the Soviet athlete. Decker said later she felt good, but the rabbit's early pace was too much for her. Forgetting her 1974 victory over Kazankina in Moscow, she permitted herself a moment of self-doubt, "This is only the second time I have raced against Kazankina," she said, "and I don't know if I will ever beat her. She is so strong." With that, however, Decker also said openly the things other people whispered. She was shocked by the sight of the Soviet women, who, she remarked, did not look like any women she had seen before. "Their muscle definition is so pronounced," she explained. "I don't doubt that they are females biologically speaking, but, shall we say, chemically, I'm not so sure." No stage whispers from Mary Decker; rather, she preferred the honest appraisal and the frontal assault. It was a way of making eye contact. If she had been unnerved by the Soviet women in Rome and Zurich, it would be the last time. They were now on notice. The battle was joined.

Might it have been an uneven battle? It always had been. The decentralized, democratic, egalitarian West had inherent disadvantages when it met the centralized, authoritarian, elitist East. Any contest posed as ideology vs. ideology, country vs. country, or form of government vs. form of government played to the strength of the weaker country because the weaker country exerted greater control of its population. In short, the totalitarian states could tell people what to do; and they told some people to run, jump and throw. It was Alice in Wonderland, in which weakness showed itself as strength, and strength showed itself as weakness. Down was up and up was down. This phenomenon became increasingly frustrating in the West after "scientific method" entered the vocabulary of the Eastern totalitarian states, and even more so in the women's events where there was no apparent limit to excess. Now, however, as Mary Decker engaged the Soviet women, the situation was adjusted when a new player emerged. The player was not a country and not an athlete. It was a thing.

As a mere thing, it might have special allegiance to one country or the other, but it had the equal potential to ignore such distinctions entirely. The thing might prefer one form of governance over the other, but it could thrive in most of them. It might prefer capitalism to socialism, but it had the means to subvert the latter to the former. The thing, of course, was the multinational corporation. The multinational corporation that entered the contest on Mary Decker's behalf was Nike. The vehicle Nike used was Athletics West, a club it sponsored for carefully selected, nurtured, coached, evaluated, and financially assisted runners, jumpers, and throwers from the United States. For the East, it was a taste of their own medicine. For the West, it was a revolutionary, private, limited, commercial incursion into international sport, largely unnoticed at the time because it came in "minor," non-revenue events, and because it was miles and massive hoopla removed from the Dream Team which was its progeny. Nonetheless, it was a critical turn: Nike vs. the Soviet Union. To some extent, that was the new reality. Pick a winner.

Mary Decker was already running for Athletics West in 1980, and was receiving its benefits. She knew that in rough weather she at last had a safe harbor, a place from which future attacks could be launched. After Zurich, she collected herself and closed the year by beating the Soviet runner Olizaryenko at 1,500 meters (4:00.3) before an unfortunate attempt to break the world record for 3,000 meters in Brussels on August 22. In that race, she was increasingly affected by pain in her achilles tendon and had to withdraw. Within weeks, she had surgery to repair a partial tear in the tendon and was out of action again. In her recovery, she swam, lifted weights, eventually started a little jogging, and expressed hopes for an active indoor season and an outdoor season that would include the 1981 World Cup. In particular, she said that Coach Bowerman hoped to teach her to run better tactically.

Before it got started, 1981 ended. Decker's shin soreness came back. She had another operation and the season got away from her. She also changed coaches. Coach Bowerman stepped away from the formal relationship, although he continued to consult and advise; and Dick Brown, an expert in running physiology, the director of Athletics West, and later a Ph.D. in exercise physiology, took over. Dick Brown was a graduate of the United States Naval Academy, an accomplished athlete in his own right, a natural jurist leaning in from his tall height to hear the detail of every argument, dignified, kind, and forbearing, but with a capacity for firmness. Blessed with a penchant for detailed evaluation, Brown had an eye for the single fact, amid the rubble of them all, that would resolve the question at hand. Brown also understood the Eastern Europeans when they spoke of the importance of blood and urine samples, electrocardiograms, electroencephalograms, and other physiological tools and tests. He was determined to take the best their system had to offer in terms of scientific measurement and adjustment while disregarding all those things that stepped over the line, including blood boosting and illicit drug use. He knew, as well, that the Eastern Europeans had, themselves, drawn from the capitalist West in designing their systems. "I talked once to an East German doctor who had left the country," Brown reported. "He said that while the Eastern Europeans base their economic system on Communism, their athletic system works because it's based on capitalism. If their athletes do better on a treadmill test, for example, the athlete and his coach both get a bonus." Thus, as the amateur code in the West was gradually distorted beyond recognition, Athletics West team members received economic reward based on performance. If financial compensation was on one level a simple matter of fairness and on another a response to the failure of the elitist social system that spawned it in England and France in the early part of the century, it was also a reaction against the East's otherwise unfair advantage.

With Mary Decker, Brown's approach was simple, balanced, nuanced, and masterful. He recognized her as a woman of unparalleled physical gifts, a natural efficiency in motion, and a powerful, strong will. He also knew that she was deadly serious about her sport, and a good learner, a person to whom one explanation, if accepted, would suffice for understanding and application. He was quoted as saying to Mary, "If we keep you healthy, no one can beat you." Therein, of course, lay the challenge. To achieve that result, Brown coached her in sections, "from the knees up, and from the knees down," in recognition of her fragile shins, achilles, heels, and feet. In addition to the watchfulness for traumatic or over-use injuries, Brown was also interested in the pioneering work of Canadian biochemist Hans Selye, M.D., who studied the effects of stress on the human body. Among other things, Dr. Selye's work distinguished short-term physiological breakdown, from which recovery could be made, and pathological breakdown, from which recovery may or may not be made; and he studied the predictable increases in pituitary and adrenal gland hormonal activity used to combat stressors, as well as the implication for recovery inherent in the process. Arguably, Dr. Selye's major contribution was to remind coaches and athletes that the training and racing assigned by a coach and performed by an athlete do not occur in a vacuum; they are only part of the athlete's experience, and, indeed, are likely to constitute a minor stressor compared to such other possibilities as domestic disputes, financial concerns, or behavioral disorders, among other possibilities. It is not sufficient to speak in terms of "over-training" or the old haunts of staleness or burnout, and look only to the road and track for explanation. Dr. Selye also reminded coaches that the reaction by an athlete to a particular stressor is individual, which is to say that some athletes will be "hot reactors" to one species of stress and "cold reactors" to another, while other athletes will reverse the order. Selye encouraged thoroughness, particularity, and caution.

In its depth, Dick Brown's background allowed him to monitor Mary Decker more closely than ever before both to antici-pate injury—and draw her back before it happened—and to design an affirmative training schedule. In the latter regard, Decker partic-ularly benefited from Dick Brown's sensitivity to each individual with whom he worked. He was not wedded to one program, "one size fits all," but rather to the condition of the person with whom he was working. This attitude meant that while he might, for example, honor the principle of the "long run," he would define it at varying lengths and paces depending on the athlete's specific situation. For one person, a long run might be eight miles while for another, with a different background, experience and physical structure, it might be twenty miles. In making the decision, Dick would work with the athlete to measure not only the benefit of the exercise, but also its risk, including the possibility of injury. Finally, Dick Brown, having been associated with Mary through Athletics West in other capacities before he agreed to coach her, proceeded with intense awareness that Mary Decker needed comfort and reassurance along the way. While others might have been wary of the commitment and the burden, Dick Brown was not because his character is nurturing and caring as well as intricate in its attention to detail. He willingly undertook the task. In all, as Dick Brown and Mary Decker began their work together in 1981, the conversion of promise to performance was finally at hand. Little Mary Decker; Mary Decker, the injured victim; Mary Decker, the woman on the mend; Mary Decker, the last, best, forlorn hope of the West; was about to become Mary Decker, champion of the world.

Decker's training in 1981 was the foundation for a breakthrough season in 1982. A review of her training shows the mixture of speed, endurance, and caution that would always characterize Dick Brown's coaching of this extraordinary athlete. Every week Mary completed a diary of the workouts, which were later summarized and broken into components including the number of miles run in any given week, the cumulative time of the workouts, the average pace per mile, the number of miles run in interval workouts, the number of miles occupied by races, and, occasionally, notes regarding body weight and body fat. For example, for the first week noted, July 26 through August 1, Decker ran a total of 37 miles in the total time of 244.17 minutes for an average pace per mile of 6:36. She ran no interval workouts and no races. For the next six weeks, she held close to that mileage and, while the pace dropped down to 5:43 in one week, it usually hovered in the mid-6:00 mile range. Beginning in the week of September 6, the weekly mileage lifted to 51, the pace hit 6:22, and interval work was added to the mix. In the weeks before year's end, she dropped only once below 40 miles a week, and that was because her knee was sore, and she never exceeded 68 miles a week. As might be expected from an exuberant talent like Mary Decker, her average pace per mile was fastest in the week she ran her highest mileage in five months, 5:34 per mile. The workouts in a specific week illustrate the quality, quantity and diversity of the workouts Dick Brown asked Mary to do:

November 8-14, 1981

Sunday: a.m. 3 miles
p.m. 5.25 miles (31:55)
Monday: a.m. 4.25 miles (24:24)
p.m. 5.25 miles (37:19)
Tuesday: a.m. 3 miles (18:26)
p.m. 6 miles (36:40,
including 2 x 3:00 min. surge and 1 x 3:30 surge)
Wednesday: a.m. 3 miles (19:11)
p.m. 10 miles (59:40) "pouring rain"
Thursday: a.m. no running
p.m. 5 miles (31:00)
Friday: a.m. 4 miles (26:11)
p.m. 7.25 miles total
consisting of 2 miles warm-up
(incl. 1.5 miles, 5 x 100 meter strideouts,
repeat jog after each); 3 x 200 in 35, 34 and 34;
2 x 400 in 69 and 68; 1 x 600 in 1:48;
2 x 400 in 69 and 68; and 3 x 200 in 35, 34,
33 (with equal recovery after each run);
1 mile warm-down.
Saturday: a.m. no running
p.m. 6 miles in 40:47.

That kind of training prepared Decker for a greatly successful indoor season in 1982. In her first race in a year and a half,
she won an easy 1,500 meters in 4:08.32 before breaking the world
indoor record for the mile on January 22, 1982 with a time of 4:24.6.
Running far ahead of her competition, she added other records that
winter: 8:47.3 for 3,000 meters, and further miles of 4:21.47 and
4:20.5. Her domestic competition developed the respectful and reasonable habit of letting her go. Outdoors it was more of the same.

Showing remarkable range from 800 meters through 10,000 meters, Mary Decker had her most complete season. She started gently. At home in Eugene, Oregon, she deposed England's Paula Fudge, who had been the top-ranked 5,000-meter runner in the world for 1981, by following her for two miles before going off on her own. The result was a world record of 15:08.26. On a subsequent European tour, she improved her American mile record to 4:21.46, ran 3,000 meters in 8:29.72 (only the second time any woman had beaten 8:30 for the distance and within 3 seconds of Bragina's world record of 8:27.12), ran a world-record mile of 4:18.08, and reduced her 800-meter personal best to 1:58.33. The 800-meter race was run on July 14, 1982, in Lausanne, Switzerland. The next day she flew from Lausanne to London to San Francisco to Eugene, a brutal schedule in itself, never mind the training and running that immediately preceded it. Nevertheless, on July 16, Decker could not resist the lure of an all-comers meet that featured a women's 10,000-meter race. Arguing her case to the judge, Dick Brown, she got him to agree to the race on two conditions, that she wear flats and not spikes, and that she stop at the first sign of trouble. She wore the flats and there was no trouble. Using the "race" to substitute for the seven-mile run she might otherwise have run in training that evening, she coasted the first 5,000 meters in 15:55 and followed directly with a second in 15:40.3 for a final time of 31:35.3. Evenly distributing her energy, she ran the mile splits in 5:06, 5:08, 5:09, 5:05, 5:06, and 5:02. A race that others might have cherished, she dismissed lightly. "I am surprised," she said, "because it was my first 10,000 on the track. It just proves that the records aren't real stiff yet." For the year, she ranked first in the world at both 5,000 and 10,000 meters. At the championship distances of 1,500 meters and 3,000 meters, however, she was not where she needed to be. In the 1,500 meters, she was only ninth. Seven Eastern Bloc women were in front of her, including four from the Soviet Union. The best time of the year, by Olga

Dvirna, was 3:54.23, at least reminiscent of Kazankina's world record 3:52.47 if not particularly close to it, and nine seconds faster than Decker's only 1,500-meter time of the year, 4:03.37. At 3,000 meters she ranked fourth, but still found herself behind Eastern Bloc women, two from the Soviet Union, including Svyetla Ulmasova who ranked first with a world-record 8:26.78, and one from Romania, Maricica Puica.

In order to get closer, Decker needed to stay healthy long enough to train properly for the 1983 outdoor season. The season was particularly important because it would include the first IAAF World Championships of Track and Field. Working with Dick Brown, she accomplished that goal, picking her way through occasional soreness and resting when minor illnesses suggested the need. She ran a low-key indoor season and then set her sights on The Athletics Congress (TAC) National Championship meet in Indianapolis, Indiana. Approaching the date, she toyed with the idea of doubling 1,500-3,000 meters, not only there but in Helsinki. Once again, the judge bowed to the inevitable. This time, Brown's condition was that the 3,000-meter race, which would be run within an hour of the 1,500-meter final in Indianapolis, would be run temperately—specifically, that Decker would not run to the front, not run away from everybody else, but would stay in the pack for a while. He thought this would be good for Mary, saying, "I'd like for her to go out and run with the pack and then let her kick handle it. It would be good for her to run with the pack and get a feeling of what it's like with other people around her." This, in fact, was Mary Decker's unique problem when she ran in the United States, much as it had been for Doris Brown a generation earlier. She ran way out front too often in domestic races, and suffered competitively when she went overseas and found herself surrounded by runners of comparable ability. What Dick Brown worried about was the possibility that Mary could be jostled unexpectedly, or fail to protect herself in a crush, or perhaps that, as had happened to Doris in Mexico City, she would come to a critical point in the race and be grabbed by a hand she never anticipated because, for so long, other people's grabbing hands had been far away. As to the attitude of the other American women, Margaret Groos, formerly of Virginia but now running for Athletics West, said, "I don't think it would matter if Mary tripled. I wish for her sake we could give her some competition." She then added the obvious, "We've learned to pretty much let Mary do what she wants to do. If you can't do her workouts, you certainly can't fool yourself and try to race with her."

The problems of the judge are trying indeed. The woman who pled her case so eloquently would not, indeed could not, abide by the conditions he imposed. In Indianapolis, Mary Decker beat the nearest runner, Cindy Bremser, formerly of the University of Wisconsin, by more than 6 seconds in the 1,500 meters, and then came back 50 minutes later to win the 3,000 meters. Needless to say, she led both races. In the 1,500 meters, she shot through the first 400 meters in 62 seconds before slowing to 65.3 and 67.2 for the next two splits and a finishing time of 4:03.50. In the 3,000, she ripped the first lap in 67 before settling into a 70- and 71-second rhythm. She finished in 8:38.36, the leading time in the world and the second fastest time ever run by an American (to her 8:29.71 the prior summer). Without a hint of chagrin at her failure to run with the pack in either race, Mary said that she was surprised at how easy the efforts had been. "It was good strength work," she said. "I'd like to run 3:59 in L.A., and I feel like this helped me. I feel like the season is just starting for me." About that 3,000-meter run, the one where she was supposed to settle in and let somebody else do the work, she felt the earlier 1,500 meters had actually been helpful. "I went into the 3,000 meters more relaxed than I usually go into an event because I used up a lot of nervous energy running the 1,500 meters," she said. "You could tell I had nervous energy the way I went out in the 1,500. It was far too fast."

The day after the TAC meet, Decker flew to Nashville, Tennessee, and the next day went to Los Angeles to put the finishing touches on her preparation for the US-East Germany dual meet. The dual meet was a big race because it offered Decker the chance to make a statement before Helsinki. At 1,500 meters, it was also an opportunity to make sub-4:00 seem more ordinary by doing it in the United States relatively early in the season without the impetus of European crowds. Decker's training was now exceptional, as she rushed from triumph to triumph, many of the sessions serving as private joys. On the first Wednesday in Los Angeles, for example, she hammered an easy ten miles in 55:00. The next two days she did strideouts and short dashes, and on Saturday against the East Germans she delivered her message. Running against Christiana Wartenberg and Astrid Pfeiffer of East Germany and teammate Cindy Bremser, Decker led through splits of 64.5 and 65.5, and 3:15 at the 1,200 mark. When Wartenburg tried to pass her with 300 meters left, Decker would not permit it. Holding Wartenberg where she was—securely in second but only there—Decker ran the last 400 in 60.3 and won 3:59.43 to 4:01.29. She had done what she set out to do.

There was still more ahead, and her training showed the way. No matter the distance, she was running free. In the week after the East German meet, she emphasized fast over-distance before turning to speed and sharpness the next week. The week of July 27 through July 3, inclusive, included the following runs:

June 27:	10 miles in 59:01
	(upon return to Eugene from L.A.)
June 28:	a.m. 5 miles in 31:00
	p.m. 5 miles no time
June 29:	p.m. 10 miles in 56:08

June 30: p.m. 13 miles in 1:14.10
July 1:   a.m. 5.25 miles in 31:25
          p.m. 5 miles in 29:10
July 2:   a.m. 10 miles in 55:44
July 3:   7 miles no time and strideouts

The next week, turning the screws tighter, she maneuvered around two sharp workouts on the track, July 7 and July 8:

July 7:   a.m. 2.5 warm-up with strides; 1 x 200 in 30; 1 x
          1,000 in 2:40; 1 x 600 in 1:35; 2 x 200 in 30, 30;
          3 miles warm-down.
          p.m. 2 miles easy
July 8:   a.m. 2 miles warm-up and strideouts; 2 x 200 in
          31, 31; 2 x 800 in 2:12; 2:12; 2 x 400 in 65, 65;
          2 x 200 in 30, 29; 2 miles warm-down.
          p.m. 3 miles easy

It was like Margaret Groos said. If you could not train with her, why would you think you could race with her? People thought they could; and people who watched people thought those people could. Prognosticators (people who watch people) who looked ahead to Decker's races in Helsinki did not rate her highly. They still liked the Soviets. In the 1,500 meters, the collected experts at Track and Field News said simply, "A Soviet sweep is expected..." At 3,000 meters, they predicted Ulmasova would win. Decker was merely acknowledged: "She [Decker] can run the pace, but can she stay with the kick? She hasn't been in this kind of competition since her teenage days as an 800-meter runner, except for a good stretch run against Christiana Wartenberg in the DDR dual at 1500."

Leaving the doubters behind, Decker skipped her way to Europe. She left Eugene on July 18, stopped briefly in Los Angeles and Houston for promotional work, and then flew to London, arriving on the morning on the 20th. Hours later, she left for Stockholm, Sweden where she was scheduled to race 1,500 meters on Tuesday, the 26th. Her training before the race continued the earlier theme of fast over-distance on some days and short work on the track on others:

> July 21: a.m. 5 miles in 31:15, 6 x 100 strideouts; 800 jog
> July 22: p.m. 2 mile warm-up; 0.5 jog and stride; 2 x 200 in 29, 29; 2 x 290 in 44, 44; 2 x 200 in 29, 29; 3 x 200 in 31, 31, 31; 2 mile warm-down
> July 23: p.m. 6.5 miles in 41:13
> July 24: p.m. 8 miles in 50:01
> July 25: p.m. 6 miles in 35:40, 5 x 100 meter strideout; jog

The 1,500 meters in Stockholm on the 26th was a triumph. As part of the US-Nordic track and field meet, Decker went immediately to the front and drew the 14,399 fans along with her. She led through laps of 62.61, 2:06.94, 3:10, and finished fast for a new American record of 3:57.12. Brit McRoberts of Canada was second but she was almost 11 seconds behind. As every race in early 1983 was prelude to the World Championships, Decker was asked what she intended to do there. She said her best chance to win was in the 3,000-meter run but she would also run the 1,500 meters "for fun." While she did not dismiss the East European women, neither did she fear them. "I think I have a good kick," she said, "If I have to kick, I will be able to kick. I'm fast and strong enough. They will not run away from me." Decker made her point emphatic five days later when she ran an American-record 800-meter run in Gateshead, England. Despite a sore right achilles tendon and a developing cold, she hit the 400-meter split in 57.0, 600 meters in 1:27.42, and finished in 1:57.60, 0.3 seconds under Madeline Manning-Jackson's 7-

year-old record. Feeling unwell after the race, she said, "I feel so bad, I'll take any time under Madeline's record."

Four days after the race in England—somewhat the worse for wear but with two new American records behind her and several more days of rest and recovery in front of her—she left for Helsinki, Finland, and the first IAAF World Track and Field Championships. Given the boycotts that affected the Olympic Games in 1976, when many African nations withdrew, and in 1980, when many Western countries withdrew, the meet in Helsinki would be the largest and finest track meet since 1972. More than 1,500 athletes representing all five continents and more than 41 countries entered the competition. The tension was further heightened when the IAAF announced that random drug testing—rather than tests of medalists, for example—would be performed. Primo Nebiolo, President of the IAAF, said that the element of surprise was a key part of the operation.

Newspaper reports as late as July 1983, said that Tatyana Kazankina had retired. She had not competed in the 1982 European Championships where the Soviets went one-two in the 1,500 meters—Olga Dvirna in 3:57.80 and Zamira Zaitseva in 3:58.82—and one-three in the 3,000 meters—Svetlana Ulmasova in 8:30.28 and Elena Sipatova in 8:34:06 separated only by Maricica Puica of Romania in 8:33.33—and no word came from her in early 1983. Nevertheless, when the runners went to the line for the heats of the women's 3,000 meters in Helsinki, Kazankina was there. She had taken time away from the sport to have a second child and then had been injured, the Soviets explained, but she was back in training and was ready for her inaugural 3,000-meter race at the international level. Kazankina had, however, run 8:32 in July in Moscow. In Helsinki, Tatyana Kazankina and Mary Decker ran in the second of the two heats, and finished together in 8:44.72, qualifying easily for the final. World-record-holder Svetlana Ulmasova of the Soviet

Union won the first heat in 8:46.65.

One day separated the heat from the final, a time for rest and a time for figuring. Decker and Kazankina were in, of course. The way they finished the heat, side by side, combined with the way Decker had run in the weeks prior to Helsinki and with the fact that Kazankina was running at all made them objects of fascination and interest for the final. Where had Kazankina been? Was she fit? Could she run 3,000 meters as well as she had the shorter distances, which had been her specialty? Could Decker hold together in her first major international championship? Was it possible for her to take on the Soviets, virtually unchallenged since 1976, when Decker sat sadly on the sideline? What of Ulmasova? Was she not the world-record holder? Surely, neither Decker nor Kazankina could stay with her? And finally, what of the third Soviet, Natalya Artyemova, who barely qualified for the final? Might she be a rabbit planted in the field to assure a fast pace for her two teammates? It was the kind of roiling possibility that made a rest day uneasy and edgy, as coaches and athletes anticipated events.

Decker settled on a strategy. She would lead the race and accelerate progressively in the later stages in order to control the tempo and take the sting out of her rivals' kicks. The progressive acceleration was a suggestion from Bill Bowerman, which Dick Brown and Mary Decker accepted. When the gun sounded, the strategy unfolded. Decker headed to the front, unmindful of the clustered runners behind her. Later, she said that this had been "a good feeling compared to being way out front. You can't make mistakes, and you sure keep alert." She led rhythmic laps of 66, 70, 71, 71, 71, 70, a little faster initially than she wanted and then a little slower, but still close to her targets and likely to have the effect she wanted. The field began to separate until only the two top Soviets, Brigitte Kraus of West Germany, Wendy Sly of Great Britain, and Agnese Possamai of Italy remained in contention. The first kilometer split was 2:51

and the next two runners through were Kazankina (2:51.27) and Ulmasova (2:51.51). As the pace slowed slightly in the second kilometer, Decker went through in 5:48.89, followed now by Kazankina and Sly at 5:49.13. Ulmasova was still close in 5:49.35 as was Kraus in 5:49.73. When the field approached the bell, conventional wisdom said that Decker was finished. She had jackals at her back and she had done all the work for them. Food for the kill, that's what she was.

Nothing was further from the truth. Decker had worked her plan to perfection. The pace had been steady if not sensational, and Decker had accelerated at the 600-meter mark. The bunched runners behind her at the bell, including Wendy Sly who was almost abreast with her, and Kazankina, Kraus, Possamai, and Ulmasova, were tired by then, and when Decker accelerated again going into the last 400 meters, she tormented them, sending little pinpricks of pain through already enervated legs and arms. Nevertheless, they responded, no one dropped back, and everybody who ever had a chance, still did. On the backstretch, Kazankina was boxed on the inside by Wendy Sly, and Ulmasova was boxed by Possamai and harassed by Kraus. Less experienced runners would have been unnerved but the Soviets were patient. They knew that one of two things would happen, that an opening would appear or that they would force one. They waited as long as possible in the hurrying crowd for the first eventuality, the one they expected and preferred, but nothing happened, no gap, no failure of will from the leader, no fallen runner; so finally, on the last homestretch, with no distance left to spare and time running out, Ulmasova sprang from her fifth-place position into an open outside lane. It was late and she would have hoped for better, or at least for sooner, but, no matter; she had a clear path in front of her to the tape and Decker was in her sights. Kazankina, responding to the late bustle, was even better positioned. When Wendy Sly finally fell away, Kazankina moved through. She was on Mary Decker's shoulder with 50 meters to run. The race was

Kazankina's after all. She and not Ulmasova would handle the usurper. In the crisis, the announcer permitted expectancy to enter the call of the race: "and—here—comes—Kazankina!" drawn out as herald, and then quickly to prevent the message from being overtaken by the event, "here/comes/Kazankina," "here/comes/Kazankina." Self-congratulation entered the voice of the announcer, as it must have done. Did he not tell his listeners before the race that this would happen, that Decker would fold before the Soviet onslaught. And now the time has come, and it must be described: in deep, quick tones with greater urgency as the runners come up the straight together, the words rush fast enough to keep pace with the race, then the single word that tells all: "Kazankina! Kazankina!" Horseman, pass by. War, famine, pestilence, and death, the end of Decker's short reign arrived in the presence of the one runner who was too strong for her, the runner she would never beat. The great Kazankina emerged at last, ready to strike. Kazankina the totalitarian to make order from chaos.

Was it the Russian Pavlov, one of the two major influences on the Soviet sporting theory, who made dogs salivate by repeating patterns and rewards? "And—here—comes—Kazankina!" they had said in Montreal, and two times Kazankina had run around the field to victory. They had said it again in Moscow, "And—here—comes—Kazankina," and she had finished like fierce wind across an open prairie. And it came therefore to pass that in Helsinki in 1983, as Kazankina poised for just the barest second on Mary Decker's shoulder, there wasn't a dry mouth in the house. Pity Mary Decker, exposed in a low, flat place with no shelter.

Just then a strange and illogical thing happened. How could it be explained? For Kazankina came to the precipice, close enough to see, really, what was possible, and then she hung there, so briefly, before being knocked back by a force that she neither saw nor felt, but which occupied the field next to her own. Mary Decker "took a deep breath, relaxed and went." Could it really be as easy as that? Decker's stride was smooth, level, and unexcited, all her energy was directed to forward motion, and she blew away to a shocking victory. Stymied and surprised by Decker's speed, strength, and courage, Kazankina faltered near the end, and Brigitte Kraus passed her on the line. That remarkably, it was over, quick as an execution or a coup bubbling up from the people. The Soviet distance runners had been toppled by two women from the West, two democrats. Decker's final time was a relatively slow 8:34.62 with a last lap of 60, while Kraus took 8.5 seconds off the West German national record by running 8:35.11. Kazankina ran 8:35.13 in her first big 3,000, while Ulmasova, who lacked the last-lap punch of the other women, finished fourth in 8:35.55, a long way behind her world record of 8:26.78. After the race, Kazankina was forthright. "I was sure I would win it. But I lost in the final sprint to the American Mary Decker, who proved to be stronger at the finish." Decker herself professed never to have doubted the result, saying, "I wasn't worried when Kazankina came up on me in the stretch because I know I have a good kick."

The Western media reaction to Mary Decker's victory was instantaneous and enthusiastic. One of our own had brought down the bullies. Said one major report, "Mary Decker proved two important points in this race: that, given the ability of course, it is still possible in a major championship to run the legs off your rivals from the front...and that even the great Soviet women runners are not unbeatable. What an inspiration the 25-year-old American is to Western girls who for so long have suffered from an inferiority complex toward the Eastern Europeans, and what a marvelous advertisement she is for the sport."

The marvelous advertisement for the sport still had a race to run in Helsinki. All along she had said she would run the 1,500 meters for fun, but if anybody ever believed that before, they no longer did. The fun would come in the winning, and after easily advancing to the final with the fastest qualifying time (4:07.47), she lined up with the Soviets again: Zamira Zaitseva, Yekaterina Podkopayeva and Ravilya Agletdinova. All three had the potential to win the world championship, as Zaitseva had run 3:56.14, Podkopayeva had run 3:57.14, and Agletdinova had run 3:59.13. After a false start by Zaitseva, the field sprinted up the first turn, hesitated slightly looking for a leader on the backstretch, and then deferred to Mary Decker as she took her now-customary position. She passed 400 meters in 64.1, 800 meters in 2:11.0 (66.90), and 1,200 meters in 3:16.7 (65.7). The pace was fast without being withering and the Russians were still in attendance, all of them reassured that they were each at least one second faster than Decker in an open 800 meters. At the bell, Decker led and Zaitseva followed closely. Too closely, Decker said later, "She hit me practically every stride the whole way. Not obviously, but just brushing elbows, touching shoes." Still, Decker controlled herself and the tempo, accelerating into the penultimate turn and heading for the backstretch, making it impossible for any but Zaitseva to get to the front and making it hard even for Zaitseva to manage it. Nevertheless, the race looked once again set up for Decker to falter. She was in front, in contact, had led the whole way, and the pursuer had the advantage of both surprise and superior 800-meter speed. The conclusion, foregone but unfulfilled in the 3,000 meters, was sure to happen on this day. The patient Soviet would explode past the even-tempo leader and dash away from her on the homestretch. In her discouragement, the leader might even find herself prey to the last-minute attention of the dashers behind her and end up out of the medals, disconsolate and discouraged, full of self-recrimination for having been bold enough, audacious enough, to try twice in a major championship the tactic that never works, leading from the front. The foolishness of such a thing was evident and Zaitseva was its proof. There on the backstretch, she was awaiting her moment, not running smoothly but jagged and rough—like a person who could jolt into top speed and come with a rush.

And she did. On cue, Zaitseva did rush past Mary Decker approximately 170 meters from the finish line, did jump her for a quick lead of five meters coming into the homestretch and did sprint ferociously toward the end, her legs driving powerfully, her face contorted in determination, her one good chance for a world championship set out in front of her, and no obstruction in view. The hand that held the dagger had stuck it in the back of her neighbor, to paraphrase an even more outrageous act of plunder. If you asked Mary Decker, she would say Zaitseva's five-meter lead and her clear view of the finish line was ill-got gain, the profit from cutting her off on the last turn. "I don't think it's personal. It's just the way they're trained....She was running with me and leaning on me and I had to back off." When Zaitseva cut in on her, the chop in Decker's stride, necessitated by the nearness of Zaitseva's move to the pole position, was barely detectable, but running at speed is a precision sport. Even a minor adjustment can cause a major decline in speed, cadence, and momentum. It would have been possible, of course, for Decker to fend Zaitseva off a bit, just touch her slightly to warn her of the encroachment at the critical stage, but she dared not, "It was a mistake, letting her cut me off. But I didn't want to have to make a sudden move. I stay more relaxed if I move into my sprint gradually. So I had to let her get a little lead, and then she surprised me by cutting in." Making the decision of the moment—the decision not to touch Zaitseva and not to protect herself from the interruption in her race—was Decker's fear of disqualification and her fear that she might overreact, "If I was more aggressive," she said, "we'd be punching (each other) through the turn." So, in that moment, the moment when Decker fell victim to her inexperience and her apprehension, the race was decided. Decker had, in fact, run her race for fun, refrained from fisticuffs and physical battle, and now it was completed. Silver was good, and Zaitseva was a forceful and dynamic victor even if she was Soviet! That is what the eyes and the mind said as Zaitseva fled for home—except, that is, for the one detail that began slowly and then with gathering momentum to reveal itself. Decker was sprinting.

In the rough stride that took Zaitseva past Decker, a role reversal occurred instantaneously. Decker the pursued became Decker the pursuer. Decker the defender became Decker the attacker. That the reversal occurred in just that way was a credit to Mary Decker, for in almost every other case the reversal takes another form, as the bold leader becomes a defeated, straggling follower. How was it possible for Mary Decker to shift mental gears so fast and attack once beaten? In part it was her disposition, in part it was an aspect of her physical gift, in part it was because Zaitseva's move had been anticipated in Decker's race planning, and in part it was her anger. Zaitseva had broken the rules—she had cut in early—and she must not be allowed to get away with it. Two meters down as they entered the stretch, Decker's sprint closed the gap to one with 20 meters to the finish line. Remarkably, Decker held her smooth stride, maintained its length neither too long nor too short, and increased her turnover ever so slightly, looking down at her legs a time or two to see that all was going well, grimacing slightly in concentration and, within a long reach of the line, closing her eyes and pulling mightily with the last one or two arm swings before she was across the line. Zaitseva did not withstand the counter attack. When Decker came back at her, Zaitseva instinctively lengthened her stride, lost control of it, and jumped down as much as out toward the line, for all the world a child in an apple tree who reaches toward the fruit in the tallest branch, loses her balance, and tumbles to the ground. When she fell, Zaitseva maintained second place only because she rolled across the line. Decker's winning time was 4:00.9

while Zaitseva was 4:01.19, a gap that illustrates the difference between sprinting across the line and rolling across it.

Mary Decker was the two-time world champion. Her race at 3,000 meters had shattered the myth of Eastern Bloc invincibility, and her victory at 1,500 confirmed the earlier result. The races established Mary as not just a fast, strong runner but as a competitor of the highest order. The victories had great value in and of themselves and should have been savored. In fact, they were celebrated and praised and recounted in high words and glowing terms, but they were not truly savored. They were not treasured in their own right. Instead, they were almost immediately set in shadow. The object that shadowed Mary Decker's triumphs in Helsinki was the Olympic Games scheduled for Los Angeles, Mary's hometown, in 1984. When Zaitseva rolled across the line, the Soviets began to speak of 1984. "Mary has prepared very well this year. I think we will change our tactics and find something new. We will change," said a translator speaking on behalf of either Zaitseva or Podkopayeva, depending upon which account you read. And Mary herself fed the fire with statements emphasizing how special it would be to run in Los Angeles at the Olympics. Asked what her strongest impression was from the competitions in Helsinki, she answered, "Well, I have a lot more confidence for next year, for the Olympics." An article written at the end of the athletic year described her reactions at Helsinki in similar terms, "That done [victory in the 1,500 meters], Decker immediately turned her full attention to doing it all over again, and better, at the 1984 Olympic Games in Los Angeles. In her post-race interview, she allowed that it was wonderful to be the first-ever world champion in her events, but that people had to understand she had missed the 1976 Games in Montreal with injury, missed 1980 in Moscow through boycott, and that she had been brought up from the age of 10 near Los Angeles," a situation she described as "perfect." Mary's reaction and that of other people to her Helsinki victories was normal, predictable and unavoidable given the warping significance of the Olympic Games, but it is saddening as well. One would wish for a champion to have at least one triumph that is truly final, one that satisfies all debts and answers all questions. Unfortunately, sporting accomplishment is by its nature transitory, and the highest triumph often provides the platform for the longest fall.

For Mary Decker, the shadow aside, the remaining races in the European season were successful. She sprinted through the races undefeated. In more than 20 races in 1983, she never lost a final. At year's end, she was ranked first in the world for both 1,500 meters and 3,000 meters, and was showered with honors and awards. Back home in Eugene, she rested from hard training in the fall of 1983 and then turned her attention to the Olympic Games. She was, as she did so, keenly aware that others were still throwing fuel on an old fire, even as they celebrated her accomplishments. "The only things missing from Decker's stat collection," said one customary remark after Helsinki, "are Olympian in nature: an Olympic title and a World Record at an Olympic distance (1,500 or 3,000 meters). Guess what's coming up in 1984."

The date an Olympic event flings itself into full-scale hype is impossible to identify. Perhaps it starts before the potential host cities float the possibility of a bid; or when the floated bid, surviving the trial balloon, defines itself in specific detail; if not then, surely after the bid is accepted; and thereafter in a building, accumulating rush that sweeps all reason aside in favor of interest, however measured. When Los Angeles was selected to host the 1984 Games, the only certainty was that a town famous for, if not founded upon, the manipulation of images would bring new heights to Olympic hucksterism. Imagine, then, a runner with a worldwide reputation for excellence, an attractive young woman tanned and blond (if the light was right), who had struggled back from injury after injury, had regained her form, and had taken on and beaten the best women runners in the world, including the previously invincible Soviet corp; imagine a young woman who was photogenic, honest, vulnerable, articulate, intelligent, and unwise enough to say what she thought on controversial subjects like drugs. Mary Decker, who was all those things, was simply irresistible. As early as August 1983, she was featured with Carl Lewis in *Newsweek's* look ahead to the Olympics, "The Making of America's Best." The remarkably balanced article captured the major themes of Mary's career. "Mary Decker," it said, "is the queen of middle distances. With her blond mane bobbing behind her, she has streaked to a world record in the 5,000-meter run...and she holds the American records at 10,000, 3,000, 1,500 and 800 meters as well as the mile." Later, the writer added a particularly striking description of Mary Decker's world, "The sight of Mary Decker in action generates the kind of delicious anxiety that once came from a new Alfred Hitchcock film. She is, after all, a pretty young woman traveling at unsafe speeds in a conveyance that can't be trusted." In subsequent articles and advertising material, Mary Decker's profile was driven higher and higher.

One aspect of Mary Decker's image was her potential reaction to physical conflict. Years before, articles included quotes to the effect that given a choice between hurting herself or hurting someone else, she would hurt herself. This, she suggested, was a sensitivity born of her own disappointments. Somewhat consistent with this theme was the idea that Mary Decker would not protect herself from the pushing and shoving of international competition. On that point, however, the evidence was mixed. The *Newsweek* article described an indoor meet in New York's Madison Square Garden when "Decker dispensed with a lapped Puerto Rican runner who failed to yield the inside track by suddenly giving the woman a hard shove," a "gratuitous maneuver" that caused the crowd "that had been cheering her to gasp in horror." A former coach, one of the several that followed Don DeNoon but preceded Mary's re-emergence at Colorado, was quoted as saying, "What you've got to understand about Mary is that she judges her worth as a person solely by what she accomplishes on the track. It's scary to contemplate, but the competitive nature that we so admire in this woman is actually a huge personality flaw." On the other hand, Decker did not push Zaitseva in Helsinki, as she had the right to do if Zaitseva cut in too closely. In a long career, contradictions are inevitable, and this was one as the Olympic year opened. Was Mary Decker a heartless competitor who would push people aside in her quest for a gold medal, or would she defer when push came to shove? Either way, the paradox in Decker was part of her appeal and fascination.

In the run-up to the Olympic Games in Los Angeles, the Soviet Union withdrew and took with it most of the other Eastern Bloc nations. The Soviets said they were worried about security, and in fact they may have been, given the paranoid quality of the totalitarian state. More likely, however, they were either retaliating for the US-led boycott of Moscow, or they were worried about the increased drug testing that was proposed for Los Angeles. Whatever the explanation, the media attention on the remaining athletes necessarily intensified. In addition to Mary Decker, one athlete upon whom particular attention focused was Zola Budd.

Zola Budd was born in 1966 in the Republic of South Africa. When she was 12 years old, Pieter Labuschagne noticed her among a group of girls competing in a school meet. She was small for her age, and according to Labuschagne who coached a competing school, looked nine at the time. Nonetheless, he said later that he knew "where her future lay the first moment he saw her run." When she transferred to his school the next year, Labuschagne asked her to join his team. Although Zola's first interest was in netball, she agreed to run. He later described her in these terms, "Zola is a running machine. All I'm doing is improving the infrastructure, the capacity of the lungs, and the efficiency of her body. Really, all I've been doing is improving the roads and rails within her." As to her subsequent training, he emphasized that Zola was self-motivated and that a major part of his responsibility was to hold her back. "Once she realized the improvement training was having on her, there wasn't any stopping her. Now if I tell her to rest for two weeks, she's ringing me after three days, begging to run again. After a week, her mother is ringing, too. Zola's impossible to live with when she's not running." The training to which Labuschagne referred was based on the schedules established by Arthur Lydiard of New Zealand. A prominent part of the regimen was distance work on the roads, a workload enhanced by the 4,568 foot altitude of Zola's countryside. In an article written in the first wave of excitement about Zola Budd, the phenomenon, the training prescribed by Labuschagne was contrasted with that performed by Mary Decker in her youth. "In this," referring to the extended distance on the roads, "she was wonderfully fortunate. Decker, by contrast, was thrown at an early age into hard interval and speed training, voluminous racing. That resulted in promising marks followed by a host of injuries." Even to a comparison of youthful training techniques, the two were becoming enmeshed.

At 13 Zola had operations on both feet to remove a small bone in each arch; but otherwise she trained steadily under Labuschagne until her breakthrough, which came when she was 15. At that age, she improved her 1,500-meter time by 9.9 seconds by running a South African junior record of 4:09.1. Between 1981 and 1984 she won more than 70 races in South Africa, but the one that brought her into the spotlight was a 5,000-meter run on January 5, 1984. Running barefoot and virtually without competition, the 17-year-old girl broke Mary Decker's world record for the distance by recording 15:01.83. Descriptions of the race convey the sense of wonder that accompanied it: "Then the January night wind came down from the Stellenbosch Mountains, flapping marker flags and buffeting hoardings....But the girl, Zola Budd, simply sets her frown of concentration more firmly and kept on. She is 17, but so slender at 5' 2" and 84 pounds, so floppy in the motion of her arms, that she seemed years younger. Yet somehow she wasn't slowing."

Zola herself had no illusions about the time. She acknowledged that "Mary Decker is out of my class at the moment. She's a great athlete, much more experienced than I, and I wouldn't feel much like racing her now. It would be silly. I know I've beaten her best 5,000-meters time but then she's only run the distance twice. If she puts her mind to it I'm sure she could run it 20 seconds faster than she has. But, in time, perhaps I will too." As the Olympic year stirred, Zola's mature caution was ignored. Instead, she got caught up in a swirling controversy that included at least the following components: she decided to leave South Africa and seek international competition, despite the ban on such competition imposed on her country as a result of its apartheid policy; she decided to use her father's British citizenship to become a citizen of Great Britain as a way to avoid the ban on South African participation; and she decided to seek membership on Great Britain's team for the Los Angeles Olympics. Amid all this "decision making" was the fact that Zola was arguably too young to know her own mind. The controversy she engendered was heightened by the involvement of a London newspaper. This latter aspect of Zola's case was described by the newspaper in these terms, "The newspaper would extend a hand of friendship to the Budds and advise them to the best of its ability what course to follow, in order for them to apply for Zola's British citizenship." Perhaps this is usual, but it did not strike many people that way. Rather, it appeared to be an attempt to carve out special privileges for a young runner who might, or might not, be old enough to handle the attendant responsibility. It hardly mattered in any event because in short order Zola became an international celebrity. After she was selected for Great Britain's Olympic team, the spotlight shone even more brightly in her direction. Along the hard way, she was picketed, protested, and threatened by overheated sections of the British citizenry who blamed her for being South African. It was a grotesque and shameful overreaction to her planned activity: running seven and a half laps around a track against suitable competition.

Meanwhile Mary Decker's Olympic Games were shrinking. The schedule of heats, semifinals, and finals in the 1,500 and 3,000 were jammed too close together for a reasonable double. When Mary tried a similar schedule at the United States Olympic Trials, the unthinkable happened. She won the 3,000 meters without incident in a fast time—8:34.91, close to what she ran in Helsinki the previous year—but, fatigued from the heavy schedule of racing and suffering from an injury to her achilles tendon, she was out-kicked by Ruth Wysocki in the 1,500 meters. After considering the options, Decker finally decided to run only the 3,000 meters in Los Angeles. In that race, most people understood that Mary's primary opposition would come from Maricica Puica of Romania, one of the few Eastern Bloc contestants in Los Angeles. Puica was the World Cross-Country champion, had excellent half-mile speed, and extensive experience. Zola Budd, on the other hand, was not a threat to Decker; she was a media event composed of many elements. In addition to her precocity and the political brouhaha that surrounded her escape from the apartheid ban, there was the fact that back home in South Africa she had slept in a bed with a picture of Mary Decker posted on the wall behind it. That moved people for some reason.

More knowledgeable people looked less at Zola's overall speed, cared less still about her political situation, and barely noticed the posters hanging over her bed. They thought instead of the one salient feature of her participation in Los Angeles, and that was her tendency to set the pace in her races. An experienced athlete and writer described the dynamic in advance of the race, "...the impatient natures of Budd and Decker may create a spectacular race, one that isn't tactical and jostling and infuriating and won with a late sprint the way the men's races will certainly be. Decker loves to lead. Budd has never done anything else but lead. If each is equally uncomfortable in the wake of the other, each will pass, and be passed and repass."

Returning home to Eugene after the trials, Decker had an injection of cortisone and turned to alternative exercises because of the injured achilles tendon. Until five days before the Olympic Games opened, her workouts were performed in a swimming pool, and were designed to match as nearly as possible the effect of training on the road or track. Equipped with a mask and a tank to simulate altitude training, and wearing weighted gloves on her hands and shoes on her feet, Mary ran in place in deep water using the buoyancy to protect the leg while gaining the advantage of resistance. Although she gave up the training benefit of gravity, the workouts were very hard. When they were concluded, coach and athlete had sufficient data to know that Decker was fit and ready to run in Los Angeles. If there was any doubt about the matter, it was removed when Mary set a world best for 2,000 meters only two days after she got out of the water; and further relieved in a final speed workout, which was supposed to include 2 x 200, 1 x 400, and 1 x 200, but which was curtailed after Mary ran her 400 meter in 54 seconds. The goal had been 58, a time which in itself would have proved that the athlete was sharp. The training behind her and only race days ahead, Decker spoke of her injury and her determination to overcome it. "It's a miracle I'm here and able to compete," she said, "but you can bet when I come down the homestretch I'll be fighting."

Arguably, the women's 1,500- and 3,000-meter runs were the races most seriously affected by the Eastern Bloc boycott. Runners from the Soviet Union in particular might have dominated both finals, notwithstanding Decker's triumphs in Helsinki. Without them, the United States placed three people in the 3,000-meter final. Decker, Cindy Bremser, and Joan Hansen all went through. They were joined by Puica and Budd, as well as Lynn Williams of Canada, Agnese Possamai of Italy, Aurora Cunha of Portugal, Dianne Rodger of New Zealand, Brigitte Kraus of West Germany, Wendy Sly of Great Britain, and Cornelia Burki, originally of South Africa but competing for Switzerland.

Mary Decker and Dick Brown were confident before the final on the evening of August 10. Mary had run well in qualifying. Furthermore, to Dick Brown's eye, Maricica Puica did not look quite right. Something in her leg movement was awkward, he thought, like she was somehow past her peak. In the circumstance, it made sense for Decker to run her usual aggressive race. She would lead if she could do that strongly and without interference, and she would drive for home with 1,000 meters to go. With 600 meters left, she would kick. The idea was to dispatch both Puica, the strength runner, and Kraus, who had a fearsome kick. Budd played no substantial part in the planning. She would be "permitted" to take the lead anytime before the sixth lap "if running at the proper speed." The "proper speed" was that which would produce for the winner, i.e., Mary Decker, a final time of 8:29.

From this vantage point, as the race is about to begin, even as the runners go to the mark, reflect a while on Olympic history. Do not think of Paavo Nurmi this time, or Jack Lovelock, not of Herb Elliott or Vladimir Kuts, nor of Tatyana Kazankina and Nadezhda Olizaryenko. Think instead of Ralph Hill, who was fouled, and of Ben Eastman, who ran the wrong event; think of Eulace Peacock who was hurt, and of Rudolf Harbig and Harold Davis, favorites who never got to run in their prime. What of Sydney Wooderson, Dave Sime, and Ron Clarke? Consider Wade Bell, the impressive year he had in 1968, but sick at the wrong time. Include Jim Ryun certainly, twice if you like, Steve Williams at 200 meters and Eddie Hart in the 100, perhaps Mike Boit or Filbert Bayi. Think of entire generations silenced by the wars, and reach out for the women who never ran at all. Collect finally all the gold medalists who could have been but never were, and add Mary Decker's name to the list.

Here is what happened. Decker led for the first 1,600 meters, but she was erratic, first running too fast for her intended result, and then slowing down too much. During the early running, the entire field hovered just at her shoulder and immediately behind her. The splits were 66.9 for the 400 meters, 2:15.5 for the 800 meters, and 2:50.5 for the kilometer. No one dropped off the pace. In fact, the lap before the 1,200-meter mark was only 70.4, and the field was getting edgy. Two hundred meters later, slightly back in the pack, Joan Hansen clipped Aurora Cunha's heel and stumbled before recovering. It was a sign. Somebody needed to stretch things out. At 1,600 meters in 4:35.9 both Wendy Sly and Zola Budd had the same idea: pass Decker. Wendy tried first but hesitated just long enough at Decker's side for Zola Budd to hustle past and go for the front. Decker held her off for half the turn, then relented and conceded the lead. Decker did not, however, concede the inside lane, and neither did Zola take it. Rather, as the front pack of Budd, Decker, Sly, and Puica began to separate from the other runners, Budd had only the outer edge of lane one, while Decker clung to her on the inside. Coming off the turn and perhaps 30 meters into the homestretch, they clipped each other. No apparent damage was done, although some later said that they detected a slight wobble in the next strides. Most observers did not see it. Instead, they saw both runners regain their balance and keep running. Either way, the two leaders were still too close to each other. Wendy Sly ran wide because she was sure "there was going to be some bumping," and she wanted to be well away from it. The danger should have been more apparent to Decker, who had Budd in front of her, than to

Budd, who led and had only the sensation of Decker's continued closeness. Later, people would say, Zola should have stayed outside or Decker should have backed off, or Decker should have tapped Zola lightly as if to say, "Hey, I'm here, be careful." But much of that was hindsight and would not have been mentioned except for what happened five steps later. At that point, the two collided and this time Mary Decker fell. She tried to get up but there was too much pain in her hip, so she stayed behind, anguished and crying, while the field hurried on. Zola Budd, who caught sight of Mary Decker falling, cried too. She was still in the race, and she ran hard, but there was no way to hold back the tears. Many of the 85,000 people in the Coliseum that night poured venom down on her, a heartbroken, shocked, sobbing, slight teenage girl who had given up her home for this chance and had seen it turn to ruin. The veteran Puica saw her chance in the turn of events. Weathering efforts first by Zola and then by Wendy Sly, she sprinted away with 200 meters to go and took the gold medal. The time was 8:35.9. Sly took silver, while Lynn Williams fought past Cindy Bremser for the bronze. Zola Budd slowed on the last lap and finished in the seventh spot, still creditable all things considered. But no one cared about any of that. A new cauldron was boiling. Who would be responsible for the loss of Mary Decker?

The English refer to the stiff upper lip. They and others might also refer to class or dignity or control, even to self-abasement and modesty of expression. In athletics, sportsmanship is the quality. In many respects, sportsmanship is a charade, but so also are the manners of everyday life. In any case, the rules are well settled and everyone can rely on them. After she tangled with Zola Budd, Mary Decker was required to say, even if she did not mean it, even if the words burned her throat on the way up, and brought to her eyes tears of new shame, anger and resentment, "It was no one's fault. Racing in tight quarters is perilous, and these things happen. I am unhappy with the result, and grievously disappointed, but I do not blame Zola Budd, for whom I have the greatest sympathy and respect. I just hope that the incident did not break her concentration and cause her to run less well than she otherwise would have." So easy now, so distant from the events, so many years, and so much time for consideration and crafting, it may seem unfair even to write the words. Still, they flow naturally because, being what sportsmanship required, the words are rote. And, as events unfolded, they, or any like them, were totally impossible for Mary Decker to speak on the evening that mattered, and indeed on the day that followed. Her emotion bubbled to the surface as bile. The incident on the track was only a fall. What followed was much more serious. It was a fall from grace.

Don Steffens, a press steward and a high school friend of Jim Ryun, himself a victim of an Olympic fall in 1972, described the scene as the runners from the race straggled through the tunnel and left the track, "A number of runners came over to Mary in the tunnel to offer their condolences. Then I think someone—the Swiss runner—said, 'Well, it wasn't Zola's fault.' Mary said, 'Oh, yes it was. You know it was.'" When Zola herself approached hopeful of some sign of acceptance, Decker waved her off with a curt, "Don't bother!" A more detailed description of the scene, the essential points of which appeared in multiple publications, had it as follows: "...Budd came by, saying nothing yet—only offering sympathetic looks. 'Don't bother,' Decker told her. 'Get away from me. It was your fault. I know it was.' Budd went out of the tunnel, past the drug-control station and sat behind an adjacent booth. After several moments, friends picked her up, whisked her away in a car, and she was gone." Remembering how young Zola Budd was, how small she was, and how shy, it was as if Decker was kicking a puppy, although it must be said that she denied saying anything to Budd beyond "Don't bother."

The moment of truth: Mary Decker in Los Angeles, 1984.

Two hours later, when the press had the first opportunity to speak with her, Mary was unrelenting, saying, "Zola Budd tried to cut in when, basically, she wasn't ahead of me. I think her left foot caught me, and to avoid pushing her, I fell. When I think of it now, I should have pushed her. But then tomorrow's headline would have read, 'Mary Decker pushes Zola Budd.'" She added a forthright conclusion, "I do hold Zola responsible. I was fit, and I was running a good race." To similar effect, "I don't think there's any question that she was in the wrong...she was not in front. You have to be a full stride in front and she was cutting in around the turn and she wasn't anywhere near passing. And I do hold her responsible for what happened because I don't feel I did anything wrong." In context, "responsible" is not a word of causation; it is word of blame and intention.

Initially, the organizers accepted Mary Decker's view of events. They disqualified Zola Budd. Soon, however, the view of the British team was preferred. The British team manager filed an appeal that took two pages to list all the reasons why the disqualification should be set aside. More briefly, he stated the case to the press, "I don't see how a young lady leading a race can be disqualified when an experienced athlete tried to go past on the inside. Zola was emotionally drained and upset that a great athlete went down on the track. But when a driver rams his car into the back of another he's at fault. It was not willful obstruction on Zola's part, and she had the lane. She has scratches on the back of her left leg to prove it." While Dick Brown and Decker denied that Decker had tried to force her way through on the inside, the jury of appeals reinstated Zola Budd. More important, the wave of public opinion swelled in her favor. John Holt, general secretary of the IAAF, expressed his view strongly, "Decker was her own victim."

Although he personally believed that Zola shifted slightly in her lane and caused the accident, Dick Brown recognized the danger of making the point too strongly to a press that might, in the situation, be unsympathetic. He urged Mary toward graciousness and otherwise tried to fix the mess. At one point, he was quoted as saying, "Nobody associated with all of this feels that anything was done intentionally. It was just very unfortunate." But nothing he said could draw his charge away from her bitter recrimination against Zola Budd. Even her most conciliatory statements had an accusatory edge, as in this remark made one day after the race, "It was an accident. It was caused by another person. I'm not angry at the other person. I'm angry that the situation happened." By now, however, the video of the race had been scanned thousands of times. It was no longer possible to go beyond the first statement Mary made: "It was an accident." Everything else was merely hurtful. When the Games wrapped up, one columnist caught the prevailing mood when he said, among other things, "We found the woman, I think, in Mary Decker. She whined, she cried, she blamed everyone but herself for her Olympic disaster... I don't feel sympathy for Decker anymore. I feel sympathy for Budd, who so many people will blame for the mishap. No matter whose fault it was, Decker should know better than to publicly wallow in self-pity, blaming the world for her own misfortune."

Few people would know how close Mary Decker and Zola Budd came to reconciliation before the Olympic Games closed and memories hardened, but in fact, it almost happened. Negotiations between the two camps—Decker in the one and Zola in the other— brought an agreement that the two athletes would march together in the closing ceremony. It was intended as a gesture of friendship and sportsmanship and could have washed away much of the bitterness. At the last minute, however, the plan collapsed, either because third parties with a financial interest hoped to exploit the controversy at a later date and did not wish it resolved, or—another story—terrorists threatened Zola's life and she was sent away as a precaution. In either case, Zola Budd and Mary Decker remained apart when the athletes marched, and a publicly unforgiving Mary Decker was unforgiven.

Rarely had a sporting figure plummeted in such a way and hit the ground so hard. The memory recoils from the senselessness of it. Zola Budd was the young girl, the person with muted sexuality, the natural wonder. Zola Budd was the tomboy and Zola Budd was promise. Zola Budd was a force of nature, the veldt, open spaces, the reminder of God's whimsy. Zola Budd was Mary Decker, as she was so many years ago; and Mary Decker, bright, intuitive, and sensitive, would have loathed her and loved her and thought nothing of her, and turned away from her as a shy person avoids a mirror. When Mary Decker and Zola Budd tangled legs in Los Angeles, it was proximity that did it. And when the dream ended for Mary Decker, it was she who killed it. She would not push Zola Budd aside, nor even tap her slightly on the shoulder. She would not push her other self away as she had been pushed by the larger, older Soviet woman at whom she had thrown her baton; and she would

After the fall, Zola Budd struggles for breath and composure.

not suffer, later, the pain of blaming herself for what she must have known was an essential act of gentleness even as the consequence was so harsh. If it was Zola's fault, it was Mary's fault. If it was Mary's fault, it was Zola's fault, and it was all too much. Decker's anger and pain, her cutting language and her blaming, were not associated with an incident on the track, not even with the loss of a cherished, public ambition. It was the pain of suicide—the end finally of Little Mary Decker—and the first stirring of rebirth, forced upon her by extraordinary, cruel circumstance.

Ironically, as Mary Decker began the long process of putting herself back together after Los Angeles, another woman with whom she is linked, Tatyana Kazankina, also took a great fall. The year 1984 had been great for the Eastern Bloc women, notwithstanding the boycott. The Soviets, in particular, had done what they said they would do. They went back home after Helsinki and got better. With no Mary Decker to stop them, her season having ended with the stumble in Los Angeles, Soviet women roared to the front. At 1,500 meters, they occupied the seven top spots in the world rankings for the year. Kazankina was only seventh with a best time of 3:58.63, but that was faster than the one fast time Decker ran before Los Angeles, 3:59.19, and both were seconds behind Nadyezhda Raldugina who ran 3:56.63. In the 3,000 meters, however, Kazankina was supreme. She obliterated the world record by running 8:22.62, almost 7 full seconds faster than the second best time in the world for the year, which was the 8:29.59 by teammate Svyetlana Guskova. It was also, just to add salt to the previous wound, faster than three more of Paavo Nurmi's old records for the distance as he got progressively faster in his career. This time, however, he got to point. After a 5,000-meter run in Paris in early September, Kazankina was requested by the IAAF to report for a drug test. She refused. Actually, it would be more accurate to say that the Soviet official accompanying her refused because it was he who adamantly refused to go forward. He argued that the test could be conducted only if a Soviet doctor was present; as there was none, Kazankina would not be tested. Although IAAF Secretary John Holt called the official's stand "bloody foolish" and appeared to set the whole thing down as a misunderstanding, it had more serious consequences than that. IAAF rule 144-5 read: "An athlete ... must, if so requested in writing submit to doping control. Refusal to do so will result in disqualification from the competition and the athlete will be deemed to have rendered himself ineligible for competition as if a positive test has been obtained...." At 32, Kazankina was banned for "life." Like most people banned for life, she would return occasionally, as she did in 1986 to finish fifth in the fourth IAAF Women's Road Race Championships in Lisbon, but her dominating years were ended.

The next year, 1985, Mary Decker rose from the ashes. Once more, she sliced into the Eastern Bloc women. She ran 3:57.24 for 1,500 meters and 8:25.83 for 3,000 meters, in both races beating Maricica Puica. She was undefeated at both distances and ranked first in the world for each. The performances could not regain what had been lost in 1976 to injury, in 1980 to boycott, and in 1984 to accident, but they cooled the pain.

One race promoter in the year after Los Angeles told Mary Decker that if she ran fast enough people would forget all about what happened at the Olympics. He might also have said, if you run long enough, people will forget what happened at the Olympics. The first suggestion is cynical. It suggests that people love a winner and a winner is forgiven every offense. The second suggestion is more neutral in its implication. It suggests only that our capacity for memory is limited, and that "old" information can be either overborne or given context by "new" information. Taking either suggestion into account, Mary Decker has now run long enough to take the sting out of 1984. After the date, to be certain, she was never again what she had been, never again the unquestioned darling of American track and field. But over time it has become evident that she is something more critical. She is the one person who carried the sport from infancy to age, crashing through social barriers, economic hurdles, and competitive challenges as quickly as she confronted them. In the course of her progress, she acquired fast friends, attracted detractors, and left a great many people simply confused and confounded.

No one, however, can deny her greatness as an athlete and few people will deny her influence. Even today, several Olympiads past Los Angeles, when she runs along the trails or on the track in Eugene, Oregon, home to many world-class athletes, it is to Mary Decker that eyes turn. If Doris Brown is the mother of American women distance runners, Mary Decker is the older sister. In that role she is popular, talented, unpredictable, in turn aloof and protective, inviting and forbidding, endearing and infuriating, unavoidable and unapproachable. In her complexity, she is the model against whom all her sisters are judged. Or more simply, as Zola Budd once said, "It would be wonderful to be so pretty." Even when Mary Decker became embroiled in controversy concerning an unreliable drug test after the 1996 United States Olympic Trials, reasonable people did not recast her career as chemically dependent. In that regard, the girl was mother to the woman. The talent of the young Mary Decker was divine. Openly displayed in countless forums in a steady, progressive development, so also was the talent of the woman.

One is tempted to end a descriptive section on Mary Decker with the question to her: "When did you become Mary Decker?" because of all the figures in American sport, she is perhaps the one who most clearly has become "something," although the precise definition of what that something is shifts throughout her career. One refrains from asking the question, however, because the facts that begin an answer to the question are discomforting. They may lead to a conclusion that we—all of us who permit other people to carry our burdens, our expectations, our dreams, our vitality— loaded too much, too early, for too long on the slender, though strong, shoulders of a young person, and that in the process, we damaged her. We do not wish to hear it.

With all that, what does the career of Mary Decker say to the young women who follow in her path? What did it say, for example, to Stephanie Herbst in the summer of 1984, as Stephanie pondered her freshman year at the university and Mary suffered her misfortune in Los Angeles? Arguably, it said this: "All things are possible."

When directed to the young, could any sentiment be more merciless? For some it is song, for some the song of the siren; for some it is promise and for some it is threat; and nowhere is it written who may go forward and who must hang back. All go. To give the matter sight, picture a diver suspended in flight above a clear pool who asks herself at the top of the arc: Is the water deep enough? Too late, for that matter is fixed. For safety's sake, ask instead of the diver and the dive, for in that combination is the outcome.

NINE

It is impossible for the future to change the past.

Anonymous

When Mary Decker fell in Los Angeles in 1984, curious eyes turned to the infield where she lay crying. Even the television cameras, which should have followed the race assiduously, pulled back for an occasional glance at what had happened, rather than following what was and would happen. After all, a running race was only an occasion for human drama, unworthy of its own respect, and the human drama was now holding her leg. The race was a distraction to be abided. Even now, do you, a special person by virtue of reading this book, remember who finished fourth in the Olympic Games 3,000-meter final in 1984? Or will you be required to flip back through the last chapter to find the name of Cindy Bremser, USA? You do her a disservice if that is the case, for in some respects the journey of Cindy Bremser was more unlikely than that of Mary Decker and her achievement more remarkable.

Cindy Bremser was not in California when the Cheetahs and the Blue Angels and the other clubs offered an opportunity for young girls to run. As a young girl, she was not permitted to choose between fast work on the track or slow runs on the road, not entitled to dreams of indoor tracks, cheering crowds, international travel, and weekly coverage, with a world panting for her next accomplishment and her promise. Cindy was playing softball with her brothers in

Wisconsin. That changed only in 1973 when Peter Tegen, a German with an exotic background that included a love for track and field, walked into the office of University of Wisconsin assistant athletic director, Kit Saunders, and asked whether he might help coach women's track. "He had just finished coaching in something like 14 countries, and I thought, I can't believe this is happening," Ms. Saunders said later. Fortunately, she acceded to his request—"welcomed him with open arms," as she describes it—and he was on his way. As the new coach he was given an insubstantial but appreciated budget, and he was told that his runners, jumpers, and throwers could share uniforms with the basketball team.

With this encouragement, Peter Tegen posted a sign in the gym. To the women at the university, the sign said something to this effect: If you want to compete in track and field for the University of Wisconsin, sign up below. The placard then added a short description of the various events so that the volunteers would have some idea what was involved. Cindy Bremser, who was enrolled in the nursing school as a junior, signed the form. She and 11 other students thought it sounded like fun. With Tegen, that meant, as Cindy soon found out, running short sprints on the track, varied exercises on and off the track, and longer runs on the roads and trails. It also meant climbing up stairs sideways with a weighted vest, being towed by a moped to increase turnover, or being subject to any number of other strange practices designed to test a new theory Peter might come up with. In the varied workouts, in the directed conversations, the prerace tactics, and in plans for the future, working with Peter Tegen meant inspiration and enthusiasm and experimentation. More important, it meant that Cindy Bremser could apply her considerable will toward the single goal of finding out how good she could be. That precisely was what other women had traditionally been denied.

At first, Cindy Bremser "looked like a quarter-miler type"

Cindy Bremser of Wisconsin: only one may be first.

to Peter. She had good speed. She was strong. She had courage. Before they could make much progress, however, Cindy broke a leg in an accident unrelated to her running. She resumed workouts the next summer. For her and for the other young women in the early days, the first goal was general fitness, which they uniformly lacked as a result of inexperience and lack of opportunity. By the fall semester, Cindy Bremser no longer looked like a quarter-miler. With the additional strength and conditioning, she looked like a middle-distance runner. Peter soon recognized an unusual challenge. His new middle-distance runner was completely untutored, so he would be able "to teach a junior in college from the ground up how I thought one should run." For Peter, this meant an emphasis on fundamental principles. He believed, for example, that biomechanical efficiency was instrumental to success, and that it could be taught "from the inside out," that is, starting with those parts of the body that are near the center of gravity. He worked with his athletes to achieve "proximal stability" by strengthening the abdomen, back, shoulders, and hips, and finally the legs and arms. With regard to the central muscle groups, he would say, "We must have a strong foundation and attach all the other things to it." Peter also believed in functional strength, by which he meant strength directed toward the requirements of the specific motion or event. The exercises would be different, for example, for a thrower and a distance runner, but the principle would be consistent: do the exercise or activity that promoted strength in a way that was proximate to the demand of the event. For his middle-distance and distance runners, he might recommend stair-running, running with weighted vests, running while holding rocks, lunge-walking, bounding, and an assortment of other work against resistance. The weight room, when it was necessary, would be used in a way that was integrated with the other work and, again, specific rather than general in its effect and intention. Peter did not believe in wasting an athlete's time or energy. Peter also began to work with a concept he called "dynamic running." Although the system is almost endlessly varied, dynamic running can be described as a program designed to contest and deny every pattern that might allow a middle- and long-distance runner to settle into a comfort zone.

For her part, Cindy was inquisitive—frequently asking, "What do I do next?" and "Then?"—and wanted to know each detail of the work she was assigned, how it fit into the pattern of previous work, and what benefit it would produce. Peter spent more time with Cindy Bremser than with any athlete that followed her. After a short year together, she was the first Wisconsin woman to be named all-American, having finished third in the AIAW National Championships in the one-mile run. After graduation, Cindy continued to work with Peter. She earned a spot on every US national team between 1975 and 1988. And as a member of the United States Olympic team in 1984 and a finalist in the 3,000-meter run, Bremser knew precisely what to do when Mary Decker fell. She surged. Before the accident, she was running in either ninth or tenth place as the field strung out behind Budd, Puica, Decker, and Sly. Within 100 yards of the accident, Bremser of Wisconsin was engaged with Lynn Williams of Canada in a fight for fourth place. As it happened, both Williams and Bremser eventually passed the disconsolate Budd in the last lap, and the battle between them was for the Olympic bronze medal. Cindy Bremser's immediate response to Decker's fall and to the changed environment of the race was characteristic of a Tegen-trained athlete. Peter Tegen believed in minutely considered tactics, but he also schooled his charges to expect the unexpected and be ready to react. Although Cindy could not stay with Lynn Williams, the close finish was a reminder of how far she had traveled after adding her name to Peter Tegen's sign-up sheet. He had reason to be proud of Cindy Bremser's fourth-place finish in Los Angeles.

Interestingly, Peter Tegen did not consider himself a middle-distance coach when he arrived at the University of Wisconsin. Born in Germany in 1940, Peter experienced the "good war" from the wrong side. His father was a German paratrooper who was eventually taken prisoner by the United States; and Peter's residence was close enough to Dresden for him to see the bombs fall on that cultural treasure. After the war, he and his family joined the massive, unorganized, troubled shunt of refugees throughout Europe, trudging 200 miles to be reunited with Peter's father upon his release from internment. After a childhood that included scarce resources and close family, as well as an athletic career that included sprinting, gymnastics and soccer, Peter emerged with an undergraduate degree from the University of Koln, and graduate university degrees in English and sports sciences from the university in Freiburg, an attractive city situated along the western edge of the Black Forest. Graduation accomplished, young adulthood followed. Peter traveled in Europe, Africa and Latin America to teach clinics on track and field, attended the 1968 Olympic Games in Mexico City, and eventually became a national coach in Peru. While coaching the Peruvian women's team, he took them to the Pan-American Games in 1971 and the Olympic Games in 1972. He was particularly proud to have coached the South American women's champion for 100 meters; and it was in the explosive sprint events that he felt most comfortable. Only the accidental appearance of Cindy Bremser turned his attention to the middle and long distances, and only his profound sense of obligation carried the issue to its successful conclusion. Seeing her talent, he did not want to make any mistakes so he studied the literature, applied his own facility for critical thinking to what he read, and began to develop practices and exercises for his teams.

In the years since 1973, Peter Tegen has established the University of Wisconsin as one of the three or four premier programs for women's cross-country, and track and field in the United States. Between 1973 and January, 1999, his teams won two

National Cross-Country Championships. His Badger teams enjoyed 22 top-ten national finishes in indoor and outdoor track. The women scored in every National Track and Field Championship since 1975. In cross-country, Tegen's Wisconsin teams qualified 22 times for nationals, and never finished lower than tenth. Tegen has coached three Olympians; developed 23 national champions in either cross-country or track and field, and watched them win a total of 42 titles; produced 66 all-Americans who were accorded the honor 227 times. Over the same 1973-1998 period, the Wisconsin women won 13 Big Ten cross-country championships and 24 Big Ten track and field Championships. A remarkable 203 individuals won Big Ten titles in either cross-country or track and field. Five of his athletes were Academic all-Americans, and 175 of them were honored as Academic all-Big Ten in either cross-country or track and field. In both 1984 and 1985, Peter Tegen was named national cross-country coach of the year by his peers. In 1989, he was honored by induction into the Wisconsin Women's Athletics Hall of Fame. In 1994, he was named to the Drake Relays Hall of Fame, and in 1995, he was honored by induction into the Wisconsin High School Coaches Hall of Fame for his contributions to Wisconsin high school programs. By any estimation, Peter Tegen is a leader in his profession.

· · · · ·

Timing is not everything, despite the cliche, but it is something. Perhaps it could be said that, if the timing is wrong, much of what is regarded would go unregarded. This is a way of circling an issue that begins with the recognition that if Cindy Bremser had been a junior at the University of Wisconsin in 1963 and not 1973, she almost certainly would not have run on an Olympic team. Just as well, if Peter Tegen had stopped his wandering and arrived in Madison, Wisconsin in 1963, he would not have coached women in intercollegiate athletics. The timing would have been wrong. Both Peter Tegen and Cindy Bremser, who embarked together on an adventure in 1973, benefited from work other people did, and events they did not control.

Intercollegiate sport for women is push and pull. Sometimes it pushes the issues; and sometimes it is pulled along by forces well beyond the campuses. Bearing that fact in mind, it remains possible to bring collegiate sport out of the whole and look at its landmarks singularly. Those landmarks arguably begin with golf. In 1940, a woman named Gladys Palmer of Ohio State University decided that college women should have their own golf championships, distinct from prior collegiate competition among women because it would be sanctioned and structured. She set about the task of making her dream real. Ms. Palmer had an advantage of course, in that golf was a traditional sport for women and relatively inoffensive, but her championship was still a work of pioneering impact. In relatively short order, Ms. Palmer's national event became institutionalized, was held every year except the war years, and began to rotate among various host cities. It also gathered moss, in its case a welter of alphabet-soup agencies. A "Tri-Partite Golf Committee" was organized to take responsibility for the tournament. The committee itself had representatives from three other organizations: The Division for Girls and Women's Sports (DGWS), the National Association for Physical Education of College Women (NAPECW), and the Athletic and Recreation Federation of College Women (ARFCW, eventually CWS). The success of the golf tournament raised the question whether a similar concept could be used for other sports. Springing from the alphabet agencies ("the Tri-Partite Agencies") came the National Joint Committee on Extramural Sports for College Women (naturally and memorably known as NJCESCW!). NJCESCW reviewed events that brought college women together for competition, and began to establish standards for the events. Meanwhile, the DGWS recognized in the 1960s that times were changing and that an opportunity existed for more women to compete. It also recognized that prior policies had discriminated against highly skilled women athletes, who were forced to seek competitive opportunities off-campus. DGSW amended its "Statement on Competition" to enlarge the possibilities. As some of the earlier agencies fell away, DGWS increased its activity even further in 1967 when it formed a Commission for Intercollegiate Athletics for Women (CIAW) within its agency. The initial purposes of the commission were to encourage colleges and universities to govern intercollegiate competition for women at the local, state, or regional levels, to hold DGWS National Championships as the need for them became apparent, and to sanction closed intercollegiate events in which at least five colleges or universities participated. Inevitably, committees were formed to research the goals and to work toward their implementation. By December 1967, the chairperson for CIAW announced that the group would sponsor national championships for women. Championships were held in 1969 for the first two sports: gymnastics and track and field. Championships were added for badminton, swimming and diving, and volleyball in 1970, and basketball got its national championship in 1972.

As participation grew, so also did the need for a more structured and specific governing body to set standards and provide leadership. The Association for Intercollegiate Athletics for Women (AIAW), an institutional membership organization, was formed in the 1971-72 academic year to fill the need. Two hundred and seventy-five schools joined in the first year of operation. By the second year of its operation, 367 schools had joined the AIAW. The AIAW remained a part of DGWS and an affiliate of the American Association for Health, Physical Education and Recreation (AAHPER), although those relationships became a matter of almost immediate controversy as interest in intercollegiate sport for women intensified. The intensity of interest originated in two primary and related sources: the passage in 1972 of Title IX of Public Law 92-318, and the growing involvement of the National Collegiate Athletic Association (NCAA) in women's sports.

Title IX says that no person in the United States shall, on the basis of sex, be excluded from participation in, be denied the benefits of, or be subjected to discrimination under any education program or activity receiving federal financial assistance. As relevant to this discussion, Title IX mandates equal opportunities in athletics for women at most colleges and universities that receive federal funds. After Title IX became law in 1972, the federal Department of Health, Education and Welfare was obligated to issue regulations and to enforce them. HEW issued the regulations in 1972, and it gave colleges and universities six years to comply. Many colleges and universities spent the six years complaining about the regulations rather than complying with them. They said, among other things, that the regulations were so vague that they did not know what constituted compliance and what did not. Amid the confusion, the six-year deadline expired without enforcement, after which HEW returned to its drafting. Title IX remained more promise than performance. Meanwhile, the NCAA recognized the potential impact of Title IX. Because college competition organized and sanctioned by the NCAA did not at that time include events for women, the impact promised to be revolutionary. If Title IX was taken at face value, it would mean that resources for athletic competition would be allocated among men and women in a strictly mathematical calculation that would, arguably, tear a hole in existing programs for men. The most notable effect would be on the revenue sports of basketball and football. When NCAA member organizations and the NCAA itself made these arguments, they were inevitably scorned by people who saw the expressed interests as chauvinistic, power-based, economic, and oppressive. Figuratively and sometimes literally, the enforcement of Title IX was cast as "women's rights" vs. the "all-male NCAA."

Ironically, even for women as the intended beneficiaries, the move to economic equality did not come without cost. Some members of the AIAW were particularly concerned that the implementation of strict economic equality with the male model NCAA would inevitably lead to a "modeling" that would disregard the AIAW's prior commitment to its educational model, which attempted to foster sport as an incident of a full academic and social experience, and not as an end in itself. One early example of this process occurred in the context of athletic scholarships. The AIAW did not permit the award of financial aid to a woman based on her athletic ability. This policy was based on the idea that athletic scholarships would tempt colleges and universities, as well as individual athletes, away from academic achievement. However, the AIAW was sued in federal court in 1973 by a tennis player in Florida who wanted to receive a scholarship for her sport and be permitted to compete in intercollegiate competition. Faced with litigation and with the impact of Title IX, the AIAW's Delegate Assembly voted to permit female athletes to receive financial aid. The controversy over financial aid split the AIAW at a critical moment in its existence, as suggested by a comment published in 1974 by Carole Oglesby, the President of the AIAW during 1972-73: "The AIAW, in its structure and function in the commitment seen of its officers, is devoted to dramatically increasing the athletic and other movement-oriented programs for women as part of the total diversification of life-style opportunities for females. Many women may not accept that this is so. The divisive effects of the controversy over athletic scholarships have placed AIAW often in an adversary position vis-a-vis women's political groups, numbers of students, some of the brightest most able women in the field. One may support the policies against athletic scholarships for women and yet be heartsick over the misunderstandings of interest and purposes which the policies fanned."

A further weakening of the bond that held the AIAW together occurred when the NCAA acted, at last, to do something about Title IX and the painful necessity of including women in sport. In 1975, the NCAA council introduced a resolution on women's athletics to its annual convention. The resolution requested a report and plan on the several issues involved in the administration of women's intercollegiate athletics at the national level, including a possible pilot program of national championships for women. When the resolution passed, the NCAA had taken its first step toward control of women's collegiate sport. Over the next several years, the athletic departments within the NCAA member institutions began to combine the men's and women's programs, which had the effect of weakening the autonomous control of women's programs by women. Finally, in October 1979, the NCAA appointed a special committee to consider possible accommodation of women's sports within the NCAA and to propose the development of appropriate programs and services. The committee decided that it was feasible to bring women's programs into the NCAA and recommended that it be done. In 1980 and again in 1981, the issue was presented to the voting representatives of the NCAA: Should the NCAA sponsor its own national championships for women? Among the inducements, the NCAA included a promise to subsidize team expenses for national championships; an agreement not to charge additional membership dues for the women's program; a statement that the women could use the same financial aid; eligibility and recruitment rules that applied to men, so that administration and enforcement would be simplified; and the prospect of additional television coverage for women's sports. By a narrow vote, the NCAA membership approved the resolution. That vote shouldered the

AIAW out of the way and marked its effective end. The organization was extended further life only long enough to witness a decline in its championships, the loss of sponsorship, and ultimately the loss of acknowledged purpose and function. While it might still have argued that its policies were a more respectful way to accommodate the diverse interests of women, the AIAW was an economic and organizational redundancy.

Writing in 1982, when the AIAW ceased operations except for the prosecution of an ultimately unsuccessful anti-trust lawsuit against the NCAA, Dr. Ann Uhlir, the executive director of the AIAW in its last three years, described the effect of the NCAA's decision to sponsor its own championships. "The NCAA, the organization that sought to dilute the impact of Title IX, had in three short years devastated the AIAW." To this she added a eulogy for the AIAW. "It assured student-athletes both vote and voice in all sports committees and major forums. It gave the nation the first and only bill of rights for student athletes, assuring protection for student rights and due process in balance with the rights of institutions of higher education." Finally, Dr. Uhlir surveyed the scene in 1982, and wrote dolefully, "The growth in women's collegiate sports has passed its zenith for the time. Although women comprise one-third of all college athletes, cutbacks—caused by ever-burgeoning costs of college sports—are being shared equally. And the independent voice of women has been stilled—now that the NCAA has rejected autonomy for women either within or outside the NCAA."

The AIAW was a noble undertaking. If one word characterized its mission, it would be balance. If one concept epitomized its challenge, it would be reconciliation. If one circumstance foretold its demise, it would be conundrum. Which way would you have it: compete or nurture? Is it possible to do both? Which way is glory?

In her 1974 article, Carole Oglesby described the tension that arose from competing values: "Another aspect which should occupy some effort is the redefinition of sport and athletics as a form of mutual self-development rather than symbolic warfare. Sport-as-battle is very familiar in forms as diverse as the terminologies and slang of sport (witness "killing" one's opponent, "smashing" the bird or ball, "wiping out" an opponent, and the like) and forms including the very form of sport itself. As examples, note the number of sports built around a theme of protecting one's home base or territory from incursion and, conversely, attempting to violate or take the opponent's space. For many reasons, sport-as-battle has a pervasive connotation of masculinity and exists as a domain into which women have tried [to move] most uncomfortably. And yet the agnostic ideal of Greek athletes (the well-spring of so much of Western sport) was rooted in the concept that only through the magnificence of one's opponent's struggle could winning provide ultimate meaning. Such a conception of sport cannot be dismissed as an idealistic absurdity."

The issues described by Ms. Oglesby are as time-worn as they are valid. What is the limit of competition? What is the purpose of sport? The AIAW had its day for women, short though it may have been. The day being extinguished, the memory lingers of a time when, at an institutional level, the essential questions were asked with seriousness of purpose. What are we doing? Why are we doing it? What is the value of what we are doing? What is the cost? Carole Oglesby once wrote that the AIAW was "a product and a producer of the two most characteristic, frightening, exciting aspects of society: liberation and change. It is the child and the mother of liberation and change in women's collegiate athletics." After 1982, mother and child were gone. Father was in charge.

TEN

Now give me a wise and understanding heart.

2 Chronicles 1
Solomon

These are the earliest generations of mankind, says the Book: Adam, Seth, Enosh, Kenan, Mahalalel, Jared, Enoch, Methuselah, Lamech, Noah, Shem, Ham, and Japeth. Several generations passed before the world got to Nimrod, who was said to be a great hero. After Nimrod, with the derisive meaning currently attached to the name, skip ahead a few generations, bring in a different author, choose a more recent reference book, and see what happens to the developing world. Who could be more reliable than James Joyce and what book more pertinent than Finnegans Wake? "The great fact emerges," says Mr. Joyce, "that after that historic date all holographs so far exhumed initialed by Haromphrey bear the sigla HCE and while he was only and long and always good Dook Umphrey for the hunger-lean spalpeens of Lucalizod and Chimbers to his cronies it was equally certainly a pleasant turn of the populace which gave him a sense of those normative letters the nickname Here Comes Everybody." Perhaps it is only a coincidence but beginning in 1973, Peter Tegen began putting together just such an assemblage (HCE). Like the great runner whose performance is the accretion of many runs, each one of which contributes something to the outcome but is distinct from any of them, Peter's success at Wisconsin is built of many single performers and performances, but it is the aggregate that impresses most. The line of his runners—his somebodies and everybodies that keep coursing through fields and slicing across finish lines—now stretches over three decades, a fact that tempts the weak-minded to refer to the Bible, and its predilection for names and lineage, and, of course, to Mr. Joyce and his endless Wake, which spun the concept and the personage of HCE. Now, of course, finicky readers will say: HCE was a man! which is true enough but he was merely a foil, wasn't he, for Anna Livia Plurabelle, the regenerative female who waked him to a new day? So: leave it there. It's all the same and altogether different. And that is the point.

At the University of Wisconsin, the everybodys began with Cindy Bremser, and then traced a bloodline through and including fine middle-distance runners like Rose Thomson, an eleven-time all-American who could run well at any distance from 800 meters through cross-country; Maryann Brunner, an eight-time all-American who led Wisconsin relay teams to several indoor and outdoor 4 x 800 meter national championships; Cathy Branta, an eleven-time all-American, winner of five NCAA titles, four TAC national championships, and a silver medal at the World Cross-Country Championships; and Katie Ishmael, a seven-time all-American. Despite the reference to genealogy, the process of taking those individuals (and others too numerous to list in the middle- and long-distances, and many more in the sprints, throws, and jumps) and building from them a consistent program was not, of course, biology. It was chemistry, the combining of elements over many years, precariously, sometimes one miscalculation shy of an explosion, but more often a propitious series of additions and multiplications creating energy in the first place and synergy in the next. Although occasionally an athlete came from a distant state or country to run for Wisconsin, Peter Tegen generally constructed his program from the clay that was available in the state of Wisconsin and

Cathy Branta (left) and Katie Ishmael (right.)
apply the pressure over the hill and field.

from neighboring states in the upper Midwest. He received young
women from towns and cities like Janesville, Wauwatosa,
Waukesha, Oconomowoc, and Chippewa Falls who had faith that he
could make them strong, fast, and calm in a crisis; young women
who asked him to make them what they ought to be, which is, what
they could be. Through the decade of the AIAW, during the uncertain years when the NCAA and the AIAW circled each other warily,
after the shuttering of the AIAW, and later when the NCAA assumed
control, Peter Tegen continued to build the program at the
University of Wisconsin. The Wisconsin women were in motion no
matter who organized the events.

Without putting too fine a point on it, it is easy to identify
in Peter Tegen some of the elements that make his teams successful

year after year: his ability to attract and retain able assistant coaches who believe in the program; the ongoing support of the administration at the University of Wisconsin; the pool of talent from which he draws; the strength of the Big Ten conference; the strong academic reputation of Big Ten universities generally and at Wisconsin specifically; and his own professional ability, including a thorough knowledge of the events, a special expertise in kinetics and human motion, a willingness to study the literature for helpful advice, a risk-taking temperament that permits him to try new things, an analytical mind, and an openness to confront error and to make corrections. However, similar elements are present at other universities than Wisconsin. They therefore do not entirely explain Peter Tegen's success. For better explanation, it is necessary to consider the intangibles, no less real for being beyond proof. Simply, Peter Tegen is a great coach because he possesses a personal magnetism that persuades his athletes that he can be trusted—with their talent, with their time, even with their lives. This quality, the communicated sense of trustworthiness, is characteristic of all great coaches, from Dink Templeton to Brutus Hamilton, Arthur Lydiard to Percy Cerutty, Waldemar Gerschler to Mihaly Igloi, Franz Stampfl to Jumbo Elliott, Pat Connolly to Ella Krzesinski. No matter how idiosyncratic any other aspect of personality may have been, the ability to evoke trust was (and is, for those still coaching) essential to healthy coaching relationships. Peter Tegen has that quality. He earns it through his seriousness of purpose and through his enthusiasm for the sport. He earns it by his confidence, and by his honesty with his athletes, and he earns it by his reliability. He also earns it by the satisfaction he takes in watching his athletes perform and by the pride he feels for them. Ultimately, there is in the relationship between Peter and his athletes a reciprocity in which the giving and receiving become interchangeable. As a result, when a Wisconsin athlete responds warmly to Peter's enthusiasm, she is finding the mirror of her own emotion. When she runs well for Peter, it is her own dream she pursues. When she places her trust in Peter Tegen, she is recognizing his trust in her.

The question of trust is raised first in college athletics when coach and athlete, coming from different directions, enter the bewildering world of recruitment. At the conclusion of the process the real question is: who do you trust? In Wisconsin's case, that world opened up for women track and field athletes in the academic year 1977-1978 when five athletes received partial scholarships for cross-country and a total of eight athletes received partial scholarships for track and field. In the 1978-1979 academic year, the first full scholarship was awarded to a University of Wisconsin woman track athlete, Pat Johnson, a long jumper, who won three national championships and was an all-American seven times.

The Scots and the Jews are cheap; the Irish are loutish drunks; the English are stiff and pretentious; the Italians are emotionally labile; the Spanish are hot-tempered; and the Germans are meticulous and calculating. Only it so happens that none of that is true about any national group, although it may be true of individuals within each national group; and it is equally true that any national group will include people who possess all of the stereotyped characteristics and many more. It is not hard, for example, to imagine a person of any heritage (American would be a good one) who is close with a dollar, drinks a good deal, ranges erratically between emotions, including hot temper, and yet, in more subdued moments, measures the opportunities sharply. What could be more pretentious? So it is that Peter Tegen, who ought to be meticulous and calculating because he is German, and, in fact, is meticulous and calculating so far as certain aspects of his training regimen is considered, rejects the stereotype when he recruits an athlete for his program. In the field of recruiting, Peter has few, if any, rigid criteria. Obviously, he appraises the athlete to determine whether she has sufficient basic skill so that, with work, she can become an athlete capable of competing in an ambitious Division I program. That evaluation does not, however, tempt Tegen to recruit only from the most accomplished high school athletes in the country. While he will take such an athlete if he thinks either that her current level is high enough to compete well or if he thinks she can improve, he is also drawn to less accomplished high school athletes. These are the women who have done moderately well but, in whom, he detects talent. The space between high school honors and ultimate potential is the headroom within which coaching and milieu can make the difference. More generally when considering an athlete, Peter looks for young women who believe in his program and want to attend the University of Wisconsin; he appreciates a good sense of humor as a hedge against the tough times that accompany any relationship; he tries to match the incoming woman with the other women on the team and with the coaching staff and its philosophy, so that the chemistry is good; he hopes the athlete will be likable; and he looks for the quality of the person taken as a whole. If he misses and brings a woman into the program who does not fit, who is not happy and makes the other people around her unhappy, he knows that it will be a long four or five years, a circumstance to be avoided if possible.

In the spring of 1984, Peter Tegen could feel satisfied by his progress as a coach and his program. Cindy Bremser was an international star who would qualify later that year for the Olympic team. And his team at Wisconsin was sprinkled with stars, the most prominent being Cathy Branta. A native of Slinger, Wisconsin, Branta was a junior at the University of Wisconsin and in the middle of an extended breakthrough that began with an eighth-place finish in the 1983 NCAA Cross-Country Championship and a third in the TAC Cross-Country Championship. The TAC finish earned her a spot on the United States national cross-country team to compete in the International Amateur Athletics Federation (IAAF)

Championship, where she finished tenth in the late winter of 1984. Returning to Wisconsin, Branta won the TAC indoor two-mile championship, and added the NCAA indoor 3,000-meter title before moving outdoors. Continuing her astonishing season, she won the NCAA outdoor 3,000-meter championship, finished fourth in the 1,500 meters at TAC, and almost made the Olympic team herself. She finished fourth in the 3,000-meter trial in a collegiate record of 8:49.94. While others might have been surprised by Cathy Branta's success in the academic year 1983-84, Peter Tegen was not. If anything, he thought that Cathy would have emerged a year earlier but for injuries. Patiently, he waited and when the injuries healed, he got Cathy back on track. He rationed her mileage, pointed her toward major competition, and rested her in smaller meets. As always, he gave her a detailed strategy for each important race. When people remarked on the variety of her tactical moves, Cathy pointed to Peter, "I have developed a lot of trust in Peter. He changes the tactics from race to race, which makes my strategy unpredictable for competitors and challenges me to try new tactics and improve as a racer." Peter accepted Cathy's credit and trust with aplomb. "Sometimes she thought I was crazy," he admitted, but she always accepted the strategies and she won with them.

Another established runner on the Wisconsin team in the spring of 1984 was Katie Ishmael, Branta's junior by one year. Katie was a high school student from Madison, Wisconsin, who enjoyed success at that level, and then transferred her talents to the University of Wisconsin. By the end of her sophomore year, she was already an all-American several times, was the Big Ten champion outdoors for both 5,000 and 10,000 meters, was second in the NCAA 10,000 meter, and was second in the Olympic Trials 10,000-meter exhibition—only an exhibition because there was no women's 10,000-meters in the 1984 Olympics, despite persistent protests, lawsuits, and pressure. In the Trials 10,000 meters, she ran a collegiate record

Peter Tegen

of 32:37.37. Ishmael also won the TAC national championship in the 5,000 meters in 1984. With Branta, Katie Ishmael formed a deadly one-two punch for the Wisconsin cross-country teams and for the distance events on the track. They were joined by other talented runners for the 1984-1985 season, including Birgit Christiansen and Kelly McKillen.

Meanwhile, Stephanie Herbst in the neighboring state of Minnesota was considering her future. Her father wrote letters to the University of Minnesota, hoping to entice that school to interest. Strangely enough, nothing happened. Many other colleges did show interest, which Stephanie found both flattering and a bother. She later said that during her entire freshman year in college, she regretted taking a scholarship because of "all the trouble I went through to get it." She was especially displeased that her preoccupation with college caused her grades to drop in the last months of high school. She was just too distracted and nervous to pay attention. She was also badly informed. When the letters poured in from colleges and universities, she had no way to distinguish the schools in which she was interested from those in which she was not. To learn more, Stephanie and her father packed up the car and went on a road trip. Her initial focus was Stanford, which had an outstanding academic reputation and a premier cross-country and track program for women. They went to take a look, but Stanford did not offer Stephanie a scholarship. Stephanie also seriously considered Arizona State, Northwestern, and the University of Missouri. At Mizzou, she was bothered when a coach said that, as a freshman, she would not be expected to challenge the first two runners on the team. The coach wanted only to take the pressure off Stephanie, to make her feel comfortable for a year while she acclimated to college academics and athletics, but Stephanie did not accept the help. She wanted pressure. She wanted people to rely on her. And she did not intend to defer to anyone, no matter how good they were.

Several college coaches warned Stephanie off the University of Wisconsin. They said that the program was "high pressure." They were talking to the wrong girl. Father and daughter added Wisconsin to their list, a decision made easier by Wisconsin's excellent business school. Having only flown over the state of Wisconsin in the past, Stephanie and her dad now stopped at Madison on the way to see other schools. Stephanie Herbst met Peter Tegen when she and her dad were on campus and was impressed. Although it was obvious that the Wisconsin women were serious about their sport, Peter said that he never pushed the freshmen. She would be expected to improve at her own pace but not be held back. Surrounded by national-class runners, coached by a proven commodity, she liked the sound of that. Peter also liked what he saw of Stephanie and what he heard from her. Later, he said, "I was completely fascinated by her as a person. That is very important. I think it is more important to find people who are interested in other people and sincere rather than finding the ones who are just athletically talented. You can't become a great athlete unless you have a great personality." While that last point is arguable, it shows the favorable first impression Stephanie Herbst made on her future coach.

The agreement was not sealed on the first trip to Wisconsin. Stephanie needed more time to think, and Peter needed to see more. He needed to see her run. It was one thing to have a string of Minnesota State High School Championships, it was another to have the talent the University of Wisconsin demanded. Peter did not visit athletes in their homes. It was intrusive and not his nature. He rarely went out of town to watch athletes run. This time, though, he did. On a cold, blustery day, he climbed in his car and drove north to see the young woman who had fascinated him in Madison. Arriving in Chaska, he attended a workout. Stephanie was impressed with Peter for coming up to Minnesota but she could not believe the day he picked. It was "horrible," she says and adds, "I thought, 'How can any coach be impressed with someone on a day like this?'" At the track, Peter remained aloof from the runners. He watched and timed an interval workout. Stephanie was, of course, nervous about his presence, but she was also having fun running with the boys. The wind was ripping across the field. The memory of the scene is still fresh in Peter's mind. "There were probably 30- to 40-mile-per-hour winds in the spring in Minnesota. And here was this young girl totally relentless—and when you talk to her and see her, that is the last thing you would expect. When I saw that, I was totally baffled. I said, 'She's got something!' I don't know what, but there was certainly some kind of tenacity visible throughout this workout. She wasn't putting on a show for me, I know that." As to Stephanie, she saw him timing her workouts and she ran a bit harder than usual to make the intervals fast enough to impress Peter. When she later remarked on this to Peter, he laughed. He had, in fact, been timing the rest breaks, and seeing how long it took her to recover between intervals. All the while she was running harder, she was extending the time it took her to recover, and just making things worse! She did not know that Peter was looking for the things she could not manipulate. He was looking at the way she moved on the track in order to assure himself that she was biomechanically sound. If she was, and if her cardiovascular and respiratory systems were strong as measured by an ability to recover between hard runs, and if her personality was open, and if she wanted to improve, he would have the base material he needed for championship running. By all these measures, the workout on the harsh day in Minnesota did the trick. Peter Tegen wanted the baffling young lady for his Wisconsin team.

The next job was to persuade Stephanie to attend the University of Wisconsin. Peter knew that most high school seniors have, at best, a vague familiarity with the good programs, and almost no data about the specific coaches with whom they may be working. To give Stephanie more information about Wisconsin, Peter invited her to make a formal visit to the campus. When she arrived, she spent time with Cathy Branta. Stephanie knew that Cathy was Wisconsin's top runner, and she might be cool to an incoming freshman; but instead Cathy was warm, engaging, and relaxed. Very down to earth, Stephanie thought, and she was sold. She accepted a scholarship to run for the University of Wisconsin beginning in the fall of 1984.

Stephanie had always run in the summer to prepare for the upcoming cross-country season, so she was ready to do the same before her first semester in college. Now, however, the summer running could not be characterized as "extra" or voluntary. It was expected of her. This made things different. As she says now, "I thought I'd be conscientious and do summer training. It was very important for me to do well for Peter. Very different from my high school coaches, I determined that it was important to make this man happy. Also, when you talk about a scholarship, you know you're

Many times a champion, Cathy Branta leads
a Wisconsin sweep in this race.

being paid so you don't want to come in and be a big disappointment." Good intentions or not, Stephanie was in for a surprise that summer. As she describes it, "I thought I was doing very well by continuing to run in summer, but because I had no idea what athletics in college was like, those summer runs were like a half-hour long and it wasn't every day and it definitely was not twice a day. And then halfway through the summer, we get this summer training and I was floored! Because I had intended to take whatever he did and add to it! Then I looked at it, and I actually talked to my dad and some other people, because I thought he must be showing us the worst, like 'they won't be able to do the whole thing; but they'll do a portion of it.' So I thought, if he said 45 minutes, he really meant a half an hour. Some days I would do the whole amount; other days, I'd do what portion I could." Only youth could begin with the intention to add distance to each workout, end up subtracting it, and accomplish the result so innocently.

After that confusing summer, Stephanie traveled to Madison, Wisconsin, for her first semester as a college student and her initial experience as a scholarship athlete. She says ruefully, "I arrived the first day nowhere near the shape I should have been." Whether that statement is true or not, Stephanie, in her anxiety, is the echo of every college freshman who preceded her, and the precursor of all who follow. Stephanie already knew what Doris Brown meant when she later spoke of the effect of a college scholarship, "If you are going to take something, you should be willing to give. It's a law of nature. If you're going to put yourself in the spotlight, you should accept what happens. It reflects on you, on your family, on your school, and on the sport." This is tough, plain talk, and the truth of it was already part of Stephanie's nature. She knew the deal. She would honor her obligations. So too would Peter Tegen. Doing so, they would learn together the breathlessness of steep ascent, more harrowing in some ways than a sharp fall.

ELEVEN

As I would not be a slave, so neither would I be a master.

Abraham Lincoln

Mr. Lincoln sits quietly on the University of Wisconsin campus, nicely situated to have a view of the city of Madison down the slope from his position. Campus ribaldry, standard fare from university to university really, is that he jumps up from his chair every time a virginal co-ed passes; and yet he remains still, ignoring the joke at his expense and refusing to be drawn into another controversy about morality, as he had been once before. He is pleased, is Abe, merely to have a place to rest. The city whose view he commands is reputed to be the best place to live in the United States, measured synthetically; and the university, whose approach he marks, is an outstanding example of public education, serving approximately 40,000 students each year. A major research center, the University of Wisconsin is well-known for its liberal arts department, where sociology, education, social work, psychology, political science, history, and public administration draw high national ranking; for its College of Agricultural and Life Sciences, always highly regarded; for its science programs, including computer science, biology, chemistry, and nursing; and for its business school, which is among the best in the nation in both undergraduate and graduate departments. These and a great number of other courses of instruction are conducted on a 900-acre campus, which itself is one of the most beautiful in the country. The campus borders Lake Mendota, which provides not only scenery but a variety of recreational options, including walking and jogging on the trail that runs the full length of the campus waterfront. The University of Wisconsin Arboretum, a nature study and hiking area, adds 1,224 acres of trails and field. All this, the size, the richness, the variety, the bewildering academic and social choices, the great spaces, staggers any incoming freshman with its implication. For Stephanie Herbst, coming from her high school of 800 students, it was something entirely new. If in high school she had been able to control her external environment, here she would have to turn inside for control—to screw herself tightly into selected places and to let the rest rush over and around her, unnoticed or ignored. In time, she might know the location and the purpose of Bascomb Hall, but she would be unlikely to learn that its architecture was Italian Renaissance or to value the use of stone, copper and concrete in a contemporary design; she would know that the Memorial Union was something special, but not glory in the great rathskeller, including its authentic beer hall with brick-vaulted ceilings, pillars, arches, and the view of Lake Mendota.

She would enjoy the terrace outside the Union, and sit occasionally, but she would not permit herself the luxury of lingering in consideration of the serious and mock-serious issues that occupy maturing students. She would see without noticing—at least in the first days—the visual diversity of the campus, its masonry and sandstone styles mixing the Renaissance Revival of Bascomb with the Victorian Gothic Revival of the Music Hall and the Romanesque Revival of the Science Hall, upon which a young Frank Lloyd Wright once worked. She would walk the lower campus without knowing that it was formerly the muddy, isolated scene of bonfires and romance in the days before, during, and after the apocalyptic years of the Great Depression, the prewar tension of the late 1930s and early 1940s, the war itself, and the tremendous growth and confusion that accompanied the veterans' return and the first wave of VA-financed university education.

She would not pause to consider the paved plaza, the benches, the clock tower, and the red granite fountain, nor to wonder how they came to be, nor from what idea or instinct or design they sprang. When registration came, she would join the chase for favored courses and professors. She would hope that she was doing the right things, but she would never be entirely sure. In the first days, only one fact pressed in upon her as a reality. She was in a big place with many people she did not know a long way from home with burdens she did not entirely understand, obligations she could not define, and expectations she could not control, even though they were her own. For protection, she had only the sense of herself, a careful boldness, and discipline. Eventually, she would measure this place. When that time came, she would do more. But for now, she would set a rigid priority of things that must be done day in and day out with no excuses. She would study and she would run. The rest would have to wait. People she might have known as friends would move past her. The girls would walk in clumps of four and five in the mile from campus to the Capitol and visit the restaurants and bars looking for the boys who were looking for them, but Stephanie would not be among them. Surrounded by 40,000 students, she would be alone. She would run and she would study. She had cast the die. "I'm going to be successful as a runner," she told herself, "and I'm going to be successful in school. And I will keep the whole rest of the world out, to focus on these two things, to make sure they happen." Many people may think it; some may say it, but Stephanie Herbst meant it.

She arrived at school about ten days before registration and the beginning of classes. She located Lakeshore Dorm, met her roommate, who was a volleyball player, and began the unsettling task of settling in. Running alone on campus, she came across three other women on the team who were also running. When they introduced her to Stephanie Bassett, another incoming freshman, Stephanie was already uneasy, feeling that "they" already knew each other and she was a stranger. To make matters worse, she struggled to keep up with them as they ran six or seven miles together. This was a scary time for Stephanie, and it did not take much to knock her back. In short order, she also faced her first formal meeting with Peter Tegen, the man she "needed to keep happy." At a full meeting of the track and cross-country teams, one of the assistant coaches spoke first. He was light-hearted, and the team relaxed and waited for the main event. When Peter did speak, the tone of the meeting changed abruptly. Cathy Bremser had once said that upon first meeting Peter, she was afraid of him, tipped slightly off balance by the German accent he still had in 1973. By 1984, the accent had softened but the essential man remained. In presentations to his team, he was direct, clever, possessed of a dry sense of humor, and capable of a winning charm.

When Peter talked to the team in 1984, some of his remarks were designed to amuse, but most were serious. He told the women plainly that this Wisconsin team would excel. In the fall, a national championship in cross-country was possible. They had the talent. He would prepare them to win. The rest was up to them. Sitting quietly with her unfamiliar teammates, Stephanie got the message immediately. It was time to get her act together, to get herself going, to get in shape. Looking around, she saw that the other members of the team heard the same message. They would respond to Peter's words the same way she would. Sadly, Stephanie guessed that the girls in the room would not be her friends. "That's not what this is all about," she said to herself, somewhat surprised by the force of the revelation and the impact it would have on her for the next four years.

Stephanie was young, and she was nervous. She was certainly intimidated, as she later admitted. It was possible that she misread the clues at the first meeting with her teammates, but she really did not think so. She had accepted a scholarship, as had many of the other women in the room, and it was time now to earn it. Peter did not say that, of course, but that is what she heard. She had to justify his faith. So did all the other women in the room. They were together as a team, yet pitched against each others as individuals. In that case, she was required to ask herself: in a world defined by competition, what was she worth? She was worth, she concluded, exactly what she produced on the field. So be it. From obligation and from pride, she would not flinch. "I made my decision; this is what I wanted, and now I will do what is required." As quickly as that, a young woman who only months before was pleased that her high school opponents wished her well before the state high school meet, now pushed even her own teammates away. Friendly but not friends, they would fight with her for a place in the top seven on the team, for esteem, and for Peter's approval. Joined with Stephanie's earlier decision to concentrate exclusively on studies and running, her characterization of the team's ethic and code of conduct was one more turn of the screw. Stephanie's world was contracting in almost direct proportion to the pressure she accepted. As each new opportunity repositioned itself as a threat, she closed off and squared up in order to protect herself from diversion and from harm.

Peter would later describe the extraordinary years of 1984 and 1985. There was an air of excellence in the program. Everyone knew that the teams would be successful, and everyone wanted to contribute. Stephanie Herbst was not the star of the team. Cathy Branta was the star. If she faltered, Katie Ishmael would pick up the load. And if Katie fell, the other excellent runners from the prior year—Kelly McKillen, Birgit Christiansen, and Sarah Docter— would step up. If further help was needed, it would probably come from Stephanie Bassett, who was the Junior National Cross-Country champion at 3,000 meters and an Indiana State High School champion in 1984. Although Stephanie Herbst was also a state champion, she had no national credentials. If any runner on the team was expected to wait her turn, it was Stephanie Herbst. Or at least that would have been the case but for two intangibles. The first was Stephanie's pure, untapped talent. And the second was her energy and initiative. From the very first day, she was driven to do well. She might accept initially that she was not the major contributor on the team, because she had no choice given the reality Cathy Branta created, but some day she wanted to be, and that made all the difference. Later, when the workouts with the team started, if she saw women running faster than she was, or doing workouts of greater volume or intensity, or speaking of higher ambitions, her reaction was to say, "Yes, I have to do that." In both workouts and races, she was impatient, pressing, pressing, pressing. She wanted to be a better runner immediately! The old expression is that you can see a distance runner coming from a long way off, referring to the fact that improvement in the distance events comes gradually as strength, speed, and experience increase. Stephanie Herbst wanted no part of that.

Stephanie now says that when she signed a scholarship with the University of Wisconsin, she hired Peter Tegen to make her the fastest runner she could be. If that is the case, she chose wisely. Perhaps no coach in America was better prepared to do as she wished. With Stephanie, however, he would not have an entirely free hand. Peter Tegen did believe, for example, in the adage that Stephanie Herbst rejected, the one that said that distance runners could be seen coming from a long way off. Given his preference, he would move an athlete slowly through the stages. Tegen often reminded fellow coaches that prime performances did not (or should not) occur until an athlete is in the middle-to-late 20s, and that it is a mistake to rush an athlete before he or she is ready, thereby threatening to end the career at 18. But even Peter Tegen is powerless in the face of nature, and Stephanie Herbst was a force of nature. In her development she would progress at her own pace, as Peter had promised when she was recruited, but her own pace would be very fast indeed. In some instances over the next several years, it would be faster than Peter would have chosen, and faster than he would have permitted had someone else's foot not been reaching for the accelerator. He was left, however, with the steering wheel, and that he held firmly.

At the heart of Peter's beliefs about middle- and long-distance running is that many accomplished athletes can handle the overall tempo of championship running; that most championships are won in the later stages of the races; and that, therefore, the ability to change pace and to sprint is critical to success. He is not an advocate of long slow distance running because he fears that any program directed to such a goal will succeed, which is, it will be likely to produce runners capable of running long distances slowly. For his part, Peter likes speed. Perhaps this is the result of his background as a sprinter, or an aspect of his nature, but more likely it is an appropriate recognition that in any sport, speed kills. Therein of course lies its paradox and its fascination because the reference to the murderous quality of speed cuts both ways. An attempt to develop speed that includes too much volume, or mingles speed work imprecisely with strength work, over-distance, or pure endurance exercises, is more likely to "kill" the athlete subject to the regimen than it is to promote improved performance. On the other hand, a properly applied program that leads to a healthy, fast runner "kills" the opposition. The separation between the two results is fine.

Peter's response to the challenge posed by speed is the dynamic running program. Peter's nemesis in running is the pattern that comes from repetition. As he said in one publication, "Running will create movement patterns, some good and some bad. Distance running is prone to creating dynamic stereotypes, or auto patterns, and we are fencing ourselves in with slow patterns and locked at one pace. This is not at all constructive. DESTROY THE PATTERNS!" Peter attempts to destroy the patterns by manipulating space, time, and force with accelerations, decelerations, surges, and shifts in tempo. His work is hard, but it is balanced, as when he refers to acceleration and deceleration in the same sentence, and when he reminds people moving toward top-end speed to "just touch it" and then come back down. His workouts, too, show the cautious balance that the development of speed requires. In a handout prepared for fellow coaches, Peter gives an example of workouts he might use for distance runners:

Some of the typical dynamic runs might look like the ones below. 1x10' or 2x5' would be steady state pace sections ('=minutes, "=seconds). The number in parentheses means the surge time after each of these sections. The run is continuous.

Early Fall: 1x10'(2'), 3x5'(1'), 5x3'(45"),
   1x5 (30") 5x1'(10"), 1x10'
Late Fall: 1x10'(1'), 2x5'(40"), 4x3'(30"),
   8x2'(20"), 5x1'(10"), 1x10'
Spring: 1x10'(45"), 2x5'(30"), 3x3'(15"),
   5x2'(10"), 10x1'(10") 1x10'

There are countless variations in designing a Dynamic Run. The examples above just happen to be about 60' long, but shorter versions of 25 to 30' in the beginning and later 35 to 50' are certainly very advisable. In general, there should be longer steady state sections in the beginning of the run followed by longer more moderate surges. Towards the end, the steady state sections become shorter with shorter but more intense surges to follow.

Essentially, the dynamic run is a highly structured fartlek effort. Although athletes report that the time goes by quickly when they are working through a "dyno," it is in fact a hard run and should be followed by a recovery day. To this, Peter adds a complement of track work, long running at Sunday pace, and strength work, which often includes hill running. For years, his teams used the apparently endless steps at the nearby Blackhawk Ski Jump. Promotional materials for the team often included a photograph showing a long row of Wisconsin women toiling up the ski-jump steps. The knee lift and the arm swing vary among the women but the heads are identically bowed from fatigue and concentration, and all the eyes look straight down at the next step, which would cause injury if it was missed.

In fact, the possibility of injury or of its near-relation, illness, haunts each of the athletes every day. It is there when they run before classes, there when they walk carefully from class to class, there when they break away in mid-afternoon and report to the track, there when they tentatively check the damage at the end of every workout, there when the evening meal comes, and there at the end of the day when they sleep. Let me remain uninjured, is the prayer. Always, they are watchful for the sore muscle that might pull, the sniffle that might be the first sign of flu, the shift in mood dangerous in itself, a pain in the ball of the foot that could presage a stress fracture, or perhaps just a slight tension in the arch that might announce plantar fasciitis. They are frightened by the possibility of injury or illness because, coming at the wrong time or costing them enough preparation, it can wipe out years of effort. It can make a special person ordinary. The task, then, is to reach as far as they can for fitness, yet remain healthy. Each of the women must run far enough, fast enough, often enough to become a champion, but they must not, any of them, run one step too far, or too fast, or too frequently, for fear of injury or illness—for fear that they will crack from the stress rather than adapt to it gradually and grow strong. To the athlete, there is only one certainty in any of this. The work they do will tantalize them, tease them, promise them success, and then it will injure them or make them sick. They will cross a line they did not see. The solution is clear enough. They must have someone watch the line for them, someone to warn them of the approach. They must have a coach. The coach will draw the line on which they walk: Do this much and you will win; do less and you will fail; do more and you will fall.

In turning to a coach for control and balance, athletes delegate a matter of great delicacy. The job requires a thorough knowledge of the practical, technical, and scientific facts and theories relevant to the athlete's event; extraordinary personal skills; and good judgment, particularly in defining the role of coach and athlete carefully and in maintaining appropriate boundaries. However, if one factor among the many does dominate a job description for coaches, it is an understanding of stress, in all its complexity. As Pavlov and Lesgaft and Selye, and perhaps Darwin in a different context, suggest, stress is the central fact in a runner's development. When it provokes adaptation, stress explains much of the progress that is made. When it overwhelms the possibility for adaptation, stress explains much of the illness and many of the non-traumatic injuries that cause all progress to cease. In that regard, stress is Dr. Jeckyl and Mr. Hyde, the good seed and the bad seed, and the cruel divorce springing from a loving marriage.

Accepting that the first task of a coach, like that of any other person, is to "do no harm," the second is to "do good things," which in context means to establish training conditions that permit an athlete to improve. The idea is for the coach to hit the perfect spot every time between health and harm. In order to achieve the result, the coach not only accepts certain stress within the program, he or she manufactures it in order to develop strength, or sharpen speed, or teach tactical responses, for example. At the same time, the coach attempts to eliminate or control all the other stressors that are inconsistent with adaptation, growth, and success.

In order to understand the magnitude of this part of the

coach's job, it is only necessary to examine a list of some (but not possibly all) of the potential stressors that might affect the performance of an athlete on a university scholarship: the physical and emotional toll of intensive and regular training; the athlete's personal ambition to succeed; a high level of anticipated or actual competition both within the team and from external competitors; financial dependence; peer and family pressure; media attention; the creation of a "public" self, which may diverge from the person's view of herself, and create unrealistic expectations and characterizations; motivations provided by and through coaching, including but not limited to the desire to please the coach and not disappoint her/him; academic pressure; social life and relationships, real or potential; lifestyle choices related to the accumulation of the above factors, and from interaction with them, such as sleep schedules, diet, personality changes, the construction of defenses to stressful situations (e.g., a person might rein in her emotional responses to maintain an even keel, and in doing so, increase the pressure rather than release it); physical and emotional fatigue; the enforced structure of workouts; physical injury; the threat of physical injury; success itself, including the discovery that it changes life less than one expected; the time limitations inherent in a college schedule; the ever-dwindling number of years available to accomplish the task at hand (i.e., the reach of a four- or five-year college career and the sure knowledge that the chance to compete at this level will not come again and therefore must be maximized); the burden of individual psychology, attitude, frame of reference, and character; the self-imposed pressure from such things as an athlete's internalization of a difficult situation; general relationships among and with team members and with athletes from other schools.

The coach absolutely controls none of the illustrative items on this list. The most that can be said is that the coach contributes to the scale and magnitude of some, but not all, of the stressors. In fact, many of the stressors are directly proportionate to only one thing: the desire of the individual to succeed as an athlete. If an athlete wants to succeed, and cares deeply for the achievement of that ambition, the other stressors will almost certainly be correspondingly high. Additionally, every athlete will make autonomous choices based on her own risk-benefit analysis: what must I do to get from "here" to "there," and how much risk is associated with the available courses? In an athlete's analysis, nothing is beyond question. The benefit one athlete perceives in a situation may mean nothing to another athlete. The risk in one situation may frighten one person away as it draws another closer to the challenge. In either instance, the calculation depends on the value system of the individual. From the core conclusion of what is valuable and what is not, the athletes will unfurl dozens of decisions every day. They will decide whether to do the morning run or to sleep in; if they do it, they will decide how far the run will be, how fast the tempo, whether they will attempt any aspect of dynamic running within it; they will decide whether to run alone or to run with a teammate, and if the latter is the choice, whether to race the workout or resist the temptation. They will decide what to eat, when to eat, even whether to eat, what to weigh, how much to care when disappointment comes, how much to sacrifice and how much to indulge. On major and minor issues, proceeding from the questions of "whether, where, and who" to "how" and "why," the athlete makes the call. Interested individuals, including family members, friends, administrators, and, prominently, coaches will help direct the analyses occasionally but that fact changes nothing: the conclusions must be those of the athlete. They are part of the intricate pattern of decision making that governs an athlete's participation in college sport.

An emphasis on the athlete's right to control the decisions of her own life, even if part of that life is spent on athletic scholarship, does not discount two other factors of similar weight and importance. The first is that the coach has a right to do his or her job. If the athlete's decisions are incompatible with that fact and with the welfare of the team, the coach may be required to address the situation. So long as the athlete understands that her decisions may have negative consequences, it is not unfair to impose those consequences if good faith permits the response. The second is that an athlete's right to make autonomous decisions works better when the athlete seeks to withdraw from the sport, or to modify her participation, and less well when she insists on doing things in the course of participation that could cause her harm. An athlete under stress can, for example, suffer physical injury, mental breakdown, depression, cognitive dissonance, academic failure, social estrangement, and conduct disorder, including any number of eating disorders. In the event the coach is persuaded that physical or emotional harm is threatened, the coach faces a quandary: whether to defer to the athlete—and honor her right to judge for herself the risk and benefit of her situation and her right to accept the losses that might be occasioned by her choices—or to intervene, to protect her safety above all else. Perhaps it is best to start with the recognition that any harm to an athlete is inconsistent with the athlete's success, which is the purpose to the relationship and its only justification, and inconsistent with the coach's position as an educator. These points may be sufficient justification for the coach to disregard the athlete's opinion. If the athlete wishes to train on her own, or to compete in events independently, that is her choice. But she does not have the right to require anyone else to bless the enterprise.

Even if the rights of the coach and the college administration are admitted, however, the timing and the act of intervention are not simple matters. When an athlete is making progress and sees the prospect for more, she may be difficult to dissuade. She may even hide the threat of injury or illness from her coach by not telling him the truth about her activity, her training, or its impact on her. That possibility, and others associated with the difficulty of knowing precisely what to do in each developing circumstance, are cautionary. They are a warning that the variables in any potential intervention are simply too complicated; the point at which danger presents itself too difficult for definition; the degree of danger too unpredictable for sureness in anything but intention. And while autonomy is not an absolute ethical value, it may create a presumption in favor of the athlete's choice. The possibility that harm may result from that choice does not transform the coach's deference from an act of good faith and respect into one of neglect, ignorance, or cruelty. In the best of circumstances, things will sometimes go wrong simply because ambitious athletes—the dreamers—take big risks.

If one factor minimizes risk and maximizes the possibility of success, it is the commitment of both athlete and coach to tell each other the truth. This obligation is not merely the avoidance of misrepresentation, it is the duty to tell the other party everything that bears on the decisions being made that affect the two of them. The coach, of course, honors the duty of truth-telling by conscientiously evaluating the ability of the athlete, by designing a program intended to maximize the athlete's potential, and by telling the athlete what is going on. The athlete bears at least as strong, if not a stronger, duty to tell the truth. The coach cannot do his or her job in a vacuum, and the information that needs to fill the vacuum in order for the athlete to succeed is extensive. The coach needs to know all the facts about an athlete's life that would reasonably be expected to affect training or racing. Imaginably, this could be seen as intrusive by the athlete. As a matter of propriety if nothing else the athlete must draw the line somewhere, but she should consistently remind herself to be fair to the coach to whom she has delegated responsibility. Further, the athlete must receive and act on information from the coach honestly. If she agrees to do a workout, she should do it as assigned and not with modifications that strike her as appropriate, or that her sense of duty or conscience tell her are necessary. If she does modify a workout, she should tell the coach what she has done so that the two can discuss the reason the choice was made and make adjustments in future training as might be necessary. It follows from the duty of both athlete and coach to tell the truth, as a predicate of trust, that they must communicate effectively. For the coach, it is the duty to explain and the duty to listen. For the athlete, it is the duty to speak when silence would be misleading.

Regrettably, some athletes, especially young ones, have difficulty speaking forthrightly to a person upon whom authority has been conferred. This is not necessarily a failure of trust or a breach of faith, although it may be. More likely, it is a failure of social skills and self-confidence. In the situation, small issues may go unaddressed in the press of other business, or on the theory that no news is good news; and they may grow until one day they rise up as crisis, too late for the solution that would have been easy if only anyone had known. Effectively, the failure of an athlete to talk to her coach, and the failure of a coach to notice and to force the issue, can mimic a failure of trust, a circumstance that leaves both parties wondering what went wrong.

Interestingly, Stephanie Herbst, for all her anxiety and her uncertainty, was fully conscious of the choices she exercised when she entered the University of Wisconsin, when she accepted Peter Tegen as her coach, and when she surveyed the room and realized that competition was the order of the day. She accepted the situation and threw herself into it. If it meant she must withdraw from other activities that she might otherwise have pursued, that was a fair exchange for the opportunity to run well. It was left only for Stephanie and Peter to negotiate the precise nature of their coach-athlete relationship. Here, too, Stephanie was in position to make a decision. She knew what she wanted from a coach, and she knew that she could get it from Peter. She made one choice, from which she did not intend to depart. She would not haggle. So far as it involved athletics, she would give him every authority. Stephanie had seen athletes and coaches collaborate on training and racing, and in doing so close the distance between them, but she considered those relationships soft. She rejected them. She wanted someone with knowledge and experience to tell her what to do. While she might from time to time raise questions or seek confirmation, she would do what was asked of her for so long as the relationship endured. The structure that Peter provided could have bothered other athletes, but for Stephanie it was a relief. Without intending offense, it might be fair to say that she had the sporting temperament of a greyhound. She was hair-trigger sensitive, intensely focused, and nervous about her success even as she strove toward it. Later, Peter would say that "with high-strung athletes, they all have to worry about their own lives. If they feel comfortable with a program, with a coach, I don't think they mind putting their fate in the coach's hands and let him or her worry about what should be. That's the way it should be. That's what they're paying me for." Stephanie accepted that view unequivocally. She described her position in dramatic terms: "If Peter said something, it was not worth rethinking the issue. That was a decision that was a lasting decision."

As a matter of sexual politics, there is something disquieting about the prospect that a man is given complete and total authority by a young woman in matters that are of primary importance to the woman and of only secondary importance to the man. The situation has a Pygmalion quality to it, a sense of patriarchy and authoritarianism that is archaic. Recognizing that much in the relationship between the scholarship athlete and the coach is inherently coercive, it remains possible that the woman in the situation is, in fact, exercising a choice about rights and interests she owns and controls. In that event, the decision and the effect is a closed matter between two people. It is not for others to color it with social policy. Furthermore, the relationship may be recast, and the social implication diminished, by defining it in the specific context of coaching rather than by reference to gender. Purely as a matter of coaching styles, the relationship Stephanie chose with Peter Tegen has strong historical precedent. By reputation, if not in reality, most university coaches worked with their male athletes from a position of unquestioned authority until the liberating 1960s. Even in those later years, however, change came hard. The idea of negotiating toward consensus was only slowly accommodated by many university coaches, who were not accustomed to challenges to their authority. Moving off campus, the coaching style of Mihaly Igloi illustrates a coaching method in which control vested predominantly, if not entirely, in the coach. Igloi enjoyed international success in Hungary as the coach of champions like Istvan Rozsavolgyi and Lazlo Tabori; but he was required to leave Hungary after the Communist crackdown on that country in 1956. Arriving in the United States, he continued to coach fortunate athletes, including the world's first indoor four-minute miler, Jim Beatty, and 1964 Olympic 5,000-meter champion Bob Schul. Jim Beatty described his coach in revealing terms: "As we talked he told me, over and over, shaking his finger at me, that it would be difficult. I would be running twice a day, twenty miles a day. He would drive me. 'Every day hard training must make,' he said. Then he agreed to take me on. On my first day of training, Igloi explained things. 'Must not discourage, must encourage. Must be patient.' He is patient and painstaking, assigning programs differently for each runner. And he has a brain like a Univac. At our daily workouts, he knows all, sees all, and plans all. Most of us in the club work out twice a day, before dawn and again after dark on weekdays. I'll walk up and he'll yell, 'Ah, Jim, finished warm-ups, yah. Then do 10 times 100 yards easy speed, and five 100 yards shakeup speed. Then three 440s, good swing tempo. Two miles 880 easy speed, then 220 jog. Sixteen times 150 hard speed.' I go do what he says and go back for more instructions....Igloi alone decides when, where, and what I will run. Once he has made up his mind and planned the training schedule for specific competition he keeps to his plan."

In another article, Beatty recounted his experience at the 1956 Olympic Trials when, before being coached by Igloi, he ran his race hundreds of times in his mind before the actual event. He showed up on the day too exhausted to compete and was well beaten. After Igloi agreed to coach him, that would not happen. "Now I relax," Jim said, "and let Igloi worry about the race I should run." The narrative provided additional insight into the method and the man; "Mihaly Igloi does not worry; he plans. With the precision of a man feeding data into an IBM computer, the coach studies the competition, the conditions, the warm-ups. Then, ten minutes before the starting gun, Igloi tells his runner what pace he should run for every quarter-mile. Then it's up to Beatty, the human machine, to deliver."

Another coach with a reputation for precision and command was Woldemar Gerschler of Germany. Gerschler was a scholar in physiology who is said to have "codified" interval training in the days before World War II. He is best known as the coach of the revolutionary 400- and 800-meter specialist, Rudolf Harbig. Harbig broke the world 800-meter mark by 1.8 seconds in 1939 when he recorded 1:46.6. Harbig's record would remain good for 16 years, until it was beaten by Roger Moens of Belgium, who was also coached by Gerschler. Harbig and Moens benefited from work that was varied, sophisticated, and intense. As to Harbig, a description of his training in Fred Wilt's book <u>How They Train</u> includes the following illuminating detail: "Harbig was coached by Woldemer (sic) Gerschler. His strength was in his iron willpower. His personal life had no shadow, and he kept no secrets from his coach." If a coach is to control the training of an athlete absolutely, he must know absolutely everything that is relevant to the experience. England's Gordon Pirie was another athlete grateful to receive the assistance of Waldemar Gerschler. "His effect on me," Pirie once noted, "was to take from my shoulders the enormous responsibility for my training which I had borne so far alone. I didn't know what I was doing until I met him." Gerschler's legacy to running is the category of training referred to as "Gerschler Interval Work," which is characterized by a high number of repetitions run with short recovery intervals, a regimen that heightens the need for a coach who is intricately involved.

Whether the example is from American universities or from private associations like those of Igloi and Gerschler, the prerequisite is that the athlete must enter the relationship voluntarily. The transfer of authority from the athlete to the coach is at the heart of every coaching relationship except those that arise from totalitarian regimes. A particularly good description of the critical transaction is given by Peter Coe, the father and coach of two-time Olympic gold medalist, two-time Olympic silver medalist, and record-smashing middle-distance runner, Sebastian Coe. "You can't drive an athlete," Peter Coe explained. "What happens is, if he chooses you and accepts you as coach, you coach at his consent. It is what he is prepared to consent to, and Seb's consent is total inside the area for which I am given charge."

So it was with Stephanie in the fall of 1984 as she evaluated the situation on the University of Wisconsin team and made her choices. The "area" for which Peter Tegen was given charge included all those matters that were relevant to Stephanie's training and racing. Within that area, her grant of authority to Peter was total.

TWELVE

While we have land to labour then,
let us never wish to see our citizens
occupied at a work-bench, or twirling a distaff.

Thomas Jefferson

The uninvited image that comes to mind when considering Stephanie Herbst on the first day of practice at the University of Wisconsin is of a young woman holding a nail and a hammer. She is confronted by hard wood and is asked to drive the nail into the wood, one minute choking up and the next minute grabbing it at the end, the task being to drive the head of the nail straight into the wood. If she missed, and bent the nail, she would start over. And if she got the nail smartly hammered into location, she would be given another of an unlimited number of nails, and asked to strike them down. On second vision, the idea of Stephanie and all those nails is simply too depressing an image, all the darker for the recognition that Cathy Branta would be there by her side, with about eight nails already safely completed and pounding away at another one, and Katie Ishmael, too, making steady progress.

Anyway, the whole picture is wrong, emerging only because it captures the incessant demand of distance running, the idea that a runner hammers every day, and that every day brings the risk of a blow that hits the target off center and ruins the whole thing; and it picks up the fact that for every nail that goes in, another is presented, and another after it, the next hope and the next dream, distinguished by sequence but mechanically alike. The work is always hard. That fact never changes. But where in all that is the satisfaction that running regularly and well brings? Where is the sense of personal freedom, growth, adaptation, and pure joy that rigorous training and competitive racing brings? Where is the life in a hammer, a nail, and hard wood? Missing entirely, and therefore inadequate. But, the hammer and nail failing, what image should carry the reader into Stephanie's freshman year?

The new vision should be pastoral; it should permit the runner to breath clean air, to experience growth, to enjoy the seasons of life, to see new things born. The clue is in the name: Herbst. In German, "Herbst" means autumn, the season of harvest. In that cycle, the cycle of planting, nurturing, harvesting, and reward, one can find much of what is good in running. Running well is an art meant to enrich life. If it is pattern, it is not John Henry but John Donne, meter and rhyme and the elements of song and poetry. "While the earth remaineth, seed time and harvest," according to Genesis 8:22, or something equally encouraging. Maybe not? Is this image too far the other way, too far from the hammer? Perhaps, then, for satisfaction, somewhere between the two images is the reality of running for a living, whether on a college scholarship or in open competition: the athlete unavoidably doing repeated tasks—running long runs at cadence, lifting weights, doing various exercises, stretching, doing repeated intervals on the track or the Wisconsin dyno on the trails—but hoping always to hold the meaning of the work, and to know that the possibility for accomplishment is buried within it. Whatever the case, let us at least admit that at some obscure place in the distance between the two images, the nail and the seed, Stephanie was standing alone in the fall of 1984 and readying herself for the signal: Begin.

At any given time the cross-country team at Wisconsin would include fourteen or fifteen women, but perhaps eight were candidates to represent the school at major meets. Cathy Branta and Katie Ishmael were, of course, among the best runners in the country. They were correspondingly serious about the work they did. Kelly McKillen and Birgit Christiansen were also talented athletes. While they would laugh and relax off the track, the two were conscientious about the workouts and cared deeply for the results, either good or bad. Holly Hering was a sophomore. She was a good runner, of course, or she would not have been on the University of Wisconsin women's team, which was of the highest order. Holly, however, had additional skills. On occasion, she could light an entire workout on fire merely by announcing to the group that "today, I'm going to beat you, and you, and you!" Of course, the two Stephanies, Herbst and Bassett, had no idea what was going on. When Holly, for example, announced her targets for a workout, Stephanie Herbst would just close off, get very quiet and reserved, and batten down the hatches.

The workouts in the cross-country season varied according to the time of the year and the requirements of the team, but had a regularity to them:

Monday:	Intervals or 20 to 25 minutes of steady-state running
Tuesday:	65 minutes
Wednesday:	A hill workout, sometimes on the ski slope
Thursday:	Dynamic run alternating hard/easy minutes and seconds
Friday:	Intervals or light workout of three miles and some strideouts if a meet was scheduled the next day.
Saturday:	Race or a short, harder run of approximately 25 minutes
Sunday:	A long, building run

To this, the women customarily added a run in the morning, weight lifting, stretching, and exercises. From these workouts, from what Peter said, and from what the other women were doing, Stephanie soon lost the illusions of the summer. Peter really did mean it when he said one hour and five minutes! Now, with the full weight of her scholarship and with the pressure to do well that came from herself, from her teammates, and from her association with a quality program like Wisconsin, Stephanie went back to her summertime ambition to do more than was required. Over the next year, for example, she increased the Sunday run to two hours. When the team ran together, she competed as effectively as she could with all the runners in terms of pace and intensity. When she had a good day and stayed with Branta, Ishmael, McKillen and Christiansen, she felt good about it. "Just to be in practice, to be running with them is great. They are so good and when you're keeping up with them, you really get a boost." She did have trouble on the hill workouts. Lean with long levers, she simply was not built for that kind of running. As a freshman, it wasn't necessary for her to lead the hills (that would come later), so she suffered from the middle of the pack. Stephanie's introduction to Wisconsin was further aggravated by the fact that she did not enjoy cross-country. She did not like the crowds, the rush for position, the bumping and jostling, the hills, the rough, uncertain terrain, and the unusual sharp turns. She preferred to open up her smooth, steady stride, and let it flow. Cross-country was the wrong sport for that approach. Over time, Stephanie would also recognize that cross-country stole something valuable from her. It took time away from her that, absent competition, could have been used for preparation, for planting the seeds that would flower during the indoor and outdoor track seasons. In effect, runners were required to plant and harvest in the same season every fall. Having done so, they were required—at least to some degree—to do the same thing in the two seasons that followed.

Nonetheless, Stephanie's life at the University of Wisconsin became routine. Awakening at 7:00 a.m., she would run four to five miles before her first class. After classes, she went to practice, where she would join the other women crowding around the bulletin board to see what workout had been posted. She would do whatever was listed and then might also lift or stretch, perhaps see a trainer if that was necessary. In the evening, she would study before going to bed early. Her eating habits during the first semester were casual. At slightly more than 5' 8" tall and weighing approximately 120 pounds, she did not worry much about calories and fat. Although it was obvious to everyone that there was a correlation between weight and fitness, and between good running and weight, however arguable the calculation and the social implications may be, the school did not institutionalize its interest in the weight of its athletes. Calipers were used once or twice a year as a rough guide to percentage of body fat, but the women were not weighed and their weights were not recorded, a practice that did occur at other schools. At Wisconsin, the women weighed themselves. Stephanie did not even keep track of her weight. She would later say that she had "the worst diet in the world" her first semester. In fact, she loved to "have something really sugary before practice. It gives me a great feeling, and I'm really hyper during my workout." In time, Peter would describe Stephanie's attitude and aptitude toward training in a highly particularized way, "She has a rare quality in an athlete. She can focus so much. She can concentrate so much. She is so relaxed. She wants to notice what is important to the coach—to run fast, place high, help her teammates, or whatever. It would not be enough to say, 'Just go out and have fun.' She would not just compete and take it lightly."

But Peter was not aware of these qualities early in Stephanie's enrollment. In the first place, this was because Stephanie did not talk about her goals, and it wasn't easy for Peter to know what she hoped to achieve. In the second place, however, this was because Peter was preoccupied with people who were first in line for his attention. Although Peter was good about extending his attention to everyone on the team, he quite reasonably concentrated more energy on the lead runners, the people who could carry Wisconsin to a national championship. In the fall of 1984, that meant Cathy Branta. Secondarily, it meant Katie Ishmael. The situation left Stephanie with ambition. "If I only get good enough, I can have that kind of personal attention," she thought.

Peter's occupation with Cathy Branta and Katie Ishmael was rewarded in Stephanie's first cross-country season. The season belonged first to Katie and then to Cathy, and finally to both of them and to the team. When the season started, Cathy was tired. She had an iron deficiency. While dealing with that she ceded the first position to Katie, who beat many of the best runners in the nation, including Cathy, when she won the Burger King Invitational 5,000-meter cross-country race. On that day, Katie broke away from the University of Missouri's Andrea Fischer during the final 2,000 meters and won by more than 6 seconds. Fischer was second, 4 seconds ahead of Shelly Steely from the University of Florida. Cathy Branta, having been overtaken late in the race by Steely, finished fourth, just ahead of the premeet favorite, Kathy Hayes of Oregon. In a ten-team competition that featured Wisconsin, Oregon, Missouri, Brigham Young, Florida, Kansas State, Iowa State, Tennessee, Minnesota, and Georgetown, Wisconsin won easily, 77 to 96 over Oregon, the team that had been top-ranked in the country. Peter was thrilled for Katie and proud of her run, saying, "I never expected Katie to do this. She was absolutely fantastic." Stephanie's contribution to the day was 21st place. At that, it was a very good day for Stephanie because it was one of the few occasions she managed to get in front of Birgit and Kelly, who finished 23rd and 28th respectively. Usually, Stephanie ran behind Birgit and

Katie Ishmael enjoys a moment to herself
far ahead of the chasing pack.

Kelly, repeating the pattern from high school in which she deferred
to a pecking order once it had been established.

As the season advanced, however, Cathy Branta re-
emerged. She (and Wisconsin) won the Big Ten title, qualified easily in the regional meet, and headed to the national championship
meet at Penn State with a chance to win. The University of Oregon
was the defending champion. Oregon arrived in University Park,
Pennsylvania, with another good team, including Kathy Hayes, who
had finished third the year before, and Leann Warren, a middle-distance runner with extraordinary range who had missed the prior two
seasons to injury. North Carolina State and Stanford also entered
good teams. Either could win, if everything broke just right. Not that
any of the various possibilities bothered Cathy Branta, who carried
Wisconsin's hopes. The night before the race, her freshman roommate watched Cathy in admiration and amazement. "It was kind of
weird," Stephanie said, "because I was very nervous, but Cathy was

very calm even though she was one of the favorites to win. She just sat there on her bed, eating cookies, and watching TV. I knew I wouldn't be able to sleep that night, but she just sat there eating cookies." It was a temperament that Stephanie would come to admire more and more over the years.

On race day, the day after the night Stephanie did not sleep while Cathy slumbered, Stanford got a bad break when one of its leading runners, Cory Schubert, went out with an injury suffered just before the meet. Oregon got an even more serious break when the starting line arc was mismeasured, adding 30 yards to the route its team members ran. Wisconsin meanwhile exercised its will. On the hilly, snow-dusted course, in a race run in near-freezing temperatures, Cathy Branta permitted Stanford's Regina Jacobs to lead the first mile. She kept a close eye on familiar adversary Shelly Steely, who shadowed Jacobs, and she waited. Farther back, the Oregon women struggled mightily to close the 30-yard gap the start cost them. Instead of racing with the field, they were chasing it. As a result, the Oregon women could not contribute to, much less control, the tempo. On an uphill spot just past the two-mile mark, Branta struck. No one could tag her and she surged toward home, drawing on strength that would also win her the open TAC championship several days later. As Cathy extended her lead, Katie Ishmael did her part. She stuck with the leaders and prepared to sprint with a field that, at the finish, would find the third through the twenty-fifth placers packed into a 30-second span. She needed to be in front of as many of those people as possible. Quickly in Katie's wake came McKillen and Christiansen, also positioned for top-25 finishes, and doing just what Katie was doing. They were steeling themselves for what lay ahead, each of them hoping to find the courage and the strength to run the whole distance and to finish hard all the way through the chute. Somewhere in the pack was Stephanie Herbst, a frail freshman contesting an event she did not like, over hills that did not favor her, in snow-covered, freezing conditions much like those that had caused her so much grief in the state high school meet only two years before. She counted, as she well knew. She was the fifth placer in a championship often decided by the fifth position. What a situation! Pressing along, carried and pushed, trying to keep her stride under her and not out front, searching desperately for one more reservoir of strength, she could not allow herself an instant's weakness, not a second of doubt. This was a chance to show that she belonged. And if she failed? The consequence was too awful to ponder. My God, what a clutter the entire event had turned out to be, runners on all sides, and hardly room to breath. Great runners were adrift behind Stephanie, struggling with problems of their own, Chris Curtin and Ceci Hopp of Stanford, Louise Romo and Kirsten O'Hara of Cal-Berkeley, Carey May from Ireland and BYU, Oregon's promising middle-distance runner Claudette Groenendaal. How tempting it was to sift back through the pack and join them. And nearby, Anne Schweitzer of Texas was so close Stephanie could feel the weight of her, and just there in front, Annette Hand running for Montana State.

When the finish line finally opened up in front of Wisconsin's women, they gathered and sprinted. They would leave no doubt of their intention or their courage. Composed, with more to give if necessary, Branta finished first in 16:16. Cathy was 7 seconds ahead of the University of Florida's Shelly Steely, 14 seconds ahead of third placer New Zealand's and Oklahoma State's Christine McMiken, and 18 seconds ahead of Regina Jacobs, Stanford's first finisher. Only Tina Krebs of Clemson separated Jacobs from Katie Ishmael, who was sixth in 16:38. In the increasingly bunched field, the women were like war planes returning from a fight, all of them low on fuel and headed to the flight deck into which they would bounce crazily before coming to rest side by side, so close that they touched, their mutual support being the only safety from collapse. In the chaos, Kelly McKillen lunged across the line in 17th place, sharing the identical time of 16:57 with two other runners and just barely avoiding six others who finished in the next 6 seconds. Behind them, Birgit Christiansen arrived in 28th place, jammed in the middle of a thick pack, everybody sprinting for the line without knowing, fully, whether it mattered or not, and not really caring one way or the other, in fact half hoping that it did not matter, that something else had happened—something beyond their control, something far away—that something or anything had happened on the other side of the course or here in the chutes that made what they did meaningless. With her own thoughts, Stephanie was still on the course when Birgit finished and began moving unsteadily through the ropes, but Stephanie was closing fast and she was not alone. With seven runners in the second or two on either side of her and no margin of error, she finished 13 seconds later, contesting every inch and every place. She finally controlled 45th place overall. With five runners in and the race continuing behind them, one frantic question remained unanswered if you were a Wisconsin fan. Where was Stanford? Who was Stanford's fourth? Where was she? Where was fifth? Were they in? Soon enough, they were all in, the course was empty, and it was time to tote it up. All that effort, the tension and the pain, the anxiety, the love and affection for each other and the day, was now a simple question of mathematics. By the numbers, Stanford was second. Wisconsin was first, and all the women of Wisconsin were skipping a ring-around-the-rosy together, Stephanie newly among them, a hair-bobbing, arm-entwined celebration to mark the University of Wisconsin's first national championship in women's cross-country. Peter was, as he had every right to be, exultant. "Can you imagine four all-Americans and a national championship?!" he exclaimed.

Perhaps no one noticed. Four all-Americans. Even as she joined the team by contributing her fifth place, Stephanie Herbst was excluded from them. She was happy to be part of the team, and she shared in the excitement of the victory, but it was not in her nature to accept minor place. She needed to do more. It was time to step it up again. The only problem was that she didn't know what to do. She only knew that she was disappointed in her contribution during the cross-country season. She did not think she was doing enough. "I had this feeling inside: Wait a minute! Why am I here? Why am I not winning? I've always been the one who's winning. I always felt that I had the ability to do it. Something must be wrong." She would, therefore, set out to discover the "thing" that was wrong and she would fix it.

THIRTEEN

It was a bright cold day in April, and the clocks
were striking thirteen.

1984
George Orwell

This time it is not nails and hammers, not autumn and harvest. It is winter. It is the still, deep water beneath the river of thin ice covered by new snow. It is the danger that a traveler crossing the river on foot never sees, or, seeing, disregards. It is the guide too far away to make the decision. It is caution, expedience, and ambition jammed into the same, tight space. It is the situation that confronted Stephanie Herbst and Peter Tegen when she went to him and asked how she might improve. After talking about her general condition and his satisfaction in the progress she was making, he did ask a couple of tentative questions—in a manner Stephanie says was "very understated." He asked her what her diet was like and whether she thought she could lighten it up. He did not press the matter, nor did he give her specific advice. His point, understood by both athlete and coach, was only that if she was lighter, she might improve.

All men and nations eat too much, Paavo Nurmi is reputed to have said, and for that reason they are not fit. In stating his view, Nurmi anticipated current opinion, especially as it pertains to distance running. For example, Ernst van Aaken, M.D., a well-known coach of such athletes as the rail-thin Olympic medalist Harold Norporth (sometimes called the human skeleton) and a man who helped popularize running for both men and women, once said that for success in the sport "the most important thing is weight. In the future, it'll be the person who has a large heart and the least weight who does best. It doesn't matter so much how much is muscle and how much is fat. It's mainly a matter of weight. Everybody is trainable. Everybody can bring their weight down, and everybody can train their heart. So everybody can bring themselves closer to this ideal." Popular and scientific literature confirms the basic notion that a runner who is light has an advantage over an athlete who is heavy although many experts place considerably more emphasis on percentage of body fat than on weight itself. Reference to percentage of body fat is especially prevalent with women because "when women train, they gain muscle mass, which is denser than fat. It takes up less space but weighs more. So as many women become fitter, they feel leaner. Their clothes become looser, but they may weigh as much or even more than they did before they started to train because their body composition—the ratio of muscle tissue to fat within their bodies—changed along with their weight." Dr. Myra Nimmo, an authority on these issues, also describes body composition rather than weight as the factor that most affects performance: "Endurance running has been shown to be closely linked to body composition; the greater the relative fat the poorer the endurance performance and it has been suggested that endurance performance is hampered if body fat is greater than 10 percent. This represents a substantial decrease in body fat for women competitors and although there are some reports of female distance runners with body fat percentages as low as 6 percent the majority of female endurance athletes will still be carrying more fat than male endurance athletes."

The advantage from a low-fat body composition comes from an enhanced ability to take in and use oxygen and from increased biomechanical efficiency. As to the relationship between oxygen uptake and body composition, Dr. Peter Snell and Dr. Robert Vaughan wrote in an influential article that "the test for maximal oxygen uptake has limited value in predicting performances...The oxygen uptake expressed in ml/kg/min will change with fluctuations in weight. Trying to maximize this figure is often where runners encounter trouble. As weight decreases, oxygen uptake increases, and performance improves. The athlete assumes 'you can't be too thin or too rich.'" Doctors Snell and Vaughan also warned, however, of the consequence that comes from accepting that view: "In cases where the athlete is amenorrheic (ceasing of the menstrual period) there exists a marked decrease in calcium absorption by the bone, often resulting in iron depletion and osteoporosis, neither of which aid performance. However, by the time either condition is manifested, it is too late for a quick reversal and years may be lost to injury or chronic fatigue. We are not aware of the problems associated with being too rich." Further the two said, "each individual has an optimal body weight and body composition for peak performances. The problem is to determine what that individual's figure should be... Certainly, no athlete in our present study ran PRs (personal records) with a body fat higher than 11 percent. For the most part, peak performance occurred with body fat readings between 6 percent and 8 percent. There is certainly a question whether elite female distance runners can maintain low body-fat readings for extended periods without negatively impacting their health. Those who are not genetically predisposed to leanness may resort to inappropriate and dangerous behavior (bulimia and anorexia) to maintain the low weight necessary for peak performance."

These references are not a survey of the literature. They are merely a starting point for analysis. That starting point is the confirmation that peak athletic performance by distance runners, male and female, is integrally related to weight (in the opinion of some) and body composition (as a matter of agreement). The next step is to

recognize that an athlete's decision to lose weight or to lower percent body fat carries risk; and that the risk for women may be higher than it is for men because it is relatively more difficult for women
to reduce body fat. The most frequently mentioned disorder related
to low body fat is amenorrhea, which is also affected by diet, the
intensity of training, and by the workload itself. At least one study
also suggests a relationship between athletic amenorrhea and major
affective disorders, including depression and the eating disorders.
Furthermore, amenorrhea may be a factor in loss of calcium and in
related structural weakness. The most frequently mentioned disorders related to diet (as opposed to body fat) are anorexia, bulimia,
and a variety of other eating disorders.

Although there is no direct relationship between running
and any of these disorders, some would argue that the pressure to
succeed is a risk factor in their development. A 1986 survey—which
is, a year at the heart of Stephanie's tenure at the University of
Wisconsin—revealed that 32 percent of female college athletes used
techniques such as self-induced vomiting, laxatives, diet pills, and
diuretics to keep their weight down. The study found that the groups
most likely to use the techniques were gymnasts (74 percent), field
hockey players (50 percent), and long-distance runners (47 percent).
Liz Natale, who competed at the championship level for the
University of Tennessee and the University of Texas in the middle
and late 1980s, was said to believe that during her years, eating disorders—either anorexia or bulimia—were considered a given
among runners, a kind of inside secret. "Some would take diuretics
before the weigh-in," she said. "Everybody talks about it because in
Division I, it's a business. So you'll do anything that you think will
make you run faster." To the extent that the characterization is accurate, some people explain it by referring to the athletes themselves.
Dr. Jack Wilmore, a physiologist at the University of Texas, once
made the argument. Admitting that eating disorders occur in the

general population, he nonetheless contended that the personal characteristics that may create them are more prevalent in athletes. "In almost any of the elite athletes," he said, "the presiding psychological profile shows that all are perfectionists, and everything is done in precise detail. Everything is black and white, total control. Being elite puts them into a higher risk category." Touching upon the psychiatric concept called "denial," which aggravates risk because the patient fails to accept the illness and the need for treatment, Dr. Wilmore noted one national study in which no "frank eating disorders" were identified, but in which two women from the study were hospitalized within six months of completing the questionnaire.

In many studies or discussions of disorders prevalent among women distance runners, there is the suggestion, if not the overt statement, that the coaches need to do more, to be more active in working with the athletes. At the least, they should not press them to lose weight beyond reason and safety. Coaches need particularly to be aware of the messages they send. A second athlete who competed in the 1980s at Texas, a woman who requested anonymity when she spoke about this issue, said that, "The main thing where coaches come into play is putting a big stress on being thin. It's not like they say 'get strong, work hard,' just 'you've got to be skinny.'" That message is not fine enough and presumably most coaches recognize today the need to present a more balanced view of weight, percentage body fat, and performance. To this, however, is added the fair caution that what the coach says and what the athlete hears is often discordant; that the line between "good"—defined by the desire to improve performance—and "bad"—legitimate desire given way to excess—is often imprecise; and that quite often the process of manipulating an athlete's body has its own life, beyond even the persuasion of the coach. Social factors may increase the likelihood that this is the case, even in the absence of a psychological component or an eating disorder. Speaking specifically of Stephanie's generation, it may be that the women entered a world of "opportunity," in which they were permitted to be both competitive and feminine, but for which an insufficient amount of time had passed for that ideal to be widely and deeply inculcated. With acceptance uncertain, women athletes would have continued to calibrate every aspect of their presentation, including weight and shape. Referring in this case only to the visual quality of thinness and not to percentage body fat, one hypothetical analysis emphasizes how tempting it is for a woman to see weight loss as a natural part of the sport: 1. While the American woman was, in fact, gaining weight as a result of better nutrition among other factors, the so-called "American ideal" for women was becoming thinner, 2. Thinness, by coincidence if nothing else, is also part of the traditional process used to feminize women athletes by keeping them away from the blocky or muscular forms customarily attributed to masculinity, 3. Thinness presents an image closely associated with the tomboy, and therefore does not bring the potential stigma to which other female athletes have been subject, 4. For people at the highest competitive levels in distance running, thinness is a tangible means of asserting oneself and staking a claim to advantage if not outright superiority, and it is a means of controlling, or seeming to control, one part of an otherwise unpredictable environment, 5. At least initially, being thin is consistent with the goal of high performance and is a positive indicator of probable success. In sum, a thin woman distance runner could come close to the media's feminine ideal; she could be strong without being threatening; she could assert at least some control over her situation; and she had a significant chance of gaining both a psychological and physical advantage over some of her competitors. Considered alone, any of these elements might be sufficient to induce dieting and weight control. Taken together, they proved (and continue to prove) compelling for many women runners. It should be added that this scenario contemplates, at least on one level, a situation in which the woman is the decision-maker, even if social pressures are also involved. If, on the other hand, the woman is coerced to weight loss, that is a different matter. All ambiguity which might otherwise mark the discussion is irrelevant, and the matter is clear. The woman is being abused.

Of course, Stephanie considered none of this after her meeting with Peter. She just went back to the dorm. She was, in fact, one of the athletes to whom Dr. Snell and Dr. Vaughan referred; she was "genetically predisposed to leanness." Or, as Stephanie says, "I had never been on a diet. I was always extremely lean, had a high metabolism, and could eat whatever I liked. I was the kind of person who could go to The Shack and eat a shake and a brownie, and that was a constant. It never occurred to me to eat any differently." Now, however, with Peter's questions, the matter of a diet flew right past "possibility" to mandate. She was going on a diet. She did not form her own opinion, but accepted Peter's inquiry—his mere questions—as the final word. Predictably, her dorm-mates were dumbfounded. With no way to know the vast difference in body weight and body fat between elite distance runners and other women, the idea that a woman who was 5' 8" tall and weighed 120 pounds might benefit from a diet was disturbing, if not bizarre. They immediately told Stephanie not to diet, that she would be "anorexic" if she lost any more weight. When it became clear, however, that she was going to change her diet, they gave her the benefit of their experience. If you're going on a diet, they advised, you have to learn to eat a lot of things you don't like. That would be a considerable adjustment for Stephanie because, in addition to the shakes and brownies, she was eating like most other students on campus, which is to say, badly. She ate whatever she could get her hands on. That had to stop, she concluded.

In the beginning, the diet was stringent. Stephanie did what the other women in the dorm told her to do. "At first, I ate grotesque foods that I didn't like: half a grapefruit, water, replaced milk with diet coke. Cut out all dairy products. Cut out all meat." After a while on this diet, she started to adjust. She changed the foods she didn't like for ones she did like. She decided that she could eat as much popcorn as she liked. She also decided that she could eat as much salad as she wanted so long as it was within the time reserved for meals. Eventually, her diet consisted largely of fruits and vegetables. Three things happened as the effect of her changed eating habits took hold. She lost weight, her energy increased, and she began to run better. Before the end of her freshman year, she was down to 105 pounds. In the course of the next year she would lose even more weight, but she would also learn better how to adjust her eating, being watchful for signs that she was going too far, losing energy, or becoming irritable. When that happened, she would increase the volume of food she took in. Later, commenting sardonically but not without humor about the eating habits of women distance runners, she would say that when she and her teammates entered a restaurant, it was no use bringing the menu. "Just bring on the salads." As to the question of body fat, Stephanie says that she never fell below 8 percent at Wisconsin.

Peter had a limited ability to monitor Stephanie during all this time, of course. Most everything of importance to the question of diet—whether Stephanie had popcorn instead of pudding for a snack, and asparagus instead of a cheeseburger for lunch—occurred outside his field of vision. He could see what was plainly before him. He saw Stephanie's weight fall, and he saw her grow faster and stronger. From time to time, he also saw that she was drawing close to skin and bone, and he communicated his concern to her. Such was the bond between them that the communication could be a "sense" Stephanie got that Peter was apprehensive about what she was doing to herself. She would adjust. Other times, he had to speak to her. Choosing his words with care, he would ask whether she was eating well; on at least one occasion, he sought assurance that she was not doing anything "strange" or "unusual" in her diet. When Stephanie told him that she was fine, that she might need to make an adjustment and eat more or exercise less but otherwise she was doing well, that was the end of the matter. He trusted her. In any event, his option if he wanted to intervene was to hold her out of meets until she was fit enough to run. But she never approached that state in his view or her own. Stephanie could look excruciatingly thin, which was her tendency, but she ran strongly in workouts and competition. Peter was not trained in psychiatry, psychology, or social work. He was trained in athletics, and in the exercise of the personal skills and judgment that would encourage an athlete to do her best on the track. With Stephanie, as well as with his other athletes, he was not likely to make a clinical diagnosis; nor would he have been comfortable with the notion that Stephanie was in "denial" when she described her eating habits. To a layman, that concept looked suspiciously like an accusation that Stephanie was lying to him. He could not imagine brushing past her version of the facts and conducting an interrogation on matters about which he already had Stephanie's assurances. Peter was interested in facts: her apparent weight, her performances in workouts and races as an indicator of fitness and health, and her statements to him.

Through the indoor season of 1985 and into Stephanie's first outdoor season as a Badger, her running improved. She was increasingly comfortable now that she was off those horrid cross-country courses and could smooth out. No hills, no irregular turns, a limited number of people on the track with whom to contend, predictable splits, and a controlled environment were the conditions she liked. For the most part, her improvement was unobserved because Stephanie was overshadowed by two of the best distance runners in the country, Cathy and Katie. Cathy's performances in 1985 were particularly stunning. Having won both NCAA and TAC cross-country meets, she represented the United States in Lisbon, Portugal, at the World Senior Cross-Country Championship where she earned a silver medal. Only Zola Budd prevented her from becoming world champion, and not even Zola could stop her from leading the United States team to victory. Indoors, Cathy won the TAC title in the two-mile, and probably would have repeated as NCAA 3,000-meter champion had she made it to the starting line. As it happened, she got food poisoning from a bowl of clam chowder and missed the meet. At the NCAA meet, however, Katie stepped up. She was runner-up in the 3,000-meter final. In the kind of performance no one noticed, the best Stephanie Herbst could do was hint at her potential by finishing fourth in the Big Ten 5,000-meter indoor championships in 16:44:42, a race Katie won in 15:50.10. Katie's margin of victory was so large that only the most sharply interested spectator would have watched the rest of finishers come across the line, no matter how significant the improvement was to any of them in personal terms.

Moving outdoors, everything pointed to two big meets. Wisconsin's goals were the Big Ten Championship, which Peter wanted to win, and the NCAA Championship in Austin, Texas. Katie, though, ran into trouble in the middle of the spring. Or rather it ran into her. Already struggling with achilles tendinitis, Katie was struck by a car on April 30, only three weeks before the Big Ten Championship. Katie was the 1984 Big Ten champion in both 5,000 and 10,000 meters, but continuing soreness in her left hip prevented a defense of either title. For the first time in her career, she was unable to run for Wisconsin. As a result, Peter was in a tight spot. With Katie out, he was 20 points short from the previous year, 10 in each of the events she won. He needed someone to get those points back.

Peter had a few options available to him. In ordinary circumstances, Stephanie would not have been one of them. She had never run a 10,000-meter race; she was only a freshman; and jumping her up in distance was premature, or at least it would be for most young runners. On the other hand, there was Stephanie's nature to consider. She clearly would not back away from the challenge. As Peter later recalled, "I didn't want to put a high school runner in the 10,000 meters, boom! That would have been somewhat unusual for me. But it was a situation that presented itself, and she didn't have any reservations about it. She didn't know what 10,000 meters was all about. Her reaction was to say, 'I've run 5,000 meters and it's no big deal.' In fact, of course, 25 laps of the track is quite a nice number. But she knew that she was that good; that she could run a relaxed pace because she would figure out that 'what we're really running is such and such, 33-minute pace, which is 16:30, so we do this twice, well, OK. Relax a little bit.' But it was partially because of her impatience that we picked Stephanie to replace Katie rather than anyone else who might have been older. She wanted it. She was always urging on for progress."

Peter made up his mind finally. Stephanie would run both the 3,000 meters and the 10,000 meters at the Big Ten. She would join Cathy Branta in the 3,000 and Holly Hering in the 10,000. Stephanie was surprised to be entered in the 10,000, saying later that "I was shocked. I found out on Monday I was going to run. It took me until Thursday to believe it, but I trust Peter's judgment." For the first time in her career at Wisconsin, she would also have the benefit of one of Peter's specially designed tactics. The tactic was directed primarily at Nan Doak, Iowa's tiny 5-foot, 88-pound champion runner. Nan was the clear favorite. No one put much stock in the thin young freshman Wisconsin entered in the event instead of Katie Ishmael. No one that is, except Peter Tegen. "I was convinced that she would win because I had seen that she was the best doing the shift exercises that we sometimes did. I just thought, if she's there, she's going to win," he explained. As to tactics, he kept it simple:

"Never show your face. Always stay back behind Nan. Never let her see you at all. Stay two or three people back. Don't rock the boat. They'll find out later." The tactic was the natural outgrowth of Peter's belief that races are won late, and the equally natural outgrowth of training that prepares athletes for that eventuality. In order to make the matter even more simple for Stephanie, Peter said that he would blow a whistle at the precise moment when she should sprint ahead. Of course, Stephanie would hear the whistle all right. But what would happen then? The trick was in the performance. About that, Stephanie had her doubts. When she heard what Peter advised, she mumbled to herself, "That's a good strategy, Peter. I'm not even a good sprinter." Still, there was something alluring about the plan. All she had to do was run. Putting her doubts to one side, Stephanie changed her attitude and accepted her fate, "Well, Peter knows the strategy. That's what I must have to do."

Stephanie went off with the field on Saturday afternoon, May 18, 1985, before a sparse crowd in Northwestern University's Dyche Stadium. Bathed by sunlight in pleasant temperatures, with only a bothersome wind to worry her, she simply tucked in. Nan Doak did much of the work. Jenny Spangler, who would make the 1996 Olympic team as a marathoner, was also in the field and occasionally drifted toward the front. Holly Hering remained close, running unobtrusively and well. Stephanie Herbst stayed put, totally self-contained, moving casually in the wake of the more-experienced runners, never even tempted to move up. She relaxed and waited, one, two, three, four, five, six, seven—the pace was slow—eight, nine, ten, eleven, twelve, thirteen—past the 5,000-meter mark and entering her very own "no (wo)man's land!"—fourteen, fifteen (extraordinary how far this is), sixteen, seventeen—still slow—eighteen, nineteen, twenty (get ready), twenty one, twenty two, twenty three... And shortly before the end of the penultimate lap, just before the gun sounded for the last lap, Stephanie heard the whistle.

Sharp enough for everyone in the stadium to hear it in the building tension of the race, it was early. Stephanie expected to sprint one lap, not one lap with the little extra bit that Peter was now requesting. She thought, "Does he really think I have the strength to go this whole way?!" Still, it was the strategy. Phrased another way, it was "what I must have to do." Quickly, Stephanie jumped into action: "500 meters," she said, "right when you came out of that turn and I just took off like a bat out of hell. And Nan Doak did not know what hit her! At first she tried to keep up, but literally I was running about as fast as my legs would carry me so I think just the shock alone set her back enough that she wasn't able to catch me."

"So I won the race," Stephanie said, "and Peter could not have been happier." In fact, his confidence had been growing as the race progressed and the pace remained slow. "This will play into our hands," he confided to friends. "They don't know about my freshman." When the time came, "his freshman" ran the last lap of her first 10,000-meter race in 64 seconds. Peter had been right, after all. She did shift pace like a winner! Stephanie's time was only 34:34.92, 45 seconds slower than Katie's conference record, but that was because of the slow early pace. Nan Doak finished second in 34:42.86. Jenny Spangler was third in 34:57.48, while Holly Hering picked up valuable points for Wisconsin by finishing fourth in 35:08.20. None of that mattered a bit. From Peter's point of view, the best thing was that the run galvanized his entire team. After the Saturday and Sunday sessions, after Stephanie had finished second in the 3,000 meters on Sunday—beaten only by teammate Branta— and after Wisconsin had safely packed up its eighth Big Ten outdoor title in ten years, Peter looked back at the 10,000 meters and said, "When Stephanie ran that sensational last lap and beat Nan Doak, that was like a great shot of incentive for the whole team. I figured then that we could do it." Stephanie herself expressed shock. She told the reporters that she did not expect to win, that she

The freshman emerges: Stephanie Herbst, fourth from right,
shadows Nan Doak of Iowa.

was unfamiliar with both the 10,000 and the 3,000, and that the
credit should go to Peter's planning.

She could say it all she wanted, and some part of it could
even be true, but it was more than Peter's planning. Anyone lucky
enough to be in Dyche Stadium that day saw the introduction of
America's next world-class distance runner. That a young woman so
fluid in her motion could explode like that at the end of a race was
startling. That she could do it one year removed from a small high
school in Minnesota, under intense pressure, in an event she had
never run, was all the more remarkable. The *Chicago Tribune* captured the spirit of Stephanie's first big victory. "Wisconsin Sub
Steals the Show," the headline read. Indeed she had. While other
people ran well, including Cathy Branta who won both the 1,500
and the 3,000, nobody made the impact Stephanie Herbst did.

The result was gratifying for Stephanie. In one stroke, one

64-second blast, she reconfigured her status on the University of Wisconsin team. If she once hungered for more attention from Peter, she had now earned it. In the moment of first triumph, however, she turned a gracious eye to Katie. She never would have won the 10,000 meters, Stephanie said, if Katie Ishmael had been there. The statement may have been literally true, given Katie's experience and ability. But the fact that Stephanie said it meant something more. It meant that Stephanie had developed affection and respect for her teammates. In the first year, the relationships stopped short of intimate friendship, but they were as close as Stephanie could get with women who were chasing the same prizes she was.

Stephanie had one more meet before the summer. Prior to the Big Ten Championship, she had qualified for the NCAA meet in the 5,000 meters by running 16:03.48. The time was good, but it was more than 30 seconds slower than the 5,000 meters Cathy Branta ran, and it was even farther behind the collegiate record of 15:23.03 Kathy Hayes of Oregon had established earlier in the spring. To make matters worse, many women had the choice between 3,000 and 5,000, having qualified in both events. When Cathy Branta decided to contest the 1,500 and the 3,000, a disproportionate number of the good runners rushed to the 5,000. All in all, Stephanie could count herself lucky to qualify for the finals. On the day of her qualifying heat, Stephanie warmed up carefully. In this regard, she benefited from Peter's attention to detail. He taught that the warm-up was a routine that needed to be mastered, and that the pre-event exercise must be sufficient to increase the body temperature to 102 degrees, at which point oxygen consumption was at its lowest and oxygen exchange at its highest. He recommended an active warm-up in order to encourage the proper oxygen exchange. Once the warm-up was complete, he worried very little about the passage of time because he felt that preparedness could last 30 to 40 minutes in case of delay. With all this in mind, Stephanie went through her paces, and Peter casually checked her progress from time to time, looking up from whatever else he might be doing. Only this time, when he looked up, something was different. There in the middle of the infield, all alone surrounded by grass, was Stephanie Herbst visibly shaking from nerves. Peter knew what to do. He dispatched Cathy Branta to settle down his freshman. Cathy went over and soothed Stephanie, telling her to relax, that she would be fine, and not to worry so much about it. Stephanie very much appreciated Peter's concern, and Cathy's help, but she could not quite get a grip on herself. "I got on the line, and I was so scared, and I just said, please don't let me qualify for the finals. I was thinking that would be the horror of horrors, to qualify for the finals!" Of course, the horror of horrors did occur. Stephanie qualified for the finals at 5,000 meters by running 16:22.29 in Austin's high heat and humidity. In the finals, though, she just ran out of steam. She finished last among the 12 finalists when she ran 16:27.61. The only other two runners who did not run faster than 16:00 were Jacque Struckhoff of Kansas State, who was 11th, and Kathy Ormsby of North Carolina State, who had been an all-American as a freshman the year before but was 10th this year. As it happened, Sabrina Dornhoefer of the University of Missouri won the championship. Sabrina had been one of two young women, along with the talented Andrea Fischer, that the Missouri coaches called to Stephanie's attention the prior year when they attempted to recruit her. They said that she would not be expected to beat either of them during her freshman year. After the NCAA, and at least as far as Sabrina was concerned, it appeared that the Missouri coaches were right all along!

The mortification of her 5,000-meter final aside, Stephanie had the pleasure of watching her graduating teammate, the woman whose kindness had enticed her to Wisconsin in the first place, win two more national championships. Before and after her stint with Stephanie in the infield, Cathy Branta won her races decisively. The

1,500 meters was particularly impressive, as Cathy made up for a relative lack of speed by forcing the pace faster than the favorites, Claudette Groenendaal and Leann Warren of Oregon, could manage. Finally, to give the week in Austin its final flavoring, Stephanie got to see Nan Doak of Iowa win the national championship over 10,000 meters by running 33:33.03. Ironically, Nan won with a big kick over the last 400 meters. Her split time was 68.7.

For Stephanie, it was the end of a long season. She had reason to be proud of herself. She had been an undistinguished recruit in a team of champions and now she, too, was a champion. She had been unknown and now she was known. She had been a follower and now she was prepared to lead. She had been afraid and now, at least, she knew of what. What was it Peter referred to when he spoke of training? Time, space, and force. Yes, that was it. Time, space, and force, not exactly the most easily controlled variables in a person's life, after all.

FOURTEEN

The sound of the sea advances, retreats
like a door blown shut and open.

Quartet
Angela Ball

In the summer of 1985, Stephanie remained in Madison to attend classes and to train. She did the workouts Peter assigned, added workouts as she thought prudent, and did sprints after every run. She emphasized her potential by winning the United States Sports Festival 10,000 meters in 33:49.77. Her former teammate Cathy Branta won the 3,000 meters at the Sports Festival, won again at the World University Games, and completed a successful two-week European tour. In the 5,000 meters, Cathy was close to the times recorded previously only by Mary Decker among Americans, and was poised for more improvement. She could scarcely have imagined that on the next tax day, April 15, 1986, her progress would skid to a halt when exploratory surgery on a sore knee revealed a 40-percent erosion of the medial meniscus and five stress fractures of the medial condoyle. The injuries, which first appeared during an otherwise ordinary set of 60-meter quick-rhythm runs, effectively ended her career. Cathy's conqueror in the 1985 World Cross-Country Championship, Zola Budd, also began to experience problems, although of a different nature. Stories began to appear in reputable newspapers and athletics magazines that Zola was simply losing the correct shape and size for long-distance running. Writing for *The London Sunday Times*, Cliff Temple reflected on Zola's relatively slower running in the prior season. The slower times, he suggested, were not the result of disappointment from the Los Angeles Olympics; they were a result of her weight. "The most curious aspect of the lackluster performances from Zola Budd in recent weeks," Temple wrote, "is that the athletics world is surprised. The Budd is merely flowering. Zola is bigger than last year, more rounded. One estimate is that she is at least 10 pounds heavier, which is a substantial increase when you remember that she weighed only 92 pounds at the Olympics." As the sporting world summarily wrote off a 102-pound woman as too large to run well, other candidates for world-class status were beginning to emerge. A resolute, hard-running Scottish woman named Liz Lynch was finishing up a term at Ricks College in Idaho and preparing to enroll at the University of Alabama. After considerable success there, she would run afoul of the NCAA's rules regarding financial reward and move back to Great Britain to continue the training that would, in time, make her a world champion at 10,000 meters and a marathoner of note. Closer to home, Cindy Bremser, still being coached by Peter, was holding her place as one of America's premier middle-distance runners; and American collegiate 10,000-meter record-holder and six-time all-American Katie Ishmael had her eyes set on the number-one position on the Wisconsin women's cross-country team, which returned four of the first five runners from the prior year's national championship team. That fact notwithstanding, the North Carolina State University women's team was marshaling its forces to challenge Wisconsin. The Wolfpack had Janet Smith, Connie Jo Robinson, and Kathy Ormsby to match up with Wisconsin's Ishmael and Herbst; they had a promising freshman named Suzie Tuffey; they had good depth; and they had a great coach in Rollie Geiger. One step away from college competition, Suzy Favor was finally entering her senior year in high school. When she finished her four-year prep career in Steven's Point, Wisconsin, she would own 11 state championships and three national junior championships. She would also have her pick of countless collegiate opportunities from all over the United States. All of these women, Stephanie, Cathy with a C, Kathy with a K, Zola, Connie Jo, Mary, the precocious Suzy and Suzie, Liz, Janet, Katie, Cindy and thousands more like them were part of the constant ebb and flow of women's running. They were moving in and out from shore, sometimes healthy and running well, sometimes not but recoverable, and sometimes not and irrecoverable, swept so far away that dry land became a memory.

For Stephanie Herbst, when summer turned to fall she was in full flow. Although she had a growing antipathy for cross-country, she was running so well that it hardly mattered. "I came in as a freshman," she said, "and joined the cross-country team, not knowing who anyone was or where I fit in. All season, I felt like I could do better. By track, I definitely felt the influence of Peter's coaching and as the season went by my confidence grew. Peter kept encouraging me to move up. I guess I was being too timid."

The summer's workouts accelerated Stephanie's progress. Throughout this period, Peter's training remained a combination of theory and practice. The theory was his, and he controlled it; the practice was that of his athletes, and they controlled it. As to the theory, a Wisconsin athlete had to be smart enough to understand what Peter meant when he started talking about what he wanted done and why. Here is the dynamic principle at the level of verbal instruction: *I believe that if you want to make someone fast, you ask yourself: who is the fastest? It is the sprinter. There are certain requirements for that: strength and biomechanical efficiency among them. Once you shift your running gear into high speed, something has to happen mechanically that relates to the ability to run at high speed. A sprinter also builds dynamic stereotypes. A sprinter who trains at the maximum velocity, and maybe does that not quite right, will fence herself in, can build limitations, walls around herself simply because that's the pattern, that's the program, and the harder she tries to get out of the pattern the harder it is to do. It has to do with neural muscular facilitation. The neural muscular patterns become programmed. We create those patterns, and if we are not careful, the ruts will grow so deep that we cannot get out of them. To get out of the dynamic stereotype you must work with accelerating and decelerating velocities so as to develop different time, space, and force stimuli. Every step you take is slightly different, and as you accelerate and decelerate, several advantages are gained: 1. You vary the stimuli. 2. You avoid the development of a monotonous stereotype. 3. You get out of prior patterns. 4. The neurosystem is permitted a free-wheeling recovery that offers you the opportunity for replenishment. Certain fuels are used for only a limited period of time, but by surging, accelerating, decelerating, you have control. You accelerate but only for a few strides and relax as soon as you hit maximum. Then come back down. In the next few seconds, your nervous system is permitted to recover. Pure speed must never be permitted to cause fatigue. You must provide yourself ample opportunity for replenishment and recovery.*

Having absorbed the theory, the women were supposed to put it into action. The Wisconsin concept of dynamic running, the regulated shifts of acceleration and deceleration in a planned workout, was only the most discrete application of Peter's theories. The theories were, in fact, pervasive within his coaching.

One element of Peter's philosophy, however, clanged into an equal and opposite force. The element of philosophy was that the nervous system must be permitted to recover and to replenish. The equal and opposite force was the inclination of his team members to beat each other's brains out in training. Girls will be girls? When Stephanie reviews the regular workouts from those days and the suggestion is made that some days seem lighter than others, she rejects the implication immediately, "If that's what your Monday, Wednesday and Friday are like [referring to the workouts that seem easier], imagine your Tuesday and Thursday because you're not going to let these people beat you." Responding to the generally competitive atmosphere created and sustained by the women on the team, Stephanie adds, "It wasn't what you would call an easy-going group!" If not, Stephanie was right at home because she never sought an open road. She actually enjoyed the tough workouts more than anything. She liked the entire ritual associated with a hard session—mile repeats or a hill workout for example. She savored the tension she felt first thing in the morning of such a workout; the building anticipation and ready nervousness as the time approached; the company of the other women at the track, on the roads, or at the hill; when there, the warm-up and the final preparation, the checking of the gauge, the estimate of what might or might not be possible on the day; and finally the workout itself, the careful allocation of resources over the entire course of the session, not too much on the first effort nor too little on the last, but always something tucked away for later use; and, at the end of the day, the languorous, satisfied warm-down among equally exhausted and exhilarated companions. The women, including Stephanie, shared those experiences as if in premonition of middle-age, all the while trying to get a leg up, an extra step, or a bit of ownership or influence that might be helpful later. Day after day, Stephanie and her teammates gathered together in their shared, but not entirely mutual, purposes. It diminishes what they were doing to call it working out; they were engaged in a much more comprehensive and demanding task. They were preparing physically and mentally for competition, for battle, with each other and for the University of Wisconsin. In fact, Stephanie and the other Badgers running together and against each other bring to mind the image created by Ezra Pound in *The Coming of War:*

Actaeon: "Over fair meadows/Over the cool face of that field/Unstill, ever moving/Hosts of an ancient people/The silent cortege." Perhaps that is a bit strong, but there was in the 1985 Wisconsin cross-country team the hint of an approaching conflict, in which casualties would be inevitable.

The conflict was natural. Inside the team Katie and Stephanie had to sort out between them who was the alpha for the pack. They also had to accommodate the interests of the other returning athletes—national-quality runners like Birgit Christiansen, Kelly McKillen, Holly Hering, and Stephanie Bassett—and at the same time adjust to yet another talented freshman. The talented freshman was Lori Wolter of Sauk Prairie, Wisconsin. Lori was a six-time state champion in track and cross-country, was the winner of the Junior National Cross-Country title at two miles, and was the Wisconsin Class A 3,200-meter record holder in 10:12.30, much faster than Stephanie ran in high school. Of Lori, Peter would soon say, "She's a very intelligent young lady who likes to be challenged mentally and physically. She is not intimidated by the fact that she is a freshman." That must have been just what the sophomores, juniors, and seniors on the team wanted to see walking onto the track—another freshman who would not be intimidated! Outside the team, the conflict came from the schools that hoped to prevent the Wisconsin repeat at Nationals, particularly Iowa State and North Carolina State.

The question of internal leadership resolved itself quickly. Stephanie was the alpha, perhaps a bit more nervous and high-strung than the usual alpha but a pretty good fit for this bunch. First, she began to assert herself in the workouts. While the previous year she conceded place, particularly in the sessions that were hardest for her like the ski slope, now she felt compelled to stay close to the front if not to actually take it for herself. In all of the running, there was an additional sense of responsibility, the idea that it was her job to lead. As the season progressed and especially as some of the other runners experienced minor injuries or illnesses, Stephanie described what happened for her. "Suddenly," she said, "it was a HUGE jump. I had to start leading in practices. I had to learn paces myself. There was a lot of learning because of that." Katie, as it happened, accepted early in the season that Stephanie was going to be the number-one runner; and she was going to be number two. She and Stephanie developed a strong personal relationship that was positive and supportive toward each other.

In the early cross-country meets of 1985, Stephanie relied heavily on Katie. Both of them and the team as a whole absorbed a difficult loss in October, when North Carolina State ambushed them at the Rutgers Invitational in New Brunswick, New Jersey. In that meet, Stephanie lost to NC State's freshman Suzie Tuffey 16:31.3 to 16:32.8. The team lost 29 to 33 even though Wisconsin had four runners in the first eight across the line. It was the first defeat for the Wisconsin women since 1983, but Peter was untroubled. He commented that the race could have gone either way, that his non-scorers could run better, and that, in any event, "the pressure has now shifted to NC State and given us a new goal for the Nationals at Marquette in November."

Three other important races came before Nationals. The first was the Badger Classic, which Track and Field News called the finest cross-country meet of the year. At home, Wisconsin faced teams from Arizona, Tennessee, BYU, Kansas State, Michigan, Iowa State, Texas, Stanford, Northwestern, UCLA, and West Virginia. To quote the fellow who was coaching girls and women in the '60s, to whom reference was made earlier, "not a dog in the bunch!" Peter's strategy was simple. He asked Stephanie and Katie, the defending champion, to stay with the pack for the first couple of miles of the 5,000-meter course, keep a good pace, and to use the hills in the last mile to break away. And that is precisely what happened. Katie and Stephanie got away from the field and then Stephanie moved inexorably ahead, winning 16:54 to 17:05. After the race, Stephanie said that she had not been sure what to expect. "I just wanted to take the lead and see how it would go," she said. "Katie and I worked together and that makes all the difference because she's such a strong runner." Behind the two stars, Lori Wolter announced her presence on the national scene by finishing fourth, 40 seconds ahead of Oregon's extraordinary freshman Cathy Schiro. The team championship went to Wisconsin over Iowa State, 50 to 96. One of the spectators at the Badger Classic was Dan Herbst, Stephanie's father. He was doing more running himself these days, and keenly appreciated his daughter's performance. "She's even a stronger runner than last year," he noted. "Stephanie has developed into a disciplined runner with a strong finishing kick."

Later in the season, Stephanie added the individual Big Ten cross-country championship to her collection and led Wisconsin to the team title over Northwestern, which had been ranked fourth in the nation prior to the race. At the Big Ten, Lori Wolter raced past her senior teammate Katie Ishmael to finish second to Katie's third; and the team total of 22 points was the lowest in meet history. Birgit was seventh; Holly was ninth, and Kelly was thirteenth in the scoring for Wisconsin. Remarkably, the Badgers did not need Kelly's thirteenth place in order to fill the complement of five scorers. Northwestern scored 83 points. A further triumph came in the NCAA Region IV meet in which Stephanie, as an individual and Wisconsin as a team, again won easily. The only cloud on the horizon as Nationals approached was the status of Katie Ishmael. She was struggling with fatigue and had to be held out of the regional meet. Asked by a sportswriter whether Katie was "burned out," Peter remarked dryly, "Not to my knowledge." All things considered, Peter counted his team's performance one of the best of the year—"particularly because we didn't have Katie and the rest filled

Rush hour at the NCAA cross-country chanpionship in 1985.

in very well"—and was hopeful that Katie would be back for the national meet. As for Stephanie's performance, Peter was spare in his description. "Stephanie was fantastic again and just ran away from everyone."

Going into the NCAA Cross-Country Championship, the University of Wisconsin women were in good shape. They had beaten many of the best teams in the country already; their only loss had come narrowly to North Carolina State, which as a result now carried the pressure of being top-ranked in the premeet calculation; the meet was scheduled for nearby Marquette University in Milwaukee; and, as Peter added with a nice touch of humor and warning, there was the matter of weather, "It would be good for us if it was cold," he joked. "Our major opponents are coming from those pussy-foot schools."

Cold weather was good in theory for Wisconsin, but it was not good for Stephanie Herbst. She was already feeling the inevitable pressure to perform, and the idea of running in wintry weather with her hands and feet frozen, her face immobilized, and the wind chilling every effort to relax and get into her motion did not help. In his heart, Peter almost certainly knew that Stephanie would not win the race. She was not robust enough for a sport that made such physical demands. But he carried on just as if he expected her to win. For her, as for every other runner on the team, he set out his expectations and prescribed a tactic. The plan was for Stephanie to stay with the lead pack and try to win the race, and the plan for her teammates was to run as a pack and to move gradually up through the field. Wisconsin's chances improved when North Carolina State lost Connie Jo Robinson to injury; and they diminished, if only slightly, with a starting line assignment on the fringe of the field, a position that might create as much as a ten-yard deficit. For Stephanie personally, her chances diminished the morning of the race when she looked out the window at the weather and when she tried out the course later in the day. It was the common Upper-Midwest mess, sure enough: snowy, wet uncertain muck and ice, troublesome wind, low temperatures. Nevertheless, when the gun went off, Stephanie set out on her assignment. She and her teammates had to work harder than ordinary because only the center strip of the course was free of snow, while the fringes were still covered. The Wisconsin runners, therefore, were snow-plowing until they could extricate themselves by getting up front and slicing toward the middle. By the 1.5-mile mark, while the other Wisconsin runners fell into their roles slightly farther back in the stampede, eventually settling in together near places eighteen through twenty-three,

Stephanie churned directly toward the point. She looked fine at that stage, but the only real indicator for success was already off-kilter. She "thought" her start was bad. She did not "think" she could win. She "thought" the weather was unbearable. "I mentally just did not have it," she later admitted, "I just got in there and I thought: there's no way."

As the race settled into an order, the leaders included Stephanie, UCLA's Polly Plumer, Wake Forest's Karen Dunn, Boston University's Lisa Welch, North Carolina State's Suzie Tuffey and Harvard's Jenny Stricker. Liz Natale from Texas, Regina Jacobs from Stanford, and Christine McMiken of Oklahoma State were also close. At two miles, Suzie Tuffey, who professed not to mind hills or cold weather, assumed the lead. She controlled the race the rest of the way, shucking challengers as they emerged. Regina Jacobs moved up through the field in the last mile. She passed four people and set her eyes on the only one left, a freshman who had no business leading a national championship event. But Suzie noted her, marked her, and rebuffed her. She won by 6 seconds over Regina, 16:23 to 16:29, and by 7 over third placer McMiken. As for Stephanie, she lost her way in the last mile. Not that she was misdirected or anything so dramatic. It was that she lost heart. She was running hard, and yet she wasn't. She finally chugged across the line in seventh place overall and with a final time of 16:37. That is not, of course, a bad result for a sophomore at NCAA Division I. It was just not what she hoped for and what she knew was expected. "From the start," she explained later, "I was mentally fighting it. If you start playing games in your head, you've lost, and I played mental games. Once somebody passes you, you have that breakdown, 'Oh, I've been beat. I'm losing it.' I knew I wasn't up there and I wasn't going to make it up." More wryly, she assessed her performance. "I also started realistically evaluating where I fit in later in the race, and it probably wasn't a real good idea." Speaking of the race more

Stephanie leads, but Suzie Tuffey (extreme right) is irresistible.

than ten years after its finish, she retains a puzzled, disappointing memory. "I was doing well within the group. I took the lead in the race. But at a certain point I was passed and it released that feeling, 'I don't care. Who wants to pass me now? Go ahead!' I basically just said, 'I'm going to get up that hill. I don't care.' The last couple of people passed me right before the finish and if I'd tried, I would have beat those two! But again it was one of those things where I said: 'I can only do so much. That's all the better I can do today.'"

Having finished the race, the worst part of Stephanie's day was yet to come. She watched first for her teammates to arrive, each of them clawing for every advantage and place, and then she and they awaited the calculation, all with the same questions. Had Stephanie saved enough up front despite her black dog mood? Had the Wisconsin pack held tight, had each of them driven past enough people in the last terrible uphill of this god-awful course? Where had North Carolina State gone? What word from Iowa State? Could there be anyone else? All the questions continued until it became clear. Stephanie had done enough; the pack had held together; each of them had picked up critical places on the finishing hill; and North Carolina State was undone, injured first by Connie Jo's absence and then by a fall suffered by one of their leaders, Kathy Ormsby, who did not finish. And Iowa State? Good, very good, but not enough today. The final total was Wisconsin 58, Iowa State 98, and North Carolina State 103. The women of Wisconsin had repeated as national champions. They joined the men's team from the University of Wisconsin which had won its own title 30 minutes earlier. It was a Badger sweep in Milwaukee, Wisconsin. If anyone had reason to feel good about the result, it was Peter, who brought his crew through a tough fall, taking into account the pressure to repeat the prior year's victory, the early loss to NC State, Katie's late-season malaise, the difficulty of keeping his sophomore phenomenon on a level course, and the incorporation of new runners into a championship mix. Specially, there was the performance of Katie Ishmael, who finished 15th, to acknowledge. Peter counted six runners Katie passed in the last half-mile. Maybe it would be good to say that Katie reclaimed for Wisconsin the two places that got away from Stephanie and then added four more for good measure. That, after all, is what teammates are for, to pick up after each other when one or the other of them gets a little sloppy. And the freshman, Lori Wolter, was due praise for finishing 22nd overall and earning all-American honors her first time out. Kelly McKillen stayed right in the fight, ending up 31st, barely outside the top-25 finish that would have made her, too, all-American again. Finally, Holly Hering ran well. She took her share of the victory by holding Wisconsin's fifth spot and by bumping an Iowa State or NC State athlete a notch or two lower than they otherwise would have been. Holly finished 36th. Similarly, Birgit who finished 44th and Stephanie Bassett who finished 78th ran well. And Stephanie Herbst, their leader, who was asked to do it all and merely did a great deal, will one day see the

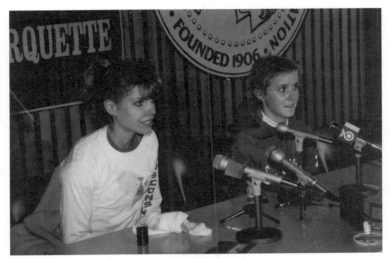

Stephanie and Suzie meet the press.

glory in the event. Each did what was required on a hard day. After the race, Peter said all that was necessary: "There is something very special about this team."

For North Carolina State, the day brought an unhappy result. A good thing that might have happened, that could have happened, that they worked to make happen, that they hoped would happen, did not happen, and the day being complete unto itself, never would happen. At that, they got the better of the deal because it fell to the Iowa State team to reveal the depth of sorrow possible on a day when things do not happen that might, and other things do happen that ought not.

An airplane carrying members of the Iowa State women's cross-country team crashed on its return trip to Ames, Iowa, killing team members Sheryl Maahs, Julie Rose, and Susan Baxter, as well as head women's coach Ron Renko, assistant women's coach Pat Moynihan, physiotherapist Stephanie Streit, and the pilot, Burton Watkins.

FIFTEEN

May God bless your journey.

The Way of the Pilgrim

Hurrying across the great frigid windblown distances of the Wisconsin campus late in the first semester of her sophomore year, clutching her books tightly and avoiding eye contact with the men who might otherwise approach, Stephanie Herbst had a lot on her mind. The first concern was finals. Impossibly, they were right on top of her. She had her attention fixed on graduate school, and she needed her grades up. This whole exercise—college—would cave in on itself if she did not find a way to wrench her attention back from running and pay attention. Still, she had to admit it. That race in Milwaukee bothered her. She had failed. Other people might dress it up, and even she could find ways to move the facts around to make herself feel better, but there was no way around the central fact of doing less than she was capable of doing, and of endangering her team's chances for a second national championship. If it wasn't for Katie, Lori, Birgit, Kelly, Holly and Stephanie Bassett—and especially for Katie—a sharp focus would have fallen on her run, and she would have been cut up. She, the best runner on the team, the first runner across the line, a woman who improved from forty-fifth to seventh in one year, would have been to blame. What an ironic consequence to spring from success. Stephanie was rediscovering gravity. When she climbed, it pulled. It was quite ridiculous really.

Thankfully, she escaped when the team won. While many of the stories mentioned her disappointing run, they did so in the course of reporting the team victory. "No harm done," they suggested, and moved along. Peter was a special case, of course. He knew what to say. Speaking of the chasm between first place and seventh place, he shrugged it off. "Things don't always work out the way you plan," he said, "that's experience." But what if it happened again? What if she stepped up to the line carrying that responsibility the next time and she fell short? This autumn Peter had given her the special attention that she needed and enjoyed. What if he withdrew? Last year, she felt a different kind of pressure after the national meet. She knew that she had to increase her commitment to running and she needed to find the way. Peter helped her. This time was worse. She already had done so much. How much more room did she have to give, how many more minutes to allocate to her running, how many more foods to push away from her plate, how many calls to refuse, how much more emotional energy to dedicate to an essentially quixotic task? It was her responsibility to put some order to all this, she reminded herself. Ducking her head and moving from class to class, she gradually released herself to the mesmeric, timeless swirl of student life. The next time she looked up, first-semester finals were behind her; Christmas had come and gone, and she was back on campus for the second semester registered for new courses and looking forward to the indoor season. Cross-country was history. It was enough to remember the essential facts. She was seventh in the country in a sport she did not enjoy and for which she was not best suited; she was an all-American by virtue of that performance; she had led the team to a second national championship, and she had emerged on the other side of her doubt with a new opportunity in front of her.

Down south, another young runner was not as sanguine about the future, perhaps because unlike Stephanie, she salvaged nothing from the race in Milwaukee. Commenting on Wisconsin's team title, one newspaper article said solemnly that North Carolina State was hurt when its third runner Kathy Ormsby "dropped out." Another article twisted the knife by saying that if Ormsby had stayed in the race Wisconsin would have been hard-pressed to win. The words were strong, they were hurtful, and they were imprecise, however inadvertently. In fact, Kathy Ormsby did not drop out of the NCAA championship race. She did not grow tired or disinclined, did not turn from the fray, or anticipate unduly the pain and withdraw; she did not drift from the race, mingle with the spectators, and leave her teammates to fend for themselves; nor did she fake an injury and fall in a pathetic heap, hoping to encourage sympathy or pity. Conduct like that would have been unthinkable for Kathy Ormsby. As it truly happened, she did not stop at all; she was stopped.

Kathy intended to compete for a spot in the top-ten individuals. The goal was realistic because she had run well throughout the cross-country season, and especially well on the day North Carolina State upended Wisconsin at the Rutgers Invitational. All she had to do was run near that level of performance and she would distinguish herself at the national meet. The race itself started uneventfully. Breaking from the curved starting line, she felt as she expected to feel—running hard but not overextended, aware of the distinguished company by which she was surrounded but not threatened by it, excited by the tumult that followed the runners but not engulfed by it. She was also aware of the weather, the terrain, and the pressure. She was an experienced national-class athlete and it would take a willing blindness not to appreciate the critical features of the race. But beyond anything else she was deeply involved in the chase and proud to add one more splash of color—North Carolina's State's deep red—to the many colors that poured across the white, brown, and green terrain.

As the runners approached the mile, Kathy was measuring

her effort, keeping an eye out for her freshman teammate Suzie Tuffey who was, rather remarkably, barreling along up front; and she was holding a good position to move aggressively when the real racing began. People standing on either side of the corridor that marked the course would back away in time to let her go past, and they would notice that she was running well. Had they followed Kathy down the course, however, soon they would have seen her gasp as if suddenly deprived of air; and they would have seen a look of apprehension and surprise cross her face. They might also have seen a tremor or a stagger as Kathy fought to continue, and they would have seen her slow. They could not, however, have seen the full detail of what was happening. They could not have seen the paralyzing, insensitive terror that now rushed through Kathy like a current, carrying every safe thought or emotion away in its wake nor could they have known that, for Kathy, literally everything of value was at risk. Faith, hope, security, comfort, and esteem, the whole idea of doing what you wanted to do as and when you wanted to do it, were crashing around her.

Shocked by what was happening in the middle of one of the most important races of her life, Kathy did what any runner of worth would do. She tried to run through the pain and away from the problem. She reminded herself to relax. She tried to breath deeply. She concentrated on the simple motion of running. She did everything that experience, reading, and coaching told her might help. Later, she recalled the effort to keep herself upright. She did not remember falling. But she did fall, and having fallen she could not raise up because her body would not work. The race passed her by, and the women were gone. Soon they were way off on the other side of the field, revealed only by the echoing cheers that swept along after them as the spectators ran from spot to spot to see who was leading, who was falling back, how a favored team was doing, what calculations could be quickly made, and what impressions might be preserved. Kathy Ormsby was no longer part of either throng. She was not running and she was not watching. She was walking in, or would when she was able. She had not dropped out, but it would look that way in the results. DNF (did not finish). On any day, those were cruel credentials for a runner of Kathy Ormsby's talent. They were particularly so on a day when her teammates needed her and when it mattered that she fell.

As Kathy returned to the team area in Milwaukee, she was concerned about her teammates. On a team, the highest virtue is reliability. And she was not reliable, not any more, no matter how attentive they were to her explanations and how sympathetic they were to her circumstance. Beyond all that, however, was Kathy's view of herself. Her responsibility to her teammates, her regret that she let them down, her self-recrimination, obscured only briefly the true significance of what happened. Out there on the course in Milwaukee, Kathy ceased to be a decision maker in one of the critical activities of her life. She did not know what happened to her and did not intend the consequence of her actions. When the terror passed, the residual fear emanating from the loss of control and from the failed presumption that she made her own choices remained to haunt her.

Kathy had, in fact, collapsed once before. In her freshman year at North Carolina State she fell in the National Cross-Country Championship, held that year in Lehigh, Pennsylvania. On that occasion, she experienced the same terror, the same inability to move her legs, and the futile reaction to the positive thoughts she feverishly tried to conjure. She said later, "I just started feeling like, I don't know if I can finish. And then the next thing I knew, a course official came over and got me." She had blacked out. Her coach, Rollie Geiger, did not over-react. He was supportive and understanding, making her feel that her welfare was important to him. He did, however, want her to be checked out by a physician. After the race, Kathy went back home to her family doctor who did some tests and found that she was mildly anemic, although he did not know whether that would be sufficient to explain the loss of consciousness. Kathy was also referred to a physician with a specialty in young adults, and finally to a psychiatrist for counseling. She was not referred to a medical specialist to consider the possibility that either a cardiac or seizure disorder explained what happened. Nothing in the single incident seemed to require it.

In due course, Kathy returned to the spring season of her freshman year. Although her parents continued to worry that she was a perfectionist who did not let go and encouraged her to give up running, she did no such thing. She went back to running. It was important to her and she loved doing it. She tried to eat better, she enjoyed the continued support of her coach, and she trained hard and consistently. She also continued to develop an intense and consuming spiritual life. As a child, she had determined to do her best for God, whatever that meant and whatever it entailed. She prayed for the strength to do His will in all things. As she grew older and started to run, she saw the movie *Chariots of Fire*, and responded enthusiastically to its message. She may have been slight, but the "muscular Christian" was her ethic. She would permit God to use her through her running. All of these aspects of her life—her early desire to serve God by doing her best, her desire to glorify the ungendered Him by athletic accomplishments, the fact that this was the second time she had let Him down and disappointed her teammates, the memory of Rollie's kindness and understanding after the first fall, the fear that the thing that troubled her was more serious than mild anemia—made Kathy's experience in Milwaukee in the fall of 1985 especially harsh. Thereafter, in every run she took and every race she ran, she knew one true fact. She might fall. When she did, she would have no answer. She would be caught short, probed and analyzed without rebuttal or defense.

It should never have been like that. In a world of good people and bad people perfectly matched with reward and punishment, Kathy Ormsby would have been safe, regarded, and rich by every measure. Friends, family, and acquaintances would line up to testify in her behalf. She had a mother and a father who loved her, and for whom she reciprocated in full measure. She had an older sister and two brothers, one of whom showed her the way when he started running track as a half-miler and permitted her to scurry through the last 220 yards of a training run with him. She had coaches in volleyball and soccer who admired her attention to the welfare of the team, even if she did sometimes boot one or shank a shot. She had coaches in softball, a sport she played less well and less frequently, who nonetheless would have noticed her spirit and her determined nature. She had other coaches who discovered her prodigious talent for distance running and encouraged her gift, all the while holding one hand on her shoulder for restraint. She had ministers and teachers who respected and facilitated her spirituality and her sense of thanksgiving. She even had neighbors and perfect strangers who enjoyed the knowledge that somewhere out there on almost every Carolina morning, young Kathy Ormsby was running. She was running for the glory of God, she said, closer there than anywhere. "Take my feet and let them be swift and beautiful for thee." It was a song she knew. It was a song she knew that joined many other songs she knew that joined a prayer she knew that joined many other prayers she knew, for her entire conscious life was cast to heaven as due. Who would argue the point?

With or without argument, there was much to offer up. In high school, she could offer God a final ranking of number one in a class of 600. She could offer Him a state championship in her sophomore year in high school when she ran the mile in 5:09. She could offer him her silver medal in the 880 that same year, and then add from her junior year another silver medal in cross-country before

Kathy Ormsby stretches out in a high school race.

sending up two more state championships in track not to mention a mile time under 5:00 that year. She could offer, finally, a state championship in cross-country and three more state championships in track, a sweep of the 880, the mile, and the two mile. She could also offer opportunities, which she rejected, to run for Auburn or for the University of North Carolina in Chapel Hill; and finally she could offer the one thing she wanted dearly, the chance to run for NC State, to attach herself to a legacy that included Julie and Mary Shea, Joan Benoit, and Betty Springs, among many others. Among all these blessings, Kathy gave particular thanks to good friends and good coaches, Pete Pittman and Charlie Bishop, who had prepared her well.

Kathy submitted all that she earned in the kind of self-effacement that has the potential to erase the living person and to make her the scrivener for someone else's thoughts and heart. Of course, the truth is different. Behind the records, behind the prayers, behind the songs, behind the credit she freely gave to the Lord was a kind, caring young girl who worked hard to develop the talents she had been given, who was popular with her schoolmates, even as she was quiet among them, and who had a subdued charisma that drew people to her. Grown strong at 5' 5" and 112 pounds before she graduated from high school, the young girl was a talented, methodical athlete. She did not win races solely because nature blessed her, although it did. She won because she made it happen. Her God loved hard work, consistency, fierce competition, tough front-running, speed work, and long runs on Sunday morning before church. When the high school coach formed a "500 Club" to encourage, primarily, the boys to run 500 miles in the course of a summer, Kathy joined it. She ran most of the miles alone. Soon, however, she met Jackie Tanner, a local marathoner whose company she enjoyed, and the two of them ran together often. Kathy grew stronger and stronger. From time to time, the high school coach would try to draw her back in—he did not want her to run so much mileage that her speed was compromised—but most often the messages Kathy heard were encouraging and exhortatory. Go! Go! Go! was what Kathy heard, and, as she was not good at stepping back from herself and looking at things dispassionately, that is what she did. "Things just happened, and I did what seemed best," she says now. She had always been serious about her work and now she grew more so. Looking back at herself, she thinks that it was an error not to have enjoyed herself more, to hold and nurture the joyous aspects of running. But it is too late for that now. Time came and went, and Kathy grew as an athlete and a person and made her way finally to North Carolina State.

Kathy made tremendous progress as a runner at North Carolina State. She loved Rollie Geiger as a coach because he was inspiring without being heavy-handed; he was funny and caring; and he was, in her informed view, a great person. She jumped into the workouts and worked very hard, so hard that Rollie had to "fuss at her" to slow down. He would tell her that the workouts were bank deposits, from which withdrawal should be made only on race day, but Kathy made withdrawals all the time, or so Rollie feared! He encouraged her to build strength gradually and to hoard it. But what could he really do with a woman of such enthusiasms and such beliefs? Kathy listened to Rollie and she believed what he said, but she was convinced that the harder she worked the better she would be. So she pushed herself. In addition to her training and racing, Kathy concentrated on her studies. She took the preliminary courses for medical school, for which her aptitude was strong enough that she even enjoyed organic chemistry. Socially, she did relatively little in the first couple of years. She did join the Campus Crusade for Christ, but she did not participate often in the group's social activities. It was later reported that this was because the social activities did not make her a better Christian and were therefore pared away. In fact, she participated rarely in the Campus Crusade social activities because her cross-country and track teams at North Carolina State provided a full and rewarding social world for her. She was modest and reserved; she had a gentle accent that permitted her to recede into the background if she wished, which she often did; she had a fixed sense of right and wrong supported by an overarching moral and spiritual code; she studied conscientiously; she was careful in her personal relationships; she did not drink; and yet—and yet!—the essential qualities of warmth and accessibility remained. To some of the young men on the team, she was a little sister with whom they could relax. For starters, they teased her no end for being a good girl and for the qualities of dependability and conscience

Kathy Ormsby as a freshman at North Carolina State.

they secretly admired. When they, one time, carried her on their shoulders across the campus, the experience gave them a playful image to which they could return later for a rise and a laugh. Held aloft, she struggled halfheartedly for her freedom, crying again and again, "Put me down! Put me down!" In recollection, something about the key and the timber to her voice and the combination of outrage and pleasure, made everyone happy. The liberty they had taken was freely given, and no one doubted it. When they had concerns or worries, they knew they could turn to Kathy. Equally, when Kathy needed help, they would comfort her, as did one young man who came to her and stayed for hours after the mishap in Milwaukee for the simple purpose of telling her he cared. The women, too, came to Kathy. Months later, one would say that Kathy was the person they went to when they were in trouble. She would say the same of them. When she needed them, they were there, singly and collectively. In an atmosphere of mutual respect and support fostered by Rollie Geiger, her teammates gave her what she most needed. They gave her a comfortable place from which she could grow; a place where she would be valued and esteemed in the same measure that each of them was; a place to be safe. Virtually to a person, she was proud of her teammates and she treasured them. Kathy Ormsby would never count herself important in the lives of the men and women on the North Carolina State teams, but she would hold one truth fast. They were important to her.

From this combination of elements, Kathy Ormsby produced a promising athletic career. In her freshman year, Kathy ran a breakthrough 5,000-meter time of 16:24 at the Penn Relays in spring 1984, was an all-American later that year at the NCAA meet, and then followed that in 1985 with a seasonal best of 16:04 before running 16:10 at the NCAA Outdoor Championships in Austin, Texas, where she finished just ahead of Stephanie Herbst, then a freshman. She was also building a deep base for future performances. Often she ran 90 miles a week, with a long run of about 15 miles on most Sunday mornings. Almost in spite of herself, she did enjoy the training, the whole experience of being out alone or with friends on the roads with a breeze blowing into or away from them, all the changes in weather, the sense of movement itself. In fact, as her college career continued, she rarely won races. She ran well and enjoyed success when it came, but she did not judge herself by the accident of victory. Day in and day out, in races and in workouts, she asked herself the harder question. Did she run as well as she was able?

In the cross-country season of her junior year—the one that ended in Milwaukee—Kathy Ormsby was in shape. In the race against Wisconsin in New Brunswick, she saw first-hand that Stephanie had stepped it up a notch, but she, too, ran a good race. She was either third or fourth in that race, she forgets which. It hardly matters because North Carolina State beat Wisconsin on that day, and that is enough to make the recollection pleasant. Some weeks later at the Atlantic Coast Conference (ACC) meet, Kathy again competed effectively. She was in the first five overall and NC State won the championship. When she and her teammates went to Milwaukee, she and they did not know if they would win the national championship. But they knew they could.

After the fall, Kathy went back to the doctors. She went to the physician on campus. The doctor thought that the incident was related to stress. Kathy does not recall an intense medical workup that included, for example, an electroencephalogram (EEG) or an echocardiogram. She knows that she was not given a cardiac stress test. Perhaps it would be unfair to suggest that those tests should have been made. The evidence that made them unnecessary was plain enough. The patient was young, female, conscientious to a fault, serious in mien, a Christian, anxious, very thin by now at 103 pounds, and engaged in a competitive sport that sent her careening over hills and across open fields at speeds sufficient to break her

A powerful 1-2 for North Carolina State in 1985:
Suzie Tuffey (left) and Kathy Ormsby (right).

apparently frail and delicate resolve, all the while with people
yelling in her face or running at her and away. In addition, the young
woman was enrolled in one of the most competitive academic programs North Carolina State offered—premed with all the hard sciences it required—and spoke of wanting to become a medical mis-
sionary. Furthermore, from outward appearances, she had little or no
social release in her life. To put it another way, there was no fun, no
joy, or at least none easily discerned. Why, then, was there surprise

that she fell? It was the natural reaction to stress, which the woman appeared to gather around herself like a cloak, if not a crown.

Of course, no reasonable person could be satisfied by a diagnosis of stress. It did not solve the problem. It did not replace a question with a certainty. To the contrary, it left every future activity under a cloud. The terror could come again at any time so long as Kathy held her course, which she would do. She would honor her commitments to herself, to her school, to her coach, to her teammates, and to the glory of God for Whom she hoped to give witness. She would not be turned away. That being true, the terror would become part of Kathy Ormsby. It would be with her as she looked ahead, however warily, to the next semester, and as she prepared to meet it. She took three weeks off after Milwaukee and then she went back to her work. With the benefit of hindsight, the image of Kathy Ormbsy rising early each morning to run in the light fog and crisp coolness of the winter of 1986 is a melancholy reminder that the future takes sharpened pleasure to mock young people, who do not have the means to protect themselves from it. It was the spring toward which she worked, the traditional season of the lion and the lamb. It was Kathy's time and it was Stephanie's time. Never again would either of them be far from the other.

SIXTEEN

Look into the darkness and the darkness looks
As if it massed before a telescope/

Four Sonnets
Mark Jarman

Stephanie was too thin during the cross-country season of her sophomore year. Peter thought so, and Stephanie knew he thought so, but she did not make an immediate adjustment. It was not that she ignored his concerns or felt he was wrong to have them. To the contrary, she appreciated the worry as a sign of his care. Nonetheless, she was on her own course this time. Deep into a delicate season for which she had so much hope and for which she felt so much responsibility, she simply would not take the time to reconsider how she stacked and measured the decisions of her life, even if the result would make her safer. She did that a year ago. Everything had gone well since then. Certainly she was running better. Absent speculation and guesswork about facts she knew better than anyone, where were the arguments for change? For Stephanie, there were none. That being the case, it was easier to go on doing what she was doing for the time being, jacking up her running mileage, racing to the front of workouts, skimping on meals, cutting out snacks except for popcorn. And it was easier to cross her fingers and hope that she would survive. Meanwhile, however, as a sign of her grace and good will, she would keep a watch on Peter out of the corner of her eye. She would monitor his watchfulness. She would also make one more change. Preemptively, she would step back every now and again to take a look for herself. She would try to get sufficient distance to see the delicate contiguity between weight, hard work, and injury. It was a concession, a slight spalling and cracking in her otherwise total concentration on the real business of running, but she would do it. She would do it for herself and she would do it for Peter.

Poor Peter. Young as she was, Stephanie had a certain sympathy for his position. The man could not speak freely because they—all of his runners—had taken the privilege away from him. Even on the matter of weight and fitness, he had to mince through the conversation, picking words with care to avoid doing more harm than good. And that was not the end of it. Even to describe a workout carried danger. Looking back now, Stephanie smiles to herself to remember the discomfort a bunch of young women could cause a man who was supposed to be in charge, and to whom they had freely given their loyalty and confidence. "Peter knew," she says, "what a sensitive group all the women were and any subject he would even broach would be very, very difficult. You know, if he said 'run fast,' people would go crazy! He could not even say that. He'd say, 'Do this at a nice clip' because 'fast' was just too strong a word. People would have killed themselves, and then they wouldn't have been ready for a meet on Saturday. And Peter probably knew the same thing about me."

For the indoor season, Peter had an idea. He would back Stephanie off a bit in distance and see what kind of speed she had. He could move her back up when they got outdoors. In the middle of January, Peter entered Stephanie in the mile at the Badger Classic. Cindy Bremser was also running. This was just a tune-up for two athletes who had other work to do later in the year and were looking for a sign to tell them where they were. On the day, Cindy broke the meet record when she ran 4:40.87. Stephanie finished second in 4:45.88, not a bad time for a distance runner on an indoor track early in the season, but not breathtaking either. "It was really nice to have Cindy run with us today because she spent a lot of time working with us and telling us what it takes to win," Stephanie said after the run, before adding that she thought Cindy's enthusiasm had "rubbed off on them." Perhaps the better running was done in the 3,000 meters by freshman Lori Wolter, who grabbed hold of Cathy Branta and hung on. Lori eventually finished third in 9:32.19 behind Cathy, who ran 9:17.13 and Leslie Seymour, formerly of the University of Minnesota, who ran 9:18.58. Stephanie would always admire the courage of women like Lori, and like Holly Hering for that matter, who had, as Stephanie puts it, "the mental intact," or the ability to "go get it." She wished she had more of those qualities.

The objective evidence, however, is that Stephanie had plenty of whatever was needed. When Wisconsin eyed the Big Ten Indoor Championship in 1986, it focused on Stephanie Herbst, for whom expectations were high and growing higher. Katie Ishmael was still affected by fatigue, exhaustion, or by a virus, depending on what newspaper you read. Lori Wolter was relatively untested and might, in the best of circumstances, be outgunned by the older runners. Wisconsin did have some good sprinters, multiple-event performers, and jumpers, but they would all have their hands full with Indiana, Michigan, and Purdue especially. That fact notwithstanding, the Big Ten was a meet Peter liked to win, and he loaded up for the effort. Stephanie's first job was to win the 3,000 meters. She did that easily. She controlled the tempo in front of Sue Schroeder of the University of Michigan, a woman she came to admire greatly, and ahead of Katie, who responded once again in a difficult circumstance to help her team. Stephanie ran the fastest time by any college runner to that point in the year, 9:08.42. Sue ran 9:15.81 for second, while Katie ran 9:22.29. Stephanie then doubled back in the mile. After her run with Cindy Bremser, Stephanie had run a mile in 4:41.10, which was the second-fastest mile ever run by a Wisconsin woman. But she was tired by the time the event was called and she finished fourth at the Big Ten in 4:49.89 in a race so close that the winner ran only 4:48.64. Katie came back, too, placing third in the 5,000 meters behind Schroeder and Jenny Spangler of Iowa. Lori Wolter hung tight to finish fourth. The first four runners were squeezed between 15:43.56, which was also a collegiate leading time, and 15:48.15, which was Lori's result. With efforts like those from Stephanie, Katie, and Lori, as well as particularly good performances from the jumpers and multi-eventers, Wisconsin won the title Peter had his eyes on.

Next up was the NCAA Indoor National Championship in Oklahoma City. Stephanie entered the 3,000-meter run. She had one of the best times in the country, but she was not confident she could win. If the truth is known, she had little idea what to expect. In her freshman year, she ran the Track and Field Association indoor meet on the boards and judged the experience a disaster. This year, too, she was apprehensive, or as she said, "scared of the boards." Her composure was not helped by the qualifying heat on Friday. She ran 9:14.15, which was the fastest qualifier, but the run felt harder than it should have. Stephanie was also a little troubled by Liz Lynch of Scotland and the University of Alabama, who was right behind her in the heat. Alabama aspired to the team championship and hoped to maximize points by sending Liz to the line twice within the space of an hour, first in the mile and then in the 3,000 meters. What unsettled the matter further was the clear possibility that Liz would succeed. At the Southeast conference meet, Liz was given an even more ridiculous assignment, and carried it off with ease. She won the mile in 4:35.06 and the two mile in 9:50.85, anchored her team's distance medley relay to victory by running another good mile, and added a gratuitous second place in the individual 1,000

meters. This, Stephanie had to ask, was the woman Peter was sending her out to beat?

It was the woman, of course, but Peter had a strategy. He
always had a strategy, which Stephanie thought was very helpful. As
she said at the time, "I just rely on what he tells me. On each lap I
work on what he has just said. He has the whole thing worked out
for me." Privately, she continues to say that she relied on Peter
because she lacked "the mental fortitude to do it." Whatever the
case, this time Peter's idea made perfect sense to everybody but
Stephanie. He wanted Stephanie to run away from Liz Lynch.
Stephanie laughs at the memory of her conversation with Peter,
"Peter's strategy was for me to take the lead and then stay in front
and run faster, and continue to run faster and faster. When he gave
me the strategy, I was like, Peter, that's the strategy?! And he said,
yes, that's the strategy." Once more, she would do all the better she
could do, running a strategy that "must be what I have to do."

Liz Lynch played her hand. One hour before the 3,000-
meter final, she ran the mile. She sat for 1,320 meters and then belt-
ed the last quarter to finish first in 4:38.85. While she was doing
that, Stephanie was warming up, prepared to take her down in the
3,000 meters as Peter instructed. When the race finally started, it
appeared to go instantly wrong. Liz Lynch dived into the lead, no
doubt hoping to control a slower tempo in front of women who were
intimidated by her. Unfortunately for Liz, Stephanie was not distracted. After giving Liz a brief moment up front, Stephanie went
around her before the first lap even ended. Having secured the lead,
Stephanie knew that she was supposed to establish a quick pace in
the early laps and then accelerate in the later ones. She could not
quite find the subtlety to do it that way. Instead, she just hit the
accelerator and drew gradually away. She said later that she was
nervous and uptight, but nothing in the run revealed that fact. As
Stephanie moved farther and farther ahead, the only real question

was whether she would break the NCAA record of 8:58.68, owned by Christine McMiken of Oklahoma State. Before that, the record had been held by Cathy Branta and it would be nice to return it to Wisconsin. Being told of the opportunity, Stephanie tightened things up over the last few laps, striving to push her stride a few beats ahead of the inexorable clock. She was holding nothing in reserve, but when she finished more than 10 seconds ahead of Liz she still did not think she had it. Coming off the track she found Peter. She was sorry, she told him, that she missed the record. "I just couldn't go any faster."

In fact, she did get it. Stephanie's front-running knocked the collegiate record down to 8:54.98. Almost incidentally, the race was also her first national championship, and should have been at least a brief time for celebration, without the need to look either backward or forward. In the nature of things, she was almost immediately required to do both, turning backward to Milwaukee and forward to distant goals, always one step shy of completion. About Milwaukee, she confirmed her disappointment in the result and said that she might have been too hard on herself. Whatever happened on that day, however, the win in Oklahoma City made up for it! She also was asked about her weight, which was even lower than in the fall, when it was low enough. "Yes, I'm lighter, and maybe I lost a little strength for awhile. But, I'm OK now and I really feel faster." As for the outdoor season, she was moving back up to 5,000 and 10,000. Finally, as to her feelings after the big win, the breakthrough win, the one that made up for the disappointment of Milwaukee, there was the more reflective view of it, the one that was personal and quiet. "It was exciting but it was a really weird feeling because by that time I had worked very hard to get there. I had given up everything just to be there. I didn't have any social life, I didn't date much, I didn't have any girlfriends. The people who I should have been close with were my teammates and we weren't good friends. I was with Katie, and Katie was a reserved person, not the kind of person who would run up and give you a big hug, and Peter was also a reserved person. I finished that race and my parents weren't there, no relatives there. Nobody there. I tried to call my Dad to say, 'Guess what? I won!' But he wasn't home. It could not have been— I mean I thought that something great was going to happen. But it was like, hey!!" This might have been the first time Stephanie recognized that, figuratively, she was a hamster on a wheel, spinning, spinning, spinning and always in the same place. It might also have been the first time she knew that, if she did not enjoy the spin itself, she might as well get off the wheel.

After the National Indoor Championship, one thing did change. Stephanie had to address the issue of her weight, which was attracting too much attention. She was down to 95 pounds. She still felt good, but she was so close to excess that the distinction was immeasurable. She was in danger of becoming incorporeal, a trail of vapor, smoke or mist curling around the track. Looking back, she described the way things were. "I think at the end of the cross-country season, my priorities were screwed up," she says. "Running was my main priority. My weight was down. I was so uptight, I couldn't even eat. I'd sit down to eat and I'd say, 'There's so much to do. I don't have time for this.' You get to be a perfectionist in your running and then it shows up in other places, too. Your schoolwork, everywhere, and there is no time for yourself."

In the months after cross-country ended and throughout the indoor season, her family encouraged her to live a more balanced life. "They were saying, 'You don't go out with your friends; you're running every day; there are other things.' My dad wanted me to take one day off a week." Peter, too, spoke of replenishment as an essential component of training. Finally, Stephanie decided to make a change. Her diet was too routinized for significant adjustment. But she did fiddle with her training as a means of rebalancing demand

and satisfaction. The work she did remained in general conformity with Peter's instructions, but Peter left a lot of room for individual choice and variation. How hard would the dyno be run? How much distance on the morning run, and at what intensity? How far would the Sunday run be and how fast? All of those issues were, by design, left to the athlete, and it was there that Stephanie modified her conduct by backing off. "I think I slightly decreased my training," she says, "I don't think I worked out quite as hard for outdoor. And I was a little concerned about that. Whereas, indoors I could just naturally go by people on the work that I was doing. I didn't have to work that hard to beat people in a race. My outdoor season, I just didn't. I mentally wasn't there. Physically, too, I wasn't in the shape I'd been in indoors. It was interesting. People were saying to me, 'You look a lot better! You look a lot better!' because I'd put on weight, not from a change of diet but from less exercise."

Despite Stephanie's additional pounds, an outsider would still see a very thin, almost tiny woman running very fast and very strongly in the outdoor season of 1986. In competitive terms, she owned the next several months. The season began in San Diego, California, where Peter took the team for spring break. In San Diego, each individual could train without the immediate pressure of schoolwork; and the team could further develop a sense of itself as a distinct entity. As Peter said, "You learn again how to become a group that functions closely together where everybody has to adjust to make sure that things run smoothly." Of course, there was also the warm weather. Wisconsin in March is not a day at the beach. All that aside, Stephanie's days in California included much of the structure she imposed at home. She got up early for a run; she studied a bit on her own, or she toured or lounged. She might lift weights, stretch, or do some of the exercises prescribed for strength, flexibility, or range of motion. In the afternoon, she and the other team members went to the track or out to run a prescribed workout. The workouts were, however, sharper and more focused in California than they would be later. "Just because the coaches are there and available at all times, we work more with smaller groups and spread out over the whole day so that the individual athletes can get more attention," Peter explained at the time.

When spring break ended, the Wisconsin women moved into the outdoor season. One of the first important meets was in Baton Rouge, Louisiana, in mid-April. In Louisiana, the team discovered the difference between warm and hot. The day was 90 degrees, it was humid, and a wind was blowing. The wind, far from being a refreshment, appeared to drive the heat in front of it so bluntly that it felt like an aggravated assault. Nevertheless, Katie Ishmael re-emerged to win the 5,000 meters in 16:27.54 as part of a one-two-three Badger finish, the other two places going to Stephanie Bassett, who ran 16:29.82, and Kelly McKillen, who finished in 16:29.95. Stephanie Herbst, it must be said, did even better. She started the day by winning the 1,500 meters in 4:23.80, which was almost 6 seconds ahead of second place, and then she returned to the track for the 3,000 meters. In the later race, she had to contend with UCLA's highly regarded freshman, Polly Plumer. It did not make a bit of difference. Stephanie just hit the front and kept going. She set a new LSU stadium record of 9:10.79. She pulled Lori Wolter along with her to an NCAA-qualifying 9:23.01 in second. Polly Plumer trailed Lori by more than 10 seconds.

A couple of weeks later, the Badger women were back in business. At the Mt. San Antonio College Relays, which Stephanie did not enter, Lori and Katie ran 10,000 meters. While they finished seventh and eighth respectively, they did relatively well. Lori ran 33:31.9 and Katie was right behind her in 33:41.5. Back in the Midwest, Stephanie continued her tear. At the 77th edition of the Drake Relays, she was scheduled to meet Betty Springs, a graduate of North Carolina State University and one of the best women distance runners in the country. Predictably, Stephanie was scared to death. She did not know what Betty Springs looked like, however, so she looked for her during the warm-up. Seeing a likely candidate, she asked Peter whether that was Betty. He said no, that's not Betty. Is that her? No. That? No. Stephanie kept looking but she never did find Betty, not even on the starting line when she checked in and got a lane. Fine with her, Stephanie thought, as she put the best light on the situation by concluding that Betty was not running after all. Now all she had to do was run the race. The temperature was 88 degrees and it was windy, but Peter set her to a hard pace. Cathy Branta's meet record of 15:31.8 was the target. This was ambitious running, but it scarcely bothered Stephanie because she did not know what Peter had in mind until it was time to step up to the line, or virtually so. "He never tells me what I'm going to run," she said later. "He never lets any of us know until the last minute. If we know, we might tell people from other teams and they can plan their strategy. If we don't know it's hard to tell."

As usual, Stephanie led. She had some good runners behind her, including two international-caliber athletes, Mary Knisely and, of course, Betty Springs. She was there all the time. In fact, as Stephanie moved 8 seconds under record pace at halfway, it was Betty Springs who clung most tenaciously to the pace. At that, she was a full 50 yards behind. One reason Betty fell back was because Stephanie was out too fast, no doubt because she had been running a lot of 3,000-meter runs and was having to adjust to a 5,000-meter rhythm. As the race progressed, Stephanie started to slow down. While the record apparently slipped away, Dan Herbst, who was in the stands, saw the reason. "The wind was too strong," he said. "The gusts up to 40 mph would sometimes blow her right into the second lane." Wind or no wind, Stephanie stayed with it. She was battling the heat, the wind, and her growing fatigue, and she was doing damage control. Essentially, she was trying to slow down less quickly.

Vice President George Bush finally getting some understanding
of "the vision thing," with Stephanie Herbst at the 1986 Drake Relays.

The experienced 18,000-strong Drake crowd knew what was going
on and cheered Stephanie in waves. The noise came loud on the
homestretch every time she ran past and louder yet on the backstretch where the students and the athletes sat. Lap by solitary lap as
the noise rolled along beside her, Stephanie persevered until she had
a fine, quite tired victory in 15:34.36. She won by 18 seconds over
Knisely (15:52.97), Kansas State's Jacque Struckhoff (15:54.84),
and Betty Springs (16:08.06). Later reports of the event would capture the image of Stephanie, still a sylph at just under 100 pounds,
fighting the weather and the pace in an attempt to get a record that
was already owned by a good friend, a record she really didn't care
about, only that Peter said to go get it. As one report had it, "There
is no such title as darling of the Drake Relays, but if there was,
Stephanie Herbst of the University of Wisconsin would be a top

candidate." Her candidacy would be furthered by one more emotional event before the afternoon ended. Vice President George Bush was in town. This was Iowa, of course, the state known best for two things: corn and the political caucus. Before he left Iowa, the vice president would speak in traditional terms. "It's planting season—a time of hope," he said, "And hope is what I feel in the air tonight. The skies on the horizon are beginning to show some bright spots for farmers." He would also attend the relays. Wearing a Drake University jacket, he was gracious enough to present the award to one of the winners. When Stephanie Herbst approached him, some wag yelled, "Kiss her," so he did. Vice President Bush leaned sharply toward her, smiled a broad, friendly smile, caught her with both hands behind the neck, and kissed her demurely on the cheek. "I was really shocked, and I didn't know what to say to him," she admits, "I guess I just said, 'Thank you, sir.'" The vice president told Stephanie that it was great watching her run and that she did a good job. He then presented her with a vice presidential pin to go along with her Drake Relays watch. In that way, it happened that in the season of hope, in the planting season, the future president of the United States conferred his blessing on a woman named for the autumn, the time for harvest.

It was harvest time, too, in Pennsylvania at the Penn Relays. Kathy Ormsby, engaged in the Lord's work, was one of the thousands of athletes convened for the several days of the meet. After Milwaukee, she had toiled through the winter and early spring, and she was now prepared to run the first 10,000 meters of her life. She had two goals: to win the race and to run faster than 33:00 minutes, no small accomplishment in either case but nothing that would send her to the top of the sport. Starting the race, she could not have imagined, not even as an exercise, the headline that would appear the next morning in *The Philadelphia Inquirer:* "Ormsby breaks record in 10K." Nor could she have believed the detail from the article, which read, "On a sun-drenched afternoon that dimmed the memory of Wednesday's snow flurries, the Kentucky women's distance-medley team and North Carolina State's Suzie Tuffey, at 3,000 meters, emerged as champions in their first competitive tours of the Penn track. But by nightfall, their triumphs had been overshadowed by Tuffey's teammate, Kathy Ormsby, a 5' 5", 103-pound dynamo who set a national collegiate record when she won the women's 10,000 meters in 32 minutes, 36.2 seconds."

That stuff about Suzie Tuffey she would believe. She had long since concluded that Suzie was from Mars, or some other distant and alien planet, such was her talent. And the report about Kentucky would not have surprised her either. They were good and getting better. But what was that business about a dynamo and about the collegiate record? No, that she would be required to deny if only from modesty. Why, when she heard references to a CR after her race, she did not even recognize the initials, did not know that in context C meant collegiate and R meant record. Those two words had an abstract quality to her when pinned together in such a fashion. If the national record to which they referred was a prize that you had to be present to win, she might have refused to go to the podium upon hearing her name called.

In truth, it happened just as the newspaper said. Ellen Reynolds from Duke was a friend of Kathy's. Ellen was the one trying for a record. Kathy was content on the crisp evening to sit behind her lap after lap, a sound policy for a person in her first 25-lap race. The two broke away from the pack with almost half the race left to run. The whole affair had a dream-like quality, as the two circled the track methodically. Kathy was comfortable. She was waiting for the right moment. And when it came with one lap remaining, Kathy simply went around Ellen and set out for home. It was all rather unceremonious. Taking flight from Ellen, Kathy ran straight into the record books. She beat the 2-year-old standard previously held by

A racer of unusual success, Kathy Ormsby on the track.

Katie Ishmael of the University of Wisconsin. Ellen finished second in 32:40.6 while Lisa Welch of Boston University ran third in 32:41.9.

Despite its unexpected nature, Kathy's run at the Penn Relays was not a fluke. She earned the record by years of dedicated running and by her attentiveness to good coaching. Rollie Geiger said after the race that Kathy had almost always had the ability to train at the level of Connie Jo Robinson, Janet Smith, and Suzie Tuffey "because she is a strong-minded person who will push her body." He also said that she concentrated her early energy on the shorter races because he believed that an athlete should run short before she runs long. "So what you saw with Kathy, particularly over the last 600 meters was a result of the development she has had in the 1,500, 3,000, and 5,000 over the last three years," he said. As to her racing, Kathy provided a clue to her success at Penn when she admitted that too often she entered races without intending and expecting to win. "Sometimes I forget about doing that," she said. "I think about wanting to qualify or to run a certain time." At the Penn Relays, by contrast, she thought she could win and intended to do so. Kathy also thought she ran better when she remained relaxed and kept her racing in perspective. In the soft, slow Southern accent that many articles noted with apparent pleasure, Kathy said that one thing that helped her was "not placing so much importance on my performances and trying to please other people." She added that she just had to learn "to do my best for myself and for God, and to turn everything over to Him. And it seems like I have been able to do that better this track season than ever before." For Kathy, a singular benefit of the victory at Penn was the chance, finally, to give public testimony of her faith. The Penn Relays, she would say later, "was one of those moments when running is so special. I just felt like I had finally been able to really give it all over to God."

Kathy Ormsby left the Penn Relays happy with the accomplishment and satisfied that she had come closer to an expression of her faith. She also now added another pressure to her lengthy, personally transcribed and created list. The pressure was that of record holder. The implication from that status was that she had to run up to a new level of performance. Kathy hoped to avoid the pressure, but she was not entirely successful. "I tried to tell myself I don't have to do that. But things I do with my head I have trouble getting my heart to understand," she explained. Whether it was pressure or something else, the weeks after the Penn Relays and before the NCAA Outdoor Championships, for which Kathy was now a favorite at the 10,000-meter run, were difficult. On May 10, she ran her slowest performance of the year, but it should not have been a matter of concern. Kathy had just finished final exams and was bound to be tired. Rollie reminded Kathy of that fact, and encouraged her to forget the race and move on. The next weekend things got even worse. At a meet on the campus of North Carolina State, Kathy and Suzie Tuffey agreed to push each other over 5,000 meters. Kathy particularly hoped to get under 16:00 for the distance. This was a reasonable goal given Kathy's 10,000-meter pace and her personal record at 5,000 meters of 16:04. Unfortunately, Kathy passed out at the two-mile mark. "I hit my hip on the side of the track and my knee. And I didn't put my hands out," she says now, "which makes me think it was like blacking out." Understandably, Kathy was embarrassed that it happened again, and initially told her father and her coach that she merely tripped, but in short order she made it right by telling Rollie what really caused the fall. Nonetheless, this latest event was very upsetting for Kathy within weeks of an NCAA championship that would force her into a spotlight. The continued accidents also had a moral or spiritual significance to Kathy. "In my eyes," she said, "I saw what was happening as failing God." Although she was being victimized by a condition that she did not control and did not intend, she nonetheless accepted it as evidence of a personal fault. Kathy said, "I felt like I was failing my coach and my parents and I thought there was really something wrong with me—I guess with the person I was—that was causing this." Rollie Geiger took a different view; he did not blame Kathy at all. He was concerned about her. He asked Kathy to see a physician immediately. Again, as in the past, he wanted to know whether the falls resulted from a physical problem. She would do that, she said, but she also wanted to see a sports psychologist associated with North Carolina State. The sports psychologist could help with relaxation techniques. In fact, Kathy saw the sports psychologist twice before the national meet. This, then, was the appearance of Kathy Ormsby's world as she approached the biggest meet of her life, the National Collegiate Athletic Association National Outdoor Track and Field Championship in Indianapolis, Indiana, in June 1986. She was already frightened, and with good reason. It—the repeated incidents warrant no other noun—could happen again at the meet, and there was nothing she could do, assuredly.

Meanwhile back in Wisconsin, Stephanie Herbst was enjoying a different run-up to the NCAA. For her, the most significant event of the spring season was the Big Ten Outdoor Championships. The meet was being held for the first time in 38 years in Madison, Wisconsin. The University had a newly resurfaced track, without which it could never have hosted the big meet, and it promised to be an emotional experience. This was so because the impetus for resurfacing the track came from the death of Dan McClimon, the popular and successful coach of the Wisconsin men's team who died in the crash of a light plane in 1983. The new track and facilities would be officially dedicated to McClimon's memory on the second day of the two-day meet. From Stephanie's view, the result of the women's competition was a foregone conclusion. Asked about the prospect for a Wisconsin victory, she said, "It's almost inevitable." Explaining herself, she said that the team had 19 seniors and "the only time they didn't win was the indoor title in their freshman season. They'll do anything it takes to win the Big Ten title." Apparently, Peter's attempt to build team consciousness was holding! As to her personal affairs, Stephanie continued to attract attention. One article noted her appearance suggestively, "There's no mistaking Herbst for anything other than a runner. Her legs are lean, but muscular. There is no sign of fat on this body." Stephanie volleyed the remark by saying that she was not on any special diet, "but distance runners try to keep a low body fat percentage." She also continued to deflect credit to Peter. "I think my success has come because of my belief in Peter because his program speaks for itself. I'm more a product of what he puts out because the people he has had have gotten better each year. He has everything figured out. He knows six months in advance every workout. He has everything systematically worked out. It's called PPP, Pushing, Passing, and Pacing." She acquired further detachment from her own running by avoiding the sports magazines and by keeping herself largely uninformed of the athletes against whom she was competing, Betty Springs aside of course! The only hesitation that she admitted was that running cut her off from a social life. "My social life suffers," she said to one reporter. "With school and track, everything is so structured. If I'm not training, I know I have to study. There's not much time for anything else. I go to bed early and study in the afternoons."

If running involved sacrifice, it also offered compensations. Stephanie Herbst's triumphant Big Ten Championship Meet in Madison was surely one of them. She was scheduled to run two events, the 10,000 meters on Friday evening and the 3,000 meters on Saturday afternoon. Friday was enough to tell Saturday not to bother if the intention was to upset Stephanie. It would not be possible. On Friday night, she glided to the front of a large pack and drew gradually and easily away. "Smoothly running lap after lap," said one report, "Herbst smashed a Big Ten record by running the 10,000 meters in 32:54.37 in the conference meet at the new Dan McClimon Memorial Track. In doing so, the lithe sophomore repeated as champion, qualified for the National Collegiate Athletic Association meet, and established the best collegiate time in the nation this year." That last part was not true, of course. The distinction belonged to Kathy Ormsby. But the gist is plain enough. Stephanie was in rare form. That conclusion was reinforced by other reports, which carried phrases and sentences like these: "Herbst, a wisp of a woman, won the event in 32 minutes, 54.37 seconds. The effort broke both the Big Ten (33:49.35) and track (36:34) records;" and, "You might want to ask the other 1,200 or so folks who were on hand Friday, but there appears to be absolutely nothing appealing about spending more than 32 minutes sucking air and running in circles. However, with her long, gliding gait, Herbst made it look almost effortless." Stephanie, who was very pleased by the race especially because a number of people came down from Chaska for the weekend, claimed that she could not believe that she broke the records. "I was just supposed to run the pace, not go too fast, and follow Peter's splits." Peter shook his head at the run, and commented Stephanie was "out of this world today." He also offered his opinion that, had he asked Stephanie to open it up and go get Kathy Ormsby's collegiate record, she would have done so. As it was, her time made her the 13th fastest collegian ever. The race in Madison was, by the way, the first 10,000 meters of Stephanie's season. She used it merely as the excuse to implement her favorite strategy, which was to get out front and run fast, remaining perfectly relaxed and concentrating always on what she was doing. "I'm conscious of everything when I'm running," she said. "You have to. You have to know where everyone is and what everyone is doing." In Madison, everyone was a long way behind, although it should be added that a freshman teammate ran a good race in her own right. Lori finished

An unruffled Stephanie Herbst winning one of her
two championships at the Big Ten outdoor championships, 1986.

second in 33:40.53 to join Stephanie as a qualifier for the national meet. Referring to Stephanie's front-running, Lori gave it full credit, "She always does that. She just goes." The next day, Stephanie did it again. She won the 3,000 meters by 6 seconds over Sue Schroeder of Michigan by running 9:08.64. Sue did, however, have the pleasure of winning a distance event on Wisconsin's track—a rare feat—when she beat Lori Wolter and Kelly McKillen in the 5,000 meters. Of course, nothing Sue did could change the team result. Wisconsin won. The team beat Purdue 130 to 106. It was Wisconsin's ninth title in 11 years.

Stephanie was cresting at the right time. She was qualified for the NCAA meet in the 3,000, the 5,000, and the 10,000, and could take her pick. In any of them, she would have a good chance to win. In the 3,000, her indoor time from Oklahoma City was faster than any collegian had run outdoors. In the 5,000, she had a best mark of 15:31.09, and again no collegian was faster. Finally, at 10,000 meters, she had her only time—the one from the Big Ten— and anyone who saw the race knew there was a cushion. She could run faster. Actually, in the longer race she might have to do that. Kathy Ormsby's time was out there as the collegiate record but Christine McMiken had an even faster time. Christine ran 32:17.1 in a race that did not qualify for record consideration because it included men. Also, Ellen Reynolds' time of 32:40.6 was faster than Stephanie's, as was Lisa Welch's 32:41.9, both of them recorded behind Kathy at Penn. A number of other women were close, as well, including Janet Smith from North Carolina State who ran 33:10.8 for her qualifier. Taking a close look at it, the 10,000 at Indianapolis could turn into a pretty good race. Not that Stephanie Herbst paid much attention. She knew who Kathy Ormsby was but not much more than that, and her familiarity with the other runners was fleeting and remote. It simply wasn't safe to have too much information. She would look for Peter to tell her, in his own time, who to watch and what to do. From that point it would be as ever: On Wisconsin!

SEVENTEEN

It were sparrowlike and childish after our deliverance to explode into twittering laughter and caper-cutting, and utterly to forget the imminent hawk on bough. Lie low, rather, lie low; for you are in the hands of a living God.

The Varieties of Religious Experience
Williams James

Not unusually, places of great sadness are consecrated and marked. A visitor is invited to overlook the blank spaces of Auschwitz, for example, or the barracks at Dachau, to walk past the window where Oswald lay the stem of his rifle, to stand in the low indentation of an open field in France, or to ponder the beaches at Normandy. More regularly, for events less collective, no mark is made and nothing remains of sadness but memory, which fails for a reason. There is a bridge in Indianapolis, beneath which flows the White River. A long line of traffic going to and from downtown crosses the bridge each day, but no one looks down and no one stops. People have forgotten that, years ago, at the base of the bridge, a college student tumbled headlong over the railing and fell to the ground below, mere feet from the forgiving water, which continued on its way.

. . . . .

Wednesday, June 4, 1986 was a perfect day for an accident. It was a fine day for things to go horribly wrong. Which is not to say that on other days in other circumstances things did not go equally, horribly wrong, nor that on all such days as this they did. It's just that the day had a portentous quality to it. It had high temperatures, a building pressure in the atmosphere, a sense that release was imminent, and a proportionate sense that the release would be, or at least could be, explosive. It was in the air for everyone to feel. It was the first day of the NCAA Outdoor Track and Field Championships in Indianapolis, Indiana. The next morning the local newspaper would report that the severe thunderstorm that struck Indianapolis ignited a $100,000 fire at a west side apartment complex; that torrential rain undermined the foundation of a local nursing home, causing a 30-foot section of the wall to collapse; that rescue efforts in the community were delayed by high water; and that 5,500 Indiana Power and Light customers lost service. The newspaper would also report that the track meet had been delayed three hours at mid-afternoon when the thunderstorm, which sounded like a train coming in, struck the Indiana University Stadium on the campus of Indiana University-Purdue University (IUPU). The newspaper would fail, however, to report at least one other important event that occurred on the evening of June 4, 1986. It would carry no article on the fate of Kathy Ormsby. She missed deadline.

The 10,000-meter run for women was the only championship final scheduled on Wednesday. The event was stuck at the end of an agenda that otherwise included heats and qualifying for events as diverse as the hammer, the men's and women's 400-meter hurdles, women's 200 meter, 3,000-meter steeplechase, men's and women's 800 meters, and the various events that constitute the first day of the women's heptathlon. The scheduled time for the 10,000-meter run was 9:40 p.m. In the days and on the night before the race, Stephanie Herbst was a bit more reserved, even, than usual because she had a cold. Slowing down to conserve energy, she nonetheless prepared for an all-out effort. So too did Kathy Ormsby. In the last full week of training, she did precisely what she needed to do. She maintained sufficient mileage to keep her confidence high; she sharpened, and she started a long taper that would leave her rested for the first national competition in which she would be introduced as holder of the American collegiate record.

Arriving in Indianapolis, Kathy met Rollie on Tuesday evening to go over the race plan. Jotted minutes capture the essential message of the meeting: "Get out but not too fast." "Behind but close." "On rail." "Relax." "Watch others: breathing, when will they go? 1000? 800? Last lap?" Kathy clearly planned to follow and kick, a tactic perfectly suited to counter a relentless front-runner like Stephanie Herbst. No one on the North Carolina State team noticed any special apprehension or depression in Kathy as she and Rollie discussed their strategy or as Kathy withdrew to make her final, personal preparations. The next morning, Kathy fell easily into a routine. She always made a list of things to do on the day of a big meet. It helped her relax to have a fixed idea of the day before it began, and there was some assurance in checking the items off one by one—done, done, done—as the important event approached. Otherwise, with time on her hands and no small tasks to absorb her, she might fret and waste nervous energy.

On this race day, the schedule included a short run, stretching, a shower, a starter course of banana and coffee, a walk, breakfast and the newspaper, as well as reading, quiet time, and naps. Later in the afternoon, she scheduled shopping. "Get something for after the race," she wrote to herself. Leaving nothing to chance, she also reminded herself to eat a meal at three in the afternoon and to order a pizza and perhaps dessert after the race, even if the hour was late. Kathy was particularly mindful of nutrition because she had to run a heat of the 5,000 meters on Thursday and could not afford to

go without food on the day before that race, no matter how concerned she was about the 10,000 meters.

In the afternoon, Kathy's parents dropped by the hotel for a
visit. Later, as evening approached and the time to leave for the track
grew closer, Kathy borrowed a tape player. She turned off the lights
in the hotel room, rested on her bed and three times played a song
by The Imperials: "Not to us Our Lord/Not to us Our Lord/But to thy
name give glory/To thy name give praise/As children of a mighty
king/we make our lives an offering." Within the song, Kathy sought
the eye of the hurricane, a quiet and still place safe within the fury.
Kathy also repeated the visualization exercises given to her by the
sports psychologist. She encouraged her mind to see the details of a
successful, uneventful race. She could overlook herself standing
with the other competitors, experience from a safe distance the start
of the race, feel the deep, easy draw of her own breathing, hear the
sound of the crowd and the encouragement of her friends, pull from
a supply of carefully hoarded energy, enjoy an easy running motion
with a composed arm carriage, and she could see—there before
her—a swift, complete finish. In caution, however, Kathy also
looked squarely to the possibility that "it" would happen again. She
practiced methods of self-control that might permit her to stave it
off. Failing that, she practiced acceptance. Come what may, she
would be fine, she reminded herself. To similar effect, she remembered a presentation by the famous University of North Carolina
miler, Tony Waldrop, who once said that under pressure it helped
him to concentrate on a small, pleasurable detail of life not threatened by sporting success or failure. In his example, the mere
prospect of a peanut butter and jelly sandwich could put him at ease.
Finally, Kathy tried to relax by getting a clear view of the goal for
the evening: she did not have to win. She prayed only that she be
allowed to do her absolute best, win or lose. That would be sufficient
for anyone who mattered to her. Kathy later summarized her mental

state. "I was scared," she said, "but I was trying for all it's worth not to be." She had, in fact, done everything possible to prepare herself, and had no sense of serious danger or impending harm. To the extent she had anything to do with it, she was ready to run no less than anyone else who lined up on the grim, humid night.

Neither Stephanie Herbst nor Kathy Ormsby would have been careless enough to believe the race was between the two of them, however. The field was too strong for that conclusion. Christine McMiken was there with her low 32 time, faster in fact than Kathy's and missing from the record-book only because it was run in a race that included men. Ellen Reynolds from Duke was entered and still running well. Connie Jo Robinson, sorely missed in Milwaukee, was healthy now and running for North Carolina State, a companionship that pleased Kathy even as she faced the possibility of being the second-best finisher on her own team. Atlantic Coast Conference rival Clemson had a good runner in Ute Jamrozy. In all 24 women would start, and all of them were capable. Wary of such a big field, Stephanie's instructions from Peter were simple. Stay close but stay back; let the race settle in. Depending on how the race went, he would decide whether she should use a long option, in which case she would move into the lead and drive for the finish line with eight laps to go, or a short option, in which she would move with three laps to go. He would signal at the eight laps one way or the other. Stephanie gave no thought to Kathy Ormsby nor indeed to anyone else in the race. She was waiting for a sound.

When the race started, Stephanie coasted to a spot near but not at the front. From that point, she fluttered through the early running until the field thinned, finally, to four contenders: herself, Ellen Reynolds, Kathy Ormsby, Christine McMiken. The pace was fast but not alarming, at least not to Stephanie. Despite her cold, she was comfortable, pushing but not pressing. Around her in the tight cluster of runners, she could hear the footfalls and the breathing, mingled with calls from the sidelines and the stands. It was dark and the lights were on. The light was sharp enough to illuminate the scene yet it fell softly over the athletes, enshrouding them in whiteness sufficient to set them apart from those who merely watched. Within the structure of the developing race, Stephanie ran smoothly, almost as softly as the light itself and as ephemeral. Most of the other runners who surrounded her were equally composed and quiet as they concentrated on the work and the passing laps. Only one drew attention to herself by a slight irregularity. It was her breathing pattern, which was odd. The breaths came shallow and quick, almost as if the woman was hyperventilating. With little effort at detection, Stephanie discovered that the runner was Kathy Ormsby. Stephanie paid little attention to the matter; for all she knew, that was normal for Kathy. As the race progressed, Stephanie's attention focused increasingly on the pace, which Christine and Ellen were alternately leading in the range of 78 to 80 seconds per lap, and on the signal that she expected to get with eight laps to go. In preparation for that moment, she drifted up to the front. As she did, either memory or the many retellings of the race convince her that she noticed just a slight shift off the back, and Kathy Ormsby was suddenly gone. That was fine with Stephanie. Whether she saw it or not, she noticed in time that Kathy was no longer with the group, and then she forgot all about it. She had two runners still with her, and eight and a half laps left to get rid of them and complete the job. The signal would come soon. Stephanie braced for it.

She was surprised that it did not come. She just kept on running, of course, but now she was a little curious about what had happened to Peter, who was always so reliable. She could not have known that Peter had troubles of his own, albeit minor. He was standing at a railing in the curve near the backstretch. When he looked up to give the signal, he saw Kathy coming off the track and approaching him, or so it appeared. "I thought she was running

directly to me," Peter recounted later. "I thought she may have confused me for her coach. I was wearing red and white, the same colors as NC State. There were eight and one-half laps to go. I know
that because I was supposed to give a signal to Herbst then. I missed
giving it because I was watching Ormsby." Turning, he watched
Kathy continue toward the stands, climb up a full set of stairs, and
disappear from view. "It was eerie," he said. "Her eyes were focused
straight ahead. She didn't look right or left."

Stephanie remained confused that the signal did not come,
but she did not panic. There was time enough. She was, however, on
her own. In the circumstance, she decided to act unilaterally. She
worked a bit more toward the front, just giving the pace a slight
bump. She felt a little guilty about it, though, because she knew that
her decision would not have been Peter's. "Well, I figured I better
go," she said. "I didn't know what was up with Peter, but I better go
because otherwise the strategy won't work. Because I didn't hear the
whistle from Peter which would have made me start up, I slowly
started increasing the pace, which was very risky, and would not
have been consistent with what Peter would like to have done." She
was not, however, wholly dependent on the gentle acceleration in
rhythm. She still had the short option. Sure enough, with three laps
to go she got a whistle and, being prepared for the event, took off
again. After the succession of 78- to 80-second laps, many of which
had been led by either McMiken or Reynolds, Stephanie's first fast
lap was 71.9. With that kind of burst, she immediately detached
from Ellen Reynolds and Christine McMiken and went sailing for
home. The only problem was that the officials had miscounted the
laps. When Stephanie re-emerged in the homestretch after one lap of
strong running and with the idea that the board would say "2," it still
said "3," a message repeated by a shout from the side: "Three to
go." Surely, that is most distressing news for a person measuring
energy against distance, and so it was for Stephanie. "I was scared

to death," she said after the race. But she also held together. "I just said to myself that I had to keep on going. It didn't make a difference physically, but it kinda did psychologically." Physically and psychologically, what it eventually did make was a national championship for Stephanie and a new collegiate record of 32:32.75. Stephanie's winning effort in Indianapolis beat Kathy Ormsby's old mark by 3.5 seconds. The time also beat the championship record, formerly held by Kathy Hayes of Oregon. Christine McMiken finished second in 32:51.71 and Ellen Reynolds was third in 32:52.52. After the race, Stephanie said that it took a lot of concentration and a lot of praying for the victory, but she also admitted that she never really doubted that she would win. It felt good, she said.

By the time Stephanie crossed the finish line, Kathy Ormsby, the woman whose record she beat, the woman who departed the race as Stephanie took control of it, was already in darkness. After she ran off the track and up into the stands, Kathy came out the other side of the stadium, crossed a softball diamond, found herself confronted by a 7-foot fence, climbed it, and kept running. She ran west down heavily traveled New York Street for two and one-half blocks before arriving at a bridge that crosses the White River. In the late evening of June 4, 1986, with the sound from the stadium echoing behind her and with the lights visible in the great distance, Kathy Ormsby jogged or walked approximately 75 feet onto that bridge. She stopped there. She did not cross the bridge nor would she ever. Rather, she toppled head first off it and fell 40 to 50 feet onto the rain-soaked flood plain below. She landed only 20 feet from the river's water.

Kathy's parents were spectators along with 1,500 other people to the race. They saw Kathy leave the track. When she did not come to them and they did not see her, Sallie Ormsby sought the assistance of a university security officer, who took her description and broadcast it. Rollie, too, saw Kathy leave the track. Under the impression that she was crying when she left the track, he attempted to follow her. When she climbed the fence, she lost him. He returned to the stadium and spoke to a police officer, who arranged to have her paged. When she did not respond to the page, Rollie went back out of the stadium to search. Very soon, he found Kathy where she fell. He flagged down a passing motorist and then clambered down the slope to be with her. When the officer arrived and asked what happened, Rollie could only say what Kathy said. She said she jumped. Only 10 minutes had elapsed from the time Kathy left the track. It was 10:10 p.m. In the fall, Kathy suffered a broken rib, a collapsed lung, and a fractured vertebra in the middle of the back. She was permanently paralyzed from a point just below the shoulders. Stephanie and the other women were still running. Indeed, had they been listening during the race they would have heard the page for the young woman who, by rights, ought to have been among them, and not lost. Had they known the danger she was in, they would have kept her safe. But they did not know. Or, more accurately, they did not immediately know they knew, that deeper knowledge coming only from hindsight and empathy.

Kathy Ormsby knew more, of course, than they did, but even she was and remains mystified by the events that evening, which began with the ordinary act of running a proposed 25 laps of a 400-meter track. She ran well for the first laps. As other runners fell behind, she remained in the lead pack. Eventually she ran with only three other women, Stephanie, Ellen, and Christine. She knew of Stephanie and of Christine, but she knew Ellen personally and liked her very much. She and Ellen had even run together in Durham, where Ellen went to school at Duke. All in all, the race was going well, and she was comfortable. That is, she was comfortable until she began to feel herself slip back from the first three, to sense—again as before—that she could not move. She was running hard but getting nowhere, or so it appeared to her, and she felt again the terror that came upon her in such circumstances. This time however she would not faint or fall because her reaction was different. A volcanic flow of emotion ran through her; and in that flow was embarrassment and frustration and anger. The complex mix was different from anything Kathy had ever experienced and so difficult to understand or explain that, years later, she reduced and simplified it. "All of a sudden—this is the best way I can tell you about it—I just felt like something snapped inside of me," she explained. "And I was really angry. And I felt like it was so unfair. All of a sudden, I didn't feel like this was me because I didn't usually have reactions like that. That was not a reaction I had as a person, ever."

Struggling against the new emotion, the one that was not like her, Kathy ran one more lap and then she could not make her body run any farther. In the moving race, she was thrust aside, a solitary person completely on her own. Incapable now of logic or understanding, she was driven by the single thought that she had to get away, not to any particular destination but to anyplace or anywhere that was not the track. Her memories from that point are, at best, like snapshots. She has no recollection of much of what happened. She only vaguely remembers leaving the stadium, and she reacts with wonder that she was able to climb the fence. "I don't see how in the world I climbed that fence," she says. "Before that happened, I felt like I couldn't run and now I was running harder than I had in the race. I just ran. And I just don't feel like that person was me. I know that sounds strange, but I was just out of control. I just couldn't face everybody. I felt like I had let everybody down. I really don't know how to explain what happened except that I don't think it's something I would have done." Kathy does not remember the run to the bridge, nor whether she stood when she got there and looked over its side, or even whether she saw it was water or land that awaited her. In fact, she does not know that she jumped, only that she suddenly was over the side headfirst, conscious always, and contrite. "I know," she recalls, "that when I went off I was headed down head-first. But I also know that the part of me, the part that was me, remembers apologizing to God and saying I'm sorry. Because it was like I was watching everything that was happening and I could not stop."

Psychiatrists later opined that Kathy's dreadful experiences in Indianapolis, Milwaukee, Lehigh, and Raleigh were caused by panic attacks, which are related clinically to anxiety and depression, and are often characterized by the feelings of terror that Kathy describes. One of the psychiatrists with whom Kathy worked after the accident described the effect of panic disorders in summary terms as "a sudden feeling of impending doom, of something terrible that's going to happen. There's a fast heart-rate, there's difficulty breathing sometimes, a feeling that you're choking or things are getting unreal." Many times a person subject to a panic attack will hyperventilate, in which case air hunger, lightheadedness, carpal spasms, and even loss of consciousness can result, a frightening set of physical consequences that can make the whole episode that much more damaging. Anxiety and panic disorders are often caused by and associated with serious medical conditions, including a variety of cardiac and seizure disorders, as well as any number of gastrointestinal, respiratory, neurological, and endocrine conditions. In fact, as many as one-quarter to one-half of all people who suffer from panic disorders are also affected by mitral valve prolapse, a condition that causes heart palpitations resulting from the failure of the valve to close properly. Because of the strong organic component in panic attacks, a complete medical examination designed to rule out, or exclude, the various medical problems is often encouraged before a behavioral health approach is taken. Even if a behavioral health diagnosis does result from the medical evaluation, the symptoms often respond well to medication, to relaxation techniques, and simply to an educational process that makes the affected person understand that she is not, in fact, "weak," or "going crazy," or otherwise flawed. Ironically, physical exercise is one of the customary interventions for a person suffering from panic attacks. The release of endorphins—the body's naturally occurring narcotic, by some accounts—is purported to induce a feeling of wellness and euphoria.

．．．．．

Because Kathy told Rollie she jumped and because the rail at the bridge was 4-feet tall, some people concluded that she intended the act and its consequences. Many stories even referred to the incident as a suicide attempt. That is far from the truth. By any standard definition, suicide is an act of intention. For example, an old Webster's Dictionary says that suicide is "the act or instance of taking one's own life voluntarily and intentionally especially by a person of years of discretion and of sound mind." Kathy was very young when she was injured. Whether she had enjoyed "years of discretion" is a complex issue, although the best-considered answer is probably that she had not. She may have had the years but not the opportunity for an exercise of discretion. As to the soundness of her mind, only the sliver of time during which she was affected by panic and terror casts doubt on the matter; and then the doubt is limited to that time. On that question, in any event, Kathy has provided the answer. She did not even recognize herself in the person who left the stadium, crossed the field, climbed the fence, and approached the bridge. There is nothing in the act or its description that suggests intention. Surely, a person who intended to destroy herself would have troubled to look over the edge to see whether water or land was below, a thing that Kathy does not remember doing. The question of intention, at least so far as it involves deliberation, is also answered by the notes that Kathy left for herself. Order pizza and maybe dessert. She did neither, of course, but it was her intention to do both. And then, of course, there was the 5,000-meter run. On Thursday morning, Kathy had intended to stand and to run, possibilities now removed from her.

On the known facts, a conclusion that Kathy Ormsby attempted suicide at the bridge in Indianapolis would be unfair and unreasonable. That much should be clear. But what, then, drove her to the act, however haltingly it is measured or understood? Kathy provided part of the answer, or perhaps it would be more accurate to say that she spoke of a single aspect of the incident, which can be understood and appreciated because it is within the experience of us all. She spoke of anger. More specifically, she spoke of an anger directed to unexplained, unaccepted injustice. She was not angry because one thing went wrong on one occasion. She was angry because critical things went wrong repeatedly with nobody and nothing to say why. Was it too much to ask that she be permitted to run one lousy race to the best of her ability—without being interrupted by this nonsense—with her parents in the stands, her coach at the sideline, her teammates hopeful about the result, and her friends at home waiting expectantly? Why must she suffer this attack now of all times? Why again in a national championship? Why not at practices or at home or when she was alone? Why any of this when she worked so hard, studied so hard, did so much, lived modestly, aspired to kindness, and hoped to do good things with her life? Why would she not be permitted so slight a grace as this one race? Why was she being treated in this way? Unfortunately, no answer ever comes to such questions. Injustice is not rational, and no person subject to it finds satisfaction in thoughtful answers. Satisfaction comes, if at all, when the emotions, being permitted to burn, are exhausted. But that is a dangerous and uncertain process. Simple anger is red hot, but it promises to burn brightly and fail. Despair, on the other hand, is a most distorting kind of anger. A stranger to proportionality, it is white hot, the result of many unquenched fires. Those fires burn low and then leap into rage. When despair seeks comfort, it finds only pain, a mocking world that acknowledges no value and no self. Memory submerges; context evaporates; hope recedes; even words lose shape; and soon the idea of jumping off a bridge, for example, becomes no thought at all, but as natural as the next breath, which it neither accepts nor rejects but merely foregoes. From such a world, despair tosses its victims over the edge. "Release me from this dark night" becomes prayer, explanation, and apology in one.

Despair in the face of injustice creates a particularly heavy burden for a Christian who has placed her entire trust in God, for is complaint not a rebuke to Him in His wisdom and His intention? "Oh, for the years gone by when God took care of me, when he lighted the way before me and I walked safely through the darkness, yes, in my early days when the friendship of God was felt in my home." The lesson of Job is our own. To lose hope, to know anger, to doubt, to rail against injustice, even to sulk at offenses committed against us, is humanity itself. For a Christian, only modest acquiescence to God's will is perfection. But it should be remembered that perfection is not a human state, and to aspire too highly, to fail to forgive even ourselves the occasional transgression, is mere vanity. And vanity is yet another sin. So, each of us in our time and place make our peace and move on. Asked to explain the inexplicable, we attempt it, knowing that the alternative is an accidental world, a prospect more frightening than ignorance.

Kathy Ormsby would not run again, neither would she walk. She would spend many hours receiving care and rehab. When she was able, she would finish her undergraduate and professional education, she would become a caring member of the medical community as an occupational therapist, and she would continue her determined effort to be a good person and a good Christian. As the years passed, she would study the events of the night that turned her world upside down; she would search her heart; she would pray to God, and she would accept, if not the act itself then its consequence. She would understand even her parents' admonitions. "Ever since Kathy passed out in her first race," Dale and Sallie Ormsby recounted, "we [had] been very concerned about her well-being. Distance runners as a group tend to be thin, with very little body fat. We felt she was not getting the proper nutrients, and this was substantiated by her need for iron supplements. We must have had a hundred talks about this." And later, after the accident, Kathy knew that her parents served as a lightning rod for other parents with daughters about whom they were worried, girls and young women who wanted to run, and about whom the Ormsbys heard much. "Since Kathy's accident," they said, "several parents of runners and runners themselves have told us of physical changes they had that made them severely depressed for a short period of time, even to the point of not wanting to live. We feel Kathy's problems started from being on a razor's edge physically, with very little reserve to draw on. A lot of things came together at that particular moment, including a burning desire to do well and the fact that the bridge was there."

Kathy agreed that the accident sprang from all those elements and others as well, including her mental, emotional and spiritual status, the pressure, the heat and humidity, accumulated fatigue, the chemistry of her body, and her own sense of responsibility. Highly combustible, they awaited only a trigger. Furthermore, move any element slightly, or change the way they related to each other, and it might not have happened at all. One thing emphatically was not a factor. The accident did not happen because Kathy was disappointed at not winning the race. She wanted only to do her best. She did not begrudge the victory of any runner who beat her, ever. In fact, for the women who ran with her on that fateful night, she worried. She worried in a special way about Stephanie Herbst, who she feared might suffer harm on her account.

In the meantime, it would become an arguable proposition, if not a fact, that what happened to Kathy Ormsby at the White River Bridge in Indianapolis on June 4, 1986, was the most important single event in the developing sport of women's track and field in the United States. To all the women who dared to dream and to hope, to work hard, to sacrifice, to seek the satisfaction that comes from exhausting effort and conscientious training, and to all those who worked with them in the fulfillment of their ambitions, what happened to Kathy was a marker. On the marker were five simple words. For God's sake, be careful.

EIGHTEEN

but the sea/does not change/
and she goes forth out of hands and/
she returns to hands/

Amores, III
E.E. Cummings

   The difference between a jump and a fall is intention. The difference between falling and being pushed is a matter of proximity. Kathy Ormsby may have jumped, she may have fallen, and she may have been pushed. She may have been faint from the heat of the evening, the great tension of the race, from the stress of her own heavy expectations and from the misapprehension of other people's best wishes and her reconstruction of them as demands. She may have been physically unprepared for the challenges by virtue of her light weight, her eating habits, a faltering heart that fluttered once or twice at the wrong instant and left her; and she may in fact have felt the terrible brunt of depression, anger, and despair. And yet, from all the possibilities, she picked only one when she said to her coach at the base of the bridge, I jumped. It was a mechanical explanation which was misleading by its simplicity. It had only the virtue of bringing to Kathy Ormsby accountability for her own action, and incidentally of freeing any other person of blame. It also relieved the sport itself, and the conditions it engendered, from scrutiny. In that regard, Kathy's statement was a selfless, brave act. Of course, no one believed her. Certainly, the other women did not. They would have believed the simple fact of the statement, that she jumped, but no one believed that the jump, if any, was the conduct of a person acting in response to singly felt impulses. Empathy, understanding, and shared experience, as well as the instinctive sense among many runners of the day that they, too, could have traveled Kathy's road, foreclosed that conclusion. Kathy Ormsby got in trouble because the demands of her sport, inseparable from the demands of her nature and of the larger social environment, brought her to the bridge and impelled her. That ultimately was the determination made by Kathy's parents. It is the view that Kathy has approached in the many years since the accident. Without delay, however, it was the shocked and chastened sentiment of many of the women in Indianapolis with Kathy. They never understood the event any other way. Speaking with reporters, the women had the choice to stand with Kathy or apart from her. They stood with her, even as they regretted the consequence of the accident. In fact, they drew Kathy across the terrible divide of her unique experience and into a world they identified as their own. As a result, the building story of June 4 was written from an epicenter and then in expanding concentric rings. The epicenter was Kathy Ormsby, whose sparely rendered life provided the opportunity for endless speculation. The next ring was composed entirely of Stephanie Herbst, the winner upon whom survivor's guilt might be visited. The remaining rings gathered up the other women in the race, then women distance runners as a group, and finally women athletes generally. No woman in any sport was outside the last circle. To visualize the media reaction, throw a pebble in a still pond. With more time, visit Vienna, Austria. Start at the Cathedral of St. Stephen and walk away.

In the first ring, Kathy was an historical collection of words and phrases selected to build a picture of anxiety, nervousness, and tension—definably, a person who tried so hard to be good that she was bound to break under the strain. She was, the reports indicated, unforgiving of herself, a pusher, a serious Christian woman who pulled pressure in on herself and then struggled to find an air pocket. "Running and school are her life," one college teammate was quoted as saying. "She'd even bring her notes to our workouts so she could study." One of the coaches from North Carolina State referred to the record and its effect: "She's a perfectionist and being the record holder for the 10,000 meters put too much pressure on her. It gave her a tremendous amount of pressure she couldn't handle." Her father, Dale, agreed that it was "a question of pressure," which originated with Kathy's desire to succeed. As to the accident itself, he felt "it was physical, and maybe it was mental, and it blotted out the ability to think rationally. I know she wanted to do well, and it was important to her. Her coach always told her to run within herself. But that was hard for her." Administrators, teachers, friends, and coaches from her hometown were also called into the account. This was, after all, a young woman honored at her high school with "Kathy Ormsby Day" shortly before her graduation, and an athlete whose number had been retired by the school, the only time that had happened. A friend from the school described Kathy as quiet, intense, deeply religious, unassuming, and as his "hero." One of her former coaches said that Kathy just would not complain, not even if she was injured, because she thought she would let her teammates and coaches down. "She pushed herself so hard," the coach said, "that we tried to get her to let up." An assistant principal added her impression, "Kathy was a strong, driven lady. She drove and drove herself." Capturing nearly identical images, another teacher and coach said that Kathy had always "driven herself very, very hard," and that "she's not the type of person who can accept second best for herself. If there's any pressure, Kathy was putting it on herself. She's always been very much a perfectionist. She was always very, very serious about everything she did." The high school's athletic director summed up Kathy's athletic persona when he said that "as far as who worked hard to be better than anybody else, I've never seen anybody like her." Finally, a high school math teacher described Kathy as a special person. "She was perfect; she was really perfect," the teacher said. "She was the most conscientious student I ever had. I don't think she competed with other people. I think she competed with herself. She wanted to excel. She just pushed herself too hard and was expecting too much from herself. And I think she kept a lot of things inside. She was quiet, a quiet girl." All the people back home were surprised and shocked about the events in Indianapolis—shocked that at the 6,500-meter mark of the 10,000-meter final the quiet girl just disappeared, figuratively carried away when the rain of many days became the flood of one day.

Any reference to Kathy's personal history tended to explain the event in terms of that personal history. Which is, Kathy had the accident because she asked too much of herself, felt too keenly the disappointment of a bad race, and over-reacted. The contrary view, or at least the view that provided balance, was that Kathy competed in a sporting environment which, in and of itself, uniformly asked a great deal from the participants and subjected all of them to risk, although the nature and extent of the risk varied from person to person. This case became stronger as fellow athletes, coaches, and teachers at North Carolina State softened the image of Kathy Ormsby by making it clear that, although she worked hard and aimed to do her best, she was also dearly loved by her teammates, as Rollie Geiger said; that she was sweet, courteous, diligent, sensible, and not afraid to reach out for help if she needed it, as her physics professor said; that she was caring enough even as she lay in her hospital bed—embarrassed, stunned, worried, in considerable pain, and struggling to adjust to a new physical reality—to write a note of encouragement to Janet Smith who was entered in the 5,000 meters on Saturday night; and that she was capable of earning the compliment of Ellen Reynolds, who stated directly that Kathy

Ormsby was and remained one of the nicest people she knew. Kathy's image was also enhanced by the report that she was an all-American and the most valuable performer for each of her first two years on the NC State track teams, accomplishments that were possible precisely because she faced many nerve-racking athletic tests without flinching; and by reports that she accepted the news of her paralysis courageously, puzzled and anguished by what had happened, but not broken. These bits and pieces of information about Kathy made it difficult to dismiss her as a stern perfectionist unsuited for the unpredictable, uncontrolled world of competitive athletics. To the contrary, the more complete information identified Kathy Ormsby as the sort who would flourish if given a fair opportunity; a person who would not, in fact, panic in the face of adversity or flee from the fight, but would turn intentionally to face it. That was her record. The conclusion that she was a fighter overborne by events outside her control would have been even more clear if her prior experience with falls and blackouts had been immediately available, which it was not.

The testimony from her coach, from her teammates, and from other athletes, as well as from her prior performances, confused the question of causation. It was obviously not going to be sufficient to look only to Kathy Ormsby and leave the matter there. Connie Jo Robinson of North Carolina State, who finished sixth in the 10,000 meters, took the next step necessary to focus the evaluation correctly. When asked about the reaction by other runners, she presented Kathy as merely one among many. "No one has come up to me and asked why," said Connie Jo in the days after the accident, "They've just come up and said we're sorry and we're praying for her. Athletes don't need to know why. They know why. We're all in the same boat. We all have the same pressures." After Connie Jo visited Kathy at the hospital, she was asked whether Kathy explained what happened. Kathy had not, nor was there any need to do so.

"She knows we understand," Connie Jo said. The runners understood because they stood where Kathy did, felt what she felt, and did not fall—they had to wonder—only by God's mercy. This point was ironically emphasized by a small, unverified report that appeared in the local newspaper two days after the 10,000 meters: "NCAA RECORDS: Wisconsin's Stephanie Herbst had a meet record (32:32.75) to win the women's 10,000-meter run on the opening day of the NCAA Outdoor Track and Field Championship in Indianapolis. Boston College senior Michele Hallett became disoriented during the race, ran out of the stadium and was found at the White River Bridge of New York Avenue about 1,000 feet from the Stadium. Indianapolis Fire Department Capt. Robert Eads said Hallett was taken to Wishard Memorial Hospital where she was treated for heat prostration. He said she was expected to be released today. During the race, temperatures were in the mid-70s and humidity was high." Accepting the report as written, there were two women at the bridge that fateful night. One was stopped before she suffered serious harm; the other was alone when she needed help.

When the athletes spoke of Kathy as a nice person capable of eliciting tremendous affection and loyalty; when they spoke of her courage and her unflinching attitude in the face of her new, awesome challenge; when they spoke of her past successes as an athlete; when they spoke broadly about the pressures in the sport; and when, by doing so, they swung the debate away from the individual and toward the general conditions that governed competition, they inadvertently increased the light being shined on Stephanie Herbst. If the sport itself was the issue, everyone was curious to know what the winner would say, what the person would say who suffered no disappointment and had no reason for bitterness or recrimination. They were curious for a reaction from the exquisitely thin, finely tuned woman who had run exactly four 10,000-meter races in her career and won each of them in progressively faster times. What would the national champion and new collegiate record-holder say? Was the pressure excessive even for her? Very quickly, it became apparent that Stephanie would be scrutinized more closely than anyone else, save Kathy who was unavailable to the reporters because she was in the hospital and strictly monitored.

Initially, Stephanie was in no position to answer questions. On Wednesday night, she did not hear the news at all. She finished the 10,000-meter race, said a silent prayer for having survived the confusion over the laps, warmed down routinely, enjoyed the congratulations of coach, teammates, family, and friends, and then went back to the hotel. The qualifying heat for the 5,000 meters was scheduled for Thursday and she needed to rest. It was not until the next morning at breakfast with Peter and another Wisconsin coach that Stephanie knew the full story of the race that would become known as her "dark victory." Over a light meal of unbuttered toast, she heard them tell her that Kathy Ormsby of North Carolina State dropped out of the 10,000 meters the prior night and that she attempted suicide by jumping off a bridge, which was the story that was circulating based on a police statement to that effect. The news was startling but Stephanie did not understand what she was told. Describing the conversation, Stephanie says, "For some reason what Peter told me missed me entirely. I didn't hear it at all. I didn't get it. I just continued to talk as if nothing had been said." Under enormous pressure herself, she had closed off again. Later, however, the bubble burst when she went to the track and found the reporters waiting en masse for her. Did she know what happened to Kathy? Did she feel responsible for what happened to Kathy? What did she think about what happened to Kathy? Did she think the same thing could happen to her? The respectful and proper questions came at her as quickly as the ones that were unfeeling and unkind, and Stephanie was at a disadvantage. As she says now, "I did not have that time where you think through something like this. What happened to

In Indianapolis, Stephanie Herbst surrounded
by reporters, friends, and relatives.

Kathy? Is she OK? Why would that happen? What will happen now?
All those were thoughts that I wanted to have. But I was just too
mixed up." Mercifully, the heat of the 5,000 was canceled because
Kathy, who had been entered, could not run, and because Ellen
Reynolds of Duke, also a qualifier, withdrew. Safely into the final,
Stephanie had time to regroup before the race on Saturday.

  She needed every minute of the time because she was now
completely off balance. Reflecting, she says that this was an "awful,
awful" time. "I first considered not running the 5,000. Then I considered whether I would finish it because I wasn't able to focus or
get myself prepared; and I wasn't able to get through all these feelings I had for Kathy. I just never got my act together." Stephanie
needed time to think, and did not get it. Instead, she had to prepare
to run a national championship and to deal with the reporters. In

some respects, it would have been better if Stephanie had said that Kathy Ormsby had nothing to do with her, and that she had no information that might be useful in understanding the event. She could then have gone about her business. Of course, few young people respond to questions like Watergate burglars, and Stephanie certainly did not. She answered the questions openly and thoughtfully. Self-interest aside, Stephanie turned out to be perfect for the interrogation about Kathy, about the sport of women's distance running at the collegiate level, and about the strains of training, lifestyle, and competition. The reporters sensed in her an enticing combination of strength and vulnerability, and they descended on the young woman later described with such words and phrases as fragile-looking, polite, soft-spoken, and thoughtful. As she fended them off, not only in Indianapolis but for months and years afterward, Stephanie's answers to the various questions created a mosaic that connected her to Kathy Ormsby like colors in a pattern.

When the reporters first came to Stephanie for answers, only the mechanical facts of Kathy's accident were known. She had pulled out of the race, left the stadium, hopped a fence, ran to the bridge over the White River, plummeted over the 4-foot-tall side rail, suffered serious injuries, including one to the spine, told her coach she jumped, and investigators considered the incident a suicide attempt. Local and national outlets summarized the known facts in predictable language. In the print media, sample headlines included: Runner Hurt in Suicide Attempt; Runner Races Off Track, Leaps from Bridge; Favored Runner Tries Suicide; Runner Quits Race, Leaps from Bridge (Called Suicide Attempt); Runner Hurt in a Leap; Ormsby Paralyzed by Leap; Suicide Attempt Still a Mystery; The Last Desperate Run of Kathy Ormsby. With few exceptions, the stories referred to the event as an attempt at self-destruction. Even when a publication was circumspect and the word suicide did not appear, there was the implication that Kathy did this intentionally. In that context, some of the articles were carefully and sensitively written in an attempt to discover what happened and why. But even in those articles, the writer's task was to explain the suicide attempt, and not to evaluate the essential characterization in terms of decisional capacity, deliberation, intention, or state of mind. The questions to Stephanie were therefore unambiguously directed to the matter of suicide. It is difficult to imagine a topic with more twists and turns.

Although suicide is not consistently viewed across time or culture, it has been traditionally disfavored in Western culture at least since St. Augustine argued in <u>The City of God</u> that no Christian had authority to commit suicide in any circumstance whatsoever. Augustine said, "If, when we say, thou shalt not kill, we do not understand this of the plants, since they have no sensation, nor of the irrational animals that fly, swim, walk, or creep, since they are dissociated from us by their want of reason, and are therefore by the just appointment of the Creator subjected to us to kill or keep alive for our own uses; if so, then it remains that we understand the commandment simply of man. The commandment is, 'Thou shalt not kill man;' therefore kill neither another nor yourself, for he who kills himself still kills nothing else than man." However arguable any of those individual propositions may be, the influence of St. Augustine on the church, on its believers, and on Western society at large is inarguable. In fact, the spiritual condemnation of suicide was strong enough to be embodied in English common law, which made both suicide and attempted suicide unlawful. Early American case law followed English common law. In 1816, for example, an American judge instructed a jury in the following terms: "Self-destruction is doubtless a crime of awful turpitude; it is considered in the eye of the law of equal heinousness with the murder of one by another. In this offense, it is true the actual murderer escapes punishment; for the very commission of the crime, which the law would otherwise punish with its utmost rigor, puts the offender beyond the reach of its infliction. And in this he is distinguished from other murderers. But his punishment is as severe as the nature of the case will permit; his body is buried in infamy, and in England his property is forfeited to the King." Consistent with this harsh sentiment, most states in the United States long considered both suicide and attempted suicide illegal. In the last years of the twentieth century, however, suicide is a concept undergoing reconstruction. The right of the individual is ascendant, and the individual claims the prerogative to live or die as an exercise of autonomy. Simultaneously, the grip of Christianity on law and custom is weakened both by its own condition and by an increased reference to other religious and spiritual beliefs, some of which hold suicide in different regard. Perhaps most prominently, social attitudes toward suicide are modified by modern medical technology, which has the apparent capacity to blow oxygen through a cadaver and call it life, a prospect that many people find unattractive for themselves. As a result of the shifting attitudes, neither suicide nor attempted suicide is now a criminal act in any of the United States. Furthermore, the way people think of suicide is becoming variegated, as people grapple with the endless circumstances that might permit a person to terminate his or her own life without censure, shame, or sanction. In fact, the ethical and legal right of a person to take his or her own life now assumes constitutional status; and the right to be assisted in the event may soon be established because people argue that, otherwise, they are unequally protected by the law if it does not take into account their incapacity, frailty, or other inability to act for themselves. All this is said only for the purpose of pushing it to one side in order to get a clear view of Stephanie's situation in 1986 when she was asked questions that involved suicide. Whether it was a matter of conscious appreciation or not, she was being asked to comment on an event that had one foot in history—suicide was murder and attempted suicide was attempted murder—and one foot in the future—no other person's life belongs to you and the action of that person in regard to his or her own life is not for you to judge.

In this complexity, Stephanie's answers for and about Kathy speak exceedingly well for her. In important respects, she took Kathy's burden as her own, and she did not presume to make a moral judgment on the alleged events. Although Stephanie spoke at different times to different reporters, each of whom quoted her separately, the individual statements can be combined in a coherent, single paragraph to make the point that what happened to Kathy, while disturbing, was understandable in context: "I heard it at breakfast. They had to tell me several times before I really started to believe what happened. My reaction was mostly shock—and a little depression that it's not really so unusual. It is not as isolated of a case as you would think. A lot of people who get deeply into distance running have problems. Running is their life. I had as many problems as anyone. This year during the cross-country season especially. There were a lot of expectations, a lot of pressure. It gets to be so much that you get to be a perfectionist. You have to go out and get that run in no matter what. It has to be long enough; it doesn't matter what the weather is; it doesn't matter how you feel. You have to get it in. I hope [Kathy] realizes that we sympathize with her and that there's a great deal of understanding that every long-distance runner feels. The public was [surprised] by what happened, but I don't think anyone involved in the sport was. People see the glamour of running but that's not all there is. The highs are definitely there, but the lows are something you really have to deal with. Any athlete who says they have no idea of the pressures that might have led Kathy to go to such an extreme is probably lying. Anyone holding a collegiate record in a race with other top athletes and facing the possibility of not placing or not keeping the record has to have tons of pressure. It's a public loss, not a private loss."

Stephanie also told the various reporters that she tried to protect herself from pressure. "I don't read track magazines," she said. "I don't know my competition. I really do prefer it that way. If you don't know who's there, you don't worry about them." Following the same theme, she told one of the reporters, "It's one thing to go into a race against this person or that person, but if I don't know who's there and who's good, I'm always going into the race fresh and saying, 'All I can do is the best I can do.'"

Stephanie also thought that if she ascribed importance to every meet or paid attention to her competition, she could easily get psyched out. "You start thinking, 'I'm only second best.' It's such a mental thing." While acknowledging the various ploys, Stephanie was also aware that they sometimes did not work. "Do you know something really ironic?" she later said to one columnist, "Three weeks before, Kathy did a half-hour television program on how long-distance runners handle stress." In reality, Kathy never did a television program like that; she merely contributed to print articles that mentioned the additional pressure accompanying her American record. But everything about Kathy was immediately rumor and lore in Indianapolis after the accident, and it would take years for the facts to catch up.

For her own part, Stephanie was answering the questions with imperfect attention. No matter how overwhelmed she was by concern for Kathy, or by questions about her, or by the general implications of the event, she had to force herself to concentrate on the Saturday final at 5,000 meters. The environment for the race was so distracting that even as she was pulling on her spikes and going to the starting line on Saturday, people were still shouting questions at her. A meet official came to her twice and asked her to get moving because the race was starting. If ever in 1986 Stephanie Herbst was ripe for the taking it was that Saturday and the 5,000-meters final at the NCAA. And Sue Schroeder from the University of

Michigan, whom Stephanie respected as both athlete and person, almost got her. When the race began, Stephanie simply slipped into automatic pilot. She led most of the way, reduced the field to five by the 2,000-meter mark, and then increased the pace. She led by 35 meters at the 4,000-meter split with Patty Murray of Western Illinois and Sue Schroeder next. As Stephanie continued to run steadily but without passion, Sue was emboldened to take a shot at her. With 800 meters to go, Sue started to move up, and the gap closed measurably. The crowd noise and perhaps her own inattention kept Stephanie unaware of the threat until the last curve, by which time Sue was in striking distance. At that point, Stephanie at last saw Sue's shadow. At about the same time, she also heard Peter shout through the crowd noise for her to pick it up. Stephanie changed gears. She was the model of a dynamic runner trained to sprint when necessary, and she was soon safely out of reach. She glided across the line with no additional threat. It was as if Peter had said to the expectant crowd, "all right, break it up, move along, excitement's over," because all the fun that comes with watching one runner work her way through the pack and then sprint to the front never had a chance after he stepped in with a loud voice. This was Peter as kill-joy. Stephanie's winning time was 15:42.36, 2 seconds ahead of Sue and almost 6 ahead of Patty. Wisconsin teammate Lori Wolter finished eighth in 16:22.51, an excellent time and place for a freshman. Stephanie's remarks after the race revealed her lack of intensity. "I wanted to forget the time," she said, "and just go to win it. I definitely didn't feel up to tops. I didn't feel strong enough to do a good kick. I wasn't scared, but I was disappointed with my time. The 10,000 was more of a strategy race. I just like to make sure to set a fast pace if I want a good time." She also admitted that she went into every race "a little scared and a little unsure," adding that she did not have enough experience to be confident of anything. As to her general reaction to the two national championships, Stephanie said that it was a nice feeling but also a sad feeling. "I can't look at this as a positive championship. There are more negatives than positives. I have a lot of feeling and respect for Kathy. Those were her races." Stephanie also said, more pointedly, "because of what happened to Kathy, I can't get really psyched up. The championships came as a result of someone else's tragedy."

The championships did not, of course, come as a result of anyone else's tragedy. They came as a result of Stephanie's hard work over many years, her good coaching, her attention to detail, her talent, and her composure under pressure, among other factors. Still, there could be no question that Stephanie was punished by her experience in Indianapolis. She immediately decided to pull back from running for a while. Rather than run the TAC meet two weeks after the NCAA, a course that was urged upon her and might have led to further competition in Europe against open athletes, Stephanie decided to go home to Minnesota. Her father, for one, thought that was best. "After Stephanie won the double in Indianapolis, they wanted badly for her to compete in the TAC meet in two weeks, [but] she was planning this break and she needed it. She had been in constant training for competition since last August. I told her, 'Forget the TAC. Get away from it for a while,'" he said. Stephanie described the decision this way, "If I [had] gone to the meet, it would have been a great opportunity. Everyone says that and I'm sure it's true. It's a great opportunity. I think my coach was disappointed. 'You mean you're not going to run?' But Kathy was the last straw. You've got to notice. But I don't know if the people involved have really sat down to evaluate it. After it happened, I talked to other runners and I said, 'Look, this is a typical situation. This isn't right.'"

Actually, Stephanie was wrong. Kathy Ormsby's situation was not typical. But she could not have known that, and, in any event, it hardly mattered. The fact is that it looked typical to many of the women who were running long distances at the collegiate level. If, as the reports said, Kathy Ormsby despaired and threw herself off a bridge, they did not find that surprising. And the fact that they did not find it surprising is the story from Indianapolis in 1986. Years later, Kathy Ormsby's accident would appear in a magazine article as an example of sport being permitted to assume exaggerated importance among women. The last paragraph implicated both Kathy and Stephanie. "Sometimes we look at a race as being the whole world. That's distorted. Think about Kathy Ormsby. How many people know who won that race she ran out of? How many care?" Here is the myth that Kathy Ormsby attempted to harm herself because she could not win; and here also is the pronouncement of a new myth, which is that no one cares who wins and who loses. No successful athlete believes that.

The reality of Kathy Ormsby's loss and Stephanie's victory is complicated. Harm and gain both originate from the volatile, unreliable mix of the individual into the environment of the sport. Some of the pressure does come from the environment. To make the point, Rich McGuire, a track coach from the University of Missouri with an academic background in sports psychology, once remarked, "Anyone who thinks that competing in a national championship is an outlet is naive. This is a totally serious business, and maybe it shouldn't be." On the other hand, some of the pressure comes from the individual and from other causes unrelated to athletics, however structured. Pioneering sports psychologist Bruce Ogilvie sounded this note when he was asked to comment on Kathy's accident. Dr. Ogilvie said, "You have to look for multiple causes. The answer is not going to be found in a single explanation that as an athlete there was some intense pressure." Dr. Ogilvie said also that parents and coaches of elite athletes "must be careful to understand that extraordinary achievement is no shield against other emotional aspects of life. You can't hide inside an athletic career. Getting the goal changes nothing. Make sure you're seeing the person under the athlete." As to the specific injury suffered by Kathy Ormsby, Eugene Levitt, a clinical sports psychologist associated at the time with the Indianapolis-based American College of Sports Psychology, concluded without hesitation that "this was an act of impulse. If it had been calculated, it would have succeeded." Meanwhile, coaches and administrators were synthesizing the information from Indianapolis to see how it would change the way they performed. One university coach spoke of a new sensitivity. "It slows you down," he said. "It makes you realize, 'I've got to deliver the message clearly.' As a coach, you want to make sure they do their best but that's all you can ask. You've got to tell them so they understand, 'Do your best and if that's first or last, that doesn't matter. You've got to remember there are people starving in Ethiopia. This is a game. Push yourself but remember, it's a game.'"

The sentiment is important. The watchfulness it promises is welcome. But, it must be said, the message is a tough sell. How can a coach ask an athlete to run thousands of miles in preparation; have her make endless social and personal sacrifices; change the way her body looks and works; send her on the long walk to the line in front of thousands of people who, in fact, do care to one degree or the other what happens, and then persuade her that the whole thing is a game? In fact, it is not a game, not when college scholarships have financial and educational implications for students, when open athletics promises direct compensation for elite performers, and when competition is increasing along with expectations. But neither is it life and death. Somewhere between the two, between the game it once was but is not now, and the life and death it must never become, is the balance that is sport. And, as always, lost in the message about what happened to Kathy Ormsby is Kathy Ormsby. All she ever wanted was the chance to do her best, first or last, as the coach said. All she wanted was a fair shake. All she wanted was a just world.

The repercussions from Indianapolis and from what happened to Kathy Ormsby would endure. People who never heard her name would benefit from the hard-earned lesson she taught. Stephanie Herbst, too, played her part. She was winner and survivor. Now that the immediate event was over, she went home for a rest. She said she would take a month off. Before the month even started, however, Stephanie admitted that she was getting jittery. "That's the danger in distance running," she said. "It can become obsessive."

NINETEEN

And I, who formerly would never flinch
At flying spears or serried ranks of Greeks,
Am now alarmed by every breeze and roused
By every sound to nervousness, in fear
For this companion and this load alike.

Aeneid, II:726-9

"I guess I never feel that I'm in the best shape or at my full potential," Stephanie said in January, 1986. "You reach one level and then you move on to the next. That's the nature of running." It was, in any event, the nature of running for Stephanie Herbst, who moved swiftly up and through the levels from state champion, to reliable collegiate performer, to Big Ten individual champion, to highly regarded national competitor, and finally to national champion in three different events over the course of the indoor and outdoor seasons of her sophomore year. At that, however, she pulled up short so close to the next level that she almost tripped on it. When the TAC meet was run in Eugene, Oregon, June 18-21, 1986, Stephanie stayed home and left familiar faces to compete for spots on the United States team scheduled to run in the Goodwill Games in Moscow in July. At 3,000 meters, Cindy Bremser surged to the front shortly after the 2,000-meter mark in an attempt to shake Mary Knisely, who, however, would not be shaken and dashed away on the homestretch for a three-meter victory in 8:46.18. In the 5,000 meters, the triumph belonged to Betty Springs who let PattiSue

Plumer set the pace for almost all of the first two and one-half miles, covered a move by Lorraine Moller in the last half-mile, and then sprinted the last 120 meters to a definitive triumph. Her final time was 15:30.99. And, at 10,000 meters, Stephanie's rival from the Big Ten meet her freshman year won the TAC National Championship. Nan Doak, now running for Athletics West, fought a fierce last-lap battle with Lynn Nelson to win by less than a second in 32:29.86. To take nothing away from the three winners, it remains fair to point out that Stephanie had beaten them all at various times and that her times at the various distances were comparable. The decision to return home was therefore significant. It was a step away from a path that virtually any other runner would have fought to hold.

Even as Stephanie was back in Minnesota engaged in active rest, another young woman was lining her up, if not consciously then as a matter of coincidence. She and Stephanie would be in the same place at the same time doing the same thing. The woman was Suzy Favor. Having completed a smashing senior year in high school, Suzy decided to remain in Wisconsin and run for Peter Tegen. For Suzy Favor, the levels through which Stephanie was moving so quickly had even less meaning. She collapsed them like a tall building imploded as a means of clearing ground, with each floor falling onto the floor beneath it until the field was level. For all of her years in high school, she was so distinguished that she was virtually an event unto herself. State championships meant nothing to her. She was always a national performer. She was ranked first in the country among high school milers her sophomore, junior, and senior years, and she won three successive TAC National Junior Championships. In her senior year, she ran 4:18.62 for 1,500 meters and the equivalent of an indoor mile of 4:44.2. Her 1,500-meter time was more than 5 seconds faster than the time recorded by the second-fastest high school girl in the country, Darcy Arreola, although Darcy was also a fine runner destined for a long and successful career. Internationally, Suzy finished ninth in 1,500 meters at the world junior meet in Athens, Greece, and she represented the United States junior team in the dual meet against Romania. All things considered, she was one of the few women who evoked comparisons, however disputable, with a young Mary Decker.

Her decision to enroll at the University of Wisconsin was a tremendous triumph for Peter Tegen and an equal challenge because everyone would be watching. Peter knew the situation, which he described this way, "I thought Suzy was unique the way she came out of high school. It was obvious to everyone. You didn't have to be a coach with any particular ability to see that this was the whole package. That is a kind of a risk." Whatever apprehension he may have had for himself, his primary concern was for Suzy. To ease her transition into college, he assured her that she did not need to hurry nor to carry the college team; a leader was already in place. When asked about her first semester experiences, Suzy said that she was under less pressure than she had been in high school. "Of course, school itself is harder," she said, "but as a runner it's easier because they aren't expecting me to do everything here... I'm not the top runner here. Stephanie Herbst is." Peter was satisfied that Suzy would handle the situation well. Her adjustment from high school to college would be smoother, even, than Stephanie's had been. "When Stephanie was a freshman, she did not have this experience and credibility," he said. "Suzy comes in with a load of experience and a lot more exposure." Gauging the effect of having two stars on the team, Peter was comforted to think that the two personalities complemented each other. After watching them together, he knew that he was right. "They both get along very well and they are sensitive to each other in competition." In fact, Suzy would eventually report that having Stephanie with her was like having an experienced sister to tell her what to expect on trips and in meets. With attention focused closely on preparation and competition, Peter could be a

Suzy Favor

little vague on such matters as travel times and reservations!

Meanwhile Stephanie took two weeks of her intended three-week summertime break before getting anxious and starting again. "It was a wonderful feeling," she told one columnist, "I couldn't wait to get back into my shoes. The first day after my break, I went out and ran ten miles. I wasn't going to go that far but it just felt so good." Training throughout the remainder of the summer, she was interrupted occasionally by good news. She was named the University of Wisconsin female athlete of the year for 1985-86. She won the Jesse Owens Award as the athlete of the year in the Big Ten, an honor she shared with Chuck Long, the University of Iowa quarterback who led his team to the Rose Bowl. She was named to the GTE Corporation Academic all-America team for her performance on the field and in the classroom. She was among a handful of collegiate women nominated for the Broderick Award. And, finally and most important, she was admitted to the University of Wisconsin's School of Business. With the admission, her academic course was clear. Before the school year started, however, Stephanie permitted herself one more foray onto the track. In August, she entered and ran the 10,000 meters at US Olympic Festival in Houston, Texas. The meet was an important event that attracted a mixture of established veterans and emerging stars. The highlight of the three-day competition was the new world-record established by Jackie Joyner Kersee in the heptathlon, an accomplishment made more meaningful by the weather conditions. One report had surface temperature at 126 degrees while the air temperature was 102 degrees. Humidity made things worse in Houston's traditional miasma. Most of the noteworthy female distance runners prudently shied away from the 10,000. Instead, a group that included Mary Knisely, PattiSue Plumer, Sabrina Dornhoefer, Cathie Twomey, and Brenda Webb ran the 3,000, which Mary won in 8:58.80. In the 10,000 meters, Stephanie ran with Sue Schroeder of Michigan and others of national accom-

plishment but she did not have to manage competitors with international credentials. In that event, she won a controlled race in
34:26.16. It was the first 10,000 in five efforts that was slower than
the one that preceded it, but that was not a concern. Stephanie was
five for five. It was time to go north toward home, time for a new
team at Wisconsin, and time for a new Stephanie.

Partly in response to what happened in Indianapolis and
partly in response to her own unease, Stephanie had decided to open
up socially. Speaking of the experiences of her sophomore year,
Stephanie acknowledged problems. She had, she said, been forced
into a leadership position before she was ready for it. "I had always
been the third person behind Cathy Branta and Katie Ishmael. But
Cathy had graduated, and Katie was injured and all of a sudden—
boom!—I was supposed to lead the team." Not only did she feel that
she had to lead every workout and every race, she had to deal with
unfamiliar attention from television, radio, and print. "The media
had never been interested in me, and all of a sudden everybody
wanted to interview me," she explained. "I think that [cross-country
season in her sophomore year] was the hardest season I've had ever
since I've started running." She later described the impact. "During
the cross-country season, if I wasn't studying, I was running. I never
allowed myself time to sit down and relax. I lost a lot of weight. I
never got out with my friends." Track season was better, she
thought, in part because she took a lighter academic load and in part
because the sport itself tended to distribute pressure more evenly
among participants in many different events. Still, she needed to
address the core issues in her personal affairs. She needed more people in her life, more activities, and more things to do and think about
than running and studying. For her, a complete, diverse relationship
with her teammates was an unlikely solution. "I like to isolate
myself from other runners," she said, "You're around those people
so much during the day. And those are the people you're competing

against. It's hard to socialize after competing. It gets to be like a game. 'What time are you going to sleep?' 'What did you have for dinner?' Or, 'You're going to drink?' I try to stay away from all that." As a sophomore, she stayed away from all that by taking a single in the dorm and burrowing into it, but by doing so she played into her intense nature and became, in her view, more and more a loner, which was not a situation she viewed as healthy. Her lifestyle particularly concerned her if she read the Kathy Ormsby experience to mean that unreleased pressure eventually found an outlet in self-destruction, which was the common interpretation of the incident before the full facts were known. As a result, Stephanie decided to change entirely the way she lived before it was too late. Comprehensively, she would get out more frequently and she would meet new people. The first thing to go was that single dorm room. Stephanie traded it in for the second story of a house, which she shared with four roommates. The next step was even more bold. Stephanie, the woman who sometimes made campus life sound like the cloister, would go through rush and pledge a sorority! Working her way through the lines of post-debs and social aspirants, she confessed that her face was exhausted from wearing a false smile. She was also dumbfounded by the questions she got. "I'm getting questions like, 'Do you really run more than five miles a day?' I feel like saying, 'Yes, when I'm not polishing my nails.'" At the end of rush, and presumably with a slight adjustment in attitude, Stephanie did find a sorority she enjoyed, and she moved to a more balanced university life.

Stephanie also learned to deal with increased public attention on campus. As early as the previous winter, a columnist for the university paper wrote a paean about her. "If you are a student at the UW you see thousands of faces every day. Maybe at this very moment you are packed into the basement of Bascomb Hall," the article began, "waiting to get into a business class that's sure to be closed. Anyway, after spending enough time in Madison you devel-op the ability to discern those people who stand out from the rest... What happens is that after you have made several thousand or so journeys up and down Bascomb Hill, you get good at recognizing a winner. There's something about the look in their eyes that instant-ly tells you that the person is someone special. Somehow a single glance or a brief exchange of hellos can transmit confidence, poise, and superior ability. Take one look at Stephanie Herbst and you know you're looking at a winner."

Bearing in mind that the article was written before any of the three national championships, it had a prescient quality, but the tone could embarrass a college sophomore who was trying to keep herself contained. Other university references were more subdued and amusing, as when a student columnist described the registration process on campus. "Like any other year, once I trotted out of the Stock Pavilion I had a mile sprint down Linden Drive toward my assignment committees. Only this year I found myself running neck and neck out of the barn-style starting blocks with none other than National Collegiate Athletic Association 10,000-meter titlist Stephanie Herbst. The scene was similar to that of a Laurel and Hardy movie. At 5-foot-6, 115 pounds (sic) Herbst resembled the slender Stan Laurel. She made up my one-block head start in less than two blocks, passing me wearing a walkman around her ears and victory in her eyes... After she passed me in front of Babcock Hall and I saw exactly who I was up against, the adrenaline started to flow. I tucked my briefcase under my arm and rambled forward... She was still within sight as I huffed and puffed up Charter Street, but time was on her side. My legs twice the size of hers, I used my bulk to gain ground going uphill on Observatory Drive, past the Social Science building. Alas, it was too late. Herbst had reached her assignment committee destination—either Bascomb Hall or the Commerce building (I couldn't tell for sure because by this time my eyes were sweat-filled)." Stephanie also attracted long-distance suitors who wrote her admiring letters. "Dear Stephanie, You don't know me. I'm a fan of yours. My name is _____, and I'm 23 years old. You're probably thinking, 'Well, why is this doof writing me this stupid letter?' Well, the reason why I'm writing is to wish you luck at the NCAAs next week. I know you're going to do great. As far as the young female runners in the world, you're tops," and on and on in the same vein. Stephanie was even "adopted" by the fraternity boys at a college one state away. The honor was dubious.

The cross-country team at Wisconsin in 1986 was a powerful collection of women. Not only was Stephanie back, but so also were Kelly McKillen, Lori Wolter, Holly Hering, and Stephanie Bassett. Katie Ishmael had graduated and Birgit Christiansen decided not to use her remaining eligibility; but Suzy Favor slipped into Katie's position and the team had sufficient depth to overcome the loss of Birgit. Kris Favor (Suzy's sister, a good runner operating in a rather long shadow), Carole and Laurie Harris, and Mary and Maureen (Gordy) Hartzheim also added power to a team that went 18 members deep when all of them dressed out. Although both Hartzheims were excellent, versatile runners, Mary had the potential to bring the quickest results. She had been eighth in the Kinney National Cross-Country Championships while a senior in high school at Minocqua, Wisconsin. Mary might even have had a state high school championship or two to her name but for the ravenous appetite of her new teammate, Suzy Favor, who was always there first. In its revised form, the team was Peter Tegen as alchemist, working with the elements to combine new athletes with old. He had a third national championship for cross-country in his sights, and he would do everything proper to get it. But Peter must also have known, either consciously or intuitively, that it was time to relax the team culture. Toward that end, he wasn't about to run out and get a beat poet, but at least he could recruit and encourage a few more strong girls who would laugh, and grin, and giggle behind his back, rebel, and obey, and question and subvert, and agree. He could get girls who would fight, work hard, step down and away, recriminate, grouse, and celebrate. So he went out and got them. These new girls, women by the time they owned the team, would turn the attitude slightly to the left, not so far that another bomb would go off on campus—no one liked to be reminded of the Students for a Democratic Society or the Weathermen—but women who were live-ly, respectful of authority but not awed by it, and likely to judge for themselves what was wise. Stephanie laughed to herself when she saw what was happening. The joke was on her. New promises were being made, Stephanie knew, but she had no idea whether she could rouse herself in response to them. Even after a summer of relative ease and of training she genuinely enjoyed, and even taking into account the lifestyle changes she had initiated, she was competition-weary after six seasons in two years: cross-country, indoor, outdoor, cross-country, indoor, and outdoor, with two summer races thrown in for good measure, a succession unlike that imposed on athletes in any other sport, all of whom have time to recover between seasons. Taking into account the sacrifices she imposed on herself as the price for success, the fine, coiled quality of her temperament, and the unsettling events in Indianapolis, the seamless experience of a collegiate long-distance runner pared Stephanie down to the nerves, a fact that would become more evident as the academic year unfold-ed. For Peter, too, this was a time of uncertainty; the promises of the future were inchoate. He would need to manage somehow the swing from old to new. To describe what was required of Peter, let us leave the laboratory and give him air. Let us say that he was like a sailor tacking across rough water toward smooth.

At first, the year was promising. Stephanie trained well and raced well, and Suzy settled into a safe place behind her. In the first major test of the season, the Midwest Collegiate Championships in

Kenosha, Wisconsin, Stephanie broke her own meet record from the previous year by 4 seconds, and Suzy finished second in her debut, but was only 3 seconds behind. As a team, Wisconsin unveiled quantity and quality that was even better than the two championship years. The Wisconsin women beat second-place Ohio State 21 to 91. The university paper reported the result in glowing terms, including a note that "while the performances of Herbst and Co. up front need no further comment, equally indicative of the squad's talent were the efforts of the second five: Mary Hartzheim, Holly Hering, Stephanie Bassett, Maureen Hartzheim, and Kris Favor. That's ten Wisconsin runners in the top twenty-one. If that isn't impressive enough, get this one: Kris Favor, the tenth runner, would have finished first for eleven of the teams in this meet. Also, eliminate their top five finishers and Wisconsin still wins the race."

The second meet of the year, against generally stronger competition, produced an even better result. At the eleven-team Indiana Invitational, Wisconsin beat the University of Kentucky 22 to 76 and put five runners in the top ten. Stephanie again was first and Suzy was a close second. Lori Wolter was fourth, Carol Harris sixth, and Kelly McKillen ninth. At that point in the season, Peter allowed himself optimism. "I am extremely impressed," he told reporters. "We had a lot of depth last year, but at the moment, we're better off depth-wise than last year's team." The next big race was the Wisconsin Cross-Country Classic, which Wisconsin won each of the prior years against nationally ranked competition, and which, individually, first Katie and then Stephanie won. Before that race, however, things started to go wrong. The first casualty was Lori Wolter who was ruled academically ineligible for the meet because she dropped below the required 12-credit mark. Suzy also encountered difficulty. She had been experiencing pain while running, and it was finally determined to be a stress fracture. Suzy went to the pool for her workouts, much as Mary Decker did before the 1984

Olympics. She said that people looked at her funny because they didn't know what she was doing, but she was able to maintain fitness. Finally, even Stephanie went down to injury, although it was none of her doing. She was running in Madison when a bicyclist blindsided her, sent her to the ground, and then fell and rolled on top of her. She fractured her tailbone, a painful injury. As late as the next indoor season, she was still affected by the injury. "I had to lay off for two weeks. But even after I got back I was in pain. I had to take a pillow with me every place and it was difficult to sleep." She also gained weight during the period of inactivity. The speculation was that neither Stephanie nor Suzy would run in the Classic.

Perhaps neither of them should have, but Stephanie did while Suzy could not. In the major home meet of the year, the reduced Wisconsin team took on a tremendous field that included national-favorite Texas, as well as BYU, Kansas State, Florida, Clemson, Washington State, Iowa State, Northwestern, Penn State, and Missouri. On a picture perfect day, Stephanie gave it her best shot, although she clearly was not herself. She led as usual until the end when Anne Schweitzer and Liz Natale of Texas drew away to go one-two for the Longhorns. Stephanie finished 14 seconds later in third place overall. Asked about the rare defeat, Stephanie refused to excuse herself because of the injury. "I felt okay but I guess I just didn't have it today. I'm not happy with my race, but I'm just going to keep an open mind. Texas has a good team." On this day, she said, they were too good for her. They were also too good for her teammates. Texas beat Wisconsin easily, 30 to 85. Texas coach Terry Crawford was happy with the victory no matter the circumstances, "Wisconsin is rated highly but head-to-head is a good indication of how we stand. I realize Wisconsin didn't run everyone due to injuries but it was a real good team effort from all seven of our runners and I'm pleased." Wisconsin could find encouragement only in the performance of its younger runners, who stepped up to the challenge. Carole Harris who was eighth and Mary Hartzheim who was nineteenth ran particularly well.

In truth, Peter was not disappointed in the performance of any athlete once she got to the line. The problem was getting them to the line at all. For the next major event, the Big Ten Championship, Lori Wolter returned but Suzy Favor was still missing. On race day, it didn't matter anyway. Running at Ohio State, Stephanie outran Kathy Monard of Kennah, Wisconsin and Ohio State, to win her second successive Big Ten Cross-Country Championship. The contest with Kathy had been closely watched, in part because Kathy was from a Wisconsin high school and had left the state, and in part because Kathy won her previous four races in course-record times and was clearly prepared to move it up a notch. As usual, Stephanie led and hoped she could get rid of Kathy before any damage was possible. "The turning point," she said after the race, "was at the hill at the three kilometer. That was the big test. I didn't feel like I had it won until I couldn't hear her breathing on my shoulder anymore." Cresting the hill, Stephanie gradually pulled away to complete a nine-year period in which a Badger won every women's Big Ten title, a streak that began with Sally Zook, continued through Rose Thomson and Cathy Branta, and now included two by Stephanie. The customary flow of Wisconsin women followed Stephanie and Kathy across the line in 1986: Carole Harris in third, Lori Wolter in seventh, Mary Hartzheim in ninth, and Kelly McKillen in tenth, for a comfortable team title, 30 to 114 over the University of Iowa. Peter professed himself reassured by Stephanie's race, given the continuing nature of her injury, and highly pleased by Carole's development.

Next up for Wisconsin was the NCAA District IV qualifying race, which was held in Normal, Illinois. Peter was still worried about the numbers, but not about the quality of his runners. "If we finish with five runners we should win it," he said. He had an ace up his sleeve. Suzy Favor returned. He did not, however, have Stephanie in the shape she should have been. As the season progressed, she was increasingly vulnerable. For one thing, the calls from reporters were persistent. Many times they wished to speak of Kathy Ormsby and of the pressure, which was now taking on a life of its own, a media image of embattled women competing in a sport that drove them too far. In Indianapolis, Stephanie had said that she was on a highwire, so it was natural that people—especially reporters who were paid to do this kind of thing for a living—would watch to see if she would fall. The university tried to restrict her telephone number but it did not work. It was to the point that Stephanie had to fit the calls into her schedule just as she did running, studying, and personal life. "I try to work them around running and studying, but anytime I break up that standard procedure, it's hard for me. Then I have to take out time from sleeping or skip lunch or something. I have really strict study habits." In this whirl, she continued to defend her inclination to leave decisions about running entirely to Peter, a situation that occasionally aroused an observer to curiosity if not doubt. "Herbst seems to have complete control over her academic and social life," remarked one writer, "and a purpose and a reason for everything she does. How ironic then that she should turn over total control of her running to Tegen." The writer in question eventually did accede to the wisdom of Stephanie's delegation, or at least concede that it was not as "ironic" as the first glance suggested. Peter took pressure off Stephanie, he admitted, by making running-related decisions for her. No matter the tone any writer or observer may take, Peter had no reason to apologize and little reason to explain his working relationship with Stephanie. After all, he did not take anything from her. Rather, he accepted the authority that she granted him, and he acted responsibly in the exercise of it. He and Stephanie did meet regularly; she did have opportunity for input, and the fact that she, most often, deferred to him was consistent with his greater expertise, his authority, and his employment. Stephanie was, he said, sure of herself and knew exactly what she wanted to accomplish. The interesting fact is, however, that Stephanie's decision-making process, her relationship with Peter, the way she allocated her personal time and energy, and the attempt she made to find emotional and physical balance were a matter for public discourse in the wake of Indianapolis and as a result of the spotlight the accident shined on Stephanie. That kind of scrutiny is wearing, and Stephanie was feeling the effect. Add the accident, the injury, the pain, the inactivity in the heart of the season, the weight gain, her own thoughts about the sport and its proper role in her life, and the worry over doing her best, and Stephanie was struggling as the cross-country season drew toward its climax. Peter thought that Stephanie also carried a special burden in reacting to Suzy because, when she came back out of the pool, it was increasingly obvious that she was as talented as advertised. Stephanie, a three-time national champion who had sacrificed everything in order to make her place, might be the second-best runner on her own team. Although they were in different events in indoor and outdoor track, they would compete in cross-country. Peter felt that might be bothering Stephanie. As a matter of fact, his interpretation of events was that Stephanie worked particularly hard in the cross-country season her junior year in order to prove that she was tough enough to handle the situation created by the incident in Indianapolis and by the entry of Suzy into the team structure. Doing so, she might again have made excessive demands on herself, as she had in the prior cross-country season. Or maybe it just wasn't her sport and she was running against the grain in taking it on.

Whatever the precise reason, Stephanie ran a poor race in Normal. She and Suzy ran together for much of the course, but Stephanie was not aggressive. She led the race without pushing it, without actively trying to get people off her, and as a result the pack stayed relatively thick. When the end came into sight, Suzy sprinted and took Carole Harris and Kathy Monard with her. Stephanie fell back into fourth place. She stayed there. Suzy won in 16:42; and Carole and Kathy passed the line before Stephanie finished 12 seconds later in 16:54, a little shocked by what had happened but not, really, surprised by it. Despite Stephanie's drop-off, Wisconsin easily won the team championship 26 to 120 over Iowa. Wisconsin's women now had the chance for a third successive national championship in cross-country. They enjoyed a legitimate prospect. They had Stephanie returning as a top-ten finisher from the prior year and as a three-time national champion in track and field; they had Suzy Favor who might outrun even Stephanie; they had Lori Wolter, who tended to load up at big meets and run very well; they had an emerging Carole Harris, and they had good depth throughout the top seven. If they had been beaten earlier by Texas, the defeat had an explanation. Furthermore, Stephanie, at least, ought to take some comfort from the site of the race. It was Tucson, Arizona, where the weather would be warm.

For Wisconsin, the National Cross-Country Championship in Arizona, when it was all over, was a race that a Badger just had to pack up and leave behind, because if he or she studied the result with any care it would be the occasion for crazy regret, with every slight turn of events producing a different, and altogether more pleasing, result. But the facts are what the facts are. Wisconsin lost to a fine Texas team by the narrowest margin in the history of the event, 62 to 64. At the gun, Stephanie, Suzy and Carole joined a sizable lead pack for the first mile. Carole was out a little too fast and fell back; Lori Wolter, who was not with her teammates in the early running, was out a little too slow—back near 50th place in the early stage—so she moved up. While those two crossed each other coming and going, Stephanie and Suzy held on to the front of the race, which of course meant that Suzy was doing the right thing and

Stephanie battles two Longhorns in Arizona.

Stephanie was doing the wrong thing. Stephanie should not have been holding on to anybody or anything. She should have been driving along from the front as she usually did, trying to create a gap. Nevertheless, at two miles both were close enough to see the unheralded Angela Chalmers of Canada and Northern Arizona University sweep away, and both were in position to chase, which Suzy did rather more successfully than Stephanie. To the very end, Suzy hoped she might win with a big kick, especially if Angela slowed, but Angela did not slow, and, although Suzy kicked, it only drew her nearer and not past. Angela Chalmers, who had been affected all season by a sore achilles tendon, held her lead and won the big race. "I just tried to stay relaxed in the first mile," she said after the race. "In the second, I started concentrating on breaking away and winning. In the last mile, I heard the crowd and my teammates saying it was my race to win." Her time was 16:56. Suzy finished second in 17:02, 6 seconds ahead of third place. Texas' first finisher was Sandy Blakeslee, who finished fifth in 17:18. Stephanie slipped one place from her 1985 finish. She was eighth overall in 17:19, a time she shared—essentially—with two other runners, both of whom, unfortunately, were placed in front of her in official times marked as 17:18.27 (sixth), 17:18.55 (seventh), and 17:18.75 (eighth), as if cross-country courses and chutes lent themselves to such particularity. Stephanie was 1 second ahead of Kathy Monard, who continued her excellent season with this all-American run, and she was 3 seconds ahead of Texas' number two, Liz Natale—Liz who was in the middle of an anguished struggle to control her own body, which naturally ran at 130 pounds but willed itself down to 116 when the pressure seemed to demand it. Within a flash of Liz, Trina Leopold sprinted across for Texas in 15th place with a time of 17:27, and Anne Schweitzer arrived in 19th at 17:38, a time she shared with Lori Wolter who was 20th. It was close all the way through the ranks, but Texas now had four finishers while Wisconsin had three. Carole Harris closed the gap, however, when she dived into the chute to claim 27th place. Texas still had an advantage, but it was precarious, and much depended on the fifth woman from each team. In fairness, Mary Hartzheim did her part for Wisconsin. She was 36th and Texas' fifth was 43rd, so Mary beat her woman, but still when the places were adjusted to remove runners from non-scoring teams and the places were counted it looked like this: Texas (3-7-10-13-29) and Wisconsin (1-6-14-19-24). From Wisconsin's side, the question must be asked: how is it possible to lose a national championship cross-country meet when you gather five women from one to twenty-four? From Texas' side, the question must be asked: was any other result possible with four runners in the top 13 scorers and the fifth in before 30? In any event, there was nothing to be done about it. Texas won, and that was that. Whatever anybody else might have said about the shoot-out in Arizona, Peter put the result in a proper perspective, telling people at home that "second place in the NCAA is really something outstanding," which it was. Rather than go looking for those two lost points, the University of Wisconsin counted them irretrievable. Hook 'em.

Stephanie did not run a particularly good race in Tucson. Neither, however, did she run a bad race. She simply ran a race without vigor. She drifted at precisely the moment when she might have been gathering herself. This was, of course, a matter of concern, but she had no idea how to address the situation. She went back with the team to Madison, she concentrated on her studies, she enjoyed the brief interlude offered by the holidays, and then she returned to the track when the indoor season announced next call.

All the while, Stephanie Herbst suspected the truth: she had nothing more to give. It was enough to make her cry. Still, from obligation and with no clear idea what else to do, Stephanie turned away one more time and kept on running.

TWENTY

*I told my little brother that when you die you cannot breath
and he did not say a word. He just kept on playing.*

A child's composition quoted in One Art,
The Letters of Elizabeth Bishop

Each afternoon Stephanie checked the board and looked at
the instructions that only a member of the team could understand.
[Sprints/Quarter/Jumps/Hep.] (1) WLS; (2) X's; (3) 2 x 6 diag's, R5
act. in betwns. (4) j.d. [Throws] (1) WLS; (2) see event coach. [Half]
(1) WLS; (2) 5 McLaps of WS in N-Straight; (3) 1-3-5-3-1 McLaps,
Fast Strides on all odd laps, R 2,3,3,2; (4) LJS; (5) j.d. and LIFT.
[MD/LD] (1) WLS (2) 6 McLaps with WS in N-str.; (3) R7, 5
McLaps (—->2h, 1e, 2h), R7, 8 McLaps (—->4h, 1e,3h), f.j.;
(4) LJS; (5) j.d. and LIFT. [Suzy and Mary] see above, except on (3)
—->instead of 8 McLaps—->Do 8 McLaps 2h, 1e, 2h, 1e, 2h.
Earlier in Stephanie's enrollment, the board revealed, item by item,
clue by clue, how she might fulfill her dreams. Stephanie knew that
the completion of the individual tasks would accumulate over many
days, weeks, months, and years. Together, they would bring fitness
and permit great achievement. The result was the foregone conclusion of all the work that anticipated it. Now, looking up at the board
in January 1987, Stephanie saw numbers, and behind those numbers
she saw tasks relevant only to the single day, a gathering of things she
had to do before she could go home. A sense of obligation rested

where inspiration formerly burned, and the determination to hold on replaced the desire to make progress.

As the new academic semester began and the indoor season approached, Peter could see that Stephanie was drifting away, but there was little he could do. A coach cannot stoke a cold fire. Looking at the situation, he sometimes wondered whether Stephanie had ever enjoyed competitive running for its own sake. From the beginning, she said that her priorities were academic and professional, and that running was a means to those ends. If her success as a runner had not turned her head and rearranged her priorities, she might calculate the future and walk away some day soon. Peter hoped not. But if Stephanie did withdraw, he would honor her decision. As a young girl battling the high winds in Minnesota, she puzzled and fascinated him, and she still did, but she had the right to make her own life. Anyway, he was getting practiced at this. Other women on the team were not only pulling away but leaving. Birgit Christiansen, who had been an important part of the two national championship cross-country teams, was again eligible in 1986-1987 but did not participate. Kelly McKillen, too, decided to leave the team. After serving only as an alternate for the cross-country team in Tucson, the two-time all-American left the program. Kelly was finishing her degree in elementary education, involved in student teaching, and simply lacked the time for championship training and racing. Another promising runner, Sarah Docter, also decided not to continue. A member of the 1980 United States Olympic team when she was 14 years old as a speed skater and a bronze medalist in the World Speed Skating Championships in 1981, Sarah had also run 4:36.1 for 1,500 meters, 10:12.1 for 3,000-meters, and represented Wisconsin in the NCAA cross-country meet one year. But that was the end of it. With eligibility left, she decided not to run in 1986. Of course, Birgit, Kelly and Sarah left for reasons of their own. None of them faulted the program or Peter, for whom they expressed high

The new generation: Mary Hartzheim and Suzy Favor
join Peter Tegen for a laugh.

regard; they merely came to the end of a road, the length of which
was personal to them. The most that can be said, commonly, is that
within the context of their individual lives, running at the university
level eventually became more burdensome than rewarding so they
stopped.

Standing outside all this and observing was Suzy Favor,
who did not stop, and who would have been troubled by the suggestion. If Peter doubted that Stephanie really wanted to be a runner,
there could be no doubt about Suzy Favor. She was a runner through
and through. "I want to run the rest of my life," she once admitted.
She did not dismiss the pressure in her sport, but much of it slipped
past her because she kept her perspective. "I don't want to get too
intense about it. You have to enjoy practice, and some people I know
don't enjoy practices and that's half the work right there." She tried

to be as much like "anyone else" as possible by going to movies, sailing, and dating. In short order, she started dating steadily a Wisconsin student who pitched for the varsity baseball team. Pulled into his life, she had less time for obsession over her own activities. In such ways, Suzy Favor kept her balance when others might have fallen. Doing so, she served as an example for her teammates. Later, her time at the University of Wisconsin would be called "the Favor years." The reference is normally to her many accomplishments, but it might additionally have been a reference to her personality, to the collection of personal qualities that permitted her to pull teammates her way when it was healthy for them, and to permit herself to be pulled their way when that was healthy for her.

As her freshman year continued, Suzy still looked to Stephanie for friendship and advice, but she also became close to the Hartzheim sisters, who shared with her a spirit that permitted them to compete hard without turning destructively introspective. Suzy and the Hartzheim sisters, joined by Carole Harris, were the critical mass for a new Wisconsin distance corp. They were also the course along which Peter was steering. This is not to say that any of the young women on previous teams had been more or less intense than Suzy and the Hartzheims, although some had. It is merely to say that the chemistry of the team, particularly in Stephanie's sophomore year, was more intense than was comfortable for women who were not willing to dedicate themselves to the sport unconditionally. In that event, it was ironic that Kelly and Birgit withdrew just as Suzy Favor began to assert herself at Wisconsin because, in many respects, they resembled Suzy in their attitude to athletics. Both came out of high school not only as fine athletes but as homecoming queens, with all the inference that status generates. At Wisconsin, they were good students; they dated frequently, and they attempted to maintain balanced lives. But when Cathy Branta graduated, competition for place on the team became volatile and overheated, and they were not able to get control; their own interests soon shifted; and when benefit and loss were measured, they left. A similar statement might be made regarding Sarah Docter, who occasionally tried to curtail the tendency of her teammates to race the workouts but was never able to do it. Sarah never could have done it, no matter how persuasive her arguments. At Wisconsin, the fastest runner set the pace in more ways than one. No runner could impose her will on the team of distance runners until she got to the front. It wasn't enough to be close; it wasn't enough to be funny or smart or good looking or well-intentioned. The leader was the leader.

Entering the indoor season, Stephanie was neither here nor there, not one of the women who had withdrawn from the team nor one of those who, clearly, had sufficient life left in them to move on. She was in limbo. And she ran like it. In the Badger Classic, she attempted to run 3,000 meters for time, but could not get rid of tenacious Lori Wolter who sprinted three separate times in the last lap before finally winning in 9:25.58 to Stephanie's 9:25.67. Even at the Big Ten indoor championship, Stephanie responded only with difficulty. In the 3,000 meter, she not only lost to Lori again, but also to Collette Goudreau of the University of Indiana, who won the race. The times were 9:11.77, 9:17.25, and 9:25.99. All three times pale by comparison to Stephanie's record run at the NCAA indoor meet in her sophomore year, which was 8:57.12. Stephanie did come back to win the 5,000 meters in a collegiate-leading 16:18.84, pulling Lori into second and Holly Hering into fourth and giving Wisconsin the valuable points it needed in order to win its ninth (of the total of ten ever held at that time) Big Ten Indoor Championship. Nonetheless, it was clear that Stephanie was still feeling the effect of the back injury from the previous fall, that she was not as fit as formerly, and, perhaps, that she just could not find the hope and the desire any longer to train and race at prior standards. Those facts were all confirmed at the NCAA indoor meet a few weeks later. In the preliminary heats of the 3,000 meters, Stephanie failed even to qualify for the final. She finished a dismal fifth in her heat in 9:22.01. Although she spoke afterward of her injuries and her lack of fitness, it was disinterest and disinclination that did the job. Stephanie did not want to qualify for the finals. When she should have been sprinting for the available qualifying spot, she was talking to herself instead. "I'm not going to do this to myself another day," said an interior voice that was loud enough to obscure even Peter's voice coming at her from across the arena, "Go, you've got to get up, go, go!!" She heard him alright, and she understood him. But Stephanie had decided. She would not. She could not. She should not. Anyway, she did not. She ceded her 3,000-meter title to Vicki Huber, an emerging sophomore sensation from Villanova University who later in the year would add the outdoor title at 3,000 meters to her list. Indoors, Vicki ran 9:06.45; outdoors, she ran 8:54.41. Asked about her improvement, she explained that she lost 15 pounds. One report said that Vicki lost weight because she gave up ice cream. Whatever the explanation, Vicki plunged from 125 pounds to 109 in a year's time. "I can feel the difference when I run," she enthused. "I feel lighter and quicker." The more things change, the more they stay the same, as the saying goes.

Meanwhile, Stephanie had crossed a line. On one side was a former version of herself; on the other was a new one. The new Stephanie was like the old one only more honest with herself. Coming to a turn in the road, she finally made the decision that made all the difference. It was the hardest thing she ever had to do at Wisconsin.

. . . . .

Have the other young women in the house retire for the evening. Permit Stephanie some time alone. Despite the lateness of the hour, make her restless. Imagine correspondence.

Date: spring, 1987

Michele Herbst
College of St. Thomas
St. Paul, Minnesota

Dear Michele,

I hope that everything is well with you. Some day, I will inquire properly on the subject. Not tonight though—-this letter is of a different kind and I'm shifting into gear fast, no time to delay. This is me telling you what sure hell my life has become. I wouldn't do this to anyone else, and I might not do it to you, except that you spend all your time in class talking about vocations, religion, and theology, so you're fair game when your very own sister is troubled. This is your last chance to turn back. If you read the next sentence you have to read the whole letter. I quit the track team. (You read it.) Did Dad already tell you? Anyone else reading the letter might think this is an insignificant event, but you know that it was difficult for me to do. Officially, I have an injury, and that's good enough for now, but I wonder if I can ever make it back. I might if the other girls asked me to return because I do hate the feeling of having abandoned them. Beyond that, however, I am determined to make this decision based on what is best for me and not for anyone else who may have an interest, no matter how much I love them or respect them, or how much confidence I have in them. So this is what I want to talk about. I want you to understand why I did this.

It seems like such a long time since you and I started running together, but in fact it is only seven years at the outside. Who could imagine the way things would go? To amuse myself, I sometimes try to remember what it was that either one of us had mind. I

know what I said. At least I know what I said in my senior year—
that story about using track as a way to make business contacts, but
I have some trouble giving myself credit for such calculation. I'm
thinking that it was something else: that we actually enjoyed running. I know that I enjoyed training to run. And I think you did, too.
But the competition is another matter. Did we like it? We liked winning, but that is something quite distinct, and no particular credit to
either of us. Did we like the actual race, the measuring of ourselves
against the other girls? I know that when I started to run well, some
people said that I was a natural at the sport, but I wonder about that,
too. I was always so nervous. The only salvation then was that no
one, or let's say few people, cared or noticed much what we did.
Dad, yes, and maybe the other girls on the team, and the girls we ran
against, but nobody else. Not really, even though we sometimes
acted like the whole world was watching—or at least I did, getting
so edgy and tense. Do you remember the cold day when I lost the
state Meet in cross-country. How absurd it all was, but it was the
best I could do on the day, all things taken into account, including
my failure of temperament, which is how I analyze it now.

When I started running here, people did notice, and because
I was running well and sometimes winning, they got an idea what it
meant to be Stephanie Herbst, and what they could expect from her.
Only thing is, I got a little behind them. I knew why they thought I
was this person who could be expected to act in this certain way, and
perform to a particular specification, but I had no idea that I could
make things come out that way. What if everything of value to you
hung always in balance and if you had no idea why the balance held,
when it did, and why it fell, when it did? What if success and failure looked much the same to you because, in either event, you could
find no sure way to control the outcome? Would you become shy of
any activity for fear of inadvertently tipping the scale? Or would you
wade in and take your chances with some conduct—any conduct—

so long as it was affirmative and forceful? I don't know either. I was just asking. What I am saying is that I no longer feel safe. I need a little certainty. I don't even know why I run well anymore (when I do, that is). Is it because I'm innately strong, something in the gene pool? Or because I'm built light? Or my legs are long relative to my trunk, or my motion is efficient? Is it because of my workouts? We have one woman on the team who swears by a pair of jeans she wears the day before every competition. Is she wrong? The balance between success and failure is so imprecise that I won't hazard a guess. Almost all the people on the team have different things like that, saying that, this thing—whatever it was—is what made me do well. And I was like that, too. I had superstitions because you'd say: gee, how'd I get here? And you'd try to figure out what element it was that got you there.

I probably made a mistake. I had Dad and Peter and I let them carry too much weight. I wanted them to provide the answers for me. It seemed better than wandering off on my own. In some ways, they controlled me, Peter more so than Dad. If Peter said something, it was not worth rethinking the issue. That was the decision that was a lasting decision. Whereas, when Dad said something, I did question it, and I think he wanted me to do that. But they definitely—in fact, some people have said to me that "those two"— that's the way my friends speak of them, although I know it has a sinister tone to it—were in control of your life. Those two controlled you. You have to get away from those two. That sort of thing. And my friends miss the point, I think, because neither Dad or Peter are that kind of person, but I put myself in the position that I made them. I created that power. I created the situation in which I didn't trust my own judgment. I needed somebody to tell me; and it was going to be one of those two people, and primarily Peter. And here's the thing. I run hard, I really do, but I don't race as well as I'd like to. I get nervous about myself, and lose confidence, and the littlest things can throw me off balance, so I want to be prepared as well as I can be, and Peter is absolutely the best coach in the country if you want to run fast. I still think that. It's just that this decision has more to do with me than with running. I hope I can find a way to make Peter understand how much I appreciated his help, taking me where he took me; and Dad too. I get down on myself. You know some of the other girls here. I wish I had half the fortitude that Suzy has or Holly Hering. They always have themselves ready to compete. I might have been better off if only I had a break now and then, but the seasons just keep on coming. You'd think that one season would help keep you in shape for the other, but that really doesn't happen, or it didn't for me anyway. I got exhausted, and finally, lately, it's to the point that I just couldn't respond in a race. It gets blurred a little. You should be able to run as fast as ever, but sometimes you literally forget to hit the accelerator, or maybe you don't want to hit it because the last time you did, nothing happened, and you were out there getting slagged and all alone with everybody watching and saying what's wrong with her today and you want to shout leave me alone, and you don't want to feel that way again, so you just don't. You don't bother with the effort that exposes you so pitiably. You're running, I guess you could call it that, but you're not racing. If that's what you want to do, what are you doing out there? You need to come off and try to find out what's going on.

This whole year, really since last summer, has been awful. People act like it's so strange that I want to make some changes. They talk about track and running, as if that's all there is, but—and I know I should have mentioned this a little earlier—there is the personal stuff. I have been worried even about you. Does that surprise you? And grandmother's death, and all the other things that crash in on us. Actually, I think I may be less confused now that I decided to stop running for the team than I was six months ago when I first started to worry about things so much.

Get past it. That's what people say, and you might feel the same way by now, but Indianapolis shook me up. It wasn't just me either. Sue Schroeder from Michigan—why didn't you tell me that was such a good school?—is a sensitive person and she and I were talking about it. So I knew that she was asking the questions too. But when I won the 10,000 meters, things changed. People called it a dark or a black victory. They even said that to me on the first day after the accident. Well, just this negative feeling came over the race. I hadn't even processed that, or worked through what happened, and they were asking me to explain it to them. I had no idea, really, what was going on. Even though I took time off after the NCAA, I don't think I got it processed completely before the cross-country season. I didn't feel responsible for what happened to Kathy, and I said so to some of the ones who asked, but I couldn't shake the feeling that if there wasn't something there they wouldn't have asked the question in the first place. Should I have taken that burden as my own? Should I? That aggravates me. I compete; and Kathy competes. One part of the deal is that we compete fairly; and another part of the deal must be that we take the results as they happen. They belong to each of us as individuals. I bet Kathy would feel the same.

How could it be any other way? How could I step aside in a field of fourteen runners, and say, who among you is going to be emotionally devastated, if only for an unfortunate minute, if she loses this race? And if someone says they will be, I step aside? Is that it? I just can't see it. And until I do, some of the questions people asked me in Indianapolis, and since, were unfair. But, Michele, they hurt me.

I was younger then, I'm growing up fast now, and in the heat of the moment my heart went out to Kathy. You know, you view things like this two ways. The first is compassionate, something direct and human: 'I hope she's alright. I'm sorry that happened. Is there anything I can do to make it better?' But pretty closely, and for some people almost simultaneously, you start to ask what it means to you. I'm not talking about compassion any longer, or warmth, or caring or charity of thought, but maybe it's an aspect of empathy, some sense that you look at what happened to someone else and feel for them because you are able to extrapolate from your own life experience to know better what happened and to get some approximate sense of how it must feel. But when you do this, it brings all the scare straight home, and now I can't find a way to make it go away. What if it was me? Could it happen to me? What can I do to avoid that? What am I doing wrong that might make it happen? Thoughts like this get mixed in with everything you do, and some of the things that used to look innocent now leer at you; a different look and feel altogether, and frightening, Michele. I'm sorry to leave all this with you, but I wanted you to know what's going on.

After Kathy got hurt, I was sad. Sad. I wanted to say the word simply. I almost said "profoundly sad" or "shaken" or "disturbed," and all of those words and phrases might work, but the plain word comes closest to what I felt. But I was also alarmed not only for myself but for all of us. I saw too much in what happened that was general. You remember the newspapers quoted me as saying that the fans saw only the glamour in the sport and not the lows. What I said—I was the "winner," after all, the so-called champion—made it impossible for people to write Kathy off as a singular person with a singular experience and then move on to something else. If the experience was general, if it sprang from conditions that prominently existed in women's athletics, then something had to be done. Of course, that can make people uncomfortable. The first thing is that people have to say: what we did before was not as it should have been. That is not to say, "we got it wrong," or that "we were unconcerned" or even that "our sport is out of balance," but only that we can do better. That still looks like a confession, and some people didn't want to give one. Even a confession isn't worth anything unless you are prepared to make changes. Anyway, I said too much after Kathy's accident. People asked me questions and I answered them, but then they started to watch me. Maybe I appeared a little too vulnerable, admitted too much. I should have closed off. Or maybe they thought they were on some kind of death watch, but it got crazy, even back here in school. The phone calls, Michele, never stopped coming. I took my phone off the hook, but that cut me off from everybody I did want to talk to. So, I had all this extra pressure on top of everything else, and I got myself stretched out a little too thin. It was inevitable, I guess. You take your victim as you find her; and I was not the kind of person who could walk away from Indianapolis without noticing that something important happened there.

I think the press was...it's a weird feeling...because the press kind of brings you up—you're not this person but they make you this person...and they don't do this to men as much. If you win, they say you're beautiful, you're sweet and you're nice; and you're also doing well in sports. Not that you're a good athlete, but that you are coincidentally doing well in the sport. They build you up to something you're really not, and it's like 'Wow!! Is that me?' You'd like to believe that's you and you take on that persona and think maybe that is me, but you're not. And then when you don't do well, they funnel you back to this horrible person that you're not either. You're like, Wait a minute—where am I?—I'm somewhere in between!!

Maybe it's me. But you're 18 years old, you come to college, you're basically being paid, it's your first real job, somebody's paying for your education. You still have to do well in school because, number one, you've got to get a job when you get out; and two, you've got to stay on the team, so there are the two parameters. And then to be a "good girl," you have to do well in school. Those are only the basics. On top of it, you've got to be a good athlete, among the best. That's just tough. And during my first two years, it wasn't this jovial atmosphere. You didn't have the support of your teammates, or didn't feel that you did. Peter is a wonderful coach, probably the best coach anyone could ever have, but he isn't an emotional man who hugs and kisses you, good job and I'm there for you. Or maybe he is, but the school wouldn't let him act like that anyway; everything is so closed off. Sometimes, the way I am, you get left. And that's OK because you're an adult, you can pick up the pieces and run with them yourself, but I think maybe I wasn't ready to run with it myself. I never did get a grip on the whole question of balance. I knew it was out there as a concept, but it escaped me. How much to run, at what pace, at what weight? The old questions: how much is too much; how little is too little? Of course, I turned to Peter for the running questions, but you know from your own running that Peter couldn't very well follow us around in a car and know what we were doing. Or know what we were eating, or what time we went to bed. And no matter what happened, the expectations kept building. I take that back. I guess it would have been possible to lower expectations by performing badly but what kind of charade is that in the long term? Finally, and circling around a little, the killer: some of the other women (I might, honestly, add myself to this because sometimes I was right in there with the rest of them) going too far. One of the articles I saw after Indianapolis had a coach who said that he knew runners who had the pills in their hands with a glass of water; and he knew women who took the first pill. I believe him. You know another woman on our team just left. She ran the indoor season because Peter thought she could pull out of it, but then she decided to take some time away. I am talking about Lori Wolter, who is one year behind me and an extraordinary runner, very, very tough in a race and an all-American for both of her cross-country seasons as a freshman and a sophomore. (She beat me this year indoors! She slides along, she hardly lifts her legs but somehow she goes fast when she needs to!) She can tell her own story, but to me it looked like she was losing herself in running, that her nature and her personality were in danger of being overthrown by the pressure to win, or to do well, or to meet her obligations to the program, or maybe just to be what she always had been—before she got here, that is. She was the best. She was not alone, of course. We all had been, at least on some level, but when we came here we didn't catch immediately what happened. We were NOT the best anymore because, even though we kept getting better and better, somebody moved the standard. What a concept it turned out to be: the best. Good, better, best, and it really comes to nothing. How do you measure such a thing? Is everybody in the group? Ever? Anybody ever? When is the decision going to be made? How long will the decision endure? How can I be the best runner today and not tomorrow, changed utterly by a night's sleep? Time, place, circumstances, grouping, the nature of the test, measurement, preparation and fortune, and the meaning gets away. It's all so transient, or at least it seems so from here. I'm sick of it. I'm also sick of knowing how wrong I am about all this, and how tired I am of working in shadow, because the fact is that, ultimately, there really is a time and a place and a circumstance when the concept becomes absolutely clear. You really are going to find out who is the best, and there is no uncertainty. In fact the possibility of winning—of being the best—is so remote and the calculation of loss so certain that you scratch around to invent ambiguity. You need to do something, anything at all, to make the race smaller and less revealing. It's not the uncertainty that causes the problem; it's the certainty. It's not the meaninglessness of the contest that breaks you up; its the meaningfulness. So there was Lori—there we all were—running along, training our eyes on the ground 10 feet in front of ourselves, concentrating, turning in, trying not to look too far into the horizon, only occasionally looking all the way up and out. And then, every great while, we might check ourselves to ask whether any of it had value, and if the answer didn't come back yes, yes, yes, it was time to stop. The tilt came out wrong, and when that happened there was nothing to be done about it. The change had been coming for a while. You argued with it, turned it away, denied it, and then it forced itself on you. You weren't any more in control of that decision than the one that started you down the road to begin with. I'm exhausted. I wonder if Katie Ishmael would say the same thing. Katie, Lori, and I are alike in one respect. We all have the ability to tighten things down and hold it, to concentrate on a long-range task and then to attack it day after day. But there may be a question how long we should hold that intensity. This isn't Peter, of course, because Peter talks about replenishing, but the concept is hard to hold onto when you feel this terrible responsibility and this ambition. Replenishment and rest mock you. Somebody else is always out there training harder than you are.

Anyway, I quit a race. I've been kind of beating around the bush about that. I think only Peter really knew. I could have qualified for the finals at the NCAA Indoor meet but I didn't. I supposed you might have guessed what happened. Even after that, I was supposed to run the outdoor track season, and I actually started in that direction. I just didn't get very far! The irony of everything is that outdoor track is where I'm best, what I enjoy the most. I have had a knee problem and soreness in the achilles tendon on one leg, and I do still have some soreness from getting run over by that ridiculous bike, but Peter didn't take any of my current injuries seriously. He probably shouldn't have because it was mostly in my head—but the doctors were saying that you shouldn't run, you'll make it chronic—so I'd taken some time off. When I took time off—I'm sorry this is so long—it wasn't really time off. I was still doing water running, strenuous workouts twice a day, lifting weights. I was still very involved. And I just decided one night that I wasn't going to do it anymore. I was going to give it up. I felt like I had no social life. I had just joined the sorority because I wanted to change that situation. I started dating because I wanted to change that situation. I started to spend more time on school because I wanted to do well in business school. I don't know, Michele, I just couldn't do it anymore. It was too much.

I called Dad and told him. I want to quit running. He started trying to persuade me that it was a bad decision. I said, "No, you don't understand. I am quitting running." I had gotten myself to the state that there was no possibility of change, the decision had been made. It was done. I said: "I'm injured. I'm quitting running. It's over. I can't do this anymore." And I even used Kathy as an example. I said I don't want to be the next Kathy. I can't take it all. There's too much pressure. I'm injured. I'm quitting. Dad was very upset about everything and emotional but I was determined. I then called Peter with Dad on the phone with me. And I said the same things basically. I posed it as "I've got these injuries." And Peter started to say, Stephanie, a lot of people have injuries, I'm a strong believer that many injuries are a matter of mind (like mine, for example!) and I said: "No, Peter, I'm quitting." He said I needed to take some time off; and I said, "No, I don't need time off. I'm done." And he said OK; that he would miss me and all that. And then we got off the phone. I was a wreck, but I did it.

Later I took my stuff in to one of the women on the athletic department staff. That may have been the hardest part of all—to actually come in, in person, and return my uniform and say this is what I decided to do. She burst out crying, "Oh, Stephanie, what have we done?" and I kept saying, "No, it's not you." But she took it so personally, like it was something they'd done and I said, "No. I took it too seriously. I took too much pressure, and I'm just the personality that can't do that. I've gotta quit." She was real supportive, and gave me a hug, and then I had to walk out past everybody outside her office, all those people who had heard us through the door.

They heard her start to cry, and wanted to know whether we were alright. Actually we were all wondering what was going on because I wasn't so sure myself by this point. I was trembling. I don't know whether it was anxiety, or maybe it was surprise. Surprise, you know, that someone cared that much, and that it meant something after all. It was moving, actually, but I had gone too far to turn back, not this time.

Michele, this has been the hardest time. Sometimes, I think it might have been easier to keep on going! But at least I wasn't the first. Not counting Lori, a number of other women had already decided to leave the team. In some ways, I was a survivor, the last of a group. And here of course you will recognize the truth. I never stopped running at all. It's just like me, you know. I couldn't quit running. I am still running the workouts I think they are doing. It is ridiculous, absolutely ridiculous. I cannot miss a day of running. I still do my morning workout and in the afternoon I do what they are doing, as near as I can figure it. I guess I'll keep on doing this this spring and summer. I don't see an end in sight! And to think, one of my excuses is that I'm hurt. (Peter knows me very well, as you can see!)

One thing is bothering me still, though. Some people are saying that this is because of Suzy, that I quit because of her, or because she knocked me off my perch, or something like that. In fact, I was happy to have Suzy join the team. Remember I told you once that the team of distance runners at Wisconsin might have fifteen or sixteen runners, but there was a cut between the serious runners and those who, for one reason or the other, probably would not run as well; and that the competition in the first group was pretty heated. Well, Suzy came right in and checked the dynamics on the team. You take that top group of, say, eight women and all at once you get somebody who is unquestionably in the top three in everything, and she comes in and she's joking, and she's laughing, she doesn't take school as seriously. She says this is a game, this is fun, and she's talking about boys. I'm thinking: "What!?! I don't date!" It's like: "What's up with THIS?" She'd go out and party! It was a complete departure from the rest of the team; and suddenly she's in that group of three, and I was so relieved to have the tension and all of that gone. That's why I gravitated to Suzy. Because she was the person who removed that tension and made it go away. She is the friend I needed all along. She has this wonderful personality. And Mary Hartzheim, one of Suzy's best friends, also came this year. Mary brought the same quality with her. She—and she has a sister also on the team who is much like her—is a smart lady, and has this wit. Suzy and she just laugh and giggle at everything that amuses them. Mary will go to the board where the workouts are posted, for example, and she'll stand there looking up at it for a long time and then she'll start in: "If you think I'm going to do this workout, you've got another think coming!!"—mock serious but ready to surrender any minute and start the workout—and Suzy will laugh at this for five minutes straight, and it just eases the tension for the entire group. It really is a joy.

I have to admit, though, that one thing did change when Suzy came to the team, and it does bother me. Initially, I never felt any pressure from Suzy. But Peter said to me—not early on, because early on I was doing well in the workouts and in the races, and to some extent was right on track with where I had been my sophomore year—but later he said, "You know, pretty soon, Suzy will start beating you and you need to be prepared for that to happen," or words to that effect. I know that he was trying to let me down easy because Suzy is an astonishing runner, but that's when I felt that I lost Peter's support. Mentally, that just lost me. I was already so torn emotionally that that pushed me over the edge.

I tried to stay with it after that. For me it is no problem passing the baton to Suzy. There are a lot of races that she will not run. She doesn't run the 5,000 or the 10,000. And I was really more comfortable on the track than in cross-country so that was no problem anyway. I never felt myself competitive with Suzy, like "I gotta beat Suzy" because Suzy was not the kind of person you would want to do that to. You don't want to see Suzy lose. I just wanted to do well in my races, and I didn't mind coming second to Suzy. I did mind Peter saying you're passing the baton to Suzy and Suzy is going to be—not my favorite—but the one I'm going to guardian over. Emotionally, that was very hard on me, because you say: "Well, I still need your support, Peter. I still need to get there and if you're not going to support me, I can't get there."

This is all so unfair to Peter. He is doing the best he can and I am always pressing him into corners with stuff like this. Anyway, it's late. Before I go, though, let me tell you one more thing, if it does not wear your patience out. The school officials worried about me earlier this year. They worried about my weight, which I still say they shouldn't have because although I get real thin, I believe I know what I'm doing (not that it matters any more, but I gained a lot of weight in the last several months, thank you very much!) and they worried about my reaction to the accident and things like that. They actually asked me to see a counselor to talk through some of the issues they thought might affect me. I went to the counselor. He started right in telling me about other women and their problems, and I thought: well, I'm not telling this guy anything because he'll just turn around and talk about me to the next person who walks in the door! But, Michele, I didn't know how to take that whole thing anyway. Let me know what you think.

That's it, this is the end. Go to bed. When you get a chance, you can tell me all your problems to pay me back for sending you this letter. I may listen.

Love,

Stephanie

. . . . .

Ten years after Stephanie withdrew from the track team at the University of Wisconsin in the spring of 1987, she learned for the first time that well-meaning members of the medical staff associated with university athletics asked Peter not to "interfere" in her struggle to find the balance and equanimity she needed. She was astonished. Peter was, Stephanie said, the one person outside the family in whom her trust was absolute. Free, uninhibited, unregulated conversation between them was the most likely cure for what ailed her. Looking back on it now, Peter says that he always had the feeling that Stephanie wanted to tell him that she was sorry; that she was suffering with this. "She got scared," Peter remembers, "and she never wanted to say it. And she felt awful. She felt she was letting me down, and the program down, and maybe herself down by not continuing." With regard to the conversations he and Stephanie had about her weight and generally about her well-being, Peter says finally, "It would be terrible if I sat here and said I never believed her. I always believed her."

TWENTY ONE

converts pass them/pass them without pity/
watching for the wave/

Surfers
Virginia Hamilton Adair

Withdrawing from the team, Stephanie forfeit the promise of Wisconsin's spring and summer. The field having been tilled, she left it fallow. She turned her attention instead to society. She enjoyed the sorority; she dated; she attended parties; she exercised with less focus; she became more casual about her eating, and she healed. In doing so, she created from the cheer and companionship a wilderness, a place and a company to hold her separate from the pressure in her life and to keep her safe. Away from the team and from competition, she had time to think and to regenerate so that, when the call was made for her return to competition, she might respond. Neither wished nor regretted, the possibility of returning was always with her. She thought about it, and in her heart she knew she would. She could not leave things as they were because it was an offense against her. Unfinished business was not a favored concept for Stephanie Herbst. She only stepped away in the first place in order to stop the unrelenting call on her account. The decision would not have been necessary if the grinding schedule of one/two/three competitive seasons had been more reasonable. Stephanie was no General MacArthur, a son of Wisconsin who famously promised to return, because she made no promises. But she understood the concept.

The healing proceeded slowly in the spring and summer of 1987. Stephanie's achilles tendon, which had in fact been sore, improved. Her knee, which sometimes bothered her, bothered her less. Her training was mild but regular, still the mimic of Peter's regimen, and she watched the team perform in her absence. She knew in the late spring, of course, that the Wisconsin women lost the Big Ten Outdoor Championship for the first time in five years and she was unsettled, preferring of course that they should win. But she also knew that her points would not have been enough to change the outcome. Purdue won the meet by almost 50 points. Stephanie also watched her friend Suzy Favor continue to advance. Suzy won her first national championship when she won the mile at the NCAA indoor meet, the same one that saw Stephanie pull up short in the 3,000. In the outdoor season, Suzy won both the 800 meters and the 1,500 meters at the Big Ten, and then added a second national championship by winning the 1,500 meters at the NCAA outdoor meet. The 1,500 meters was especially impressive because Suzy set the championship record by running 4:09.85. Carole Harris also improved, as did the Hartzheim sisters and virtually all the other runners on the team. If they were in transition, and surely they were, they were moving at an orchestrated, smart pace.

By the fall of Stephanie's senior year, the team was almost reconstituted. Stephanie, too, was almost ready to run. If Dr. Hans Selye had been alive and in the area, he might have set her through a series of endocrinoligical tests to assure that the stress levels were reduced sufficiently to assure success. That option being unavailable, Stephanie assessed the situation for herself. Like a deer checking out a campsite, she did return to the program for the cross-country season. But she stayed only long enough to get the scent of danger, and then she danced away. She was not ready. Unfortunately, it was not possible for her to leave unnoticed. When she departed, Stephanie, Peter, and the Wisconsin team were buffeted by a series

Two friends in the open field: Suzy Favor and Mary Hartzheim.

of articles announcing her decision. Emotionally and actually, the reports were six to eight months out of date. As a result, they took the first indication of return for the proof of departure. "Although we will miss Stephanie's talents," Peter was quoted as saying, "I respect her decision not to compete. She has recognized that her priorities are elsewhere. It happens all the time. People change their minds on what they are doing." Stephanie expressed the belief that she had gone as far as she, personally, could go. She spoke of collegiate running as if it was a job she no longer wanted. She referred also to the ephemeral nature of athletic accomplishment. "You bring home a trophy, and it's good for about a week. The next week, you have to go out and prove yourself again." You could always see someone else's shadow, she said. People continued to think, of course, that the shadow she saw was Suzy Favor's, but there was nothing she could do about that.

In Stephanie's absence, the cross-country team built itself around Suzy, Carole Harris, and the Hartzheims, as well as a couple of talented first-year students, Kim Kauls and Tammy Breighner. Stephanie Bassett was a dependable contributor as well. The 1987 team won the Big Ten Championship again, won the NCAA District IV Championship, and finished sixth overall in the national meet. At the nationals, Suzy dropped back to 21st from her runner-up position of the prior year, but she was still fast enough to be an all-American, as was Carole Harris in 24th. All of the women had a right to feel satisfied that the season went as well as it did. Stephanie's presence would have made slight difference in the circumstance.

Inevitably, Stephanie's attitude shifted in the course of the spring, summer, and fall. So also did her academic schedule, which lightened. With the combination of factors in mind, Stephanie once more inched toward the team. She wanted to run. It was no longer enough to get up every morning and circle a course alone, not enough to copy the workouts in the afternoon, or to stretch idly. She wanted to really run. Finally, one day late in the fall she got up from her seat at the library. She went to the phone and she called Peter Tegen. "Can I come back," she asked. "Yes," he replied. Playing the decision out later in the press, which watched her closely and missed little, Stephanie emphasized that this was her decision. Peter did not prompt her or pressure her. She truly missed the thing that once drove her to the edge. Referring to the team, she said that she could not find the gratification she needed anywhere else. "As hard as I tried to do it through grades, something was missing," she said. "I continued to train on my own the whole time. I just didn't have the sharpness that I had on the cross-country team. When you're by yourself, you don't push yourself, and nobody I ran with could provide the same competition as my teammates." As for Peter, he could accept the rewards of patience. "You just never know what will happen," he said, "I guess I was a little surprised. But it wasn't anything that was totally unexpected. We left on good terms." He did admit that he was disappointed when Stephanie left the team, but he added that he had never been disappointed in her as a person. And that, for Stephanie, was a saving grace.

However smooth the reconciliation, the two of them confronted a serious challenge. For one thing, Stephanie weighed 125 pounds, which was at least 15 pounds heavier than when she left the program. She would be careful, but, really, some of that weight had to come off. Meanwhile, her base had to be re-established, speed tempos regained, and competitive drive re-engaged. All this had to be done knowing that Stephanie now drew her own line; she would decide when the training was excessive and she would back it off. In that way, the relationship between Stephanie and Peter was adjusted. No longer, for example, would Stephanie permit herself to be drawn into racing the workouts. She would step back from any such nonsense. "I know I can't let it happen again. If I'm working out at practice," she said, "and other people are being too competitive and I'm feeling pressured, I'll pull away. A workout is a workout, not a race." As Stephanie and Peter joined together again, they each felt satisfaction that now, indisputably, the goals were those of the runner. Peter's pride in Stephanie was evident when she said, directly, that she wanted to end her senior year at the University of Wisconsin with a good run in the NCAA outdoor championship.

Stephanie's comeback began auspiciously when she set a meet record for 3,000 meters at the Wisconsin Open Indoor meet in 9:48.05. She was, however, still a long way from fitness, as the Big Ten Indoor Championship proved. At the later meet, a solicitous official asked her whether she wasn't Stephanie Herbst. Learning that she was, he said sadly, "You used to be good, what happened?" It was a haphazardly cruel thing to say, given the 19-second loss Stephanie absorbed in the 5,000 meters that day. Nevertheless, a

The easy power of Suzy Favor: together again in 1988.

more relaxed Stephanie took the remark and the loss that occasioned it in the proper spirit. She had been up; now she was down. Of all people she knew the interchangeability of the positions. The circumstance called to mind, however, the adage of the man who said he had been rich and he had been poor, and rich was better. Stephanie had been fast and she had been slow. Fast was better. Stephanie went back to school, castigated herself for losing a race she "could have won," and dug in for good. She increased her mileage and her intensity. "I have to meet my potential. I can't do things halfway," she reminded herself. From that point, Stephanie improved swiftly. Moving outdoors, she ran 33:34.6 at the Mt. SAC Relays. She didn't win at that pace but she did qualify for the NCAA meet. She also got a boost going into the Big Ten Outdoor Championships scheduled for Ann Arbor, Michigan, at which Stephanie won both the 5,000 meters and the 10,000 meters. The weather was hot and the times were slow (16:31.44 and 34:22.87) but the two titles were gratifying contributions to the Wisconsin cause, although not enough to prevent the University of Illinois from taking away the team title. After the Big Ten, of course, Stephanie anticipated the NCAA outdoor meet, the meet she missed the prior year. How long ago it seemed! This year she entered the 10,000 meters, a distance at which she felt comfortable.

For once, the tactics for the race did not go as planned. Stephanie and Peter figured the talented but unpredictable Sylvia Mosqueda of Cal State Los Angeles was the major threat. They also knew that Sylvia tended to go out too fast and fade. Naturally, they decided to let her fizzle before Stephanie moved up to take the victory after a well-paced run. Initially, the race went precisely according to plan. Sylvia did go out fast, did draw gradually away, and was running at a pace far in excess of her previous efforts. She could be expected to fold any time now. Only thing was, she never did. Stephanie was running with Kirsten O'Hara of the University of California at Berkeley, they were helping each other along, and they were watching Sylvia. Too late in the race to do either Kirsten or Stephanie much good, it became apparent that Sylvia was not coming back, not ever. With 600 meters to go, Stephanie swung around Kirsten and set out after Sylvia but it was no good. Not only was Sylvia gone but so, too, was Stephanie's meet record. Sylvia ran 32:28.57 to take the win and the record. Stephanie finished second in 32:44.16. Stephanie was unhappy, of course. She was particularly critical of herself for letting Sylvia get that lead. "With all due respect, she starts fast and fades," Stephanie said after the race. "I was hoping she would come back. I really intended to win." As it happened, so did Sylvia, and Stephanie would have to make herself content. On balance, that was an easy task. The last year had been so long, so twisted, and yet she had come back. She did what she set out to do in November when she called Peter from the library.

Through all her fear and anxiety and her apprehension and her sense that, from time to time, she was veering dangerously off course, she nevertheless returned to her work and she ran it out. With this race, she could revise the ending to her career at Wisconsin. It was no longer, "I quit." It was now, "I have finished." To use one of Stephanie's old quotes, the career—in its four years and its completion—was all the better she could do. And what a career it was: three-time national track and field champion indoors and out; six-time all-American; seven-time Big Ten champion; former record holder for the NCAA 10,000 meters; NCAA championship record holder for the 3,000 indoors; member of two national championship cross-country teams, two-time cross-country all-American; two-time Academic all-American; two-time Academic Big Ten; Big Ten Athlete of the Year for 1986; and Wisconsin Female Athlete of the Year for 1986. When the decade ended, she would be named to the Big Ten Conference All-Decade Athletic Team for women's indoor and outdoor track and field as well as cross-country. Survivor, champion, role model, one-time Cassandra, Stephanie Herbst could look back with pride. If her time with the team was a job, she did it well. If it was a life, she lived it bravely.

After graduating with her class in 1988, Stephanie immediately accepted a position with a leading multinational corporation. As efficiently as that, a new dream was underway. Although she ran the Olympic Trials later in the summer of 1988, it was for fun. If, later in life, she ran again, the fire would erupt from embers long cooled and from new dreams, emerging in their time.

TWENTY TWO

Away a lone a last a loved a long the

Finnegans Wake
James Joyce

Stephanie. Turn and look. These are the women and the races you foreswore. This is the life you left behind.

Mary Knisely and Cindy Bremser ran for the United States in Rome in 1987. The occasion was the second World Championships for track and field. Neither Cindy nor Mary could handle Tatyana Samolenko of the Soviet Union, Maricica Puica of Romania, or Ulrike Bruns of East Germany. The Eastern European countries still cowered behind walls and produced inexplicable women distance runners. Liz Lynch had somewhat better success at the same meet. Running for Great Britain, Liz finished fifth in the 10,000 meters. She, at least, took an open and obvious beating. Ingrid Kristiansen of Norway did the job. In 1988, Regina Jacobs made the United States Olympic team competing in Seoul, Korea. So too did Vicki Huber, who joined Mary Decker and PattiSue Plumer on the team at 3,000 meters, and Cathy Schiro O'Brien, who ran the marathon. Liz Lynch was there with them, of course, because Great Britain again selected her to run the 10,000 meters. Regina didn't make the finals at 1,500. Even if she had, she would have smacked into Paula Ivan of Romania, the latest creation of that country's sports machine. Vicki Huber did better, actually. She finished sixth in the 3,000. Still, she was behind the traditional phalanx of Easterners: Samolenko, who won; Ivan, a disappointed doubler; Yelena Romanova and Natalya Artymova of the Soviet Union in fourth and fifth. To her credit, Yvonne Murray of Great Britain grabbed the bronze. Creditable, too, was Liz Lynch, now using her husband's last name of McColgan. She stormed the 10,000 in 31:08.44 for a silver medal. She lost the gold, however, to Olga Bondarenko of the Soviet Union. Internationally, the post-Olympic year of 1989 belonged to PattiSue Plumer. In a series of extraordinary races, she established herself as one of the best women middle-distance runners in the world. She also pulled Sabrina Dornhoefer along with her. The two American women ran hard-fought, no-holds-barred races that brought admiring attention to winner and loser alike. By 1991, Suzy Favor was ready to represent the United States. Running under her married name of Suzy Hamilton, she joined Darcy Arreola and PattiSue Plumer on the Tokyo World Championship team for 1,500 meters. Annette Hand, now Annette Peters, made the team, too. She ran with Judi St. Hilaire and Shelly Steely in the 3,000 meters. In the championships, only PattiSue Plumer of the American entrants survived to the finals in the 1,500 meters. Hassiba Boulmerka of Algeria won the race. She was a harbinger. Increasingly in the next several championship cycles, women athletes from the so-called Third World would be pushed onto center stage as an aspect of small nation state-craft. In part, the small countries were filling a vacuum that was, with each tremulous year, growing more expansive. East Germany, for one, was collapsed. East and West, the Germans were competing as a unified team amid confirmation and embarrassed admission that the prior "miracle" sports machine had been fueled by drugs. The Soviet Union, too, was tottering. This would be the last championship attended by citizens of that totalitarian state. Boulmerka, in fact, beat two runners from the Soviet Union and one from Romania, a farewell performance by people about to emerge from a long, disturbed sleep. PattiSue Plumer of the United States, meanwhile, was 12th in the 1,500. In the 3,000 meters, Judi was seventh and Annette was eighth. The gold and silver medals went to women from the Soviet Union; the bronze went to Susan Sirma of Kenya. In the 10,000 meters, Liz McColgan finally won her gold medal. In 31:14.31, she beat two Chinese women. After the Games, she cemented her status as the world's best female long-distance runner by winning the New York City Marathon in 2:27.32.

By 1992, they were all there, or so it seemed, the women of a college generation who continued to run after graduation. Regina Jacobs, PattiSue Plumer, Suzy Hamilton, Shelly Steely, and Annette Peters made the United States Olympic team for Barcelona, as did Cathy Schiro O'Brien. Sylvia Mosqueda almost did. In a 10,000-meter trial that Lynn Jennings won in 32:55.96, Sylvia finished fourth in 33:17.11, one place away from qualifying. It was still rough for them, of course, when they got to the Games. Boulmerka, Romanova, Dorovkikh, Qu Yunxia, Derartu Tulu formed a deadly mix of Russian and emerging powers, none of them free of suspicion, of course, about what was going on, exactly. For the United States, only Lynn Jennings broke into the medals. She took a bronze in the 10,000 by setting an American record of 31:19.89.

The next year, it was the World Championships again. In Stuttgart, Germany, the Chinese women ran wild. In fact, they ran so wild that they came as close as any tiny group of people could to ruining an entire sport. Almost literally no one believed that the Chinese performances were clean, especially given the record of cheating now commonly and openly attributed to all the former Soviet Bloc nations. Less excitedly, of course, the West looked to its own state of affairs. But no one could prove anything against the Chinese. Doubt hung over the Games and over the future of

All-American and international athlete Amy Wickus
with Peter Tegen, a word of advice.

women's distance running in an unconscionable and cruel response
to the opportunity that people like Doris Brown, so long ago, fought
to produce. That fact notwithstanding, some familiar people were in
Stuttgart. Annette Peters was there, as was Shelly Steely. Suzy
Hamilton made the team but did not run. Another emerging star
from the University of Wisconsin did participate, however. Amy
Wickus joined the United States team in the 800 meters but was
knocked out in the semifinals. Amy was back again in 1995 when
she made the team for the World Championships held that year in
Goteborg, Sweden. Suzy Hamilton also made that team, and she was
joined in the 1,500 meters by yet another University of Wisconsin
star, Sarah Thorsett. None of the three Badgers made the finals, but
that fact may be explained by the increasingly diverse and uniform
competition that characterized the women's events. Even the
Chinese dropped a notch and became more accessible, perhaps cha-

grined and warned against the danger of doing preposterous things on a track. Instead of the Chinese and the Russians, the winners were from Algeria, Portugal, and Ireland. Boulmerka was the Algerian. The Portuguese woman was Fernanda Ribeiro. The Irish woman was Sonia O'Sullivan. Sonia, a graduate of Villanova University, remained a favorite when the Olympics were held the next year in Atlanta, but a revived Russian beat her. Svetlana Masterkova brought back memories of Tatyana Kazankina by winning both the 1,500 and 3,000 meters. Suzy Hamilton was on the United States team again. Perhaps most interestingly, Jenny Spangler was on the US team as a marathoner. Jenny ran for the University of Iowa way back in 1985 when Stephanie won the Big Ten 10,000 meters as a freshman. In 1997, Suzy Hamilton, Sarah Thorsett, and Regina Jacobs represented the United States in the 1,500-meter run at the World Championships in Athens, and Regina broke through for a silver medal. In 1998 and 1999, Suzy continued to improve and make headlines, engaged now in an oscillating rivalry with Regina Jacobs. Later in 1999, with Suzy injured, Jacobs added a second silver medal in the 1,500 meters at the outdoor World Championships. Both Regina and Suzy made the United States Olympic team in 2000. Regina withdrew from the team for reasons related to health. Prior to the Games, Suzy ran the fastest 1,500 meter time in the world. She made the final for 1,500 meters in Sydney, but fell to the track on the homestretch. When teammate Marla Runyan, also a finalist, saw what had happened, she went back for Suzy, to comfort and to care. With the contest only just complete, the new image overcame the result and put something new in its place.

· · · · ·

Stephanie, of course, saw her friends and her peers do things that might once have excited her interest; but she did not regret the choices she made. In the passing time, she used her own opportunities wisely. She returned to the University of Wisconsin in 1989 and earned an MBA, she continued her business career, she married, and she became a mother twice. She also continued, inevitably, to hold her place among the best of the Badgers. She watched from a distance as Peter, year after year, produced marvelous teams and accomplished individuals. The heritage that began with Cindy Bremser, ran through Rose Thomson, picked up Cathy Branta and Katie Ishmael, and paused with her, tore into high gear with Suzy Favor. By the time Suzy graduated from the University of Wisconsin she was the most prolific winner in NCAA history. Suzy won nine individual national championships, was named an all-American 14 times, won 23 Big Ten individual championships, was the holder of seven University of Wisconsin school records, was Wisconsin Female Athlete of the Year four times in row, won the Jesse Owens-Big Ten Female Athlete of the Year three straight times, and won both the Babe Zaharias Female Athlete of the Year and the Jumbo Elliott Award. She also carried the Wisconsin team from the early and middle stages of its development into a modern, thriving program that shows no sign of relenting in its drive for excellence. With Suzy, Wisconsin got the Hartzheims who thrilled Badger fans by finishing second and third behind only Sonia O'Sullivan at the 1990 NCAA Championships in the 3,000-meter run; it got Sue Gentes who won the NCAA 1,500-meters in 1992; and it got Kim Sherman who won the 800 meters in 1993. Clare Eichner came out of Wauwatosa, Wisconsin, to complete a double-double in 1993 by winning the NCAA indoor mile/3000 and the outdoor 1,500/3,000 meter titles. The previously mentioned Amy Wickus, an extraordinary 800-1,500 specialist with great strength and personal courage, won four individual NCAA titles and two more as a relay-team member before she finished her years at the university. As the tradition continued, Sarah Thorsett, a fine runner at Wisconsin, became an international performer by dint of talent, hard work, and persistence after graduation. Kathy Butler was an NCAA champion several times over, and she nurtured Angie Kujak, Jenni Westphal, Janet Westphal, and Sara Fredrickson, all-Americans every one, and each of them the forecast of Erica Palmer, the NCAA Division 1 cross-country champion in November, 1999. Even this list is shy in describing the successes of the program. It does not carry the names of the numerous young women who entered the school with little more than ambition to sustain them and found that, at Wisconsin, that was sufficient.

Here is a story-- two, actually, but they are related. One day in the fall of 1995, Peter Tegen took his cross-country team to the NCAA National Championship meet in Ames, Iowa. It was a typical championship challenge for a team long accustomed to the routine. As the team members relaxed in the moments before the start, Peter spoke with them one at a time. Invariably, the last response from the woman to the coach was a smile and then a determined concentration on the task at hand. In the event, the last person Peter spoke to at the line was Kathy Butler. When the race was run, she was its winner, a gracious, kind, and determined champion who brought credit to the university. In her victory and in her demeanor, Kathy added luster to a program that already shined.

A year later, a visitor met the 1996 version of the University of Wisconsin cross-country team for an early fall run. The women were friendly, relaxed, open, and high spirited. They were evidently serious about the sport, but not overwhelmed by it. They joked about each other's sleeping habits, the way they ate, the way they raced, and the way they worked out. They also bragged on each other, making sure the visitor knew not how good THEY were, but how good the woman running next to them was. At one point, a team member asked the visitor what he was up to. Told that he was working on a book about Stephanie Herbst, and asked in kind whether they had heard of her, the reaction was instantaneous and enthusiastic. Heard of her! Yes, she's a legend!! They said. Could she visit with the team? The excitement and pleasure at the mere possibility that she might join them was palpable. Later in the day, the visitor passed the substance and the emotion of the conversation along to Stephanie. Her eyes widened and Stephanie Herbst permitted herself an expansive, happily believing smile. Really, she said, really? But she was obviously very pleased. She was glad to know—ten years after she won that 10,000-meter run in Indianapolis, ten years after Kathy Ormsby went off the bridge, ten years after the first reluctant thought that this sport was not right for her and that she might be required to leave—that she was still one of the team, part of the long and remarkable tradition of the University of Wisconsin women who ran for glory, for self, and for sport. She was glad to know, in fact, that she never left Wisconsin after all, had never been alone, never been abandoned, and never been forgotten.

All the years cascading through and over the great distance of time, memory, and event, she had been loved.

Epilogue

This is the ideal. No voice, once spoken, is forgotten. No experience, once acquired, is unlearned. No advance, once made, is given up. The development of women as middle-and long-distance runners is a line which is pushed further and further along by the athletes themselves, together and as individuals. Doris Brown Heritage and the women of her generation made it respectable for women to run more than a quarter of a mile at a time. Tatyana Kazankina, and more generally the women from the Eastern Bloc nations, changed the standards by which women runners would be judged and they altered the expectations to which they would be subject. Incidentally, they cast aside the presumption of innocence that might once have protected women in competitive sports. Just in time, Mary Decker Slaney reappeared on center stage. Without her, the women's middle- and long-distance events might have become irrelevant in the West as a result of what was happening behind the Iron Curtain; with her, they revived and flourished. Virtually coincident with Mary Decker Slaney's efforts and her impact, Title IX finally made its way onto college campuses. Women were permitted to accept college scholarships. To many of them, the scholarships represented obligation and responsibility as much as reward and opportunity.

The increased opportunity for women in sport changed the way they related to each other. Simply, they went from a single, shared experience defined by exclusion and limitation to a multitude of different experiences, dependent in part upon the extent to which each person decided to take advantage of the new opportunity and

what happened when they did. In competition itself, winners separated from losers, a process that immediately (if momentarily) created subclasses at every competition. That this has the potential to
cause harm is evident from the philosophy of the AIAW, which
attempted to stop it from happening by emphasizing participation
over result as the criteria for success. Just as notably, if the NCAA
rejected the AIAW philosophy and replaced it with a "male model,"
the effect was to recognize that in sports some people win and some
people lose. Beginning in 1982 when the NCAA pulled women into
its world, commerce in women's athletics entered the mainstream in
force, a process that continues. The commerce trades on the separation of women from each other.

As early as high school, Stephanie Herbst's acceptance of a
competitive paradigm for women was hesitant and compromised.
She felt that she had to win. Even as she strived toward that end,
however, she valued the companionship and approval of the people
she beat. Moving into college, the conflicts grew more exaggerated.
While companionship remained critically important to her, she
judged the situation to exclude it, at least on intimate and trusting
terms. The women on the team were her competitors; and so were the
women from other teams. Stephanie ran well and hard. Many times,
she won. But she always missed the closeness of another world. In
fact, the world Stephanie missed was arguably the vision of the
AIAW, in which the shared venture was more important than who
won and who lost. Eventually, Stephanie pulled back from athletics
in order to rest, to recover, and to get a closer view of things. In that
distance, she found companionship in the traditional and settled
world of the university sorority. She went back to the team only when
she was composed and balanced. In that state, she completed a marvelous university career. Stephanie's decision to leave the team was
an act of courage. The return is her triumph. So also is the strong relationship she formed with the other women on the team, including

Suzy Favor, to whom she gives credit for injecting humor and mutual support into a team that needed exactly those qualities.

Interestingly, the woman most associated with Stephanie Herbst as a college athlete is a woman she never knew: Kathy Ormsby. As interesting is the fact that Kathy Ormsby in the misleading filigree of image, impression, and memory is a woman who got it wrong, a woman whose interest in winning was so distorted that it overcame her sense of worth and self-preservation. Described in those terms, Kathy is the woman Stephanie might rationally have feared she would become. And yet the truth is that Kathy at North Carolina State was a social person who trusted her teammates, who did not seek to withdraw from them, but rather gloried with them in their triumphs and comforted them in their sadness, little knowing that her own sadness would become legend. With regard to the events of June 4, 1986, she is like an awakened sleepwalker, to whom people turn for explanation. It is impossible. She does not know the stranger who threw her body over the guard rail. She knows the injury only. A more heartrending circumstance is difficult to imagine, yet Kathy endures. Indeed, in the ways most important to her, she prospers.

With it all, with ambition and fear and accomplishment and risk and reward, with choices made and those taken away, Stephanie and Kathy were part of a special generation. Neither angels nor fools, they tread in the tracks left by the few who preceded them. From that frail beginning, they and their contemporaries created a future in which the later withdrawal of women from sport would be inconceivable. There were too many of them; they were too accomplished, too strong, and too caring of each other for a reasonable person, ever again, to doubt the fundamental correctness of what they were doing. They were dreaming, all of them. They were dreaming of the feeling that came when body, mind, and spirit answered the call, and they exploded with joy. They were dreaming of a world in which they could use all their gifts without notice, without reservation, without ridicule, and without criticism. They were dreaming of a wholeness that had been denied their mothers and grandmothers and great-grandmothers stretching back in time as far as the eye could see.

They were dreaming, and they were running. Barriers falling all around them, they were hurtling toward a future which—like the road that stretched out in front of Stephanie on the first day she ran with her sister in the warmth of a Minnesota summer—whispered at daybreak and shimmered like new sun. If they were in haste, who would blame them for it? They were young, and never would be again:

The Photographs: Credits

The photographs are credited as follows, in the order they appear. Chapter two: the three photographs are privately held by Stephanie Herbst Lucke (SHL) and are used with her permission. Chapter three: Time, Inc. Chapter four: the first two photographs are privately held by Doris Brown Heritage and reproduced with her permission and the third photograph is courtesy of Track and Field News. Chapter five: AP World Wide Photos, Track and Field News, AP World Wide Photos. Chapter six: AP World Wide Photos. Chapter eight: Boulder, Colorado, Daily Camera (1,2), Warren Morgan Photography, Portland, Oregon, AP World Wide Photos, AP World Wide Photos. Chapter nine: University of Wisconsin Sports Information Office (UW). Chapter ten: UW (1,2,3). Chapter twelve: UW. Chapter thirteen: SHL. Chapter fourteen: UW (1,2,3). Chapter fifteen: the three photographs are privately held by Kathy Ormsby (KO) and reproduced with her permission. Chapter sixteen: SHL, KO, UW. Chapter eighteen: SHL. Chapter nineteen: UW (1,2). Chapter twenty: UW. Chapter twenty-one: UW (1,2). Chapter twenty-two: UW. The photographs maintained in the private collections of the athletes did not include information sufficient to identify them further.

References and Acknowledgments

I appreciate the assistance of Stephanie Herbst Lucke and Kathy Ormsby in the preparation of this book. Both women were accomplished college athletes with much to celebrate in their careers, but they also had difficult experiences. For no reason but the desire to help me sort things out, they turned to the issues forthrightly and directly.

Doris Brown Heritage, Dick Brown, Don DeNoon, Suzy Favor Hamilton and Peter Tegen spoke with me at length. Each of them provided depth and insight without which the book, whatever its current condition, would have been diminished. Mary Decker Slaney spoke briefly with me in Eugene, Oregon. Although short on content, the meeting was productive and I appreciated her courtesy. I also benefitted from meeting some of the women who ran for the University of Wisconsin track and field and cross-country teams between 1995 and 1998, and most particularly from Kathy Butler and Sho Kroeger. I was powerfully influenced by watching the contemporary University of Wisconsin women compete, and by seeing their balanced reactions to success and disappointment. Kendall Smith helped develop material from the years Mary Decker Slaney spent at the University of Colorado, and Rich Castro provided several photographs from that period, as well. The University of Wisconsin Sports Information Office responded with consideration and efficiency to my requests for assistance and for photographs of Wisconsin athletes. The annual media guide published by the University of Wisconsin was a valuable resource. Erin Davis, Rare

Book and Special Collections Librarian at The Irwin Library, Butler University, Indianapolis was gracious and helpful. Joe Henderson, Janet Heinonen, Paul Christman, and Sieg Lindstrom were kind enough to read early drafts of the book and to give advice. Ed Fox of Track and Field News responded patiently to my many requests for assistance. Regarding the careers of Stephanie Herbst Lucke and Kathy Ormsby, much of the factual detail comes from daily newspapers and contemporaneous newsprint reporting. I attributed quotations from those sources as well as I could, bearing in mind that some of the articles in my possession do not include a publication date and some do not show a reliable point of origin. This is because some of the articles were collected from the athletes, who did not, of course, have copies of the entire newspaper from which the individual articles originated.

Chapter One

The ruminations in this chapter are based on interviews with Stephanie Herbst Lucke, but the words are, unless otherwise cited, those of the author as is responsibility for content. At the end of paragraph one, readers will find an allusion to E. E. Cummings, whose poem reads, in part, as follows: "love is a place/& through this place of/love move/(with brightness of peace)/all places."

1 "runs like a deer,": Patrick Reusse, "Herbst distances self from running," St. Paul Pioneer Press.

2 "I like to see how far and how fast I can go,": Andrew P. Baggot, "Herbst makes herself a runaway success," Wisconsin State Journal.

3 "her trust,": Miles McMillen, Jr., "Happy Herbst, UW runner leaves good impression," Capitol Times.

4 "like to take running as far as it will take me,": Paul Sweitzer, "Modesty meets victory for runner," Badger Herald, January 13-17, 1986.

Chapter Two

1 "I don't know what it was,": "Stephanie Herbst 5th in state 1600-meter competition," local reporting.

2 "Chaska High School may have a future state champion,": Ibid.

3 "It's a great place to train,": Patrick Reusse, "Herbst distances self from running," St. Paul Pioneer Press.

4 "I try to keep a consistent pace,": Roman Augustovitz, "Chaska sophomore sets sights high,": Carver County Herald, November, 1981.

5 "I was hoping to do a little better,": Ibid.

6 "the answer to every male runner's dreams,": Mark Moeller, "Cross Country in Retrospect," Fall, 1983.

7 "thought her teeth were going to shatter,": "Numbed Herbst takes second at state meet," Carver County Herald, November 10, 1982.

8 "Oh, I could have,": Ted Olsen, "Hawks place 1st, 2nd, 3rd at state track meet," Carver County Herald, June 15, 1983.

9 "a little less nervous than last year,": "Herbst wins state girls cross country title," Carver County Herald, November 9, 1983.

10 "I always felt there was somebody back there,": Charley McKenna, "Wodney leads state harriers in record time," Minneapolis Star and Tribune, November 5, 1983.

11 "her own decisions about how she wanted to compete,": Judy Schmidt, "Women athletes enjoy mix of sports and academic life," Carver County Herald.

Chapter Three

1 A thorough description of the process by which women gained entry to competitive sports is found in Susan K. Cahn's excellent book, Coming on Strong, published by Harvard University Press in 1994.

2 "It would probably be culturally unacceptable,": Rose and Hal Higdon, "What Sports for Girls?," Runners World, January 1970.

3 Ibid.

4 "act like a man,": Bil Gilbert and Nancy Williamson, "Are You Being Two-faced?," Sports Illustrated, June 4, 1973. ("Behind the myth that participation in sports will masculinize a woman's appearance, there is the even darker insinuation that athletics will masculinize a woman's behavior," 47).

5 "marked by voluptuousness,": Cahn, Coming on Strong, 126.

6 "That image continued into the 20th century,": Ibid.

7 "Babe didn't confine herself,": The Olympic Story, Pursuit of Excellence, Grolier Enterprises, Inc., 1983.

8 "This chin of Babe's,": "The World-Beating Girl Viking of Texas," Literary Digest, August 27, 1932.

9 "would rather sleep than run,": Girl on the Run, Newsweek, February 6, 1961.

10 "As late as 1965,": "A Startling Invasion by Women,": Sports Illustrated, March 1, 1965.

11 "the New York Times reported that event,": "Americans Beaten," New York Times, August 3, 1928.

12 "the London Times was only slightly,": "The Olympic Games," London Times, August 3, 1928.

13 "there was little harm to any of the participants," M. Leigh, "The Evolution of Women's Participation in the Summer Olympic Games, 1900-1948," Doctoral Dissertation, The Ohio State University, 1975.

14 "An early example is seen in a 1961 article,": "Tomboy out on a Limb," Life Magazine, December 15, 1961.

15 "Marie Mulder came to prominence,": "Near Miss," Newsweek, August 16,1965.

16 "The next time Marie appeared,": John Underwood, "This is the Way the Girls Go," Sports Illustrated, May 10, 1965.

17 "Succinctly, one writer says," Cahn, Coming on Strong, 138.

18 "The emphasis on grace, beauty and youth," Gwilym S. Brown,

"A game girl in a man's game," Sports Illustrated, May 2, 1966.

19 "Marie Mulder was back,": John Underwood, "Chasing Girls through the Park," Sports Illustrated, December 5, 1966.

20 "Doris and Marie,": Gwilym S. Brown, "Teenager on a Comeback Trail," Sports Illustrated, February 20, 1967.

21 "In other articles, she and her coach,": Skip Myslenski, "A PTA meeting was tougher," Sports Illustrated, December 8, 1969.

22 "My gosh, couldn't he see,": Ibid.

23 "The first question was 'when is a woman not a woman,": the historical development of this issue can be found, among other places, at: Dick Bank, "Dick Bank discusses the 'sex test', its history and why it is needed," Women's Track and Field World (1967) and Alison Carlson, "Chromosome Count," Ms., October, 1988.

24 "no unfair advantage would be taken,": Bank, Women's Track and Field World.

25 "it was absolutely firmly established that she is no woman,": Bank, Women's Track and Field World.

26 "I know what I am and how I feel,": Carlson, "Chromosome Count."

27 "The woman involved was Maria Jose Martinez Patino,": Much of the development of this issue, specifically as it relates to Ms. Patino's situation, originates with Alison Carlson's article, "When is a woman not a woman," which appeared in Women's Sports and Fitness, March, 1991.

28 "Don Caitlan of the USOC testing laboratory,": Pat Connolly, "After Sweat and Tears, Women must give blood," New York Times, July 28, 1996.

29 "even slight changes in male blood hormone,": Ibid.

30 "Studies suggest that women who value achievement,": Carol Tarvis, MisMeasure of Woman, Touchstone, 1992, at 32.

31 "For these and other women,": Ellen Kaschak, Engendered Lives, A New Psychology of Women's Experiences, Basic Books,

1992, at 195.

32 "in western society," Ibid.

33 "Some studies place the minimum,": See, e.g., Bobbie Hasselbring, "Are You Running too thin, "Women's Sports and Fitness, December, 1986.

34 "In fact, many elite women distance runners,": Dr. Myra Nimmo, "Women in Sport," Track Technique, Fall, 1989; and see also, Dr. Peter Snell and Dr. Robert Vaughan, "Longitudinal Physiological Testing of Elite Female Middle and Long Distance Runners," Track Technique, Spring, 1990.

35 "one of the repeated injunctions to boys,": Kaschak, Engendered Lives, 123.

36 "On a page devoted to fashion," New York Times, October 31, 1996.

Chapter Four

1 This chapter owes a great deal to Doris Brown Heritage, who generously spoke to me about her experiences.

2 "a heart the size of a whale,": Women's Track and Field News, September, 1967.

3 "As one girl said in 1969,": Skip Myslenski, "A PTA meeting is Tougher," Sports Illustrated, December 8, 1969.

4 "I knew that if I was going to win,": Ibid.

5 "You go against the Russians,": Pat Putnam, "They're Sweet 16 and Deserve a Kiss," Sports Illustrated, March 27, 1972.

6 "People expect it,": Ibid.

7 "This is a chance for some very fine competition,": Ibid.

8 "You can run on a bloody stump,": Doris Brown Heritage, Conversation with the Author.

9 "When for the first time I ran two laps,": B. Valik, "On the Track with Ludmila (sic) Bragina," Track and Field 11: 16-17, 1972.

10 "Another important element was the fact,": Lyudmila Bragina,

"Monologue," Track Technique, Fall 1979.

11 "Bragina and her coach Kazantsev decided,": Ibid.

12 "for the finals we decided to change our tactics,": Ibid.

Chapter Five

The statistical compilations in this and the following chapter are taken from a combination of sources, chief among them Wizards of the Middle Distances, Roberto Quercetani and Nejat Kok, published by Vallardi and Associati in 1992, Athletics, A History of Modern Track and Field Athletics (1860-1990), Roberto Quercetani, published by Vallardi and Associati in 1990, and Track and Field News. Otherwise, as follows:

1 "young physical culturalists,": Henry Morton, Soviet Sport, Collier Books, 1963.

2 "the track and field sessions were very exciting,": Alexei Srebnitsky, "Tatyana Kazankina, Olympic Champion," Canadian Runner, September/October 1984.

3 "Lesgaft's philosophy was based on the idea,": Morton, Soviet Sport.

4 "I train twice a day as a rule,": Ivan Berenyi, "Tatyana Kazankina," Athletics Weekly, October 16, 1976.

5 "frequently dead tired,": Ibid.

6 "by increasing stride length and stride frequency,": A. Samoukou, Y. Popov, "Stride Length and Frequency in Long Distance Runners," Legkaya Athletika, 3:8-9, 1980.

7 "She's a nice girl,": Track and Field News, August 1976.

8 "highly dubious chance,": Berenyi, Athletics Weekly, October 16, 1976.

9 "psyched out by Weis' run,": 1976 Olympic Games: A Close Up Look at the Track and Field Events, Runners World Magazine, 1977.

10 "stick with the leaders as much as I could,": Berenyi, Athletics Weekly, October 16, 1976.

11 "a bit lucky,": Ibid.

12 "just could not sprint,": The London Times, July 27, 1976.

13 "to start off calmly and move up,": Ibid.

14 "is this a robot straight off the conveyor belt,": Ibid.

15 "I love to shop,": Berenyi, Athletics Weekly, October 16, 1976.

16 "I will have to consult my husband,": Ibid.; and Track and Field News, September, 1976.

17 "what Hoffmeister saw,": 1976 Olympic Games: A Close Up View of the Running Events (article by Dave Prokop: The Long Races at Montreal), Runners World Magazine, 1977.

18 "my strong finish is the result of special training methods,": Berenyi, Athletics Weekly, October 16, 1976.

19 "But it may not, of course, be me,": Ibid.; also, Jon Hendershott, "She Caught the World Unawares," Track and Field News, February, 1977.

20 "All that time, I was seriously involved in a building-up routine,": Srebnitsky, Canadian Runner, September-October, 1984.

21 "it will come in preparation for Moscow,": Track and Field News, October, 1977.

22 "in the winter of 1980,": The 1980 Olympics: Track and Field, The Sports Market Limited, 1980.

23 "some reports said,": Athletics Weekly, November 15, 1980; Track and Field News, September, 1980.

24 "I knew that I was in top form,": Athletics Weekly, November 15, 1980.

25 "I will concentrate on the 1,500-meters,": Ibid.

26 "I have known of Nadezhda's potential,": Ibid.

27 "There will no Belousova in the Olympics,": Ibid.

28 "How should I know,": Ibid.

29 "So who is there,": Ibid.

30 "I wanted to win the race,": Ibid.

31 "I knew then I was capable,": Track and Field News, September,

1980.

32 "Her secret?" and "Uncompromising tempo and scorching fin-ish,": Athletics Weekly, November 15, 1980, quoting from unnamed edition of Sovietsky Sport.

33 "Naturally, just like at Montreal,": Track and Field News, September, 1980.

34 "I didn't care about times,": Ibid.

Chapter Six

1 The statistical ranking for August, 1980, is from Track and Field News.

2 "Neither the thousands of spectators,": World Athletics, February, 1962.

3 "Remember massive Tamara Press,": Track and Field News, May, 1979.

4 "It may be a coincidence,": Women's Track and Field World, February, 1973.

5 "One doctor said that three options existed,": Track and Field News, December, 1976.

6 "This is one of the reasons,": Ibid.

7 "It is a matter of conditioning,": Track and Field News, December, 1979.

8 ""Our battle against doping will be ruthless,": Ibid.

9 "despite the heaviest regimen of testing yet,": Track and Field News, September, 1980.

Chapter Seven

1 "In the sixth grade, my best friend and I were sitting around,": Kenny Moore, "Yesterday's Child: Mary Decker," Best Efforts, Doubleday and Company, 1982.

2 "a physical genius,": Ibid.

3 "an elegant mover,": Mel Watman, "The Indestructible Mary

Decker," Athletics Weekly, November 19, 1983.

4 "DeNoon was influenced by the coaching methods of Mihaly Igloi,": Don DeNoon, conversation with the author (all such conversations hereafter cited as DD).

5 "Don DeNoon's youth teams ran workouts,": Don DeNoon, "Don DeNoon Gives His Side of the Story," Athletics Weekly, December 24, 1983.

6 "she absolutely hated to 'lose' an interval,": DD.

7 "No one knows Mary like I knew her,": Don DeNoon, Athletics Weekly, December 24, 1983.

8 "curtailment was the result of Seaver's disease,": Ibid.

9 "Sabaite chased after the skinny little Californian,": Mel Watman, Athletics Weekly, November 19,1983.

10 "she had been shooed away from the starting line,": "Nice Girls Finish First," Newsweek, February 25, 1974.

11 "calmly shucked her sweatsuit,": Ibid.

12 "There wasn't anybody there,": Ibid.

13 "Mary giggles innocently,": Ibid.

14 "Similar language appears in a Sports Illustrated article,": Anita Verschoth, "Mary, Mary, Not Contrary," Sports Illustrated, April 22, 1974.

15 "Primarily through television,": Mel Watman, "Mary Decker: The Girl who wouldn't Give Up," Athletics Weekly, March 22, 1980.

16 "Robin Campbell was only 14 years old,": Ron Reid, "Thank Heavens for this Little Girl,"
Sports Illustrated, March 26, 1973.

17 "Mary no longer dazzles crowds,": Newsweek, February 25, 1974.

18 "she runs a secure race right now,": Ibid.

19 "She's the greatest female 800 meter runner in the world,": Mel Watman, Athletics Weekly, November 19, 1983.

20 "Frenn interrupted one of Decker's workouts,": Anita Verschoth, Sports Illustrated, April 22, 1974.

21 "People think DeNoon pushed me,": Mel Watman, Athletics Weekly, November 19, 1983, quoting from a prior article by Eric Olsen that appeared in The Runner Magazine.

22 "I didn't know what to do with all this body,": Kenny Moore, Best Efforts.

23 "Wearing a new Patriot Track Club uniform," Women's Track and Field News, February, 1974.

24 "At sixteen, I was a has-been,": Mel Watman, Athletics Weekly, November 19, 1983, quoting from a prior article by Eric Olsen.

25 "DeNoon once said that her whole life was running,": DD.

Chapter Eight

The description of Mary Decker's workouts in the period between 1982 and 1984 is from documents prepared by Dick Brown in his capacity as her coach.

1 "It was difficult to sit and watch,": Gary Burns, "New Lady Buff Decker Aims for 1980," Boulder, Colorado, Daily Camera (hereafter Daily Camera), January 27, 1977.

2 "in California, people were always coming up,": Ibid.

3 "we may even suggest she not run,": Ibid.

4 "right now, I wouldn't want to push myself,": Ibid.

5 "there probably wouldn't be any problem,": Ibid.

6 "Track and Field News carried a cryptic report,": Track and Field News, April, 1977.

7 "It pushes you," Daily Camera, September 29, 1977.

8 "we really don't have a superstar right now,": Daily Camera, November 17, 1977.

9 "This is elation,": Women's Track and Field News, March, 1978.

10 "Because I haven't run indoors for so long,": Track and Field News, February, 1978.

11 "No more injuries and no more losses,": Daily Camera, February 9, 1978.

12 "It's like I told everyone else all over the world,": Ibid.

13 "I really think I'm more suited to the longer race,": Ibid.

14 "sort of shrugged her shoulders,": Track and Field News, February, 1978.

15 "Mary is just too strong now,": Ibid.

16 "As a child studies a thing,": Daily Camera, February 19, 1978, reprinting an earlier Newsday article by John Jeansonne.

17 "spirited her away to his track team,": Ibid.

18 "honored to be trusted with her talent,": Kenny Moore, "She runs and we are lifted,"
Sports Illustrated, Double Issue: December 26, 1983 and January 2, 1984.

19 "marked by a mother and father who were,": Kenny Moore, Best Efforts.

20 "not as much fun as running,": Track and Field News, August, 1980.

21 "a good one in August,": Mel Watman, Athletics Weekly, March 22, 1980.

22 "I would love to win an Olympic gold medal,": Mel Watman, Athletics Weekly, November 19, 1983.

23 "The world record is definitely on my mind,": Track and Field News, August, 1980.

24 "I don't think I would have won a gold medal,": Mel Watman, Athletics Weekly, November 19, 1983.

25 "But I tried though," Ken Kesey, One Flew Over the Cuckoo's Nest, The Penguin Group, 1962.

26 "This is only the second time I have raced against Kazankina,": Track and Field News, September, 1980.

27 "Their muscle definition is so pronounced,": Track and Field News, December, 1980.

28 "I talked once to an East German doctor,": Cathy Henkel, Eugene Register Guard, August 4, 1983.

29 "If we keep you healthy,": Kenny Moore, Sports Illustrated, "She runs and we are lifted, December 26, 1983, and January 2, 1984.

30 "from the knees up and from the knees down,": Dick Brown, conversation with the author.

31 "I am surprised,": Track and Field News, Track and Field News, August, 1982.

32 "I'd like her to go out and run with the pack,": Cathy Henkel, Eugene Register Guard, June 15, 1983.

33 "I don't think it would matter if Mary tripled,": Ibid.

34 "It was good strength work,": Eugene Register Guard, June 20, 1983.

35 "I went into the 3,000 meters more relaxed,": Ibid.

36 "She can run the pace, but can she stay with the pack,": Track and Field News, August, 1983.

37 "for fun,": Eugene Register Guard, July 27, 1983.

38 "I think I have a good kick,": Ibid.

39 "I feel so bad, I'll take any time,": Craig Neff, Sports Illustrated, August 8, 1983.

40 "took a deep breath, relaxed and went,": Kenny Moore, Sports Illustrated, "She runs and we are lifted," December 26, 1983, and January 2, 1984.

41 "I was sure I would win it,": Alexei Srebnitsky, Canadian Runner, September/October 1984.

42 "I wasn't worried when Kazankina came up on me," Eugene Register Guard, August 11, 1984.

43 "Mary Decker proved two important points,": "3,000: Decker from start to finish," Athletics Weekly, August 27, 1983.

44 "She hit me practically every stride along the way,": Kenny Moore, Sports Illustrated, "She runs and we are lifted," Double issue: December 26, 1983, and January 2, 1984.

45 "I don't think it's personal,": Eugene Register Guard, August 15, 1983.

46 "It was a mistake,": Kenny Moore, "She runs and we are lifted," Sports Illustrated, Double issue: December 26, 1983, and January 2, 1984.

47 "If I was more aggressive,": Eugene Register Guard, August 15, 1983.

48 "Mary has prepared very well this year,": Ibid.

49 "Well, I have a lot more confidence,": Tom Jordan, "Interview: Mary Decker," International Running Guide, 1984.

50 "a situation she described as 'perfect',": Kenny Moore, Sports Illustrated, "She runs and we are lifted," December 26, 1983, and January 2, 1984.

51 "The only thing missing from Decker's stat collection,": Track and Field News, December, 1983.

52 "Mary Decker is the queen of middle distances,": "The Making of America's Best," Newsweek, August 15, 1983.

53 "where her future lay the first time he saw her run,": Brian Vine with Zola Budd, Zola, the Official Biography, Stanley Paul with a copyright held by the Daily Mail, 1984.

54 "Zola is a running machine,": Ibid.

55 "Once she realized the improvement,": Ibid.

56 "In this, she was wonderfully fortunate,": Kenny Moore and Peter Hawthorne, "A Flight to Stormy Haven," Sports Illustrated, April 9, 1984.

57 "Then the January night wind came down,": Ibid.

58 "Mary Decker is out of my class,": Vine and Budd, The Official Biography.

59 "the newspaper would extend a hand of friendship,": Ibid.

60 "the impatient nature of Budd and Decker,": Kenny Moore, "The Way it Must Be," Sports Illustrated, July 18, 1984.

61 "It's a miracle I'm here,": Runner's World, September, 1984.

62 "if running at the proper speed,": Athletics Weekly, August 25,1984.

63 "there was going to be some bumping,": Neil Allen, The Standard, as quoted in Athletics Weekly, August 25, 1984.

64 "A number of runners came over to Mary,": Runner's World, September, 1984.

65 "don't bother,": Newsweek, August 20, 1984.

66 "Budd came by,": Kansas City Star, August 11, 1984.

67 "Zola Budd tried to cut in,": Athletics Weekly, August 25, 1984; Runner's World, September, 1984.

68 "I do hold Zola responsible,": Runner's World, September, 1984.

69 "I don't think there's any question that she was in the wrong,": Athletics Weekly, August 25, 1984.

70 "I don't see how a young lady leading a race,": Ibid.

71 "Decker was her own victim,": Ibid.

72 "Nobody associated with all of this feels that anything was done intentionally,": Ibid.

73 "It was an accident,": Track and Field News, September, 1984.

74 "We found the woman, I think, in Mary Decker,": Mike Littwin, Los Angeles Times, August 14, 1984.

75 "bloody foolish,": Track and Field News, October, 1984.

76 "It would be wonderful to be so pretty,": Kenny Moore, "The Olympics," Sports Illustrated, August 20, 1984.

Chapter Nine

1 "He had just finished coaching in something like 14 countries,": Lisa Gaumnitz, "Going the Distance," Sports Illustrated, October 30, 1995.

2 "we must have a strong foundation," Peter Tegen, Conversation with Author (all such conversations hereafter cited as PT).

3 "Women's Athletics, Coping with Controversy: Selected Papers for the 1973 National   Convention," American Association for

Health, Physical Education and Research (AAHPER) Publications, 1974, provides much of the detail for the discussion of the AIAW and its relationship with the NCAA. The paper submitted for the conference by Carole Oglesby—"Future Directions and Issues"—is the source for the three quotes attributed to her.

4 "The NCAA, the organization that sought to dilute the impact of Title IX,": Ann Uhlir, "Political Victim: the Dream that was the AIAW," New York Times, July 11, 1982.

Chapter Ten

1 " I have developed a lot of trust in Peter,": Sean Hartnett, "Branta Had a Year to Remember," Track and Field News, October, 1985.

2 "Sometimes she thought I was crazy,": Ibid.

3 "all the trouble I went through to get it,": Paul Sweitzer, "Modesty meets victory for runner," Badger Herald, January 13-17, 1986.

4 "they said the program was high pressure," "Stephanie Herbst keeps on running," Carver County Herald, February 2, 1985.

5 "I was completely fascinated by her,": Miles McMillen, Jr., "Happy Herbst: UW runner leaves good impression," Capitol Times, Spring, 1986.

6 "How can anyone be impressed with someone on a day like this," SHL.

7 "There were probably 30 to 40 miles per hour wind,": PT.

8 "I thought I'd be conscientious and do summer training,": Stephanie Herbst Lucke, Conversation with Author (all such conversations hereafter cited as SHL).

9 "I arrived the first day,": SHL.

Chapter Eleven

The description of the University of Wisconsin campus owes much to Thomas A. Gaines' book, The Campus as a Work of Art, Praeger Publishers, 1991.

1 "I'm going to be successful as a runner,": SHL.

2 "to keep happy,": SHL.

3 "running will create movement patterns,": Peter Tegen, "Middle Distance Running," IAAF, NACAC, 1994.

4 "with high-strung athletes, they all have to worry,": Bob Berghaus, "Herbst runs on, but not with UW," Milwaukee Journal, reprinted in the Madison State Journal, September 30, 1987.

5 "If Peter said something,": SHL.

6 "Jim Beatty described his coach in revealing terms,": "The Magic of the Great Igloi," Life Magazine, March 1, 1963.

7 "Now I relax,": "Do as Igloi Says," Newsweek, February 26, 1962.

8 The description of Rudolf Harbig's training is taken from Fred Wilt's book, How They Train, first published by Track and Field News, Inc. in 1959.

9 "His effect on me,": Dr. Edmond van den Eynde, "Coaching of Distance Runners," from the book edited by Jess Jarver, Long Distances: Contemporary Theory Technique and Training, TAFNEWS Press, 1989.

10 "You can't drive an athlete,": from the video, Sebastian Coe: Born to Run, Films for the Humanities, Princeton, New Jersey.

Chapter Twelve

1 "the worst diet in the world,": "Stephanie Herbst keeps on running," Carver County Herald, February 20, 1985.

2 "She has a rare quality in an athlete,": John Aune, "Minnesota runner finds her stride in Wisconsin (The One That Got Away; or, How to Make it Big in Madtown)," Minnesota Daily, May 28, 1986.

3 "I never expected Katie to do this,": "Ishmael outruns women's field," Wisconsin State Journal, October 14, 1984.

4 "It was kind of weird,": "Stephanie Herbst keeps on running,"

Carver County Herald, February 20, 1985.

5 "Can you imagine, four All-Americans,": Don Lindstrom, "Branta, UW run to national championships," Wisconsin State Journal, November 20, 1984.

6 "I had this feeling inside,": SHL.

Chapter Thirteen

1 "very understated,": SHL.

2 "the most important thing is weight,": Ernst van Aaken, van Aaken Method, World Publications, 1976.

3 "when women train, they gain muscle mass,": Megan Atherton, "My Body, My Self," Runner's World, June, 1993.

4 "Endurance running has been shown to be closely linked to body composition,": Dr. Myra Nimmo, "Women In Sport," Track Technique, Fall, 1989.

5 "As to the relationship between oxygen uptake and body composition,": Dr. Peter Snell and Dr. Robert Vaughan, "Longitudinal Physiological Testing of Elite Female Middle and Long Distance Runners," Track Technique, Spring, 1990.

6 "each individual has an optimal body weight," Ibid.

7 "the most frequently mentioned disorder related to low body fat," Bobbie Hasselbring, "Are You Running too Thin?," Women's Sports and Fitness, December, 1986. Also see, Dr. Myra Nimmo. "Women in Sport."

8 "At least one study suggests a relationship,": Warren J. Gadpaille,M.D., Charlotte Feicht Sanborn, Ph.D., and Wiltz W. Wagner, Jr., Ph.D.; "Athletic Amenorrhea, Major Affective Disorders and Eating Disorders," American Journal of Psychiatry, July, 1987.

9 "Furthermore, amenorrhea may be a factor,": Snell and Vaughan, "Longitudinal Physiological Testing of Elite Female Middle and Long Distance Runners."

10 "The study found the groups most like to use the techniques,": Bobbie Hasselbring, "Are You Running too Thin?"

11 "Some would take diuretics,": Susan Bickelhaupt, "The Thin Game," The Boston Globe, January 13, 1989.

12 "In almost any of the elite athletes,": Ibid.

13 "the so-called American ideal for women was becoming thinner,": Bobbie Hasselbring," Are You Running too Thin?"

14 "I had never been on a diet,": SHL.

15 "At first, I ate grotesque foods,": SHL.

16 "Just bring on the salads,": Cathy Breitenbucher, "Running on Empty, Diet a concern for women athletes," Milwaukee Sentinel, Fall, 1986.

17 "I didn't want to put a high school runner,": PT.

18 "I was convinced that she would win,": PT.

19 "That's a good strategy,": SHL.

20 "Well, Peter knows the strategy,": SHL.

21 "I thought, does he really think I have the strength,": SHL.

22 "So, I won the race,": SHL.

23 "This will play into our hands,": Don Pierson, "Wisconsin sub steals the show," Chicago Tribune, May 19, 1985.

24 "never would have won the 10,000-meters if Katie had run," Ibid.

24 "When Stephanie ran that sensational last lap,": Don Lindstrom, "Special blend helps UW women win," Wisconsin State Journal, May, 1985.

25 "I got on the line and I was so scared,": SHL.

Chapter Fourteen

The description of Cathy Branta's injury comes from an article, "Not what she needed: Can Branta Come Back?", which appeared in the September, 1986, edition of Women's Sports and Fitness. Otherwise, attribution as follows:

1 "The most curious aspect,": "Is Age Getting to Zola Budd?," Track

and Field News, September, 1985, quoting from a July, 1985, article in the London Sunday Times by Cliff Temple.

2 "I came in as a freshman,": Mark Sabljak, "Strong legs carry dream," Wisconsin State Journal, Fall, 1985.

3 "I believe if you want to make someone fast,": PT.

4 "If that's what your Monday, Wednesday and Friday are like,": SHL.

5 "It wasn't what you would call an easy-going group,": SHL.

6 "She's a very intelligent young lady,": Mark Sabljak, "Strong legs carry dream," Wisconsin State Journal, 1985.

7 "Suddenly, it was a HUGE leap,": Rob Hernandez, "I wanted to run, Herbst is back on track but the pressure is gone," Wisconsin State Journal, April 17, 1988.

8 "the pressure has now shifted to NC State,": "N.C. State runs past UW women," local reporting, October 5, 1985.

9 "I just wanted to take the lead and see how it would go,": Phill Trewyn, "CC teams post Classic victories," University of Wisconsin Cardinal, 1985.

10 "She's even stronger than last year,": Gary Mellgren, "Herbst emerges as top runner," Carver County Herald, Fall, 1985.

11 "not to my knowledge,": Cathy Breitenbucher, "Uncertainty surrounds UW women," Milwaukee Sentinel.

12 "It would be good for us if it was cold,": Mike Ivey, "Badger women runners hope to repeat," The Capital Times, 1985.

13 "I mentally just did not have it,": SHL.

14 "From the start, I was mentally fighting it,": "Women's CC team repeats as NCAA champion," November 26, 1985.

15 "I also started realistically appraising,": Cathy Breitenbucher, "Badger women champs again," Milwaukee Sentinel.

16 "I was doing well with the group,": SHL.

17 "There is something very special about this team,": Don Lindstrom, "Ishmael, Herbst share Badger honors," Wisconsin State

Journal, December 4, 1985.

Chapter Fifteen

1 "things don't always work out the way you plan,": Mike Ivey, "Herbst disappointed with her finish, not team's", The Capital Times, November 26, 1985.

2 "its third runner 'dropped out,'": Cathy Breitenbucher, "Badger women champs again, "Milwaukee Sentinel.

3 "hard-pressed to win,": "Women's CC team repeats as NCAA champion," The Daily Cardinal, November 26, 1985.

Chapter Sixteen

1 "scared of the boards,": Don Lindstrom, "Herbst: With Tegen's guidance, she's become a champ," Wisconsin State Journal.

2 "I just rely on what he tells me,": Ibid.

3 "Peter's strategy was for me to take the lead,": SHL.

4 "Yes, I'm lighter,": Don Lindstrom, "Herbst: With Tegen's guidance, she's become a champ," Wisconsin State Journal.

5 "It was exciting,": SHL.

6 "I think at the end of cross-country season, my priorities were screwed up,": Doug Grow, Win at all costs: a running battle," Minneapolis Star and Tribune, June 15, 1986.

7 "I think I slightly decreased my training,": SHL.

8 "You learn again how to be a group,": Rob Hernandez, "Tegen's tracksters look to defend," The Daily Cardinal, March 19, 1986.

9 "He never tells me what I'm going to run,": Perry A. Farrell, "Running in the dark, UW coach has Herbst guessing her way to the top," Milwaukee Journal.

10 "The wind was too strong,": Gary Melgren, "Herbst win 5,000 at Drake," Carver County Herald, May 26, 1986.

11 "There is no such title as darling of the Drake Relays,": Sunday Register Iowa News, April 27, 1986.

12 "It's planting season,": "Bush presents trophy at Drake Relays," Sunday Register Iowa News, April 27, 1986.

13 "I was really shocked,": Don Lindstrom, "Herbst cruises to Drake title," Wisconsin State Journal, April 27, 1986.

14 "Ormsby breaks record,": Ron Reid, "Ormsby breaks record in 10k," Philadelphia Inquirer, April 25, 1986.

15 "she's a strong-minded person,": Track and Field News, June, 1986.

16 "So what you saw with Kathy,": Ibid.

17 "Sometimes I forget about doing that,": Ibid.

18 "was one of those moments when running is so special,": Tom Sorensen, "Paralyzed Track Star Tells Her Story: Fear of Failing God Led to Leap from Bridge," The Charlotte Observer, December 21, 1986.

19 "I tried to tell myself I don't have to do that,": Ibid.

20 "I hit my hip on the side of the track and my knee,": Ibid.

21 "In my eyes, I saw what was happening as failing God,": Ibid.

22 "I felt like I was failing my coach,": Ibid.

23 "It's almost inevitable,": Perry A. Farrell, "Running in the dark, UW coach has Herbst guessing her way to the top," Milwaukee Journal.

24 "There's no mistaking Herbst for anything other than a runner,": Ibid.

25 "Stephanie vollied the remark,": Ibid.

26 "My social life suffers,": Ibid.

27 "Smoothly running lap after lap,": Don Lindstrom, "Herbst places UW in charge," Wisconsin State Journal, May 24, 1986.

28 "Herbst, a wisp of a woman,": Andrew P. Baggot, "Herbst makes herself a runaway success," Wisconsin State Journal, May 24, 1986.

29 "I was just supposed to run the pace,": Don Lindstrom, "Herbst places UW in charge," Wisconsin State Journal, May 24, 1986.

30 "I'm conscious of everything when I'm running,": Andrew P.

Baggot, "Herbst makes herself a runaway success," Wisconsin State Journal, May 24, 1986.

31 "She always does that. She just goes,": Ibid.

Chapter Seventeen

Much of the description and detail of the routine Kathy Ormsby followed on June 4, 1986, was developed in conversations between Ms. Ormsby and the author. The description of the storm in Indianapolis on that day appeared in the June 5, 1986, edition of the Indianapolis News, in articles titled "Storm blamed for fire," and "Storm delays NCAA track." Other source notes for this chapter follow.

1 "I was scared,": Tom Sorensen, " Paralyzed Track Star Tells Her Story: Fear of failing God led to leap from bridge," The Charlotte Observer, December 21, 1986.

2 "I thought she was running directly to me,": Richard DeMark, "And Then She Just Disappeared," Sports Illustrated, June 16, 1986.

3 "Well, I figured I better go,": SHL.

4 "I was scared to death,": Ruth Laney, "Dark Victory for Stephanie Herbst," Track and Field News, August, 1986.

5 "She had, in fact, done everything possible to prepare herself, and had no sense,": Kathy Ormsby, Conversations and correspondence with the author (all such conversations hereafter cited as KO). ("Certainly, I was scared and concerned before the race, but I took comfort in the fact that I felt I had made every effort to assess the situation honestly and deal with the 'problems' in a constructive and positive manner—spiritually, physically and psychologically. I had NO sense that I would or could ever react in the manner in which I did. Had I any idea that I would react as I did I would never have approached the starting line.")

6 "Her memories are, at best, like snapshots," KO. ("From that point forward, my memories are, at best, like snapshots and I have no rec-

ollection of many aspects such as climbing steps and scaling a fence to get out of the stadium, crossing the baseball field, climbing over the railing of the bridge. I have no memory of looking over the side of the bridge to see what was below but do have an awful picture of myself going over headfirst....it was as if I was watching someone else. I certainly did not recognize myself in that person.")

7 "All of a sudden—this is the best way I can tell you about it,": Tom Sorensen, Paralyzed Track Star Tells Her Story: Fear of Failing God Led to Leap from Bridge," The Charlotte Observer, December 21, 1986.

8 "I don't see how in the world I climbed that fence,": Ibid.

9 "I know that when I went off,": Ibid.

10 "One of the psychiatrists with whom Kathy worked,": Ibid.

11 "Ever since Kathy passed out in the first race,": Dale and Sallie Ormsby, "In Their Own Words," The Charlotte Observer, December 21, 1986.

12 "Since Kathy's accident,": Ibid.

Chapter Eighteen

1 "Running and school are her life,": Wire Report, "Pressure on self led to Ormsby's jump, friends say, N.C. State runner said to be 'perfectionist,'". The Atlanta Constitution, June 7, 1986, carried the story and that is the newspaper from which I acquired it.

2 "She's a perfectionist,": Ibid.

3 "Her father agreed that 'it was a question of pressure,'": Tom Sorensen, "Injured Runner's Friends Speak with Admiration, Shock," The Charlotte Observer, June 7, 1986.

4 "his 'hero',": Ibid.

5 "She pushed herself so hard,": Frank Litsky, "Ormsby Is Permanently Paralyzed," New York Times, June 6, 1986.

6 "driven herself very, very hard,": Ibid.

7 "as far as who worked harder to be better,": Tom Sorensen,

"Injured Runner's Friends Speak with Admiration, Shock," The Charlotte Observer, June 7, 1986.

8 "She was perfect, really perfect,": Ibid.

9 "No one has come up to me and asked why,": Frank Litsky, "Teammate of Ormsby cites pressure on Athletes to Excel," New York Times, June 7, 1986.

10 "She knows we understand,": Ibid.

11 "NCAA Records: Wisconsin's Stephanie Herbst,": This paragraph ran as an incidental item in various newspapers around the country.

12 "I did not have that time where you think through something like this,": SHL.

13 "an awful, awful time,": SHL.

14 "Although Stephanie spoke at different times to different reporters,": The full paragraph is a combination of quotes attributed to Stephanie Herbst by various newspapers and periodicals. The quotes, however, shift slightly from publication to publication, as they are altered to fit the individual text, making it difficult, if not impossible, to distinguish the original quote from its later uses. Nonetheless, the following source-notes are provided: (a) "I heard it at breakfast. They had to tell me several times before I really started to believe what happened,": Patrick Reusse, "Herbst distances self from running," St. Paul Pioneer Press; (b) "My reaction was mostly shock—and a little depression that it's not really so unusual,": Ruth Laney, "A Dark Victory for Stephanie Herbst," Track and Field News, August, 1986; also, Bob Hammel, "Concerns and Best Wishes to Ormsby." (c) "It is not as isolated of a case as you would think. A lot of people who get deeply into distance running have problems,": Patrick Reusse, "Herbst distances self from running," St. Paul Pioneer Press. (d) "Running is their life," Kristy Bull, "Herbst forced to scrap plan," Wisconsin State Journal, June 8, 1986. (e) "I had as many problems as anyone. This year during the

cross-country season especially. There were a lot of expectations, a lot of pressure. It gets to be so much that you get to be a perfectionist. You have to go out and get that run in no matter what. It has to be long enough; it doesn't matter what the weather is; it doesn't matter how you feel. You have to get it in,": Doug Grow, "Win at all costs: a running battle," Minneapolis Star and Tribune, June 15, 1986. (f) "I hope [Kathy] realizes that we sympathize with her and that there's a great deal of understanding that every long-distance runner feels,": Kristy Bull, "Herbst forced to scrap plan," Wisconsin State Journal, June 8, 1986. (g) "The public was [surprised] by what happened, but I don't think anyone involved with the sport was,": Doug Grow, "Win at all costs: a running battle," Minneapolis Star and Tribune, June 15. 1986. (h) "People see the glamor of running but that's not all there is. The highs are definitely there, but the lows are something you really have to deal with,": Ruth Laney, "A Dark Victory for Stephanie Herbst," Track and Field News, August, 1986. (i) "Any athlete who says they have no idea of the pressures that might have led Kathy to go to such an extreme is lying. Anyone holding a collegiate record in a race with other top athletes and facing the possibility of not placing or not keeping a record has to have tons of pressure. It's a public loss, not a private loss,": Don Pierson, "NCAA champ Herbst puts her mind in place," Chicago Tribune, June 9, 1986.

15 "I don't read track magazines,": Ruth Laney, "Dark Victory for Stephanie Herbst," Track and Field News, August, 1986.

16 "it's one thing to go into a race with this person or that person,": Kristy Bull, "Herbst forced to scrap plan," Wisconsin State Journal, June 8, 1986.

17 "Do you know something really ironic,": "Doug Grow, "Win at all costs: a running battle," Minneapolis Star and Tribune, June 15, 1986.

18 "I wanted to forget the time,": Ruth Laney, "Dark Victory for

Stephanie Herbst," Track and Field News, August, 1986.

19 "I can't look at this as a positive championship,": Associated Press/Wisconsin State Journal, June 8, 1986.

20 "After Stephanie won the double at Indianapolis, they wanted badly,": Patrick Reusse, "Herbst distances self from running," St. Paul Pioneer Press, Fall, 1986.

21 "If I had gone to the meet,": Doug Grow, "Win at all costs, a running battle," Minneapolis Star and Tribune, June 15, 1986.

22 ""The last paragraph implicated both Kathy and Stephanie,": Judy Mills, "Cracking Up, "Women's Sports and Fitness, October, 1986.

23 "anyone who thinks that competing in a national championship is an outlet is naive,": Frank Litsky, "Ormsby Paralyzed by Leap," New York Times, June 6, 1986.

24 "you have to look for multiple causes,": Brian Settle, "Puzzle of Kathy Ormsby may not fit, expert says," Indianapolis News, June, 1986.

25 "this was an act of impulse,": Ibid.

26 "It makes you realize,": Doug Grow, "Win at all costs: a running battle," Minneapolis Star and Tribune, June 15, 1986.

27 "That's the danger in distance running,": Patrick Reusse, "Herbst distances self from running," St. Paul Pioneer Press.

Chapter Nineteen

1 "I guess I never feel,": Paul Sweitzer, "Modesty meets victory for runner," Badger Herald, January 13-17, 1986.

2 "I thought Suzy was unique,": PT.

3 "Of course, school itself is a lot harder,": "Prize Recruit: Suzy Favor," Track and Field News, December, 1986.

4 "When Stephanie was a freshman she did not have this experience,": This quote is from an article by Andy Katz in the student paper, The Daily Cardinal, and was published in the fall of 1986.

5 "They both got along very well,": Ibid.

6 "It was a wonderful feeling,": Doug Grow, "Herbst latches onto a new perspective and runs with it," Minneapolis Star and Tribune, August 27, 1986.

7 "I had always been the third person behind Cathy Branta,":

8 "The media had never been interested in me,": Mary Schmitt, "On the Mark: Badgers' Herbst has learned to cope with pressure," Milwaukee Journal, Fall, 1987.

9 "During the cross country season, if I wasn't studying, I was running,": Ibid.

10 "I like to isolate myself from other runners,": Ibid.

11 "I'm getting questions like, 'Do you really run more than five miles a day,": Doug Grow, "Herbst Latches on to a new perspective and runs with it," Minneapolis Star and Tribune, August 27, 1986.

12 "As early as the previous winter,": Paul Sweitzer, "Modesty meets victory for runner," Badger Herald, January 13-17, 1986.

13 "Other university references were more subdued and amusing,": Rob Hernandez, "Herbst wins Registration Road Race," Daily Cardinal, September 3, 1986.

14 "while the performances of Herbst and Co. up front,": Madison, Wisconsin, local reporting.

15 "I am extremely impressed,": Paul Zuziak, Cross-country to defend title," Badger Herald, October 21, 1986.

16 "I had to lay off for two weeks,": Jim Lassiter, "Herbst fails in distance defense."

17 "I felt okay but I guess I just didn't have it today," Paul Sweitzer, "UW runners finish second," Badger Herald.

18 "Wisconsin is rated highly but head to head competition," Andy Katz, "Wisconsin runners hobble to second," Daily Cardinal, October 20, 1986.

19 "The turning point was at the hill," Steve Blackledge, Dispatch, November 2, 1986.

20 "If we finish with five runners, we should win it,": Don Lindstrom, Wisconsin State Journal, November 14, 1986.

21 "I try to work them around running and studying,": Mary Schmitt, "On the Mark: Badger's Herbst has learned to cope with pressure," Milwaukee Journal, Fall, 1986.

22 "Herbst seems to have complete control over her academic and social life,": Ibid.

23 "second place in the NCAA is really something outstanding,": Wisconsin State Journal, November 25, 1986.

Chapter Twenty

The exemplar University of Wisconsin workout, which introduces the chapter, comes from Suzy Favor Hamilton's records.

1 "I want to run the rest of my life,": Andy Katz, The Daily Cardinal.

2 "I don't want to get too intense about it,": Andy Katz, The Daily Cardinal.

3 "I can feel the difference when I run,": Ruth Laney, "Huber Can Run But She Can't Hide," Track and Field News, July, 1987.

4 The letter from Stephanie to Michele is a device only. While it is based on conversations between the author and Stephanie Herbst Lucke, as well as the other many sources of information reflected therein, responsibility for content and characterization necessarily remains with the author.

5 "Peter was the one person outside the family in whom her trust was absolute," SLH.

6 "She got scared," PT.

7 "It would terrible if I sat here," PT.

Chapter Twenty One

1 "Although we will miss Stephanie's talents,": John Mueller, "Herbst calls it a career at UW-Madison," Carver County Herald, October 7, 1987.

2 "You bring home a trophy and it's good for about a week,": Ibid.

3 "As hard as I tried to do it through grades,": Mary Schmitt, "Herbst is back on track," Milwaukee Journal.

4 "You just never know what will happen,": Ibid.

5 "I know I can't let it happen again,": Andy Katz, "Herbst lives with the pressure," The Daily Cardinal, March 9, 1988.

6 "you used to be so good, what happened,": Phil Hersh, "Former champ runs on her own terms now," Chicago Tribune, May 13, 1988.

7 "With all due respects, she starts fast and fades,": Dave Kayfes, "Mosqueda has time for a record," Eugene Register Guard, June 2, 1988.

Generally, I would like to note that it would be impossible to write a book like this one without Track and Field News, which is the reliable and consistent chronicler of our sport. I also want to acknowledge the remarkable book written and compiled by Louise Mead Tricard, American Women's Track and Field, A History: 1895-1980, McFarland and Company, Inc., 1996. While I do not believe I have quoted from the book, I did benefit from its statistical compilations and from its general treatment of the subject. No person who writes about the early development of American women as track and field athletes will wish to proceed without Ms. Tricard's book as a resource. I also referred to the following source material: James Coote, Olympic Report 76, Kemps Group, Ltd. 1976; and Roberto Quercetani, Athletics: A history of modern track and field athletics (1860-1990) Men and Women, Vallardi and Associati, 1990; Roberto L. Quercetani and Nejat Kok, Wizards of the Middle Distances, A history of the 800 meters, Vallardi and Associati, 1992.

In over twenty-five years of running and reading, it is possible that I have retained images first presented by other writers in other works. I have consulted only the sources mentioned here and am unaware of any other specific sources, to the authors of which I owe a debt of gratitude and acknowledgment. If I knew who they were, I would have no hesitation in expressing my appreciation.

Index

A

Arreola, Darcy, 370, 418
Ashford, Evelyn, 76
Association for Interollegiate
Athletics for Women (AIAW), ix,
216-223
Augustine, 360

B

Balas, Iolanda, 59
Bassett, Stephanie, 240, 241,
296, 298, 321, 377
Baxter, Susan, 297
Bayi, Filbert, 199
Bell, Wade, 198
Belousova, Raissa, 123
Benning, Chris, 120, 164
Benoit, Joan, 159, 164, 305
Bingay, Roberta 52-53
Bishop, Charlie 305
Board, Lillian, 88
Bowerman, Bill, 165, 171, 183
Boxer, Christine, 120
Bragina, Lyudmila, 96, 97,
99,100, 101, 131, 146, 176
Branta, Cathy, 33, 225,
229-231, 235, 241, 256, 258,
259, 260-261, 262, 263-264, 277,
281, 284, 318, 374, 381
Breighner, Tammy 412
Bremser, Cindy, 178, 200, 210-
214, 225, 229, 285, 369, 417
Bresolles, Claire 58
Bridges, Cheryl, 56, 93, 159
Brown, Dick, 171-174,
176-177, 183, 198, 203
Brown, Doris (Heritage), viii, 53,
55, 55,, 56, 71-103, 148, 208,
236, 426
Brown, Julie 162, 168
Brunner, Maryann, 225

Bruns, Ulrike, 132
Budd, Zola, 193-196,
199-205, 284, 285
Burneleit, Karin, 96, 101
Bush, George 323, 324
Butler, Kathy 423

C

Caitlan, Don, 64-65
Campbell, Robin, 149
Castro, Rich, 155, 158-159
Caurla, Lea, 58
Cerutty, Percy, 227
Chalmers, Angela, 385
Chase, Julia, 48-49
Christiansen, Birgit, 241, 258,
259, 261, 265, 296, 298, 377, 389
Chudina, Aleksandra, 58
Clarke, Ron, 198
Coe, Peter, 255
Coe, Sebastian, 255
Cole, Pat, 56
Colorado, University of, 158
Cunha, Aurora, 199
Cooke, Charlette, 55, 84
Crawford, Terry, 380
Curtin, Chris, 264

D

Dam, Shim Geum, 58
Danboy, Anne, 152
Daniels, Billie Pat (Pat Connolly,
Pat Winslow), 75, 76, 227
Dardik, Irving, M.D., 135
Davis, Harold, 198
Decker, Mary (Slaney), viii,
142-209, 426
DeNoon, Don, 143-155,
150-151, 153, 161, 193
Didricksen, Mildred (Babe),
43-44
Diet and nutrition, 66-68
Dixon, Rod, 157
Doak, Nan, 33, 278, 279, 283,
370

Dobbins, Debbie, 93
Docter, Sarah, 241, 389, 392
Dorio, Gabriella, 116,
125-126, 132
Dornhoefer, Sabrina, 33, 282, 418
Dunn, Karen, 294
Dvirna, Olga, 176, 182

E
Eastman, Ben, 198
Eichner, Clare, 422
Elliott, Jimbo, 227

F
Falck, Hildegard, 96, 131, 146
Falcon Track Club, 79
Favor, Kris, 377, 379
Favor, Suzy (Hamilton), 33, 285,
370-372, 377, 379-380, 383,
385-386, 390-391, 410-411, 414,
418-421
Fischer, Andrea, 261, 282
Foltz, Vicki, 79, 93
Foreman, Ken, 56, 79
Foster, Brendan, 157
Franken, Al, 153
Fredrickson, Sara, 423
Frenn, George, 151

G
Geiger, Rollie, 285, 307,
327-328, 337, 343
Gentes, Sue, 422
George, Walter, 129
Gerasimova, Valentina, 110, 112,
149
Gerschler, Waldemar, 227,
254-255
Gilbert, Rose Mary, 93
Gilman, Chandler, M.D., 37
Gluth, Doris, 112, 113
Gnojevoi, Boris, 123
Goodall, Ellison, 159
Gommers, Maria, 85
Graham, Lynn, 51

Groenendaal, Claudette, 264, 283
Groos, Margaret, 164, 178, 180

H
Hallett, Michele, 356
Hand, Annette (Peters), 264,
418-420
Hamilton, Brutus, 227
Hansen, Joan, 199
Harbig, Rudolf, 198
Harris, Laurie, 377
Harris, Carole, 377, 381,
384-386, 391, 410
Hart, Eddie, 199
Hartzheim, Mary, 377, 381, 386,
390-391, 410-411
Hartzheim, Maureen, 377, 391,
410
Hawaii, University of, 77
Hayes, Kathy, 33, 260-261, 342
Heald, Debbie, 97
Herbst, Dan, 322
Herbst, Michele, 22-23, 34, 35,
394-407
Herbst, Stephanie (Lucke),
high school, 21-35
recruitment by the University of
Wisconsin, 231-234
coached by Peter Tegen,
251-255
competition as freshman,
256-283
diet and nutrition, 267-275,
national indoor champion,
316-319
outdoor national champion,
335-350,
reaction to Kathy Ormsby
accident, 352, 357-359,
362-363
withdrawal from competition,
394-407
return to competition,
412-416
Hering, Holly, 258, 277-279, 296,

298, 377, 392
Hildebrand, Klaus-Peter, 157
Hill, Albert, 129
Hill, Ralph, 198
Hoffman, Abby, 55, 82, 84, 101
Hoffmeister, Grunhild, 96, 101, 116, 118
Holmen, Nina, 116, 132
Holt, John, 203, 206
Homer, Trina, 79
Hopp, Ceci, 264
Huber, Vicki, 393, 417

I

Igloi, Mihaly, 227, 253-254
Ishmael, Katie, 33, 225, 230-231, 241, 256, 159, 258, 260-261, 263, 285, 290-291, 296, 298, 315-316, 321, 374

J

Jacobs, Regina, 263-264, 294, 417, 421
Jamrozy, Ute, 339
Jennings, Lynn, 164
John F. Kennedy College, 77
Jordan, Payton, 58

K

Katyukova, Raisa, 110, 115
Kauls, Kim, 412
Kazachova, Tamara, 149, 152
Kazankina, Tatyana, 105-140, 141, 150, 168, 169, 182-186
Kelly, Essie, 164
Kessler, Karen, 83
Klapezynski, Ulrike, 115-116, 118
Klobukowska, Eva, 60-61
Knisely, Mary, 322-323, 369, 417
Knudson, Wendy, 112, 146, 154
Koubkova, Zdena, 57-58
Kraus, Brigitte, 164, 183-184
Krebs, Tina, 264
Krzesinski, Ella, 227
Kujak, Angie, 423

Kuts, Vladimir, 134

L

Labuschagne, Pieter, 193
Larrieu, Francie, 56, 57, 94, 115, 121, 149, 154, 160,161, 164, 168
Leopold, Trina, 386
Lesgaft, PS, 108
Levitt, Eugene, 367
Lincoln (sisters), 85
Lovelace, Rose, 75
Lovin, Fita, 122
Lydiard, Arthur, 227
Lynch, Liz (McColgan), 285, 316-317, 417-419

M

Maahs, Sheryl, 297
MacDonald, Florence, 47
Malyshev, Nikolai, 108
Manning, Madeline (Jackson), 82-83, 89-91, 108, 111-112, 131, 182
Marasescu, Natalia, 120, 127, 138
May, Carey, 264
McGuire, Rich, 366
McKillen, Kelly, 241, 258, 259, 261, 263, 265, 291, 296, 321, 333, 377, 389, 391
McRoberts, Brit, 181
Merrill, Jan, 115
Mills, Kathy, 159, 163-164
Mineyeva, Olga, 125
Moller, Lorraine, 370
Monard, Kathy, 381, 386
Morton, Billy, 87
Moynihan, Pat, 297
Mulder, Marie, 49-51, 53-55, 92, 148
Murray, Patty, 364

N

Natale, Liz, 270, 294, 380, 386
National Collegiate Athletic

Association, control of women
collegiate sport, 219-223
Nikolik, Vera, 83-84, 88, 90,
96, 101
Norporth, Harold, 268
Nurmi, Paavo, 129, 140, 267

O

Ogilvie, Bruce, 366
Oliver, Judy, 79
Olizaryenko, Nadyezhda,
121-128, 168
Ormsby, Kathy, 34, 282, 285,
296, 300-312, 324-329, 331, 333,
335-350, 351-368, 375, 428
Otten, Debbie, 93

P

Packer, Ann, 134
Palmer, Erica, 423
Pangyelova, Tamara, 96-97
Patino, Maria Jose, 61-62
Pavlov, IP, 108, 246
Peacock, Eulace, 198
Pepperdine College, 77
Petrova, Totka, 120, 138, 164-165
Pigni, Paoli (Cacchi), 84, 101
Pirie, Gordon, 134
Pittman, Pete, 305
Plumer, PattieSue, 33, 370,
417-419
Plumer, Polly, 294, 321
Podkopayeva, Yekaterina, 124
Pollock, Judy, 88, 90, 112
Poor, Cyndy, 152, 154
Prefontaine, Steve, 151
Press, Irina, 58-59
Press, Tamara, 51, 58-59
Providokhina, Tatyana, 110-111,
121, 123, 125, 139
Puica, Maricica, 123, 127, 177,
182, 196

Q

Quax, Dick, 157-159, 162, 165

R

Radke, Lina, 46
Rand, Mary, 45
Ratjen, Hermann ("Dora"), 57
Rendina, Charlene, 146
Renko, Ron, 297
Reynolds, Ellen, 325, 333,
339, 354
Robinson, Connie Jo, 285, 327,
339, 355, 356
Romo, Louise, 264
Rose, Julie, 297
Rulolph, Wilma, 44, 74
Ryun, Jim, 199

S

Sabaite, Niole, 101, 146
Saunders, Kit, 211
Schiro, Cathy (O'Brien), 291, 417
Schroeder, Sue, 315-316, 333, 363
Schubert, Cory, 263
Schweitzer, Anne, 264, 380, 386
Seattle Pacific University,
77-79
Selye, Hans, 172-173, 246, 411
Severtsen, Doris (see Brown,
Heritage)
Sex testing, 57-63
Shafer, Sue, 159
Shea, Julie, 159, 164, 305
Shea, Mary, 305
Sherman, Kim, 422
Shorter, Frank, 153-154
Shrubb, Alfred, 129
Shtereva, Nikolina, 111, 113
Silai, Ileana, 101, 120, 123,
130, 138
Sime, Dave, 198
Sipatova, Elena, 182
Slater, Dana, 159
Sly, Wendy, 183, 184
Smith, Diane, 93

Smith, Janet, 285, 327, 333, 354
Smolka, Lyubov, 124, 127
Snell, Peter, 269, 273
Spangler, Jenny, 278, 316
Springs, Betty, 33, 305, 321, 322, 323, 369
Stampfl, Franz, 227
Steely, Shelly, 33, 261, 264, 420
Steffens, Don, 201
Stephens, Glenna, 93
Steroids and artifical enhancement, 63-65, 134-139
St. Hilaire, Judi, 164, 418, 419
Stirling, Rosemary, 101
Streit, Stephanie, 297
Stricker, Jenny, 294
Struckhoff, Jacque, 323
Styrkina, Svetlana, 110, 112-113
Suicide, social attitudes toward, 360-361

T

Tanner, Jackie, 306
Tegen, Peter 17, 211-216, 225-230, 240-242, 251, 293, 296, 398, 313,-315, 317-320, 331, 341, 364, 371, 377-378, 382, 383, 387, 412
Temple, Ed, 44, 74-75
Templeton, Dink, 227
Tennessee State University, 44, 77
Thomson, Rose, 168, 225
Thorsett, Sarah, 420-421
Title IX, viii, 219-222
Tuffey, Suzie, 33, 285, 290, 294, 325, 327-328

U - V

Ulmasova, Svetlana, 119, 182-184
Van Aaken, Ernst MD, 267
Vasileyeva, Yevdokya, 118-119
Vaughan, Robert, 269, 273

Vetter, Debbie, 164
Viren, Lasse, 157-158

W

Waitz, Grete, 119-120, 131-132, 164
Waldrop, Tony, 338
Walker, Judy, 93
Warren, Leann, 262, 283
Wartenberg, Christiane, 128, 168, 179
Watkins, Burton, 297
Webb, Brenda, 159, 164
Weiss, Anita, 112-113
Welch, Lisa, 294, 333
Westphal, Janet, 423
Westphal, Jenni, 423
White, Martha, 164
Wickus, Amy, 420, 422
Williams, Lynn, 200
Williams, Steve, 199
Wooderson, Sydney, 198
Wolter, Lori, 289, 291, 315-316, 321, 333, 364, 377, 381, 384-386, 392
Worchester, Cindy, 155

X - Y - Z

Zaitseva, Zamira, 124, 182, 187-190
Zinn, Elfi, 113
Zlateva, Svelta, 101, 110
Zook, Sally, 381

FRANK MURPHY was the coach of the Rockhurst College men's and women's cross-country teams for five years. He practices law and is an adjunct instructor in the sociology department at the University of Missouri at Kansas City. He is the author of A Cold Clear Day, *The Athletic Biography of Buddy Edelen.* Edelen was a former holder of the world record in the marathon.

About A Cold Clear Day, the reviewers were in agreement:

"Let an old marathoner commend to you a surefooted book. A Cold Clear Day, *The Athletic Biography of Buddy Edelen*, by Frank Murphy, moved me with what I didn't know about an important American marathoner. Then—and this was more difficult—it moved me with what I knew perfectly well about runners under stress, holding themselves together, reduced and revealed by the longest Olympic distance."

Sports Illustrated

"A Cold Clear Day is the perfect book for a high school distance runner who wants to learn something about the real work needed to challenge yourself."

American Track and Field

Murphy provides wonderful detail from Edelen's diary, research and interviews, particularly with coach Fred Wilt. His niftiest writing is his version of Edelen's thoughts during his victory at the '64 Olympic trials.

USA Today

About the Book

The text of this book was written in Microsoft Word. The layout was designed in Quark Xpress 4.04 and Adobe Photoshop 5.0 on the Macintosh computer and output to PDF files. The body text is set in Times Roman. The headings, chapter titles, and page numbers are set in Futura Light.

The Creative Director is Susan Ng Williams. She resides in Paradise Valley, Arizona.

Annette Pierce provided assistance. She resides in Boulder, Colorado.